Let It Blurt

Let It Blurt

Jim DeRogatis

The Life and Times of
Lester Bangs

America's Greatest Rock Critic

Broadway Books   New York

BROADWAY

Broadway Books titles may be purchased for business or promotional use or for special sales. For information, please write to: Special Markets Department, Random House, Inc., 1540 Broadway, New York, NY 10036.

BROADWAY BOOKS and its logo, a letter B bisected on the diagonal, are trademarks of Broadway Books, a division of Random House, Inc.

Visit our Web site at www.broadwaybooks.com

Library of Congress Cataloging-in-Publication Data
DeRogatis, Jim.
Let it blurt: the life and times of Lester Bangs, America's greatest rock critic /
Jim DeRogatis.
p. cm.
Includes bibliographical references and index.
1. Bangs, Lester. 2. Music critics—United States—Biography. 3. Rock music—History and criticism. I. Title.

ML423.B245 D47 2000
781.66'092—dc21
[B]   99-039766

Printed in the United States of America

May 2000

FIRST EDITION

Book Design by Terry Karydes

Page ii: Lester Bangs, New York City, 1981.
PHOTO BY MICHAEL MAYHAN

Page vii: Lester Bangs, Birmingham, Michigan, 1975.
PHOTO BY CHARLES AURINGER

ISBN 0-7679-0509-1

00 01 02 03 04 10 9 8 7 6 5 4 3 2

For Melody Rose DeRogatis
Matthew Hildebrandt, Emma Altman, Siri,
Isak, and Teddy Kai Keller, Allison Moerer,
and their generation of critics and fans.

Now it's your turn

Is criticism really a creative art? Why should it not be?
It works with materials and puts them into a form
that is at once new and delightful.
What more can one say of poetry?

–Oscar Wilde: "The Critic as Artist"

Contents

Contents

List of Illustrations

I have always believed that
rock 'n' roll comes down to myth.
There are no "facts."

—LESTER BANGS,
in *Rod Stewart*

Preface

Sometimes Lester was full of shit. Of course there are facts in rock 'n' roll, and they are valuable tools for deflating the myths, thereby making heroic deeds seem possible for us lowly humans. This was a pursuit that Lester loved almost as much as constructing the myths in the first place.

Lester was the great gonzo journalist, gutter poet, and romantic visionary of rock writing—its Hunter S. Thompson, Charles Bukowski, and Jack Kerouac all rolled into one. Out of tune with the peace 'n' love ethos of the sixties and the Me Generation navel-gazing of the seventies, he agitated for sounds that were harsher, louder, more electric, and more alive, charting if not defining the aesthetics of heavy metal and punk. Where others idealized the rock 'n' roll lifestyle or presented a distant academic version of it, he *lived* it, reveling it its excesses, drawing energy from its din, and matching its passion in prose that erupted from the pages of *Rolling Stone*, *Creem*, and the *Village Voice*. In the process he became a peer of the artists he celebrated, brash visionaries and dedicated individualists such as Captain Beefheart, Iggy Pop, Patti Smith, Richard Hell, and most of all Lou Reed, with whom he had a relationship that was equal parts Johnson/Boswell, Vidal/Mailer, and Mozart/Salieri (and it was often difficult to tell who was who).

I set out to meet the Lester of legend on the afternoon of April 14, 1982. A senior at Hudson Catholic Regional High School for Boys in Jersey City, New Jersey, I had been assigned by my journalism teacher to interview a "hero." The PATH train deposited me on the corner of Fourteenth Street and Sixth Avenue in Manhattan and I shouted Lester's name at the fifth-floor window as instructed. His building didn't have doorbells, and at that point he lacked a phone; it distracted him from writing, he said. After a minute he threw down the keys, and I made the long climb up to his apartment. Dominated by thousands of albums and piles of trash, it was an exaggerated version of every teenaged rock fan's lair, though its occupant at the time was thirty-three years old.

Over the next few hours I caught a glimpse of another Lester: the kind, magnetic, righteous, outrageously funny, and occasionally frustrating man behind the persona. His gangly frame carried a penetrating intellect housed in a brain so big it seemed to be pushing through the alien lump on his forehead. Addicted to contrarianism, he was a brilliantly successful failure, a doofus savant, and a self-described "compassionate humanist" perfectly capable of destroying someone with a casual blast of callous insensitivity. "He was a romantic in the gravest, saddest, best, and most ridiculous sense of that worn-out word," his friend Nick Tosches wrote. "He couldn't merely go to bed with a woman, he had to fall in love with her. He couldn't merely dislike something, he had to rail and rage against it. None of it was real, but in the end, the phantoms of all that crazy love and anger, since they weren't his to command, conquered him."

Early in his grade-school years the dictates of his mother's religion marked Lester as an outsider, and long after he split from the Jehovah's Witnesses he never really fit in anywhere. Raised in a San Diego suburb, he rebelled against both his vanilla surroundings and the hippie alternative by transforming himself into a self-proclaimed beatnik "drug punk." When he went to work at *Creem*, he embraced the angry energy of working-class rockers desperate to avoid the assembly line, but it wasn't long before he found Detroit as stifling intellectually and emotionally as El Cajon had been. Finally he settled in Manhattan. At first he thought he'd found the creative community he'd long advocated in the punk explosion centered at CBGB, but he was ultimately disillusioned when the reality fell short of his ideal. In the end he was preparing to write about life as an alienated castaway on one of the world's most populated islands.

To friends and lovers Lester sometimes confessed that he felt predestined to follow in the footsteps of his alcoholic father, who died an early and horrifying death, but he was also committed to raging against any game that seemed rigged. That's why he broke from his mother's church, and that's why he'd started to pull away from rock journalism and the image that he'd created for himself. "There was a time in my life when you would have come up here and I would have got all drunk and exhibitionistic and you might have preferred it that way," he told me. "But if I act like that, I might live a long time, but I won't live very long as a good writer."

Slumped in a ratty old chair, his posture mirroring the skew of the Cookie Monster hand puppet that served as a shade on his desk lamp, Lester seemed enervated and barely able to move, but he spoke in a passionate torrent of words. He paused for a long time when I asked him to define good rock 'n' roll. Even as an inexperienced interviewer, I was surprised that his answer wasn't boilerplate.

"Good rock 'n' roll is something that makes you feel alive," Lester said at length. "It's something that's human, and I think that most music today isn't. Anything that I would want to listen to is made by human beings instead of computers and machines. To me good rock 'n' roll also encompasses other things, like Hank Williams and Charlie Mingus and a lot of things that aren't strictly defined as rock 'n' roll. Rock 'n' roll is an attitude, it's not a musical form of a strict sort. It's a way of doing things, of approaching things. Writing can be rock 'n' roll, or a movie can be rock 'n' roll. It's a way of living your life."

I was sitting in my bedroom transcribing our interview two weeks later when I heard the news of Lester's death on WNEW-FM. This biography began that day. By the time I started working on it in earnest fourteen years later, I had established four goals for the book. The first was to tell a life story that began to intrigue me even before I met Lester.

"If all you knew about Lester Bangs were articles that he wrote, I'd have to say that you knew him quite well," Billy Altman wrote, eulogizing his mentor in the pages of *Creem*. I disagree. In print and in person, Lester was constantly changing, evolving, and battling competing impulses toward senseless self-destruction and a giddy celebration of being alive. His psychiatrist, Phil Sapienza, told me that he has rarely treated someone who assumed so many contradictory "roles," playing them all so thoroughly that they became integrated as parts of his personality. Sapienza pointed out my challenge as biographer: "If you are able to synthesize those hundred and fifty versions into a composite personality, then you have Lester."

My second goal was to chart the history of rock criticism, Lester's chosen field, and my own. That story has never really been told, despite the wealth of colorful characters, flamboyant antics, and memorable prose. The form was born in the mid-sixties, blossomed along with New

Journalism in the early seventies, and was professionalized and purged of much of its personality by the early eighties. Though much of it was as evanescent as a breath of air through a saxophone, Lester's work represented a high point that the field has yet to match. Since rock criticism's development and decline mirrors and coincides with his career, that tale runs through this book, along with goal number three: an examination of his critical ideas and aesthetic.

"His critical ideas were not the strength; it was the language that was the strength," Lester's editor at the *Village Voice*, Robert Christgau, said when I interviewed him in 1997. Again, I disagree. Two camps dominate rock criticism today: the two-thumbs-up consumer-guide careerists who treat rock 'n' roll as mere entertainment, and the academics who drain it of all the joy and fury. Both camps attempt to marginalize Lester by portraying him as a stylist, a "rockist" (as if all he cared about were three chords and a backbeat), or an elitist whose true love was "popular" music that nobody else liked. Well, they're sort of right there: The rock 'n' roll he loved most was a joyous or cathartic roar and a defiant fuck-you to the bland and bullshit culture at large. And not everybody is ready to let it blurt.

Some of Lester's peers and possibly even Lester himself came to believe that rock 'n' roll of this kind died in the sixties or seventies. For what it's worth, I disagree with them, too, but that's another book. The final goal of this one was to examine the music and culture of the times through the prisms of Lester, his aesthetic judgments, and rock criticism itself. To accomplish this I relied on skills honed during the first five years of my career as a beat and investigative reporter, interviewing 227 people who played some role in Lester's life, and poring through his many published and unpublished writings, letters, recordings, and notebooks.

Throughout the reporting and the writing I drew inspiration from my subject. In a characteristically surprising 1976 *Chicago Tribune* review of two books about Jack Benny and Doris Day, Lester wrote, "Biographies are, for some idiosyncratic reason, practically my favorite reading matter. I've read 'em all, from Malcolm X, to Tennessee Williams, to Joan Baez. And in spite of the built-in drawbacks to the Hollywood school of journalistic history, I have in my peregrinations discovered that it is possible to write a Hollywood biography and not only tell the truth but even occasionally produce an important documentation of this century's cultural climate."

From time to time friends remarked that I would be charting a very sad tale in these pages, but while there are tragic elements, I do not see this book as a tragedy. It is not just the story of a guy who drank Romilar by the gallon, insulted rock stars, then died. Absent Lester's ideas, the poetry of his writing, and his singular lust for life, this story would not have been worth telling. Those are the parts of his legacy that I celebrate, and I hope that you will do the same.

Introduction

Lester waited in the wings at Detroit's Cobo Hall, fingering the keys on the old typewriter that he hastily grabbed from a corner of the Creem House. The three shots of Chivas and the six-pack of beer he had consumed in lieu of dinner did little to drown the butterflies in his stomach. He had never been frightened when he joined Thee Dark Ages to play harmonica back in El Cajon, and he didn't think twice about hopping onstage with the Blues Train in Windsor. Now, at the age of twenty-five, he worried that he might actually lose his cookies over the act of dadaist theater that he was about to commit.

Finally the J. Geils Band bounded offstage, and there was no more time to think. One of the roadies signaled to him as the musicians regrouped for the encore. They churned out a respectable R&B groove for a bunch of white guys from Boston. In the dire bland-out of the mid-seventies they were one of the few groups you could cite for proof that, no, rock 'n' roll was *not* dead and buried. At least not entirely.

The interview at the hotel earlier that day had been a snooze until Jerome Geils lobbed an insult. "Hey, Lester, did anyone ever tell you that you look like Rob Reiner?"

Archie Bunker's Meathead—he'd heard it too many times before. "Bullshit!" Lester roared. "Don't tell me that! I do not!"

Peter Wolf laughed. "So *that's* what it takes to get him to react," the singer said.

Lester sneered. "Hell, the only difference between you musicians and us rock writers is that people can *see* you doing what you do," he said. "I can't go up in the street and say, 'Hey, honey, dig my far-out John Lennon review,' because she can say, 'Kiss my ass, Jack, how I know you wrote that?'"

Twenty-four years later Wolf recalled his response. "Detroit was like our second home," he said. "We used to see Lester every time we went through town, and he was always as colorful and eclectic as an artist. I remember saying to him, 'Well, fuck it, man! Why don't you take your typewriter and do your review from the stage?' It was almost like *Saturday Night Live* or a David Letterman sketch."

That night in the summer of 1974 Lester stomped into the spotlight and set his Smith-Corona down with great fanfare on a piano bench in front of the drums. "Plug the son of a bitch in!" he yelled. "Let's get down!" He'd dressed up for the occasion, sporting a red sweater-vest over a blue-and-white shirt, baggy blue jeans, and his usual nine-dollar red Converse sneakers. As the band sounded its first notes, he kneeled in front of the typewriter and theatrically donned a pair of shades.

Out in the crowd of thirteen thousand some six people cheered, all of them buddies from *Creem* magazine. The band played "Give It to Me," the triumphant closing track from its 1973 album *Bloodshot*. "I want it so bad/You've got to *give* it to me," Wolf sang. The tune grew harder and more soulful in concert, with an edge of desperation that marked it from the loopy reggae version that would power an annoying advertising jingle two decades later. The sound of Lester's hunting and pecking could barely be heard, though the crew had thoughtfully miked his "ax." He wasn't contributing to the music, and he certainly wasn't writing anything worthwhile.

VDKHEOQSNCHCHSHNELXIEN (+&H—SXN+(E@JN?, he typed.

"Yer doin' great!" shouted a roadie to his right.

"Vengeful bastard," Lester thought. As the song ended, he stood up, kicked over the piano bench, and jumped on the machine until it cracked in two. He'd laugh at himself when he wrote it all up—his version of George Plimpton's New Journalist heroics. But at the moment he felt like a star.

Let It Blurt

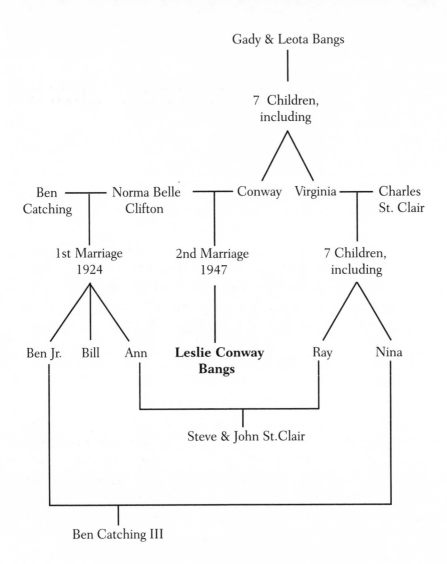

The Closed Circle

Conway Bangs needed a drink. He chain-smoked while pacing nervously in the cool night air outside Escondido Community Hospital—a fancy name for a tiny clinic run by one doctor in a wood-frame house only a little bigger than most of the others here amid the Southern California orange groves. From time to time he heard his wife cry out, and he knew that she must be hurting. Complaining about the pains of the flesh was not the way of the Jehovah's Witnesses, and Norma was nothing if not a faithful soldier.

The doctor had urged Conway to talk some sense into his wife. There were risks in having a child at age forty-three, but Norma wouldn't hear any talk of abortion. The Witnesses forbade it under any circumstances, including a fatal threat to the mother. Conway didn't have much use for his wife's religion, but for once he was glad she stood her ground. A few years earlier the prison doctor had told him he'd never have a child. Them doctors seemed to be wrong a lot, he thought, because his son was born without complications at two minutes before eleven on the night of December 13, 1948.

The baby arrived weighing eight pounds, eight ounces and exercising what sounded like an extremely healthy pair of lungs. The couple named him Leslie Conway in honor of his father, Conway Leslie. Once he saw that Norma and the boy were resting peacefully, Conway ran to spread the news to the rest of the family. "Conway was thrilled to death," said his twenty-one-year-old stepdaughter, Ann St. Clair, one of three

Conway's baby boy, January 1949.
(ALL FAMILY PHOTOS COURTESY BEN CATCHING III)

children from Norma's first marriage. "When he came up to the house where my husband Ray and I lived, he told us that he had the most beautiful son in the world. Because Leslie was born with a full head of black hair—enough for three or four babies!—I didn't think he was very pretty, but that didn't make any difference. That was Conway's baby boy."

From Ann and Ray's place Conway went to see Ben Catching, Jr., Norma's eldest son. At twenty-three Ben already had a four-year-old boy of his own, Ben Catching III. The two men drove trucks for Escondido Transit Mix. After work they would sit outside Conway and Norma's small rented house near Highway 395, drinking beer on the rickety front porch. Early on the morning of December 14 they drank a toast to young Leslie Bangs.

For several generations on both sides Leslie's forebears were migratory Southwestern farm workers. The families' roots in the United States stretched back far enough for the current members to have forgotten the Old World traditions and even their particular European heritages. They shared some Scottish and English blood, no doubt, and possibly some Irish and German as well. Basically they were the sort of people portrayed in William Faulkner's "Barn Burning" and Nelson Algren's *A Walk on the Wild Side*. At the time they would have been called Arkies, Okies, drifters, or crackers. In his less charitable moments a grown-up Leslie would call them "white trash."

Leslie's paternal grandparents Gady and Leota Bangs crossed the border from Arkansas to Texas around the turn of the century. They settled in the country between the small towns of Cooper and Enlow about ninety miles northeast of Dallas. Gady farmed, brewed bootleg whiskey, and drank, though not necessarily in that order. A broad, squat man with a penchant for oversize cowboy hats, he was as unpleasant and churlish as the plump, round-faced Leota was sweet and loving. The couple raised five daughters and two sons, including Conway Leslie, born on August 25, 1915. His middle name paid tribute to the sheriff of Delta County, but the family friend never did his namesake any favors. In fact, he was one of the men who sent Conway to prison.

Conway's first arrest came a few months before his eighteenth birthday, six years after he dropped out of school in the seventh grade. Charged with four counts of burglary, he pleaded guilty to one in return for the others being dropped. Because of Conway's age the judge suspended the five-year sentence, but the conviction stigmatized him nonetheless. One day in late 1934 a neighbor accused him of stealing some tools. Conway asserted his innocence, but the man wouldn't listen. The boy flew into a rage and viciously beat his accuser with a wooden bucket. "If Conway saw someone being mistreated, man, he would jump right in there," said his sister Imogene. "He could get angry, but usually when he got angry, he had a right to be angry. He wasn't much of a talker, but when he did talk, it meant something. And if someone beat him, well, he'd just beat them right back."

On January 15, 1935, a jury found Conway guilty of assault with intent to murder. District Court Judge Charles "Chuck" Berry sentenced him to five years for the beating and reinstated the original five-year sentence for burglary. Three weeks later Conway began serving his decade-long term at Huntsville. Among the habits noted on his prison record: intemperance, use of tobacco, and a disdain for organized religion. On the rare occasions later in life when he talked about his incarceration,

Conway spoke of being whipped, beaten with chains, and strapped to a plow like a horse. One day he begged off the work detail, complaining of a headache and a painful swelling in the groin. The guards sent him out into the fields, and the next morning he collapsed. The mumps had brought on a case of encephalitis. The prison doctor told him he'd have died if he went without treatment much longer. As it was, he'd probably been rendered sterile.

Conway completed his sentence on September 11, 1945, and he moved back in with his parents. He found work driving dump trucks on construction sites in Dallas, which bustled during the postwar building boom. His younger sisters admired his rugged good looks and compared his hardened features to an outdoorsy, Western version of Humphrey Bogart. Like his father, Conway sometimes drank to excess, but he was a docile drunk, where alcohol only made Gady meaner. The old man's favorite rant was about the new religion that consumed so much of his wife's time. Gady would stand in the doorway and curse Leota as she left for Bible study. "I hope you drive up a goddamn tree and kill yourself!" he'd shout. "Goddamn you and all your *Gee*-hovah's Witnesses!"

Leota was unflappable. "Gady, honey, you just relax, and I'll see ya back here in a little bit," she'd coo while driving off with her friend, Norma Catching.

Conway would watch these scenes and shake his head. Norma was nine years his senior. She had already buried one husband and raised three children who were living on their own, but he was struck by her youthful beauty. Her quiet dignity in the face of his father's vitriol impressed him, and he was glad that she didn't seem to think less of him because he'd been to prison. He felt like a teenager whenever he talked to her, and he hated to see her go.

The former Norma Belle Clifton was born to a family of strict Southern Baptists in the mountains of Pecos County, Texas, on September 14, 1906. When she was five years old, her parents, Hampton and Ophilia, packed the family into a horse-drawn wagon and set out for New Mexico. There Norma grew into a tall, pretty girl with a long, thin face, dark hair, and soulful eyes.

The Cliftons worked at a large ranch, and Norma was extremely popular with the other workers' sons. At age fifteen she wandered away with a boy during a communal barbecue, and he raped her. It was years before she told anyone, because she knew that her father would have sought justice with a shotgun.

Around her eighteenth birthday, Norma met a tall, handsome man named Ben Harley Catching, who had served in the Army Ambulance Corps during World War I. Nightmares haunted his sleep, and he suffered from a painful back injury that required him to wear a heavy steel-and-leather brace. The couple married in 1925 and had three children—Ben Jr., Bill, and Ann—but Ben Sr. drank heavily, and he was not a loving husband or father. "If anything you'd have to call him brutal," said his daughter, Ann. He disappeared for long stretches—off on a bender or a trip to the VA hospital—leaving Norma struggling to feed the family with a sack of flour and some hominy.

In 1935 Ben returned from one of his jaunts to find his wife praying with a colporteur, a traveling preacher who conducted Bible studies in the home. The man pitched his tent and stayed for a week, introducing the family to the teachings of the Jehovah's Witnesses.

The religion traces its roots to the 1870s and a group called the Associated Bible Students. Founder Charles Taze Russell preached what was essentially traditional Calvinism on steroids, emphasizing the coming apocalypse. No other major Christian sectarian movement has been as insistent on prophesying the end of the world on such specific dates. The first of these was 1914, and while World War I seemed to fulfill some of the Bible Students' expectations, the world did not in fact end. Pastor Russell died in 1916 without seeing his prophecies realized.

Russell was succeeded by his lawyer, Judge Joseph Franklin Rutherford. The judge helped take the movement to new heights by decreeing that every member of the congregation should participate in the early Christian practice of preaching from door to door. The Bible Students spread their message through *The Watchtower* magazine and a book entitled *Millions Now Living Will Never Die*, which set a new date for the beginning of the end. In 1925 the 144,000 saints or anointed ones mentioned at Revelation 14:1 would ascend into heaven to sit at God's side. After Armageddon the rest of the faithful would celebrate eternal life in a new paradise on earth, while nonbelievers would be doomed to the fires for eternity.

Undaunted when 1925 also passed without incident, the faithful convened in Columbus, Ohio. They updated the catastrophic calendar once more, settling on a less specific "soon" and adopting a new name based on Isaiah 43:12: "Ye are my witnesses, saith Jehovah, and I am God." When the colporteur visited the Catching family, the Jehovah's Witnesses still numbered fewer than fifty thousand. Many of the men had been jailed for refusing to serve during World War I, and this stance held considerable appeal for Ben Catching, Sr. "When Daddy came back from the First World War, he hated anything that had to do with the government," said his daughter, Ann. "When he began to read and get associated with the Witnesses, why, that just fit him perfectly. He could really separate himself from everything else."

For Norma the Witnesses promised a life with strict moral guidelines, an order that had been sorely missing in her marriage. The couple and their three young children were baptized in 1936. In the years that followed, Ben Sr. became a forceful and convincing preacher, and word filtered back to the Watchtower Bible and Tract Society, the Brooklyn-based organization that administered the religion. The elders named Ben a special minister and charged him with organizing a congregation in the fertile cattle country on the banks of the Red River in Paris, Texas.

Charles and Virginia St. Clair were hardworking ranchers with seven towheaded children who'd been reading *The Watchtower* for some time when the Catchings arrived. The two families began Bible studies together. The former Virginia Bangs remained close to her family, and she frequently made the twenty-mile trip out near Enlow to preach to her mother and sisters. Ben Sr. baptized Leota Bangs and several of her daughters into the faith, but her husband Gady and their son Conway refused to heed the call.

Under Ben's leadership the Paris congregation thrived. Few worshippers suspected that he showed one face at Kingdom Hall and another at home, and his occasional disappearances continued. On the night of July 4, 1944, he was en route to the veteran's hospital in Dallas when he had some car trouble. Some family members say he was attempting to flag down help when he was struck and killed by a Greyhound bus. Others suggest that he stepped in front of the vehicle, ending his back pain forever. "I truthfully couldn't say I missed him when he was gone," said his daughter, Ann, "because there was finally peace and quiet."

Ben's two sons had already left home. At sixteen Bill lied about his age and joined the Navy, while seventeen-year-old Ben Jr. married Nina St. Clair, one of Charles and Virginia's daughters. A short time later Ann wed Nina's brother, Ray. Brother married sister and sister married brother, as the family explained. After the war the two couples joined the westward migration of thousands of veterans, settling thirty miles north of San Diego in the rural farm town of Escondido.

Norma suddenly found herself alone at the age of thirty-nine. She spent much of her time reading the Bible with her friend Leota Bangs, and on visits to the ranch she met Leota's son, Conway. Almost a foot shorter than her first husband, Conway was soft-spoken and unassuming where Ben Catching had been bold and assertive. Although he had recently been released from prison and was not a believer, Conway struck Norma as a good man who just hadn't found the right path in life. "I guess I'm gonna have to marry the woman just to get rid of her," he told his sisters. The couple wed in 1947 at the Kingdom Hall that Ben Catching built, and shortly thereafter they joined Norma's children in Escondido.

The family trees of the Bangses, Catchings, and St. Clairs were now intertwined by three marriages, but this was not a warm, extended clan prone to communal gatherings or preserving family history. Most members believed that the world was going to end any day, and the family of God was the only one that mattered. They effectively formed a tight-knit cell inside the already claustrophobic world of the Jehovah's Witnesses. Fifty years later Ben Catching III would describe the environment that greeted his uncle Leslie as "the Closed Circle—nothing comes in, nothing goes out, and everything gets thrown away."

Conway worked hard in Escondido, but he always found the energy to push his son around the yard in a wheelbarrow or sit him atop a neighbor's workhorse at the end of the day. He loved the boy and tried to do right by his family, but while Norma never talked down to him, he always felt inferior compared to the good Christian husbands and fathers at Kingdom Hall. The worse he felt, the more he drank.

One night midway through Leslie's second year, Conway sat his son on the kitchen table, turned his back, and reached into the icebox for a beer. The toddler fell and hit his head on the floor with an awful thump. Conway rushed the screaming child to the same doctor who'd delivered him. The only damage was an ugly lump on the boy's forehead that never receded, but Conway couldn't forgive himself.

Shortly after Leslie's second birthday his father went on a binge and didn't return for several weeks. Norma had to leave Escondido and take a job as a cook on a ranch in a small town near the Mexican border. She

At the Palomar School, Perris, California, 1951.

moved into a tiny apartment adjoining the kitchen, and Leslie played on the floor while she cooked for thirty men. About a month later, Conway woke up in his car on the side of a lonely road in northern Texas. He saw someone walking toward him, and he realized it was a vision of himself. He took it as a message to sober up and return to his family.

"You're gonna take him back?" Ann asked her mother when Norma called with the news. "Of course," Norma replied. A few weeks later Ann went down to visit them. "Welcome home; you were missed," she told her stepfather. Conway cried as she hugged him. "How could you say that to me?" he asked. Ann just smiled. "Because you love my mother, and my mother loves you," she said. "We just want you to watch yourself."

From late 1951 through 1954, when Leslie was ages three through six, his parents lived and worked at the Palomar School, a boys' ranch in Perris, California, that catered to the sons of the Hollywood elite. Norma cooked while Conway kept the grounds. Leslie grew up to become a bright and curious boy with chipmunk cheeks, a black cowlick, and a sly, knowing grin not unlike Beaver Cleaver's. "You could just look at him and see the wheels turning," said his half sister, Ann. Norma read to him constantly—the Scriptures, mostly, but also some children's stories. "He could read when most children couldn't pronounce the words," said his aunt, Imogene Bangs. "It was just amazing."

When Leslie enrolled in elementary school, the teacher encouraged his mother to let him skip a year and go right into the second grade, but Norma declined. Like many Witnesses, she didn't value education beyond learning to read the Bible; she sent her son to school only because the law demanded it. In addition to attending services on Sundays and Bible studies several nights a week, Leslie often joined his mother in the "preaching work." They knocked on the doors of nonbelievers and marched in the streets wearing placards bearing apocalyptic slogans such as WHAT IS YOUR DESTINY? and DO YOU KNOW WHAT TIME IT IS?

Conway usually waited in the car. He never opposed his wife, but he confessed his frustrations to his sisters. He didn't understand why the

Norma and Leslie in San Diego, 1953.

The Bangs family, 1955.

religion forbade him from giving his son presents at Christmas, or why the Watchtower prohibited inoculations and blood transfusions. Deep down he disliked the Witnesses as much as his father, Gady, did.

In school Leslie became increasingly aware that the religion marked him as different. He was forbidden to salute the flag or recite the Pledge of Allegiance, and his mother didn't let him participate in sports or after-school clubs. These activities fostered what the Witnesses called "unwholesome relationships."

Music did not play an important role in services at Kingdom Hall, and the Watchtower frowned upon playing instruments, but Leslie was increasingly drawn to what he perceived as a force for transcendence. "Music has been a fluctuating fanaticism with me ever since I heard 'The Storm' from the *William Tell* Overture on a TV cartoon about first grade," he wrote. "Riding in the car through grammar school when songs like 'There Goes My Baby' would come on the radio . . . these are events you remember all your life, like your first real orgasm."

More than twenty years separated Leslie from his half siblings, and he never felt a strong connection to them. His closest companion was his half brother's son, Ben Catching III, four years his senior. On the clan's complicated family tree, Ben was Leslie's nephew, but the two grew up tighter than many brothers. The older boy called his uncle Les or "Skeeter," short for "Mosquito," because he always seemed to be buzzing around. Ben liked to play ball and ride his bike, but Les was a clumsy kid with no affinity for physical activities. "Skeeter was just this little guy who didn't have a firm grip on boyhood things," Ben said. Mostly they sat around reading *Classics Illustrated* comic books.

Stories such as *Treasure Island* and *Twenty Thousand Leagues Under the Sea* fired Les's imagination. By age eight he was drawing and writing in a notebook, extending the narratives past the points where Robert Louis Stevenson and Jules Verne left off. From there he progressed to writing original stories about a superhero he called Captain Applejack. One day Norma found him jumping up and down on his bed wearing a towel as a cape and yelling, "I am Superman, ruler of the world!" She chastised him, "No, *God* is the only ruler of the world." Years later he noted that the seeds of his dissension from the Jehovah's Witnesses were sown then and there.

"The drawer where I kept my *Classics Illustrated* collection was subject to stringent, arbitrary, and rather sudden swoops of censorship," Les wrote at age twenty. "Things like *The War of the Worlds* by H. G. Wells and *From the Earth to the Moon* by Jules Verne, my literary mentor of the third grade, would suddenly appear in ripped piles atop the ashes when I'd go out to empty the trash into the incinerator on a winter morning. My mother thought science fiction was demented nonsense; all the Witnesses do. They hold that since the Bible never mentions life on other planets, there just must not be any, and no one can sway them from their conclusions. Typical example of Witness logic and dogma."

Les, Ben, and their childhood hero, Bill Catching.

After serving in the war in the South Pacific, Les's half brother Bill settled in Hollywood and found work as a stuntman on films and TV shows such as *The Cisco Kid, Seahunt*, and *Bat Masterson*. He reconnected with the family after his father's death, but he dreaded visiting because his mother always preached to him. Of course Les worshipped him. Bill figures he saw his half brother only ten times in his entire life, but he made an impact, especially during Les's formative years. Bill sent Les scripts and encouraged him to rewrite them.

"I read a couple of them, and he came up with better stories than the originals," Bill said. He also gave Les a subscription to the Heritage Book Club. Every month the mail brought a deluxe edition of a classic such as *Moby-Dick* or *The Meditations of Marcus Aurelius*. The boy invented his own library system, writing four-digit codes on the covers and stamping the books with the images he adopted as his insignia: an hourglass and the Looney Tunes character Sniffles, the shy mouse.

As much as he admired Bill, Les looked up to his father even more. Conway spent as much time with his son as possible, given the hours he worked and the fact that Norma was always dragging Les off to some church function. One of Les's most vivid memories came from around age seven. Conway had to pick up a truckload of supplies in Los Angeles, and he took his son along for the trip. As they approached, they saw the dense smog hovering over the city. It made breathing difficult and caused their eyes to water, but it also resulted in a glorious sunset as the light was reflected by the clouds of pollution.

Sometimes you could find great beauty in the midst of ugliness, Conway observed. "The sky's electric gash" was the phrase his son recalled, but Les wasn't sure if it was something he came up with—a child's spontaneous haiku—or an especially poetic line spoken by his truck-driver dad. Later in life he was never certain what he actually experienced with his father and what he imagined or idealized, though he was dimly aware of Conway's binges. "Your dad isn't feeling well," Norma would say. After a few days Conway would indeed return looking gravely ill. His breath and his clothes would smell awful, and his complexion would be ghostlike.

*   *   *

In the winter of 1956 Norma Bangs convinced her husband to move to Arizona. Ann and Ray St. Clair had relocated to Glendale, a suburb of Phoenix. Long her mother's closest confidante, Ann now had two young sons, Les's nephews Steve and John, and it wouldn't be long before all the children could read their Bibles together.

Conway and his wife found jobs as the groundskeeper and cook at the Orne Ranch School between the towns of Mayer and Prescott, eighty miles northwest of Phoenix. Conway hated Arizona, and he drank heavily. "He didn't like working 'like a nigger,' as he called it, cleaning up in the kitchen and doing what he called 'menial nigger work,' " said his stepdaughter, Ann. He wanted a decent job in construction like his stepson

Les with nephews Steve and John St. Clair
in Glendale, Arizona, 1957.

Ben back in California. Norma replied that he'd never amount to any-thing unless he stopped drinking and devoted himself to the Lord. The couple separated in July 1957, and Conway left for the West Coast, promising to return for his family once he found steady work.

Ben Catching III traveled to Arizona that summer to spend his va-cation with his grandmother and uncle at the ranch school. Twelve-year-old Ben and eight-year-old Les passed the days reading comics in the woods, free from Norma's prying eyes. One morning she yelled for them to come inside, and they found her hurriedly packing their bags. She herded them into the backseat of her old Studebaker and set off for Glendale.

En route Norma turned and spoke to her son in the Southern drawl she inherited from her mother. "Your father is dead," she said in a calm and emotionless voice. "He burned in a fire, but don't worry; he had *The Watchtower* and *Awake!* beside his bed. He'll be all right, because in the end he was with God."

The Jehovah's Witnesses do not grieve for the deceased. Death is simply an event like any other in this life—an act of God's will. Les followed his mother's example and sat in silence for the rest of the hourlong car trip. He refused to look at his nephew and just stared out the window at the sky.

Conway Bangs hadn't been gone for long. He'd spent a few days hitching rides for the 385-mile trip from Arizona to Borrego Springs, California. There he'd linked up with Ralph Wagor, an old friend who had a cabin where he escaped to hunt and fish. Conway stayed there for a day or two before continuing west to Escondido. Wagor loaned him the keys to his place near Metcalf and Lincoln streets, and Conway arrived on the evening of Saturday, August 4, 1957. He dropped off his pack and went to quench his thirst at his old haunt, the Seven Points Roadhouse. When the bar closed, he staggered back down Escondido Boulevard and fell asleep on his friend's couch.

Early Sunday morning Dr. Edward Calvert was awakened by the sound of a fire. He called the sheriff at 3:50 A.M. to report that the Wagor house two doors away was completely engulfed by flames. The blaze burned so swiftly that the walls and roof collapsed before the San Marcos Volunteer Fire Department arrived. Wagor's brother and other relatives rushed to the scene and watched as firefighters sifted through the rubble and found a body burned beyond recognition. The family assumed the worst until someone noticed a wristwatch. Ralph didn't own a wristwatch.

A few hours later Ralph Wagor came home and identified the remains. The death certificate described Conway as a "transient truck driver, age forty-one." Cause of death: "partial cremation." The Escondido authorities had never thought highly of the ex-con, and they didn't work very hard to determine the cause of the fire. Conway had always been a chain-smoker, and some of his relatives believed he passed out drunk with a cigarette. "The only reason he hadn't burned himself up before was because Mother was there," said his stepdaughter, Ann.

Other family members were suspicious. "Somebody could have followed him home from that club," said Conway's sister Imogene. "We didn't do any investigating, and now I wish we did. I just live with the regret." His friend and stepson Ben Catching, Jr., suspected that Conway ran afoul of someone who took revenge through arson. No one put much stock in this theory—Ben Jr. was a good storyteller—but Les heard the talk from time to time when he was growing up.

John L. Rehwalt, servant of the Jehovah's Witnesses, presided over the funeral on August 6. For the second time Norma buried a husband who had met a grim and untimely end. "The thing that made it so horrid was that there was no good-bye," her daughter, Ann, recalled. "They scooped Conway up and sealed him in a stainless-steel box because there was just nothing left."

Norma shed no tears, but that night she insisted that her son sleep with her, and she clutched him tightly to her breast. A rush of emotions overwhelmed Les as he shared his mother's bed four months before his ninth birthday. There was anger at not being allowed to express his grief, shock in sensing his mother's adult needs, and guilt that he was somehow expected to take Conway's place. Then, too, there was the very real terror of death by fire. The Jehovah's Witnesses talked constantly of the apocalypse, but it had become such a vivid reality for Les that he would later tell intimates he saw the glow and felt the heat of the flames that consumed his father.

En route to Arizona, 1956.

Birth of the Cool

Norma Bangs had been calmly calling from the kitchen for ten minutes when she finally lost her temper one night in late 1958. Her son lay on the floor in the living room listening to some infernal jazz music. She stormed in and dramatically turned off the old console record player that came with their rented rooms. "I said, 'Will you *please* turn down that coon caterwauling!'" she screamed.

Ten-year-old Les simply looked up from his dog-eared Edgar Allen Poe paperback, flashed his sarcastic grin, and turned the phonograph back on.

After Conway Bangs's death, his wife and son left Arizona and returned to Escondido. Norma got a job at a local diner, and Les entered the fourth grade at the Lincoln School. The three years that followed comprise the darkest period of his life. The rest of the family had moved on, and Norma and Les felt isolated and alone. In addition to what he later called the "paranoid restrictiveness imposed by my widowed mother and tightened by the Jehovah's Witnesses," Les had four enduring memories of this time.

The most pleasant recollection centered on scouring dusty antiques shops in search of *Classics Illustrated*. "Anyone who has ever devoted himself to collecting something and gotten hooked can well imagine the shock of pleasurable recognition and the heartswell of satisfaction as I stood in line, grimy coins saved secretly from twenty-five-cents-a-day lunch money," Les wrote a decade later. "I never believed that anybody else in the world, much less Escondido, was possessed by the same *Classical* collectors' virus."

Another memory involved the night some bored teenagers corralled a stray cat that Les had been nurturing. They tied its head to the fender of one hot rod and its tail to the back of a second car, then slowly drove apart. Les also remembered being pummeled by the son of a Mexican migrant worker—"beaners," his mother called them—and feeling as if he couldn't fight back because he'd kill the boy. "He beat the shit out of me, but I couldn't help it," he wrote. "I pulled my punches because I was afraid of hurting him."

Finally there was the middle-aged man who lured Les into his trailer and paid him cash and comics books in exchange for sex. The encounters continued for several months through Les's eleventh year, but at the time he didn't tell anyone because he felt that his mother and the church elders would somehow hold *him* responsible. Years later, after society became more aware of sexual abuse, he talked about these experiences in the tone of a detached observer. "Was he scarred by these incidents? I don't know," said his therapist, Phil Sapienza. "It was important enough to him to mention in the therapy room, but 'scarred' is maybe too strong a word. It had an impact." Like most of Lester's closest confidantes, Sapienza believes that the death of his father, his relationship with his mother, and the feelings of guilt and impending doom bestowed by the Jehovah's Witnesses were the most potent sources of pain in his life.

In the summer of 1960 Norma announced that they were moving to El Cajon. Les happily turned his back on Escondido, "the city of my birth, my father's death, and one thousand childhood shadows." Plenty self-conscious on the page, he laughed when he wrote that line at age twenty. "Actually I'm kind of proud of this dark, distorted childhood mythology," he admitted. "Looks good on a literary figure."

*   *   *

Located in a dusty valley surrounded on three sides by mountains, El Cajon took its name from the Spanish words for "the drawer" or "the box." It experienced its first boom in the early 1900s, after a primitive wooden flume brought desperately needed water to irrigate the farmlands. An even more dramatic expansion followed World War II, when returning GIs arrived en masse in search of comfortable tract homes with nice backyards and two-car garages. "It's a red hot town with red hot prices," a hyperbolic realtor told *San Diego and Point* magazine the year Norma and Les arrived, but you could still find the odd horse pasture, vineyard, or old frame house with a handmade sign announcing BIG RED EARTHWORMS.

Every Saturday after Thanksgiving, many of El Cajon's forty thousand residents lined Broadway to watch the annual Mother Goose Parade and greet celebrity hosts such as Timmy and Lassie. But there was another side to the town that the Chamber of Commerce didn't talk about. Realtors had a "gentlemen's agreement" to keep black families out, a practice known as redlining, and though it was only thirty miles from Mexico, El Cajon displayed few traces of Latino culture. The hills sheltered the town from winter winds as well as summer breezes, and the climate that boosters called "pleasant" could just as accurately be described as "stifling."

Always renting and always hoping to find a nicer apartment, Norma and Les moved three times during their first few years in El Cajon, usually settling within a few blocks of Ben Catching, Jr., and his family. Les and his nephew became constant companions. Tall and skinny with a full head of curly brown hair, Ben Catching III towered over his awkward young uncle. Ben's interests were turning away from cowboys and pirates as he entered his teens, but Les was advanced for his age, and they shared two key obsessions: music and literature.

The boys would con Norma into driving them to the Thrifty Drug Store to buy ice cream when they were really searching for comics and albums. They'd stow the contraband outside Les's bedroom window and recover it once Norma went off to wait tables. At first Les loved the dramatic orchestral soundtracks to films such as *Around the World in 80 Days* and *Ben-Hur*—"any music that you could imagine having grand adventures to," Ben said—but the swinging theme songs from TV action shows such as *Peter Gunn* and *M Squad* eventually prompted the boys to begin exploring the world of jazz. Dixieland, blues, Kansas City, bop—the style didn't matter as long as the sounds were *cool*.

The intensity of his uncle's passions often overpowered Ben. "I had other interests—I'd go out and play catch—but music and reading were everything for him," Ben said. Music seemed to transport Les to another world. "My most memorable childhood fantasy was to have a mansion with catacombs underneath containing, alphabetized in endless winding dimly lit musty rows, every album ever released," he wrote. Records held an almost mystical attraction for him, and he imagined that each had its own personality. "Once when I was in the seventh grade I went back to visit the town where I'd lived the year before to retrieve a copy of the Henry Mancini *Mr. Lucky* album which I'd loaned to a friend," he wrote. "When I got back home I put the *Mr. Lucky* album into the record rack next to its old neighbor, the *Peter Gunn* album. Looking down on them sitting there like that, I felt glad for them. I was thinking that the two old friends, among the very first albums that I ever bought, must be delighted to see each other again after so long. Maybe they even had some interesting tales to relate."

One afternoon in 1960 Miles Davis's *Birth of the Cool* and *Kind of Blue* both turned up in the drugstore's jazz bin. Ben bought the former because it had more songs on it, and he and Les got more than they bargained for. "*Birth of the Cool* was everything we ever wanted," Ben said. "As soon as we heard that, it was all over." Les concurred. "It all started with Miles for me," he wrote. "*Birth of the Cool* and *Miles Ahead* and *Porgy and Bess* and *Sketches of Spain* and *Jazz Track*—man, I thought nobody else but me and my nephew remembered that record! The first side of that's one of the greatest things of all time, music from depths of feeling few men can touch."

The two started to become discriminating jazz aficionados. They

Ben and Les in El Cajon, 1960.

scoffed at the stodginess of *Down Beat,* but they read every issue religiously. During the early 1960s Les ran through a procession of heroes: Miles yielded to Dave Brubeck, Brubeck to John Coltrane, and Coltrane to his ultimate favorite, bassist Charles Mingus. Years later he heard *The Black Saint and the Sinner Lady* as he lay on his bedroom floor in a cold sweat, playing it ten times in a row. "This was IT," he wrote. "Babies being born, taxicabs honking, people fucking, couples fighting, the cries of lonely anguish that no one else hears in solitary rooms, children laughing, insurgents and guerrillas clashing, people of all sorts crying, shouting, and whooping for joy, stunned at the crossroads, and some of them dying."

The boys were also developing other literary interests. They read *The Catcher in the Rye* several times, but they were even more impressed with a 1960 novel called *Harry Vernon at Prep.* "Les always had a copy with him," Ben said. "It was a sacred text." Franc Smith's novel follows a con man who stumbles into a position teaching literature at a New Hampshire boarding school. It lampoons the "phonus bolonus" pomposity of stuffed-shirt academics while contending that the *real* intellectuals are self-taught free spirits like the hero, a pseudo-Beat poet. From there it was only a short jump to the Beats themselves.

Les dug the perverse humor and science-fiction imagery of William S. Burroughs and the passionate rhythms of Allen Ginsberg, but most of all he loved Jack Kerouac's romantic novels about the search for spiritual transcendence. He borrowed *On the Road* from Ben and refused to return it, but he actually preferred *The Subterraneans,* the story of Kerouac, his "spade lover" Mardou, and their quest for kicks with a gang of self-styled intellectuals and poets. "Kerouac came roaring down each new highway hollering tokay haikus like a man possessed, moving on not from a sense of disenchantment but with a voracious and insatiable hunger for experience," Les wrote. He felt a similar hunger and disillusionment, if not with American society in the shadow of the bomb, then at least with his mother's church. He had started to embrace a new religion. "For me it was always Mingus—Mingus and Kerouac," he wrote. "Those were my saints."

Before entering the eighth grade in September 1961, Les took a summer-school class called Creative Writing and Drama. Norma disliked the idea, but she needed a place to send him while she was at work. In class he met a skinny, blond, bespectacled kid one year his junior named Roger Anderson. They swapped comic books and records, and one scorching afternoon they ran around under the sprinkler in Roger's backyard shouting poetry and pretending to be Beatniks.

Les was in the process of reinventing himself. Following the model of the Beats, he turned his outsider status from a liability to an asset—or at least a persona. As he prepared to enter high school, he began to introduce himself, sign his homework, and byline his writings "Lester Bangs." No one remembers why "Leslie" became "Lester." Saxophonist Lester Young was no more of a hero than a dozen other jazz players, and Les had never especially disliked his given name (though some might consider it "feminine"). One day he simply *was* Lester, and that's how it would be for the rest of his life.

*   *   *

In 1962 El Cajon Valley High School still smelled of gas fumes from the auto shop and cow manure from the 4-H Club, but it also boasted a drama department with a separate theater, a well-appointed music building, and several brand-new tennis courts, all signs of the suburb's growing prosperity.

As in any school there were different cliques. The coolest kids were the surfers, still a relatively new group. They were followed closely by the traditional jocks and cheerleaders. No one wanted to be known as a farmer. Lester was a whole new type—a suburban version of the Beatniks portrayed in *Life* magazine—and he relished the role. He grew his hair long, drank bottles of vanilla extract to get drunk on the alcohol, and laced chocolate shakes from Jack in the Box with nutmeg in an effort to get high.

Though he was bright and talented, Lester alienated many of his teachers with a blatant disdain for authority. He could break up the entire class with a well-timed wisecrack. Once he sauntered up to the vice-principal's wife on the cafeteria lunch line and shouted, "Gimme an *OJ* baby!" He was suspended for two days for that one. Another time he was caught in biology class passing around a copy of *Naked Lunch*. That earned another two-day suspension. He had never been any good at sports, so he avoided gym at all costs. Coach Foster required a ten-page paper for every class a student missed; when Lester cut an entire week, he wrote a fifty-page story called "Hector the Homosexual Monkey." This time he got a week's suspension, but Norma succeeded in getting him permanently excused from Phys Ed. The Jehovah's Witnesses did not believe in dodgeball.

Against his mother's wishes, Lester became an active member of the drama and speech clubs. He stole the show as George in the drama club's

production of *Out of the Frying Pan* and was up
for the role of Tom in *The Glass Menagerie*.
Everyone thought he was perfect for the part,
but the director chose a more disciplined young
thespian. Undaunted, Lester entertained his fellow actors with monologues by Lenny Bruce
and Stan Freberg. Speech-club members were
allowed to skip class to practice on campus, and
Lester could often be found holding court on a
bench by the tennis courts. Here he formed his
own high-school gang of Subterraneans.

As a high school freshman.

Roger Anderson's parents were among the
most liberal residents of El Cajon, and his mom wrote stories for true-
confession magazines. Rob Houghton's father was a plumber who moved
the family west from Minnesota, and his mother wrote a column for the
El Cajon Daily Californian. Both boys looked up to Lester and listened
intently to his endless raps about drugs, sex, and music. Another pal in
speech class characterized them in the title of an unfinished story: "The
Guru, The Poet, and The Madman Three."

All of them had a crush on the speech teacher, a grown-up Gidget
named Barbara Brooks. Lester was her star pupil. In class he recited
"Howl" and "The Sunflower Sutra" in his distinctive drawl—part Southern California hipster and part Okie hick. "You are most likely the best
speech student this school has had," Miss Brooks wrote in his junior
yearbook. "You are also the most erratic, unorthodox, non-conforming
person this school has had. Both/all of these can help you to succeed—
in moderation and used wisely."

In addition to being a dead ringer for the middle-aged Anaïs Nin,
junior-English teacher Juanita Haliburton was a free spirit who devoted
part of her class to creative writing. For the exam she played an album of
electronic music and instructed students to write about whatever it inspired in them. Lester's colorful prose validated her approach, and his en-
thusiasm infected the class. "It's easy for him to be generous with other
writers because he's convinced he's the greatest writer in the world," she
told Roger Anderson, and she didn't say that she disagreed.

The following year Lester also thrived in senior English, though
George Bascom's methods differed dramatically. A conservative South-
erner fond of white bow ties, he had been a leader in the initiative to ban

the *Dictionary of American Slang* from California libraries because it contained the word "fuck." He had no use for spontaneous prose, but he believed that Lester showed promise nonetheless. "He was just weltering in the glory that he could express himself, but he was always on the same note," Bascom said in 1982. "He was brilliant. What he wanted was an education, and he didn't care where he found it. If a teacher gave him a C in a course, it didn't bother him. He wasn't going to do something he had already conquered. He knew where he was going."

In an effort to appear more writerly, Lester took to smoking Chesterfields or a pipe and wearing button-down Oxfords under a beat-up black suit jacket. He discovered a book by Aleistar Crowley and imitated the occultist poet's wild-eyed stare with the intention of using it on the dust jacket for his projected novel. "I used to dream of a critic writing somewhere that I was 'possessed of a demonic style, burning with insane ferocity,'" he wrote. "But where to score demonic ferocity in the ice-cream and television world of El Cajon?"

He fantasized about life in New York, and his friends had no trouble believing that Lester would make it there. In his 1965 yearbook Bill Swegles wrote, "One of these days, in an old café in a middle-everything town, I'll pick up a magazine and read your name. I'm going to smile then and remember, and that little part you left me with will begin to bloom (and grow into a damn ugly weed). What I'm trying to say is that I don't think you'll ever be forgotten."

Almost everywhere he went Lester carried a manila folder bulging with his prose. The poem "Bartók Images" evoked "waves of purple sound crested by mauve and dark green dragons," while the short story "Between Light and Shade" followed the adventures of a Burroughsian exterminator. Both were published in the high school literary magazine, *Thought*. What he called his "books" were actually more like novellas. *The Smashed Cathedral* told a Burroughs-style tale of a homosexual street gang that defiled a Catholic church, *The Adventures of Captain Applejack* revived his childhood character as a superhero on the side of evil, and *Death's Head Ragas* explored "a symbolic nightmare depicting the war between the life/energy instinct and the death/martyrdom instinct within myself."

His nephew Ben remembered a long poem that Lester scribbled in chalk on the roof of a rented cottage on Chase Street. Years after Norma and her son moved out, Ben still wanted to go back and copy it down. But he also urged his uncle to drop the Burroughs fixation and develop his

own voice. "My eternal critic," Lester dubbed him. By 1964 their tastes
had diverged. Ben didn't care for the rock 'n' roll that now dominated
Lester's listening, and though they shared some early experiments with
marijuana, Lester quickly outdistanced his nephew with his drug adventures.

Sitting on the tennis court bench, Lester and his friends scrutinized
the special issue of *Life* devoted to the drug menace, lusting after photos
of exotic highs such as LSD, hashish, and magic mushrooms. "This im-
patience to gain the drug experience colored everything that came later,"
Rob Houghton wrote. At the time the best they could do in El Cajon
were morning glory seeds, belladonna, and—if they were lucky—the occasional handful of diet pills swiped from Lester's new girlfriend.

A big girl with auburn hair and freckles, Andrea di Guglielmo was
funny, theatrical, and vivacious. She lived in a development called Valley
Village with her stepfather, half brother, and mom, another El Cajon
housewife who became a writer after splitting from Andy's dad. Andy listened to Barbra Streisand and Broadway musicals and loved to shop at
the malls that dotted Mission Valley. She affected a Carnaby Street look,
sporting coral lipstick and a polka-dot headband and zooming across
campus wearing a long cape that trailed behind her. The star of the
speech club barely noticed her, but she didn't care. "I was madly in love,"
she said.

To date, Lester's experiences with the opposite sex had been furtive
and few. At age twelve he copped a cheap feel from a woman in white
toreador pants in the crowd at a demolition derby. "I couldn't wait to run
back to my hot-dog bleacher seat to brag it up to my four-years-elder
nephew!" he wrote. He groped fellow Witness Sandra Wyatt under a blan-
ket in the back of her parents' station wagon after a trip to the San Diego
Zoo, and he played footsie with Judy Bistodeau underneath the desks during freshman math. The closest he got to really scoring was with one of his
teachers' daughters, a college girl who struck him as the paradigm of the
sensual older woman. They smoked marijuana as they lay on her bed listening to "Lady Gabor" by Chico Hamilton. "I've got this big sex thing for
you!" he gushed. She invited him to act on it, but he didn't know how to
start.

At the end of his junior year in 1965, Lester competed in a regional
speech tournament at Grossmont Junior College. He savagely parodied
the merchants cashing in on the assassination of JFK by selling miniature

rocking chairs and Jack 'n' Jackie salt and pepper shakers, and he took first prize for the men. Andy claimed top honors for the women, and she chose the occasion to make her move. During the bus ride home she loudly referred to herself as "a speckled wombat." Earlier Lester had written a poem in an effort to woo another girl into the prop loft, the official drama-club make-out spot. The most memorable line: "Watch out! Speckled wombats have been known to rape!"

"Where did you hear that phrase, 'speckled wombat'?" Lester demanded.

"Oh, I don't know," Andy said coyly. "I just made it up."

Lester decided it was destiny. "As we were to repeat so often in those first babbling weeks of courtship, we were 'seeds of the same flower,'" he wrote. "We both had psychic larceny in our souls." Andy eventually confessed that she'd heard him drop the term during one of his tennis court harangues, but by then it didn't matter. "She was the only chick who came forth to challenge my madman hype."

The sight of Lester and Andy walking hand in hand down Broadway during the summer break stunned his friend Roger Anderson. A few days later the couple showed up at Roger's door. "We were in the neighborhood and we decided we want to read all your writing!" Lester announced. They marched into his room, pulled a box from under his bed, and started riffling through the pages as Roger cringed. "Looking back on it thirty years later, I think it was their way of saying they wanted to be friends," he said. "It was especially typical of Lester—and to an extent it was typical of Andy—that the only way they could go about it was with this big, brusque production."

When the couple didn't have money for the movies, Lester donned a suit and went door to door seeking contributions for a fictitious school trip. "He had no shame whatsoever," Andy said. "It was wonderful!" They took the bus to downtown San Diego to catch the latest European art film or run through the streets "flying" behind Andy's cape. Most dates ended with hot dogs, sodas, and a trip to the photo booth on Navy Pier.

Andy shared many of the views of her stepfather, a conservative Republican, while Lester proudly flaunted a budding liberal consciousness, but they didn't take their spirited political debates personally. "The things we disagreed about were fleeting as opposed to what we had in common—the very nature of who we were," Andy said. "Allowing other people freedom of expression—that was what we were all about. We were

The Speckled Wombat and the Dirty Dingbat circa the Summer of Love.

both eccentrics. Neither one of us fit in the small town of El Cajon, but we both fit with one another because we didn't fit where we were."

❉ ❉ ❉

Early in their courtship Lester took Andy to see the Rolling Stones when the band performed at the Civic Theater in San Diego during its second American tour. Until his junior year Lester had professed a general hatred of rock 'n' roll. He had been too young to connect with Elvis Presley and the fifties stars, and early sixties acts such as Fabian, Frankie Avalon, and Bobby Rydell left him cold. As a jazz fan he disdained the pop charts; "popular" usually meant "crap." All that changed in January 1964 with "I Want to Hold Your Hand."

"From the very beginning, he was hell-bent for leather on the Beatles," Roger Anderson said. "Then the Stones came along, and he was just a raving lunatic." Deep down you could hear that the Stones understood jazz and the blues, Lester said as he expounded on their merits from the tennis court bench. The snarling fuzz-tone riff of "Satisfaction" was the most intense sound since John Coltrane's sax, and you could practically hear the leer in Mick Jagger's voice, he said. Lester almost came to blows with a classmate who taunted him by claiming that anyone who liked Jagger had to be "a sexual *pre-vert*." Lester knew better. He pronounced the Stones "a supernatural visitation, a cataclysmic experience of Wagnerian power that transcended music."

In the months that followed, Lester also raved about Bob Dylan's *Highway 61 Revisited* and the singles of the Yardbirds. Dylan's lyrical sophistication thrilled him, and he loved the way the Yardbirds merged Eastern drones, jazz tonalities, and amped-up rhythm and blues. "The music of the future will capitalize on a blend of forms and cultural outlooks, mating every sort of diverse form to give birth to the greatest musical age the world has ever seen," he wrote in his high school newspaper. "Rock 'n' roll—that *enfant terrible*, that ugly child, that bad noise, that raucous wilderness of amateurs grabbing a shifty buck, yes baby, rock 'n' roll has jumped up out of the manhole like the Shadow himself and bombed us all with its own brilliant musical innovators, and it's about time we got the Black Mass and desert whirlwinds and northern lights and apocalyptic dragon fires back into the music of our time."

Lester contributed several "Sounds of the Scene" columns to the El Cajon Valley High School *Smoke Signal* in 1965 and 1966, but he never considered them as important as his poetry or fiction. "The idea that Lester would become a person who wrote about music was the farthest thing from everyone's mind, including his," said his friend Roger. "He was going to be a famous mad-hatter novelist like Burroughs." But when his girlfriend, Andy, read some of his "books," she seconded his nephew Ben in urging him to be more original. "I have a talent for mimicry," he finally confessed, "but the difficulty lies in shaking off the old idols when I want to follow a new map."

Shortly after finishing a new epic called *Adventures of a Dirty Dingbat*, Lester took all of his manuscripts to the incinerator. His collection of Beat paperbacks followed his own work into the fire—everyone except for Kerouac; he couldn't part with him. It seemed reasonable that if he no longer *read* Burroughs and the others, he wouldn't write like them, and he'd decided that his own muse deserved a clean slate.

"I was just beginning to realize that I was coming up in the dawning days of a new era," Lester wrote, "when literature would turn to toilet paper, daily news would become surrealistic, and artists of all stripes everywhere would feel blissfully free to cut themselves loose from their heritage, or even not learn that heritage, because there was more relevance to be found in the splashy trash of the popular press, in the open-throated yawps and mechanical twangs of rock 'n' roll, in the chaotic inner jungles which all of us hurled ourselves into with every type of drug imaginable. I suppose I'm not a truly dedicated artist, whatever that is, and I don't want to be. I'll probably never produce a masterpiece, but so what? I feel I have a Sound aborning which is my own, and that Sound if erratic is still my greatest pride, because I would rather write like a dancer shaking my ass to boogaloo inside my head, and perhaps reach only readers who like to use books to shake their asses, than to be or write for the man cloistered in a closet somewhere re-reading Aeschylus while this stupefying world careens crazily past his waxy windows toward its last raving sooty feedback pirouette."

*   *   *

Norma stood in the doorway of Lester's bedroom again, whining in the Southern drawl that he had come to loathe. "*Oh*, I'm hungry for *something*," she said, "but I don't know *what* it is." Her son could see a hole in her life that the church did not fill, and he hated it.

Before leaving for work every morning, Norma left a note and a copy of *The Watchtower* beside Lester's eggs, bacon, toast, avocado, tomato juice, and coffee. Men paid two dollars for this kind of breakfast at the restaurant, she said, and he ought to appreciate it. No matter how well intentioned, it all grated. "It's like being wrapped in wax paper on the shelf of some musty, stifling, overheated old thrift shop," Lester wrote. "It's waking to the well-meant nag that starts your day with grinding teeth, it's complaints that your actions are leaning on her sometimes beleaguered heart, it's all the postures and movements and gestures and backs turned and doors closed and unsynched eyes with a parent who cares and gives more than most but just never will understand what this minor madness means."

Equally frustrated, Norma found it impossible to communicate with her son as he sat in his bedroom reading those infernal Beatnik paperbacks and listening to some hooligan named Wolfman Jack broadcasting

Norma and her children: Bill, Ann, Ben Jr., and Les, 1966.

from Mexico. When she stumbled across a can of nutmeg in the car, she finally confronted him. He laughed in her face, though secretly he was proud that she was that hip.

Norma kept their new garden apartment on Lexington Avenue sparklingly clean, as befits a good Christian home, but Lester abused the space she gave him. Mounds of forty-fives, magazines, comics, Coke cans, cigarette butts, and empty bags of potato chips piled up around the ottoman he used as a writing desk. She was appalled, and she didn't even know about the nook where he hid his copies of *Playboy* and *Jaguar*.

In addition to lifting the occasional five or ten bucks from his mother's purse, Lester had become an expert shoplifter. Sometimes he picked up the contents of an entire record bin and walked out the door as if he were an employee shuffling the stock. Once when he was caught putting a record under his shirt at Woolworth's, he pretended he was retarded, and the clerk let him go. Other times Norma had to pick him up at the police station. Some of his friends thought that he went out of his way to flaunt his rebellion. He robbed the contribution box at Kingdom Hall and smoked in the house. When Norma reminded him how his father had died, he hopped on the bed and pretended to fall asleep with a cigarette.

One day Lester pressured his mom into taking the gang to the beach. She wore gloves and a dress, stayed on the grass far away from the sand, and fiddled with her car keys until it was time to go home. "It was hard to be around her and the environment that she created," Rob Houghton said. "He got away with what he could get away with, and she prayed to God for whatever kind of deliverance she could get."

Convinced that Lester needed a positive male role model, Norma enlisted one of the brothers who played piano at Kingdom Hall. He came to the apartment and tried to talk about Bach, but Lester blasted Thelonius Monk, and the man never returned. Norma's eldest son, Ben Catching, Jr., was the closest father figure in the family, but he didn't have much patience with his half brother. "He would come off the job in his truck boozed up and stop by the house and hassle me about my hair with the usual boy/girl clichés and a strong tangible undercurrent of repressed violent rage like he wanted to bash some sense into my drug-soaked head with those big hamhock hands of his which have held hammers for eight, ten hours hitting one nail into the sheet rock after another for decades," Lester wrote.

"There wasn't much gentleness with Les in that family," Andy said. Norma liked her son's girlfriend—Andy seemed to be a calming influence—and she hoped they'd start a family. But though they were together constantly, the couple only had what Andy called "quasi-sex." They were waiting until marriage, though Andy did not expect Lester to be chaste. In fact, she encouraged him to get some experience so he'd be ready for her.

One night during the spring of his senior year Lester and a jock buddy from speech club set out to visit a Mexican brothel. Older boys in El Cajon bragged of crossing the border to Tijuana or "TJ" twenty-six miles to the south to get drunk, score speed, watch the cockfights, and smoke Horseshit cigarettes (the slogan: "Not a fart in the carload!"). TJ fascinated Lester because it represented the polar opposite of Kingdom Hall. He returned from his first visit wearing his goofy grin, seventeen years old and a virgin no more. It wasn't until a few days later that he felt the burning sensation when he peed.

"It wasn't a big deal," Andy said. "He just got the gonorrhea. So he went to the doctor and they give him a shot of penicillin, but the thing is, they had to tell Norma."

A week later Lester invited Roger Anderson over to listen to records. When his friend arrived, Lester announced that his adventure had been discovered and he had to go to Kingdom Hall to meet with a committee of elders. On the way Lester found some torn paper sunglasses on the sidewalk—the kind eye doctors gave out when they dilated your pupils—

put them on, and defiantly lit a cigarette. The brothers asked Roger to wait outside, but he listened through an open window as they asked his friend about his interests and whether he believed in Jehovah God. Lester said he believed in other things, like poetry and music. "They weren't being pushy or trying to bully him," Roger said, and the meeting lasted only fifteen minutes. Lester was placed on probation, but he decided to force more drastic action.

On Friday nights the congregation gathered for two hours as members took turns giving prepared speeches about the Scriptures. At the next meeting Lester began what was supposed to be a five-minute talk by reading from Deuteronomy 25: "If there be a controversy between men, and they come unto judgment, that the judges may judge them; then they shall justify the righteous, and condemn the wicked." Here he veered from the text. "You're all hypocrites!" he shouted. "You say one thing and do another!" He ranted on for about a minute until one of the older brothers stood up and said he'd had enough. With that Lester walked purposefully down the aisle and out the door.

"It was like hell had opened up and erupted right there in Kingdom Hall," said his friend and fellow Witness, Milton Wyatt. Like many of the faithful, Milton's parents forbade him from speaking to Lester again. The Witnesses' most severe form of punishment is disfellowshipment. A servant suspected of immorality or heresy is called before a judicial committee. If he is found guilty, he is barred from Kingdom Hall. The righteous may not speak to him, do business with him, or attend his funeral. Reinstatement is possible, but only if the sinner repents and sits at services in silence for a period of two years.

Although she was angry and embarrassed, Norma wore a stoic face at Kingdom Hall and generally avoided the topic at home. From time to time she would venture that perhaps her son would return to the church, but Lester just ignored her whenever she started that rap. He rarely wrote about the religion in the years that followed, but in 1978 he offered this simple observation: "I quit the Jehovah's Witnesses because I thought disease in any form more worthy of a life's devotion."

chapter three

Drug Punk

"Why don't we go down to TJ and score some Demerol!" Lester ventured to Roger Anderson one day in the summer of 1967. Lester had shoplifted a copy of *The Merck Index,* an exhaustive guide to pharmaceuticals, and he was forever thumbing through its pages in search of ingenious ways to disconnect from his senses. Almost anything he came up with could be had in Tijuana.

The two friends hopped into Roger's 1958 Hillman Minx and headed south, but the U.S. border patrol flagged them down as they tried to enter Mexico. While a guard checked their IDs, they sat in a holding room listening to an intercom that seemed to be connected to a construction site. The sound of earthmoving equipment blared through the tinny speaker. "Are you *listening* to this?" Roger asked, hip to John Cage and *musique concrète*. Lester had already registered it. "Yeah!" he said. "It's *beautiful!*"

Turned away from TJ, they resorted to Lester's backup plan. He emerged from the drugstore back in El Cajon carrying a package of Marezine, an over-the-counter remedy for motion sickness. He abstained but talked his buddy into taking ten pills. "It was the worst thing that ever happened to me in my life," Roger said. "It was absolutely horrible. I felt

Lester and Roger Anderson, 1966.

sick and I had hallucinations. I ended up at my house, totally blowing it in front of my liberal parents." The next morning Roger told his folks he'd smoked marijuana. "Dummy," said his friend and fellow psychic explorer, Rob Houghton. "Now you've ruined their good opinion of weed!"

Despite Roger's warnings Lester couldn't wait to take the Marezine himself. He swallowed a dozen pills and spent the night hallucinating tiny vicious demons wielding giant axes. "It works better than LSD!" he wrote in a prank letter to the drug's manufacturer, Burroughs Wellcome & Company. Presenting himself as the chairman of "Parents Against Narcotics, El Cajon Branch," he expressed his concern about the potential for abuse by thrill-seeking teens, and offered his help in curtailing the menace.

On graduation day in June 1966 Lester grinned for the photos in his red cap and gown, looking like an elongated version of Dustin Hoffman. In the senior yearbook he announced his intention to study journalism at nearby Grossmont Junior College. Though all of his friends considered Grossmont "high school with cigarettes," it never occurred to any of them to study further afield, nor did their guidance counselors often suggest it. Grossmont had recently made headlines for instituting a ban against Communist speakers and for firing four teachers after they shared beer and wine with underage students, but none of this bothered Lester. He enrolled only for the fringe benefits.

In January 1967 the local draft board classified Lester as 1A, available for military service. He could avoid the frightening prospect of serving in Vietnam as long as he could prove he was a full-time student. His attending Grossmont also convinced his mother that he was staying out of trouble, and he could therefore continue to live rent-free without worrying about a job. Finally, as long as he remained in school, he would continue receiving a monthly check for ninety-nine dollars from the Social Security Administration, a child-support benefit that Norma began collecting after Conway's death. "I'm ashamed to admit it now, but I talked Les into hitting his mom up for that check," Andy confessed.

Lester almost always spent the cash on drugs, beer, or records, but before starting college he made a valiant attempt to spruce up his image. He invested in a few pairs of new corduroy slacks, two sports coats with brown elbow patches, and a pair of brown loafers from J.C. Penney. Strolling around campus, the spiffy new college man hauled an armful of Uncle Scrooge comic books (he loved Carl Barks's surreal art), copies of *Life* and *Newsweek*, the latest issues of *Beat* and *Hit Parader* ("both rock 'n' roll rags and both absolutely essential!"), and the usual manila folder full of his writings. But he rarely remembered to bring his textbooks, and he never did take any journalism courses.

Aside from composition and literature, Lester hated his classes, and he attended only one session in three. He relied on his writing skills to carry him through exams and term papers. The fact that this system actually yielded decent grades seemed to confirm the contention of his old sacred text, *Harry Vernon at Prep*. Academia was a haven for "phonus bolonuses."

Shortly before the start of the Summer of Love, Lester left home and moved into an abandoned meat locker dug into a hillside behind a villa east of town. He had a mattress, a record player, and a light for reading. Power was supplied by an extension cord running to the house, which was owned by some bohemian pals from Grossmont. He romanticized the place as a rural retreat like the one described by Kerouac in *Desolation Angels*. "The party went on all summer long," Rob Houghton wrote. "We played *Sergeant Pepper*, the first albums by the Doors, Cream, Procol Harum, the Velvet Underground, Frank Zappa, the Jefferson Airplane, the Grateful Dead—the list goes on and on."

After three or four tries, Lester finally got his driver's license, and his half brother Ben gave him a beat-up 1955 Plymouth. Lester was never a model driver—he was always talking, smoking, or punching the

buttons on the radio instead of watching the road—and the gift was intended to ensure that he wouldn't wreck Norma's car. In June 1967 he
got behind the wheel and took off on his own for Northern California.
He missed the Monterey Pop Festival but spent a few weeks exploring
Berkeley and the Haight as those locales erupted with the first full flush
of hippiedom. He spent every night in San Francisco's fabled ballrooms,
but returned a few weeks later to announce that the whole clichéd psychedelic trip was a bust. "I was always pretty much of an outsider, a loner
until the spring-up of the psychedelic subculture brought the mediocre
masses to me like the mountain to Mohammed," he wrote. "That item
which functioned as my main interest, namely dope, had by the peculiar
mechanics of the passage of history become the central concern of all my
contemporaries as well."

Ever the contrarian, Lester spent the rest of the summer consuming
a drug the hippies did not embrace: Romilar cough syrup. "In 1967, when
I was a freshman in college and had never imbibed cough mixture in suf-
ficient quantities to place me among the *illuminati*, there came one day
into my possession one tab of acid and one bottle of Romilar," he wrote.
"As was my wont at the time, I threw the I Ching to find out which drug I
should take. When I asked it what would happen if I took the acid that day,
it tossed back a section called 'Inner Truth.' When I asked what would happen if I drank the Romilar, I got the passage on 'Confusion.' I took the tab
of acid, and did not get off a fraction of a flash. The moral of my tale is simple: Confusion is the only thing left which makes any sense."

The Block Drug Company of Jersey City, New Jersey, introduced
Romilar in the late 1950s to replace codeine-based cough syrups, which
those in search of illicit highs had begun to abuse. Romilar turned out to
be useful for the same purposes, thanks to its key ingredient, dextromethorphan. The synthetic cough suppressant is chemically analo-
gous to morphine, but rather than prompting opiatelike effects, it acts as
a powerful psychedelic when consumed in quantities of six to eight
ounces or more. Manufacturers discovered this in the late 1960s and
began to lace their cough medicines with chemicals designed solely to
induce nausea, but while drinking a bottle became a stomach-churning
adventure, the psychedelic trip was undiminished.

"Romilar is the ultimate street drug," Lester wrote. "Why? Because
every street has a drugstore on it, and every drugstore has a shelf loaded
with you-know-what." Dextromethorphan made him feel both numb and
jittery. "You call it a 'stone' or a 'high' because it changes your conscious-

ness and your physical sensations. But it changes them to emptiness—a total vacuum, a total absence of self." Like many psychedelics it could enhance the experience of listening to music, producing synesthesia, the sensation of "seeing" sounds as colors. But there were also less pleasant effects.

By Lester's own admission Romilar turned him into "a creep who couldn't do anything but stumble up to people and bellow 'HAW! HAW! HAW!' in their faces like a wacked-out aborigine." Rob Houghton and Roger Anderson tried it at their friend's urging and found it to be extremely unsettling, but Lester continued to imbibe. He viewed the drug as a conduit to altered consciousness, and in the spirit of Thomas De Quincey's *Confessions of an English Opium-Eater* and Aldous Huxley's *The Doors of Perception*, he began to detail his experiences in a series of spiral notebooks.

• • •

After music became a consuming passion, Lester made several attempts to master an instrument. At age twelve he tried the saxophone. He spent hours fantasizing about blowing atonal ragas while listening to John Coltrane, but he gave up after a month of lessons left his lip sore and cracked. He studied guitar for a while the following year, piano for three months a little later on, and drums for two weeks, "never meeting with much success because I was always too fired with the imperatives of inner song to bother learning music-book drivel like 'Old Black Joe' and 'My Bonnie,' " he wrote.

Harmonica was the only instrument Lester could fake well enough to jam with other people, though he could come up with some decent vocal melodies, and of course he had a folderful of smart and funny lyrics. Most of his songs were anthems to nonconformity or lampoons of stuffed-shirt killjoys. Among them: "Please Don't Burn My Yo-Yo," "He Gave You the Finger, Mabel," and "Keep Off the Grass." Jack Butler thought these tunes were great, and the two friends talked about forming a band together in senior year of high school. Butler was an accomplished musician, but Lester needed to determine whether his motives were pure. "Are we gonna get into it for the music or for the money?" Lester asked. Butler said what he thought Lester wanted to hear: "For the money!" It was the wrong answer.

"That blew him away," Butler recalled. "Right then we knew we weren't going to form a band. That wasn't even the answer I believed. I just thought I had Lester figured out. I thought he was into groups like Question Mark and the Mysterians—the garage stuff—as kind of a lark, and that he was in on the scam. I just wanted to please him."

Butler went on to cover the hits of the British Invasion bands in a group called Thee Dark Ages with another of their classmates, Jerry Raney. In 1966 the band moved into a nitery called the Hi-Ho Club. Once a fancy discotheque called Art's Roaring Twenties, it had reopened as a teen club, but it retained an ornate decor inspired by *The Untouchables*. The musicians joined the union and earned scale, but because they were underage, the club owner made them kick back most of their earnings in return for keeping the gig. It was one of Lester's first lessons on the ways of the music business.

Drunk or drugged out of his mind, Lester turned up regularly to cheer his friends' versions of "I'm a Man" and "Psychotic Reaction." He was especially fond of the latter, a blatant Yardbirds rip-off written by the Count Five, a one-hit-wonder garage band from San Jose. He had hated these "zit farmers" when he first heard them on the radio in the fall of 1966, but a year later he became a convert. He considered the reasons for his turnaround as he sat at the typewriter in his bedroom the day he finally broke down and bought the album.

"I'd always wanted to dig the song, but I never permitted myself to because I thought there was a real distinction between rock 'n' roll artists, musical workmen, and these fly-by-nights like the Count Five and the groups that played at the dances I went to," Lester wrote. "Eventually I realized that everybody steals their material and is heavily influenced by just about everybody else, and my tastes began to change radically. I suddenly found it an effort to listen to the more 'arty' rock (Beatles, Beach Boys, Jefferson Airplane) and that I much preferred the hard crude sound of groups like the Seeds, the Fugs, the Who, etc. And when I would go to dances and hear local teenagers, school friends of mine even—non-heads even!—turn around in the middle of 'I'm a Man' and roll off on a thirty-minute electric raga, plasticizing the beat, crouching in front of their amps for feedback, and knocking me out, really turning me on more than anything on record, that was when I finally was enlightened."

At every show Thee Dark Ages invited Lester to blow harp on four or five tunes. He had good energy, he could play passably well, but most important he *looked* cool. In his long frock coat and sideburns he summoned the image of a special guest from England. Following Lester's path, Milton Wyatt had strayed from the Jehovah's Witnesses, and he hoped to join Thee Dark Ages on drums. He thought his friend showed the same intensity onstage that he showed the day he exploded at Kingdom Hall. "Ever since the church thing it was like Lester could care less," Wyatt said. "I don't think he had an embarrassment gene; he just wasn't born with one."

Andy scoffed at her boyfriend's musical antics; she thought Lester was just playing the fool. Nevertheless, his appearances became so popular that Thee Dark Ages saved them for the last set of the night. The group would come back from its break and the red velvet curtains would part. Jerry Raney would shout, "Ladies and gentlemen, the best harmonica player in San Diego County!" And Lester would proceed to howl.

* * *

The meat locker was a damp and chilly place, and Lester's steady intake of Romilar didn't protect him from catching cold. In the fall of 1967 he moved back into Norma's apartment, girding against the inevitable "I told you so." But he didn't stay home for long.

Beatlemania yielded to psychedelia, and Thee Dark Ages disbanded, victims of the changing tides. In early 1968 Jack Butler formed a new, unnamed trio modeled after Cream and the Jimi Hendrix Experience. He and his bandmates lived in what they considered "a real hippie crash pad." The three-bedroom dump was one of several ramshackle houses propped up on cinder blocks and railroad ties in a dirt-road cul-de-sac.

Lester moved in with the band and spent much of the winter of 1968 in a self-medicated haze, listening to records and writing in his drug journals. He augmented his Romilar highs with six-packs of Busch and the ephedrine-coated wicks inside plastic nasal inhalers. "The cotton wick was so repellent and toxic that it was next to impossible to swallow, but if you could hold down even a little piece of it, it would shoot you the most intense speed rush imaginable," Rob Houghton wrote. Lester also mixed Romilar with Valium and Darvon purchased from the new crew of pill-pushers atop Mount Helix. "Darvons are the 'biggies,'" he wrote, so named because the large pink capsules contained an aspirin tablet in addition to the narcotic compound.

His new roommates were about as tolerant of Lester's musical tastes as his mother had been. They cranked endless blues jams by Cream and the San Francisco bands but called him a "faggot" whenever he played his new favorite, the epic white-noise assault of the Velvet Underground's "Sister Ray." He hung a giant poster of Velvets patron Andy Warhol in the living room, but one of the musicians ripped it down because he swore that the Pop artist was staring at him. "I didn't go around shoving my prejudices down everybody's throat," Lester wrote. "I just endured Cream every fucking day, 'Spoonful' and all the rest of that whiteheap bigdealsowhat. And you'd think it'd only be fair for them to endure the Velvet Underground, Count Five, *Oldies But Goodies,* the Fugs, the Godz, and I forget what other godawful racket I doted on. But they wouldn't let me have my equal portion of obnoxiousness. My music was 'bad' and theirs was 'good.' "

Musically Lester had more in common with his next-door neighbors, the San Diego or "Dago" chapter of the Hell's Angels, who occupied the house to the south. Following an alarmist report by the California attorney general in mid-1965, the state-wide biker gang had become America's most notorious outlaws. Their reputation was disproportionate to both their numbers and their actual threat to society, but the media attention prompted California authorities to crack down hard. By 1968 the dozen or so Dago Angels were trying to lie low in sleepy El Cajon.

Looking to escape his roommates' jamming, Lester would amble over to the bikers' place to drink beer and listen to the Seeds and the Music Machine. One night he took some whites and wrote one of his free-association epics in permanent marker on their walls; luckily the bikers were even sloppier than he was, and they didn't mind his impromptu redecorating. The gang was trying to recruit Jack Butler as a member, but it viewed Lester as a sort of mascot—a wacked-out college kid good for a laugh. The only trouble he had with them involved a copy of Hunter S. Thompson's bestseller, *Hell's Angels: The Strange and Terrible Saga of the Outlaw Motorcycle Gangs.*

"One afternoon Silly Willie was over at the house lecturing us all on how to be cool, avoid heat, get along, be like Angels with class, etc., and he mentioned something in the book as an example of one of his points," Lester wrote. He fetched his copy, and the Angel immediately flipped to the passage in question. Silly Willie had never seen the hardcover edition, and he asked Lester if he could buy it to replace his well-worn paperback. Lester said he'd checked it out of the Grossmont library.

"Well, shit, man, *burn* it off the fuckin' library and *give* it to me,"

Willy said. Lester unwisely demurred, and the angel smiled. "Well, then, how 'bout if I burn it off *you*, how's *that?*" he asked.

Though he had never progressed beyond penny-ante shoplifting, Lester harbored some outlaw fantasies of his own. As a child he'd heard talk of his father's prison record, and he imagined that Conway had been like Kerouac's manic car-thief sidekick, Neal Cassady. Whenever he encountered some of El Cajon's finest, Lester went out of his way to antagonize them. "Cop-hating is a passion that reaches across all levels and divisions of society," he wrote, but his only arrest in California resulted from a warrant for an unpaid moving violation. Two officers arrived at the apartment one morning after Norma left for work. They roused Lester out of bed and watched through the bathroom door as he relieved himself. Then they handcuffed him and put him in the squad car.

"I felt like I was Kid Killer Bangs," Lester wrote. "Man, I felt so bad I coulda let out a bloodcurdling Injun whoop! At the station I marched past a cell occupied by three spades slouching with profound unconcern. Maybe they were dope dealers! I could play it cool, rap like a champ, and get some respect from the dudes for this suburban white boy who chose to live by his own rules even if society tried to break him for it."

Instead he wound up sitting in a sterile fluorescent-lit cubicle, whiling away the time reading a copy of Richard Brautigan's *Trout Fishing in America*. Norma posted bail and they went home, but the mundane reality didn't stop Lester from milking the story when he told Andy and her mom. He dwelled with special indignation on the fictional part where the cops probed his ass for contraband. "Andy's stepfather Paul was the only one who saw my act for what it was," Lester wrote. "I was glorying in it."

One Friday night in March 1968 Andy picked Lester up at the band house. As they drove off, he noticed that the Angels next door were having a party, and he supposed it would be more fun than the one he was going to, yet another soirée hosted by Andy's theater pals. While the drama kids played charades, Lester rummaged through the medicine cabinet, swiping a vial of Darvon for future use; he had already popped three Benzedrines. Andy generally avoided the band house, and after the party she dropped off her boyfriend and said goodnight. Lester was sitting around with two of his roommates when Silly Willie burst through the door wearing a short kimono.

Lester had read about the Angels turning women into "mamas" who provided sex on demand for all comers; now their friendly neighborhood biker proffered an invitation. "Hey, you fuckers: How would you like to rip yerselves off a nice juicy fuck tonight? We got a broad over here and she's fuckin' with *everybody!*"

One of the musicians jumped up immediately, but the other begged off. "I didn't particularly relish the idea of being something like sixteenth man in line at an Angel gangbang," Lester wrote, "and even if I *were* that flipped-out and horny the Benzedrine I'd taken earlier would have made it pretty near impossible for me to partake in the festivities." But he fancied himself a true pop journalist, and he wanted to observe. "After all, every writer wants to have as many unusual experiences as possible."

At the Angels' door Silly Willie suddenly paused and asked his guests if they were eighteen. He sounded like the doorman at an exclusive nightclub. Lester and his friend assured him they were of age. Inside, eight of the Dago Angels and one of their girlfriends lounged around listening to the stereo. Another girl crouched with her head in the crotch of a biker. She was naked, but the only thing Lester could see was a tangled mass of wiry black hair that made him think of Archy's alley cat, Mehitabel.

The girl was the former lover of a hulking Angel who nodded off behind his shades. Lester sat down next to him on the ratty old couch. Somebody played a Motown collection, followed by Otis Redding singing "I've Been Loving You Too Long (To Stop Now)." Lester asked Silly Willie if there was any beer, but the booze was long gone. They passed around a joint. "It was *boring* in a way," Lester wrote. "No, not boring—it seemed almost as if time had come to a stop."

For forty-five minutes the girl fellated the biker. Then she began to sob. "What kinda half-ass creep job is this?" he asked angrily.

The former lover popped out of his stupor. "Clout the bitch upside the head, motherfucker," he said. "Tell 'er she better give you some proper fuckin' head or I'm gonna make damn straight she ain't alive to see the sun come up!"

"Ah, she's no good," the first biker replied.

"I said give that boy some head!" her ex-amore shouted. He rose from the couch, lifted his boot high, and brought it down hard in her face— "hard enough to bruise and pain, but not so hard that she couldn't go back to sucking cocks," Lester wrote. "He gave her another kick at the base of the spine and she hardly made a sound. This had been going on for several hours, after all."

The Angel plopped back down beside Lester, who now saw something that he hadn't noticed before. A tattered copy of an Uncle Scrooge comic from his collection lay open on the floor, its bright colors a stark contrast to the dark happenings inches away. "I had taken the whole scene in at last," Lester wrote, "nothing more to add."

·: ·•, ·:

Lester shuddered visibly the following day when he told Ben the story. Fearful that the bikers would try to stop him if they sensed that he'd been spooked, he enlisted his nephew's help in moving out. Ben in turn recruited his construction-worker dad, and the three of them went to the band house in Ben Jr.'s pickup truck.

There Lester discovered that someone had liberated his entire record collection. He quickly packed the rest of his belongings. They were loading the truck when a biker approached and flashed a chrome-plated revolver in his belt. Ben Jr. brandished the hatchet that he used to chop through Sheetrock, and the Angel backed off.

Two days later the police acted on an anonymous tip and raided both the Angels' shack and the band house. Like Lester, Jack Butler had moved out just in time. "I could tell the shit was going to hit the fan," he said. A woman the Angels gang-banged wound up in the hospital and talked to the police; Lester was never sure whether it was the girl with the Mehitabel hair or someone else. By the time the cops arrived, most of the bikers were gone. They were said to be hiding in Mexico.

Lester returned to live with his mom in a two-bedroom unit on the second floor of an apartment complex directly across First Street from the high-school tennis courts. He settled in to destroy his room and search for catharsis through writing. Drawing on the entries in his spiral notebooks, he compiled an autobiographical account of the preceding year in a four-hundred-page manuscript called *Drug Punk*. It built to a frank account of the Angels' gang bang and an apocalyptic fantasy entitled "The Destruction of El Cajon."

The hip young teacher in his humanities class often encouraged Lester to read his work, and as a result it was the only class at Grossmont that he never skipped. One day near the end of the spring semester, he read the climactic scene from his novel, but the reaction stunned him. "I would be interested in hearing you justify this complete piece of garbage you've just read," the teacher said. Several students demanded to know how Lester could have sat there thinking about his comic book while a woman was being raped. For once he had nothing to say. "What else could I have done?" he finally stammered.

Devastated, Lester dropped the class, quit Grossmont, and withdrew to his mother's apartment. "Months went by, and no one saw him," his friend Roger Anderson wrote. "He was hiding in his room, wrestling with nameless demons. It was as if he died—as if he saw himself as a dead man." Andy agreed. "I don't think Les ever really got over the rape," she said. "Part of him died from that."

Lester began to put on weight, developing a beer gut at age nineteen. His hands trembled, and he was always sweaty and clammy. He stopped bathing regularly and drank a bottle or two of cough syrup a day. When he was high, the lump on his forehead that lingered from childhood seemed to become more prominent. He called it his "whizzer" and joked that Romilar made it grow, but it was really the fact that his hair became plastered to his scalp as the drugs made him sweat.

"The fall of 1968 was such a terrible time," Lester wrote a decade later. "I was a physical and mental wreck, nerves shredded and ghosts and spiders looming and squatting across the mind." He hid in his room watching TV and jerking off to his favorite copy of *Playboy*. The only book he could concentrate on long enough to finish was *The Rise and Fall of the Third Reich*. He continued to scan *Newsweek* every Tuesday, following the war in Vietnam and the election of Richard M. Nixon, but he felt no connection to these events. He had become an amorphous, apolitical, apathetic blob, and he roused himself only long enough for the occasional visit to Ratner's or Arcade Records.

"Buying records was always a certain form of self-expression for me (I almost said 'therapy,' but you don't want to make yourself look too desperate)," Lester wrote. Two albums in particular brought him solace. *White Light/White Heat* by the Velvet Underground he dubbed "rock 'n' roll's ultimate expression of nihilism and destruction," while the improvised epiphanies of *Astral Weeks* by Van Morrison struck him as a beacon of light cutting through the murk. While Norma slept in the next room, he played both albums through the night, the volume so low it was barely audible. "I was wracked with existential anxiety spazzouts because I couldn't handle living with my mother when I hated her," he wrote, "yet for some reason I couldn't seem to summon the energy and conviction and plain *imagination* to move out and face the world on its terms instead of Mom's, mine, and the Velvet Underground's."

Andy literally tried to knock him out of his funk. "I remember I hit him in the head with a shoe," she said. They were driving around one sunny afternoon when she realized he was high. He lied and said he hadn't taken any cough medicine. "Don't give me that crap!" she snapped. "I can always tell because you act like such a *goon!*" They pulled over and began flailing at each other. She found a bottle of Romilar and threw it down the street, but he just grinned, reached into his pocket, and pulled out another.

Instead of the old carefree dates on Navy Pier, the couple sat around her parents' house watching sitcoms like *Gilligan's Island, My Favorite Martian,* and *The Flying Nun.* If Andy wasn't home, her boyfriend watched cartoons with her five-year-old brother. Lester would take his shoes off and lie on the couch, and Danny would bite his feet and laugh. One day Lester showed him a comic by R. Crumb, the story of the castrating vulture demonesses. Thoroughly freaked, the kid fell silent for the rest of the day.

Sometimes Lester felt like a character in one of Crumb's comics. Here he was with "all these hippies laying all this garbage on me about a groovy freelovechicksdopewoman paradise," and he still wasn't getting any. But the woman he loved gave him something else that he needed even more. "I don't want the kind of woman that will lay her head on my knee as I'm puking in the sink or toilet and say: 'Oh you great poet Byronic genius, how do you do it' and then clean up the house," he wrote. "I want a woman willing to put up with a certain amount of that then say: 'Go ahead and kill yourself! I don't care! But if you do you won't write shit! And you'll live through it stupid bastard for thirty years or less if you're lucky!' They make girls like that now, fortunately. Didn't use to."

Goaded by Andy, Lester finally began to pick himself up. He enrolled at San Diego State College and agreed to see a doctor about his nerves. He made an appointment with the Seventh-Day Adventist who'd been treating him since junior high. He didn't admit that he'd been lacerating his system with drugs for the past year, and the avuncular physician never suspected a thing. The old man asked him about school, and Lester told him about starting at State. The doctor concluded that his problem was college-induced stress and wrote a prescription for a dozen two-milligram tabs of Librium. Then he smiled.

"You know a lot of kids," the doctor said. "I've been thinking about this, and maybe you can enlighten me a little: How come so many of them are out taking drugs?"

Lester just stared at him; the good doctor was trying to use him as a representative of the youth culture to fill him in on the latest. "Well, I guess they're searching for something," Lester said at length. "I really don't know."

chapter four

Make It
or Break It

"I awoke from The Funk at the age of nineteen, nervous and tired, with the look of crossed eyes and queasiness peculiar to survivors of it," Lester wrote. Said his friend Roger Anderson, "It was like he'd died and been reborn."

Lester started at San Diego State College in September 1968 with the goal of becoming a teacher, a profession that would pay the rent while he wrote his novel. Situated on a mesa overlooking Mission Bay, the campus teemed with the swelled enrollment of Baby Boomers seeking to avoid the draft. For the next three years Lester took almost nothing but literature courses, and he scored some respectable grades. In the spring of 1969 he earned two A's in English Literature and Sophomore Composition, two B's in Modern Contemporary Fiction and Twentieth-Century American Prose, and a C in American English. He also withdrew from a class called Principles of Healthy Living.

Shortly before the Social Security checks cut off, Lester got a job in the women's casuals division of Streicher's Shoe Store in the Mission Valley Shopping Center. He earned $2.50 an hour plus a 1-percent commission, but there were other benefits. Squatting between the knees of a pretty teenager or her divorcée mom, he'd slip on a pair of pumps, allowing his fingers to linger for a second on a smooth, tanned calf. Once again he thought of his life imitating a comic by R. Crumb.

Debbie Rachac met Lester when she was a sixteen-year-old shopping for school shoes with her mom. She tried on twenty pairs, and she and Lester wound up dating. He was still going steady with Andy, but they had an agreement that allowed them to see other people. It was, after all, the sixties. "I suppose in that way our relationship was a weird mix of Ozzie and Harriet and the Velvet Underground," Andy said.

The majority of Streicher's sales force was comprised of middle-aged alcoholics. "These guys could corrupt anything," according to Ben, who worked in the company's warehouse. Some of them resented Lester because he was the only one who seemed to have a future. When he wrote some graffiti in the bathroom that employed the word "graffiti," the notoriously surly manager nailed him instantly. "Why do you think I did it?" Lester asked. The boss snickered. "Nobody else here knows what 'graffiti' means," he said.

Once the crew persuaded Lester to spike the manager's Coke with waterproofing spray, and the boss spent half an hour vomiting in the john. The incident became part of Streicher's lore, along with the tale of how Lester handled a particularly annoying customer who wanted to see every pair in the place. She finally requested some calf-high go-go boots in gray suede, though she'd clearly never fit into them. When Lester brought them out, she asked whether they were *genuine* suede. "Oh, no," he said. "These are made from *elephants' foreskins.*" The lady looked at him and said, "I *knew* there was something about them I liked!"

One morning in October 1970 Lester came in late after a night spent drinking wine and blasting Bob Seger's *Mongrel*. It wasn't the first time, and the manager fired him, but by then it really didn't matter. An ad he'd answered many months before had started him on a new career path. "We are interested in receiving record reviews, movie reviews, and book reviews from interested writers," it read. "Please send your manuscript with a self-addressed envelope to Manuscripts Editor, *Rolling Stone*, 746 Brannan Street, San Francisco, California 94103."

※ ※ ※

Rock 'n' roll had thrived for more than a decade without anyone to critique it. When the mainstream media wrote about fifties rockers such as Chuck Berry, Little Richard, and Jerry Lee Lewis, it was often in terms of an encroaching cultural plague, which only made fans love it more. Magazines such as *Song Hits, Hit Parader, Beat,* and *16* lauded teens' heroes by printing lyrics, photos, and occasional interviews about the stars' favorite foods and colors, but there was very little "real" journalism, and absolutely no criticism.

When it debuted in February 1966, *Crawdaddy!* was the first publication to bill itself as "a magazine of rock 'n' roll criticism." Paul Williams, a freshman at Swarthmore College, looked at the homemade magazines produced by science-fiction fans and realized that anyone with a typewriter and a mimeograph machine could become a publisher. He wrote about the music he loved in essays that were like letters to his friends, and before long his hand-stapled fanzine began to attract other aspiring rock critics. Jon Landau was a clerk at the Briggs & Briggs record store in Harvard Square, Sandy Pearlman studied at the State University of New York at Stony Brook, and Pearlman's pal Richard Meltzer was about to be thrown out of graduate studies in philosophy at Yale.

While he was still at Stony Brook, Meltzer wrote a sprawling, funny, and sometimes inscrutable treatise that analyzed rock in comparison to the rest of the art produced by Western civilization. In the spring of 1967 Williams retitled it "The Aesthetics of Rock" and printed it in the eighth issue of *Crawdaddy!* By then plenty of other writers were reviewing rock 'n' roll. Richard Goldstein penned his "Pop Eye" column for the *Village*

Nick Tosches and Richard Meltzer, 1971.
PHOTO COURTESY OF RICHARD MELTZER

Voice, Robert Christgau wrote for the New York monthly *Cheetah,* and Greil Marcus contributed to several underground papers in the Bay Area.

"In 1966 bedazzled college students like myself were helplessly dumping quotes from Plato on Beatle hits and Dylan albums, attempting to talk about the world the music seemed to be changing," Marcus wrote. "Meltzer communicated as a pointedly cynical joke, out of tune with the mandated optimism of late '60s culture."

Meltzer considered himself first and foremost a visual artist. He specialized in weird and disturbing works such as a stillborn kitten entombed in a Tropicana orange-juice bottle filled with Jell-O, but he continued sending *Crawdaddy!* sharp and funny essays such as "What a Goddam Great Second Cream Album" and "Pythagoras the Cave Painter," the first interview with Jimi Hendrix published in America. Hendrix laughed when he read the piece. "You were *stoned* when you wrote that, right?" he asked.

In the spring of 1968 Meltzer split from *Crawdaddy!* because of a dispute with Williams, but by then the editor himself was ready to quit for a stint on a commune. The magazine had reached a circulation of twenty thousand, and Williams felt that the battle had been won. "The *New York Times* was reviewing the new Beatles album when it came out, and there was no longer a need for the crusade which I had been on, to get people to try to take this stuff seriously," he said. "I had a lot of fun with it, but by then it was obvious that people were taking this stuff far *too* seriously."

Chief among the offenders were the struggling reviewers of *Rolling Stone.* Founded by a twenty-one-year-old Berkeley dropout named Jann Wenner, the biweekly tabloid published its first issue in October 1967. Early on, Wenner sought advice from Williams, who told him that readers wanted more hard information about the musicians. "I wasn't interested in giving it to them," Williams said. "To me it was about what we could learn about each other through our responses to music. I recognized from the beginning that Jann would leave me in the dust, but that was fine. I didn't even try to compete."

From the outset *Rolling Stone* published "all the news that fits," rising above the slew of new rock magazines by virtue of an old-fashioned journalistic approach. There was no reason that stories about the youth culture shouldn't be professionally written and reported, Wenner said. His mentor, veteran *San Francisco Chronicle* jazz columnist Ralph J. Gleason, convinced him to hire a skilled reporter from the *Oakland Tribune* as managing editor. John Burks started in early 1968, shortly after copy editor Charles Perry. A year after the magazine's launch the only section still lacking was the record reviews. *Rolling Stone* staffers critiqued whatever they happened to be listening to whenever they got around to it. In the first issue Wenner himself wrote eight reviews full of such illuminating assessments as "strange but quite nice," "quite well done," and "good record!" In a review of Arlo Guthrie's *Alice's Restaurant* he advised, "First, take a look at the cover of this album. If you don't dig the cover, which is incredibly funny-looking, then don't listen to the title song."

Lester didn't have much use for such criticism. "I long ago gave up on giving the other fellow's taste the benefit of the doubt," he wrote. "It led me to too many shitty, phony albums rhapsodized over by the influential sycophants serving as rock journalists in the absence of anyone with more style, taste, and insight." He read the underground press religiously, but aside from *Crawdaddy!*, he wasn't impressed with any of the music mags, including *Rolling Stone*. "People just aren't writing for me on the whole," he wrote. "Maybe someday they will be to a greater degree, if indeed *Rolling Stone* and its ilk are the prototypes of the future, but even *Rolling Stone* is crammed with the most predictable portraits of uninteresting people. In fact, the literature of the counterculture could well be the most boring of all."

When Lester saw *Rolling Stone*'s house ad, he decided that if no one was writing for him, maybe he ought to be writing himself. "So I started sending them reviews," he said in 1982. "The first four reviews I sent I said that *Anthem of the Sun* by the Grateful Dead and *Sailor* by Steve Miller were pieces of shit and *White Light/White Heat* by the Velvet Underground and Nico's *The Marble Index* were masterpieces. And I couldn't figure out why they weren't printing any of these things."

The reviews landed on John Burks's desk. The critiques didn't impress him, but he enjoyed the cover letter about being a shoe salesman and Romilar addict in some godforsaken suburb called El Cajon. He made a note to give the writer a call, but he wouldn't get around to it for another six months.

❦ ❦ ❦

San Francisco wasn't the only American city in 1967 with a dynamic rock scene and ambitious young entrepreneurs. Early that year a burly, pot-smoking jazz fan, poet, and hustler named John Sinclair called a meeting of the leaders of the Detroit underground. They formed an umbrella group called Trans-Love Energies to inspire cultural revolution in the Motor City and then the world, and maybe make a few bucks promoting concerts along the way. But the tenor of optimistic capitalism changed on July 23.

The riots erupted in the middle of the Summer of Love, and the white musicians, writers, and artists watched from their rooftops as downtown burned. "When the Detroit uprising jumped off, we thought the beginning of the end had arrived, and we were busy planning for the 'post-revolutionary construction' which would start with the victory of the insurrection," Sinclair wrote. "But the fantasy ended with the brutal suppression of the slave revolt in the streets and the gun-butts of the National Guard and U.S. Army troops, who beat our door down and threatened to shoot us all on the spot."

In the aftermath Sinclair became the manager of the city's most exciting rock band, the MC5, which he saw as a vehicle to motivate white youth toward another, more successful uprising. In August 1968 the Five was the only group to perform at the protests outside the Democratic National Convention in Chicago. The violence there convinced Sinclair that revolution would not be possible without armed struggle, and Trans-Love Energies transmogrified into the White Panther Party.

In November 1968 the new organization announced a radical ten-point program. The first point was full endorsement of the Black Panthers' agenda, but it was the second point that captured the public's imagination: "Total assault on the culture by any means necessary, including rock 'n' roll, dope, and fucking in the streets."

Two months later MC5 singer Rob Tyner appeared on the cover of *Rolling Stone*'s twenty-fifth issue, shortly before the release of the band's debut album, *Kick Out the Jams*. An impressionable young writer smoked pot for the first time with Sinclair and came away convinced that the MC5 and their manager would change the world. Suitably stoked, Lester rushed out and bought the album the day it was released. On the way home he read Sinclair's political treatise in the gatefold sleeve and concluded that the ideas were lifted from the teen exploitation film *Wild in the Streets*. "Clearly this notion of violent, total youth revolution and takeover is an idea whose time has come—which speaks not well for the idea but ill for the time," he wrote in an angry review.

The Five boasted of playing guitar the way Pharoah Sanders played sax, but instead of rock's answer to free jazz, Lester heard only inferior versions of the two-chord songs by the Kingsmen or the Seeds. "Just like anybody, you buy something you don't like and you feel like you bought a hype," he said in 1982. "I wrote this really like—'Blaaah!'—scathing sort of review and sent it to *Rolling Stone* with a letter that said, 'Look, fuckheads, I'm as good as any writer you've got in there. You'd better print this or give me the reason why!' And they did, they printed it, and that was the beginning."

Managing editor John Burks finally gave Lester a call. *Rolling Stone* still had a humble circulation of about fifty thousand, and Burks cultivated any writer who showed promise. "We encouraged a lot of people, because who knew who was going to be any good?" he said. Copy editor Charles Perry was particularly impressed with Lester's work. "He was such a slick writer compared with some of the stiffs that were writing about rock 'n' roll," Perry recalled. "He could really use the language."

The magazine published five pieces by Lester—including reviews of the third album by the Velvet Underground and Alice Cooper's debut—by the time Jann Wenner hired his first full-time record-reviews editor. The son of a San Francisco furrier, Greil Marcus had majored in American Studies at Berkeley and participated in the Free Speech movement led by Mario Savio. He looked and talked like the professor he intended to become, but he was also a devout fan of Elvis Presley. One day he complained to his friend Ralph J. Gleason about the poor quality of *Rolling Stone*'s record reviews, and shortly thereafter Wenner phoned with a challenge: "If you're so disgusted with the record-reviews section, why don't you edit it?"

Marcus took the job. "I like your writing," he told Lester the first time they spoke on the phone. "Write about whatever you want." The first issue Marcus edited, in July 1969, spotlighted two reviews paired to illustrate the strange but passionately argued aesthetic of the shoe salesman from El Cajon. Lester hailed Captain Beefheart's *Trout Mask Replica* as a masterpiece of warped blues and the work of "the only true dadaist in rock." He also railed against the syrupy strings and Rod McKuen–style lyrics of the self-titled *It's a Beautiful Day*. "I hate this album," he wrote, "not only because I wasted my money on it, but for what it represents: an utterly phony, arty approach to music that we will not soon escape."

Over the next few months Lester submitted as many as a dozen reviews a week—most of them never printed—accompanied by long letters explaining how he viewed music, writing, and the world. "I had already speculated that I might be striking the folks up north as some kind of *enfant terrible*, firing off salvos of venom at things I disliked and eulogizing things I dug as if they were the second coming," he wrote in July 1969. "And although there was some real bullshit in my style and statements (as when I laid that Burroughsian/revolutionary bit on you about wanting 'to blow up the set and start all over again'), the main barrier between what I've done and real excellence is this kind of cultural defensiveness I've always had from having to force everything from the early Stones to the Velvet Underground to all of jazz on my friends."

His goal was to write with the rhythm and energy of the music, Lester declared, incorporating "the free-flowing, imagistic quality" of his fiction into his critiques. He heralded a new movement in rock, progressing from the Yardbirds to the Velvet Underground and Captain Beefheart "on to incredible unglimpsed horizons of masterfully abstracted sound." Marcus disliked dense and distorted productions, but Lester lauded them. "You discover new things every listen that you'd missed before in the buzzing haze," he wrote. "Fact, I dig buzzing hazes for their own sake!"

Clearly Lester had a different standard for judging music—a way of finding beauty in unconventional places, just as he and his father had once been struck by the grandeur of a polluted highway sunset. "I do think the beauty of something like *Trout Mask Replica* or 'Sister Ray' or Don Cherry's *Symphony for Improvisors* puts the beauty (which is nevertheless great, of course) of, say, Van Morrison or the Byrds far in the shade," Lester wrote in late 1969. "Those are more traditional concepts of beauty, while this is the beauty of rushing many-streamed complexity which when it finally grabs you can literally take your head away so that you'll find yourself. . . . It demands *involvement* on the part of the listener. You've got to pay attention to it, it's not for the passive listener. But shit, here I go *sermonizing* again."

At the time he had yet to tell Marcus of his Jehovah's Witness upbringing.

❊ ❊ ❊

Initially the major record companies were oblivious to the needs of these new rock critics. Fewer than a dozen copies of *Sergeant Pepper's Lonely Hearts Club Band* were sent to the press in 1967, but two years later things were changing. Older publicists fearful of losing their jobs and newly hired "company freaks" were both all too happy to send piles of albums, press releases, photos, and promotional goodies to anyone who seemed to have a pipeline into the youth movement.

A decade earlier, when he was furtively hiding his records from his mother, Lester could never have imagined a time when he'd receive twenty albums a day in the mail. Now the promo copies that he didn't like he sold for beer money, those the record stores wouldn't buy he gave to friends, and the ones that no one wanted became fodder for a new game that he played with Gary Rachac, the brother of the girl he picked up at the shoe store. A few years Lester's junior, Gary carted stacks of vinyl LPs by nowhere artists to Wells Park so that his idol could hurl them across the parking lot. When the records looked as if they could still be played, Lester gave them a spin; when they didn't he smashed them to bits. "There are probably still chips of vinyl out in that parking lot today," Gary said.

Lester's early work for *Rolling Stone* generated considerable feedback. One of the members of Captain Beefheart's Magic Band called to thank him and invited him to come live with the group at its commune in Antelope Valley. Julie Driscoll sent a note of appreciation for his critique of her album *Streetnoise*. "It really did brighten my day, although I was kinda hoping she'd offer to ball me," Lester wrote Marcus. Most gratifying was a letter from Velvet Underground drummer Maureen Tucker. Lester loved the band's self-titled third album, though it was quieter and more understated than *White Light/White Heat*. Record-company ads quoted the question he posed in his review: "How do you define a group who moved from 'Heroin' to 'Jesus' in two short years?"

In October 1969 Lester, Roger Anderson, and Rob Houghton drove to Los Angeles to see the Velvets play the Whiskey A-Go-Go. Lester was flabbergasted when he handed the waitress a dollar for a fifty-cent Coke and she walked off with the change. After the show he went backstage to meet the band members, and he tried to talk drugs with them. "I think you can take *any* drug just so long as you don't take it too much or too often," he said. Singer Lou Reed scoffed. "Well, yeah, if you wanna be a smorgasbord schmuck," he said. Lester changed the subject to music, raving about the second album by the Band. "It's typical of all these people who want to go back to an agrarian society," rhythm guitarist Sterling Morrison cracked.

Despite the frosty reception Lester remained curious about the musicians as people, especially Reed, and the band continued to represent his paradigm for great rock 'n' roll. Through their early association with Andy Warhol, the Velvets made it clear that they viewed rock as art. They incorporated elements of the classical avant garde and free jazz in their music and drew on the literary tradition of the Beats in their lyrics, but they understood that what mattered most was the visceral gut reaction. They proved that so-called teenaged rock 'n' roll could be substantive and important, and that smart, passionate people could devote their lives to it.

With every review that arrived at the magazine, *Rolling Stone*'s editors grew more curious about the correspondent from El Cajon. Who was named "Lester" anymore? And "Bangs"? What a name for a rock writer: *Bang! Bang!* In the fall of 1969 they convinced Jann Wenner to fly their star critic to San Francisco. When Lester got the call, he assumed he was being summoned north for a job interview as a staff writer.

Greil Marcus and his friend Langdon Winner picked the reviewer up at the Oakland Airport. Winner was stunned when Lester got off the plane wearing short hair, a suit jacket, and a tie. "I think he was even wearing brown shoes," Winner said, "and this is at the time of Frank Zappa's 'Brown Shoes Don't Make It'!" The trio crossed the Bay Bridge and dropped by the magazine's offices. No one remembers if Lester made much of an impact on the publisher, but the other editors were just as surprised by his appearance. "I don't know whether Lester was fried from whatever pharmaceutical combination or just freaked out about being there," John Burks said, "but he certainly seemed weird."

Three years Lester's senior, Marcus intimidated him. One day as they were driving into the city, Lester cracked open a bottle of Old Overholt whiskey, a favorite dubbed "Old Overcoat" by the gang at home. "I hope you'll save some of that so that I can have a drink tonight," Marcus said. He paused a beat, then added, "I *will* not!" in an imitation of Lester's drawl. "Lester thought that was really funny," his friend Roger Anderson said. "But it was also obvious that Greil was like this middle-aged guy. This wasn't the sort of pleasantry any of *us* would make."

As Lester's editor, Marcus felt compelled to put him up at his house in Berkeley, even though his wife was eight and a half months pregnant. "Lester was the all-time oblivious, obnoxious houseguest," Marcus said. After two days he suggested that Lester might be more comfortable at Langdon Winner's place. "Lester thought he wasn't good enough to stay at my house, and he would write about this over the years to various people—how badly I had treated him," Marcus said. "But the thing that really got to him, and that he really felt betrayed by, was that he thought we were flying him up to see whether or not we should hire him at

Rolling Stone, and that had never even occurred to any of us. We just wanted to meet him, and we thought he would want to meet us."

Blissfully unaware, Lester didn't realize that his critiques were also generating some negative reactions, and these had filtered back to Jann Wenner. His pans of *Kick Out the Jams* and *It's a Beautiful Day* infuriated Elektra head Jac Holzman and CBS president Clive Davis, both of whom advertised in the magazine. Lester also dismissed the psychedelic soul of Buddy Miles's *Them Changes*, calling it "sloppy, slushily horn-y soul stock jammed with the most stereotypic instrumental and vocal clichés." After he lambasted the next two Miles albums as well, the drummer stormed into *Rolling Stone*'s offices, threw an editor against the water cooler, and demanded to see the publisher. Wenner fled via the fire escape as a secretary summoned the police.

In October 1969 Andy woke Lester with the news that Jack Kerouac had died at the age of forty-seven after years of rampant alcoholism. Lester rolled over in bed and stared at the wall; he had just been dreaming of finding a portfolio of Kerouac's unpublished writings in a dusty junk store back in Escondido. He badgered the editors of *Rolling Stone* until they agreed to let him write the obituary. "Jack was in so many ways a spiritual father of us all, as much as Lenny Bruce or Dylan or any of them," he began. "He was the first and greatest of those to write literature akin to the sound and feeling and spirit of rock." After a thousand heartfelt words he concluded, "Good night, Jack. May Gerard and all your white-robed angels sing you tenderly upward-borne forever."

The obituary was the first of his *Rolling Stone* stories that Lester showed his mother, but Norma disapproved. All of this talk about spiritual fathers and white-robed angels for a drunken Beatnik poet—it just wasn't right.

A few weeks later Lester submitted what he hoped would be his first major *Rolling Stone* feature, an interview with another of his heroes, Charles Mingus. The critical establishment had never appreciated the rogue bassist's talents as a composer, Lester contended, but his story would remedy that. "I want to make it a really polished, journalistically convincing piece of work, the kind that will leave no doubt in the reader's mind that he's *got* to hear this man's music," he wrote Marcus when he proposed the piece. He went on to spend six months on the research and writing—an unprecedented amount of time when he usually churned out a couple of reviews a night on speed.

Because he didn't know much about jazz, Marcus gave Lester's finished epic to Ralph J. Gleason, the jazz critic for the *San Francisco Chronicle*, a *Rolling Stone* columnist, and Jann Wenner's friend and mentor. "I got the feeling I was being totally condescended to," Lester wrote of Gleason's subsequent phone call. "At one point he said that the theme of evil jazz critics was an integral part of my article, that he didn't see how it could be removed, but of course it *had* to be removed. At another point he said that unless I had all the information that would allow me to present both sides of the picture, I shouldn't even *write* an article. . . . *Down Beat* and the jazz critical establishment have been forces working against jazz for years, not only in the record reviews but in their whole racist, reactionary attitude. Gleason, though he always liked Mingus, was one of the very *Down Beat* critics I was slamming. . . . I believe I'm starting to get like Mingus and wonder what the fuck is what."

The article never ran. A few months earlier Lester had sent his novel, *Drug Punk*, to Wenner, and now it came back without so much as a note. The publisher hadn't even considered running it in *Rolling Stone*, though it wouldn't have been inconceivable: Two years later the magazine would publish a not dissimilar first-person examination of drugs and decadence called *Fear and Loathing in Las Vegas* by Hunter S. Thompson.

"We didn't know it then, but politics rule the world," said Lester's girlfriend Andy. "He wasn't happy when he got that knowledge. He thought that *Rolling Stone* was a free press, which of course it wasn't. It was always an empire, and he had trouble with that."

Lester would be disillusioned one more time before 1969 ended. Determined not to be upstaged by Woodstock and anxious to deflect criticism that they'd sold out, the Rolling Stones announced that they would end their first U.S. tour in three years with a free concert in the Bay Area on December 6. The show would usher in the new decade and cap a turbulent year that had witnessed the Apollo moon landing, the exposure of the My Lai massacre, Chappaquiddick, the trial of the Chicago Eight, and the Tate-LaBianca killings.

Though they originally intended to sit out the concert, Lester, Roger Anderson, and their pal Jim Bovee got caught up in the excitement the night before the show as reports were broadcast on San Diego's hip new rock station, KCBQ-FM. At 9 P.M. they counted their change, grabbed a joint and a bottle of Jack Daniel's, and piled into Roger's 1966 Falcon for the five-hundred-mile trip north.

By two in the morning Lester was in an alcoholic slumber in the backseat. Roger lit the joint, took a hit, and passed it to Bovee, who was driving. "Shouldn't we save some of this for Lester?" Bovee asked. Roger turned and prodded his friend, but Lester merely snored. Just then a member of the California Highway Patrol sped up behind them.

Roger threw the joint out the window and stashed the booze. The officer told Bovee he'd been swerving and asked if they'd been drinking. "What is this, fucking Nazi Germany?" Lester asked, springing to attention. This response surprised the cop, but before he could say anything he was distracted by a call on the radio. He left with a quick warning that Bovee probably shouldn't be driving.

"Fine," Lester said, climbing over the seat. "*I'll* drive."

They started back up the highway, swerving worse than ever. "One of you guys better take over; I don't think I'm up for this," Lester said. He pulled over, returned to the backseat, and took a swig of Jack Daniel's. "Say, where's that joint?"

The trio arrived in the small town of Livermore, forty miles east of San Francisco, just as the sun was rising over the Altamont Speedway. The site was not the Stones' first choice, but at the last minute the owners of the original venue had demanded an additional $125,000, and the band wasn't willing to pay. The stage at Altamont was set up in a low bowl-like area near the highway, surrounded on three sides by sloping hills covered with dead grass and sticker burrs. The biggest crowd the track had accommodated in the past was sixty-five hundred. Now three hundred thousand came down its one dirt access road.

"I remember thinking all day: 'If I was waiting to see anybody but the Stones, I'd leave this fucking shitheap right now,'" Lester wrote. To Roger the place seemed like a hippie concentration camp. A line of drug dealers openly hawked their wares, peddling Seconal by the handful. The drug made people clumsy and surly, especially when it was combined with alcohol. Nixon's Operation Intercept was stopping the flood of speed and marijuana at the Mexican border, and after years when booze was disdained as an Establishment trip, alcohol was making a big comeback. Shards of broken glass from thousands of bottles of Boone's Farm wine littered the ground by eight in the morning.

At one point Lester spotted Greil Marcus in the crowd, chomping on his professorial pipe, but they didn't connect. The Hell's Angels had been hired as security, and they began to congregate around the stage as the day progressed. Most were drunk, downed out, or tripping on acid. Given his experience at the band house, the sight of the bikers set Lester on edge, but he and his friends gamely worked their way toward the stage. During a perfunctory set by Crosby, Stills, Nash & Young a boy ran through the crowd bleeding and calling for help. "We need a doctor, asshole!" Lester shouted as David Crosby rapped about peace, love, and Woodstock. Nobody paid any attention.

"I think they're gonna snuff that guy," Roger said when the Angels beat a man who got too close to the stage while the Jefferson Airplane performed. "I remember the naked sobbing girl who came stumbling down past us," Lester wrote, "shoved by some irate redded-out boyfriend up the hill, everyone ogling her and snickering. . . . I remember the freaked out kid shrieking: 'Kill! Kill! Kill!' I remember the Angels vamping on him, too, and then seeing him passed in a twitching gel over the heads in the first few rows and then dumped on the ground to snivel at the feet of total strangers who would ignore him, because the Stones were coming on in a minute which would be two hours. Nobody wanted to take their eyes off the stage for fear of missing them."

Night fell, and the crowd surged toward the four-foot-high platform, sweeping Lester and his friends forward as the Stones finally opened with "Jumping Jack Flash." Surrounded by bikers and looking as tense and wary as many in the crowd, the band tore through its set. The scuffles between the Angels and the fans continued, and the Angels always won. As the Stones played "Under My Thumb," the bikers began hassling an eighteen-year-old black fan named Meredith Hunter; some said it was because he was with a pretty white girl from Berkeley. Hunter pulled a nickel-plated revolver to defend himself. In *Gimme Shelter*, the tour film commissioned by the Stones, several Angels can be seen stabbing and beating him to death.

Like many who were there, Lester was unaware of the killing until the following day. The Stones watched as the violence spiraled out of control, but they kept playing. "What else could they have done?" Lester asked. In the immediate aftermath he was quick to absolve his heroes. "It would be easy to align the Stones with this, but false and unjust," he wrote a week after the concert. "The Stones' violence is therapeutic and removed to the realm of art, while the Angels' is a naked gash gushing blood. . . . The Stones, thank God, can really feel, while the Angels, like all violent sadists, want numbness for themselves and that only their victims should feel anything."

As he reflected on the experience in the months that followed, Lester realized he was wrong. He had no idea what the Stones really felt, and to some extent everyone at Altamont was complicit in the violence.

Why did three hundred thousand allow themselves to be brutalized by several dozen? Maybe they *enjoyed* it. Hell, he did. He had never heard the Rolling Stones play better—art in the midst of ugliness.

"It wasn't just Altamont or the Stones," Lester wrote three years later. "The whole peace brat society was wrongo to the liver. The Stones had expressed it in 'Gimme Shelter,' but they were even less prepared to deal with it than we were. . . . Death of Innocence in Woodstock Nation my ass. Altamont was the facing up."

∗ ∗ ∗

The Monday after Altamont, *Rolling Stone*'s editors met to discuss how they should cover the concert. Eager to put the event behind them, most favored a short news report or nothing at all, but Jann Wenner vetoed them. Eleven journalists, including Lester and Marcus, were assigned to document what they'd seen and interview as many others as possible. Managing editor John Burks wanted to run all of their individual accounts, but Wenner insisted that Burks play the role of an old-fashioned newspaper-rewrite man, combining the reports into one massive story that consumed the entire issue of January 21, 1970. Nobody but Wenner was happy with the results.

"Again, Lester felt very misused," Marcus said.

In the wake of Altamont, Marcus felt increasingly alienated from the music. "It was the worst day I'd ever been through," he said. "Not just in a direct, personal sense of being physically threatened and seeing awful things over and over again, but seeing everything that I had devoted myself to as a writer and an editor turn to garbage." In the spring of 1970 he angered Wenner by panning Bob Dylan's *Self-Portrait*. The publisher fired him—"If you talk to Jann he'll still say I quit," Marcus said—but after a year on the job he was happy to go.

Many writers believed that *Rolling Stone* was becoming increasingly beholden to the industry as Wenner tried to survive a serious financial crunch. CBS president Clive Davis and Elektra head Jac Holzman bailed the publisher out by each advancing a year's worth of advertising revenue. Wenner began admonishing his critics to "just write about the music," which was generally interpreted as "no-holds-barred criticism is no longer welcome." Burks, Langdon Winner, and several others resigned. "My strong feeling was that what was going on was a move from rock 'n' roll as popular culture to rock 'n' roll as sheer commodity," Winner said.

Added Burks, "There were two sets of writers on *Rolling Stone*, and the ones that Jann Wenner took seriously were the stuffed shirts. Lester was the only one that was sufficiently irreverent about the situation."

"I started getting things rejected in the summer of 1970 when Wenner was going through one of his freak-outs," Lester said in 1982. "Before that, I was so stupid that I thought you should be loyal to *Rolling Stone* and only freelance for them. And they were paying like twelve dollars a review! Then I started getting reviews rejected, and I started sending each one to a different magazine. I sent them to *Fusion* or *Creem* or whatever, and things with *Creem* started going really good."

By 1970 numerous magazines had emerged to compete with *Rolling Stone*. Based in Boston, *Fusion* was a smart and funny bimonthly featuring regular contributions from Richard Meltzer and his friend Nick Tosches, among others. *Creem* came from Detroit and the same milieu that spawned the MC5 and the White Panthers. Englishman Tony Reay worked at a head shop and record store called Mixed Media, and he convinced the enterprising young owner that money could be made with an underground music mag. At the age of twenty-five Barry Kramer launched *Creem* with an investment of $1,200—$6,300 less than Wenner had when he started *Rolling Stone*. The name came from Reay's favorite band, though the spelling was changed because *Cream* seemed too obvious.

A year after *Creem* started as a sporadically published tabloid, Reay moved on and a hyperactive twenty-year-old named Dave Marsh became the de facto editor; in the egalitarian spirit of the times, nobody at the magazine had a formal job title. Marsh published Lester's first reviews— *Golden Filth* by the Fugs and "Anyway Anyhow Anywhere" by the Who— in August 1970. A long Ray Charles retrospective followed two months later. "They were *exactly* what I was looking for, and immensely more erudite than anything I had the ability to create at that time," Marsh said. He sent Lester a letter: "Listen, kid, I've been looking at your stuff in *Rolling Stone* for a while now, and it looks really good. We might be able to find space for a young upstart like yourself, although you take way too much acid and don't drink half enough whiskey."

"I was like: 'All right, man!' " Lester said in 1982. "So then they assigned me to review *Funhouse* by the Stooges, and I wrote this endless article that ran in two parts as a record review, and they printed it. And I said, 'Well, I guess this is where I belong.' "

Boy Howdy!

In the spring of 1970 the author of *Howl and Other Poems* came to speak at San Diego State College. Afterward an enthusiastic twenty-one-year-old fan greeted him before he even set foot off the stage. "Mr. Ginsberg! Mr. Ginsberg! Hi, I'm Lester Bangs. I write for *Rolling Stone*!"

Allen Ginsberg floored him. "Yeah, I've read you," the poet said.

Lester handed him two chapters of *Journal of a Blob*, which was either the autobiographical successor to his first novel, *Drug Punk*, or part two of the earlier book; he couldn't decide which. A few weeks later Ginsberg returned the manuscript with an encouraging note scrawled on the cover sheet: "Lester: Writing is swift and intelligent in much detail, despite Salingeresque coyness, which is frivolous. The Kerouackian self-musing is mellow and mortal—whole tone is clear and your loser saints and human curiosities are immortal—the prose itself is energetic and rhythmic. Try some real yoga with a teacher, though poetics *is* a yoga—the seat of poets at composition.—Allen Ginsberg, May 26, 1970."

"Fuck the yoga!" Lester said. "One of the Beats read my stuff and he liked it!"

Andy was hoping this would give her boyfriend the encouragement he needed to get serious about writing fiction. To her, rock criticism was an obvious dead end. "He thought it was a dandy thing that he had fallen into, and I don't think that he realized that it was ultimately a trap," she said. "His entire life was spent chronicling these rock stars and not really living a life of his own." But Lester found the seductive charms of the rock world increasingly hard to resist. He had mastered the ability to crank out salable features and reviews in any state of consciousness, and the promotional gravy train nicely augmented his admittedly meager earnings.

The major-label publicity departments had started to spend lavishly, wining and dining writers and sponsoring expense-paid junkets to see forgettable acts that they hoped would sound better in more hospitable locales. In the fall of 1970 Elektra flew Lester and Andy to Los Angeles and put them up at the Chateau Marmont for a few days just so he could hear a band called Crabby Appleton. From that point on he flew out of town two or three times a month, sometimes with only pennies of his own to his name. In a sarcastic travelogue entitled "San Francisco on Two Cents a Day," he bragged of living large at the Miyako Hotel courtesy of Impulse Records while mostly ignoring the music he'd been flown in to hype. The piece was published in *Phonograph Record Magazine*, a publication owned by another label, United Artists, which meant he bit the hand that fed him twice over.

It was all too much fun to be considered work, and Lester was being accepted—hell, he was being *celebrated*—by a circle of peers who were as obsessed about music and writing as he was. Many of the members of this far-flung critical community met for the first time in the fall of 1971. The Jefferson Airplane sponsored the most elaborate junket yet to celebrate the launch of its new label, Grunt Records, and the band flew writers to San Francisco from across the country. On Saturday night everyone gathered at Friends and Relatives Hall, and Richard Meltzer chronicled the party in a chatty style not unlike that of Australian rock writer Lillian Roxon in her chatty column for *Fusion*.

Roxon was there, of course, and she pulled fellow gossip Lisa Robinson's tits out of her dress. Ed Ward, Greil Marcus's successor at *Rolling Stone*, walked around sporting a hard hat, while *Creem*'s Dave Marsh wore leather. Lester had met Greg and Suzy Shaw of *Who Put the Bomp?* fanzine a few months earlier, when he stayed at their house in Marin County and wrote a speed-fueled tribute to the Troggs called "James Taylor Marked for Death." (The couple had an "open" marriage, and Lester and Suzy enjoyed a brief fling.)

Village Voice critic Robert Christgau had recently split from his girlfriend Ellen Willis, who wrote a column called "Rock, Etc." for *The New Yorker*, and in a fit of pique he hurled his dinner at her. "Bob had evidently decided that having broken up with him, the least I could do was stay away from his turf, so he demanded that I leave," Willis wrote. "I told

Meltzer puts gum in Lester's ear, 1971.
<small>Photo courtesy Richard Meltzer</small>

him he could leave, if he felt like it, and he let fly with a paper plate full of food. Perhaps it's stretching things a bit to see all this as a metaphor for gender relations in rock-critic land, but . . ."

Oblivious to this drama, Lester and Andy cut loose on the dance floor with a step they called "the funky penguin"—just two unself-conscious kids from the suburbs with rock 'n' roll spirit to burn. Yet even on first encounter some of his colleagues noticed an edge to Lester's partying. "Man, Lester Bangs can really drink a lot," Meltzer wrote. "He can do Romilar and tequila in the same motion and he doesn't mind it when he barfs and he doesn't mind hangovers and Greg Shaw who was there too with his wife Suzy predicts Lester's got less than two years left on earth at the present rate."

Shortly after the Grunt party Lester sat in El Cajon pondering his fate. Andy and Norma lectured him constantly about "doing something" with his life. He had drawn 163, a relatively low number in the dreaded 1970 draft lottery, and now he received notice to report for his physical. He was unlikely to get a student deferment because he was still a fifth-year freshman. At San Diego State, as at Grossmont, he never completed anything but literature courses; during his last semester he withdrew from four classes and flunked the fifth. If he had remained a Jehovah's Witness, he could have registered as a conscientious objector, but even Vietnam seemed better than Kingdom Hall. "I'll cop out as a fag or a flip, most probably a flip—go down there high on Romilar or Methedrine," he wrote, but he wasn't sure the draft board would buy it.

Making matters worse, Lester was flat broke. During a trip to L.A. he borrowed a car from a friend of Michael Ochs, the head of publicity for Columbia Records. Distracted by a beautiful girl on Sunset Boulevard, he rear-ended another driver. Ochs covered the $789 in damages, but Lester vowed to repay him. "It took him years, but he paid me every penny, and I never had to remind him," Ochs said. "That's what made him a best friend."

In the midst of all this Dave Marsh called and asked Lester if he'd like to fly to Detroit courtesy of Warner Brothers to interview the much-hyped Alice Cooper. He had been freelancing for *Creem* for thirteen months, and after two years of writing four-hundred-word record reviews for *Rolling Stone*, he had found a forum that allowed him to run wild. In pieces such as "Psychotic Reactions and Carburetor Dung: A Tale of These Times," an epic homage to the Count Five, and "Of Pop and Pies and Fun," his two-part manifesto on the Stooges, he felt he had achieved the merger of hard-hitting criticism and the "free-flowing imagistic quality" of his fiction that he promised Greil Marcus in 1969. He took the assignment and spent several days hanging out with Cooper and his band.

"Lester Bangs had one of the great quotes about me for the very first album we put out," Cooper said three decades later. "He called it 'a tragic waste of plastic.' I *loved* that line, and I still use it to this day." By the time Lester wrote the *Creem* cover story, he had warmed to Cooper's shock-rock, which he described as a mix of Looney Tunes cartoons and late-night TV horror flicks. The only real surprise: Under the greasepaint, Cooper was "the perfect cherub-cheeked picture of a God-worshippin', pie-scarfin', parent-respectin' all-American boy."

Lester intended to spend two weeks in Michigan and wound up staying for two months. "Somewhere in that period it was determined that he was a great guy and should move to Detroit, with me as the one holdout," Marsh recalled. "I wanted to keep my distance, because that's my way of dealing with competition. He had the most raw writing talent I've ever seen in a young writer."

In November 1971 Lester returned to El Cajon only to pack his belongings; he had accepted publisher Barry Kramer's offer of a job as assistant editor. Andy would come east once he was settled to see if she liked it enough to join him. "I was distraught, but it was also like freedom for me, because I'd always been with him," she said. Lester's mother didn't say much at all. "There was no party or anything; he just sort of left," said his friend Jim Bovee. "We were in a state of shock, but I suppose we always knew that it was going to take him away eventually."

Rob Houghton watched as Lester performed the herculean task of boxing up his record collection to ship to *Creem*. He took pains to put all of his corniest novelty records on top to confound anyone who might open the boxes on the other end. "I really want them to wonder about what kind of weirdo they just hired," he said.

• • •

Lester arrived in Detroit wearing his goofy grin and looking like a cartoon bumpkin. He sported long sideburns, a bushy mustache, and the same brown suit coat he'd worn to visit *Rolling Stone*. His overstuffed valise was literally held together with a rope.

When MC5 guitarist Wayne Kramer encountered Lester during a party at a Cass Avenue loft, his first instinct was to kick the ass of the guy who had nearly ruined his career. "We were used to getting attacked for our political stance, but he hit me where I *lived*," Kramer said. "He said I couldn't tune my guitar and couldn't play." The group had recorded its second album—1970's *Back in the USA*, produced by *Rolling Stone* editor Jon Landau—partly as a response to Lester's review. "We wanted to prove that we could do an album where the songs were tight, the guitars were in tune, and the playing was solid," Kramer said. "That all fit into Jon Landau's thinking. It didn't fit into John Sinclair's thinking, but at that point he had his hands full with the police."

Sinclair had received his infamous "ten for two"—a ten-year sentence for the possession of two joints—in July 1969. While in prison he and two others were indicted for the September 1968 bombing of the Ann Arbor CIA office. The White Panthers' total assault on the culture had been effectively shut down. By the fall of 1971 the members of the MC5 had spent the last year distancing themselves from their former manager and mentor, but they hadn't forgotten the reviewer who first pointed out that the Panthers' vision of the revolution was jive.

Kramer approached Lester, introduced himself, and waited for the flash of recognition that would make the blows to follow that much sweeter. But instead of brawling, the two wound up drinking arm in arm—just two more drunken buddies at the bohemian watering hole, Cobb's Corner. Twenty-five years later the guitarist still wasn't sure how that happened. "It took a lot of courage on his part," Kramer said. "Rarely do people like to admit they were wrong."

Lester not only admitted it, he'd been born again. Shortly after his arrival he saw the MC5 in concert at a Detroit dive called the Frütcellar. "They weren't just fantastic, they wuz cataclysmic, and it's only now that

I completely and finally understand why so many people lose their cool and objectivity over this band," he wrote his friend Roger Anderson back in El Cajon. "THERE IS NO BETTER BAND ANYWHERE!"

"It felt like vindication," Kramer said. "Once he said, 'Damn, the MC5 really are what they said they are,' what was there to argue about? We considered him an ally."

Such was the mind-set in the city that Lester always called "Deee-troit!" To him the denizens of the Motor City appeared to be either speed-addled maniacs grinding their teeth to dust or zombies collecting drool in puddles beneath their chins. Underground cartoonist R. Crumb called Detroit "Trank City" when he came to visit *Creem*, and publisher Barry Kramer joked that the giant Firestone tire that greeted visitors near the airport should be replaced with a big Quaalude. "The whole town is like one huge mouth where all the teeth rotted out and no dentist has been 'round for years nor is one ever gonna come again because nobody cares," Lester wrote. Yet the natives took a perverse pride in it all. They sported bumper stickers heralding DETROIT, THE MURDER CITY, and when newcomers wondered why nobody cared enough to tow away the many rusted-out junkers abandoned on the sides of the highways, locals pointed out that at least they were all *American* cars.

John Lennon nailed the vibe when he performed in nearby Ann Arbor in the fall of 1971 at the Concert to Free John Sinclair. "Apathy isn't it," the former Beatle said. "We can all do something. So Flower Power didn't work. So what? We start again!"

Barry Kramer was one local who'd started something to be proud of. In its early days as a newsprint tabloid, *Creem* was indistinguishable from the many other underground newspapers of the time, offering a mix of overly earnest political commentary, awkward paeans to local bands, and ads for Kramer's record store and head shop. After founding editor Tony Reay departed, the magazine started to hone a more distinctive vision of cultural journalism based on the contributions of three unique personalities: Kramer, his cousin Nathaniel "Deday" LaRene, and nineteen-year-old Dave Marsh.

Kramer was born to a working-class Jewish family in Detroit. His father had been reclining on the floor playing with his infant son when he was stricken by a heart attack, and he cradled the boy in his arms as he died. Barry grew up to become a short and troubled man with an unruly brown shag, intense, probing eyes, and a serious persecution complex.

Barry Kramer, Dave Marsh, and Lester during his first visit to Detroit, 1971.
(Roberta Cruger hovers in the window behind them.)
Photo by Charles Auringer

He believed in hitting people hard before they had a chance to hit him. His typical greeting: "Hi, motherfucker. You're an asshole!"

Born on June 6, 1944, hence the nickname, Deday LaRene graduated from the University of Chicago Law School in 1968. He stepped off the fast track to help his cousin with *Creem*, penning witty and incisive reviews that drew praise from his colleagues, but once the magazine was rolling, he returned to practicing law. Locally famous, he cut a colorful figure in the courtroom with a flamboyant style and a wild gray mane like Albert Einstein's. Unfortunately he subsidized his pro bono work for animal rights with some notorious paying clients, and he was eventually sentenced to a year in prison for helping reputed mobster Vito "Billy Jack" Giacalone hide $410,000 from the IRS.

The third key member of the *Creem* brain trust grew up in the shadow of Pontiac Motors Assembly Line Sixteen, thirty miles north of

Detroit. When he was fourteen, GM bought all of the houses on his block to make way for a parking lot, and Dave Marsh never forgave his dad for selling instead of fighting. A frequent target of his father's rages, he sought solace in the music broadcast on WPON-AM. Smokey Robinson's "You Really Got a Hold on Me" prompted an epiphany. "The song was a lifeline that suggested—no, insisted—that these singers spoke *for* me as well as to me," he wrote, "and that what they felt and were able to cope with, the deep sorrow, remorse, anger, lust, and compassion that bubbled beneath the music, I would also be able to feel and contain."

Marsh entered Wayne State University in 1968, but the excitement surrounding the White Panthers and the MC5 soon swept him away. His obsessions were politics, music, and journalism, in that order, and he attacked them with a signature passion; his *Creem*-era girlfriend, Roberta "Robbie" Cruger, described him as "a possessed elf." In 1969 he critiqued the Toronto Pop Festival and covered John Sinclair's trial for the underground newspaper *The Fifth Estate*. When *Creem* reprinted the Toronto article without his permission, Marsh complained to Sinclair. "Let's go talk to Kramer and straighten this out," Sinclair said. "They don't have any writers, and you can write for them."

Kramer offered Marsh a job, though at fifty cents an hour, the economic reality didn't quite warrant that word. Marsh knew he wasn't going back to college, so he accepted. A week later Sinclair was shipped off to prison. Kramer did his part in the efforts to free the White Panthers' leader, helping to organize the famous benefit concert, but like Lester, he never bought into Sinclair's talk of revolution. Kramer was a capitalist. Marsh was an idealist, though he preferred the term "radical professional." The two loved to argue, and their distinctive styles combined with LaRene's irreverent humor to shape *Creem*'s personality.

In January 1970 *Creem*'s editors published a windy mission statement. "Detroit is such a unique hotbed of rock 'n' roll because the kids are so deeply involved in it; rock 'n' roll is their whole lifestyle and they know no other," they wrote. "Where do we fit into all of this? Within the community, we ought to be the stuff that runs between the subatomic particles, the tightly bound power blocs that run rock 'n' roll in this area. . . . Our bands are people's bands; similarly, we think of ourselves as a people's magazine. We want to be 'professional' only in terms of our access to information and our efficiency in putting out our magazine. We do not want to be another *Rolling Stone*. . . . We are a rock 'n' roll magazine, with all that that implies. Our culture is a rock 'n' roll culture. We are rock 'n' roll people."

A few months after Lester arrived, all of that was boiled down to a few not-so-humble words on *Creem's* masthead: "America's Only Rock 'n' Roll Magazine."

Early in Lester's tenure the magazine was housed in a three-story cast-iron loft building at 3729 Cass Avenue, near the epicenter of the 1967 riots. Kramer managed Mitch Ryder and the Detroit Wheels, and they rehearsed on the top floor, rocking the building with the strains of "Devil with a Blue Dress On." Back issues piled up on the stairs, and a demolished typewriter sat atop a pedestal on the second-floor landing, symbolizing *Creem's* approach to journalism. According to various accounts, Marsh had gotten pissed off and thrown it out the window; Marsh had gotten pissed off, thrown it at Kramer, and it had sailed out the window; or, most popular, Kramer had gotten pissed off, thrown it at Marsh, and it had smashed into the wall after narrowly missing Marsh's head.

A few weeks after Lester moved to Michigan, *Creem* relocated. The loft building had been robbed several times—during Lester's initial visit someone stole the TV set out of his room while he slept—but Kramer had vowed to stay put until the day a group of black gangsters stormed into the office brandishing automatic weapons. "They came looking for one of the guys in the Wheels because of some kind of deal gone bad," according to art director Charlie Auringer; "I'm not talking, but it *could* have happened," bandleader Ryder said. Yielding to his wife, Kramer finally followed the many white-owned businesses that had fled Detroit, though the publisher preferred to think of it in terms of the San Francisco hipsters trading the commercialized Haight for idyllic Marin County.

Kramer bought a 120-acre farm at Thirteen Mile and Haggerty roads, thirty miles northwest of the city. Just barren and remote enough to qualify as "the country," the small town of Walled Lake struck Lester as "Dogpatch without the charm." Kramer and his wife, Connie, lived in the nicer of two farmhouses with Charlie Auringer and Ric Siegel, a friend who pasted up the magazine and served as the publisher's confidant and henchman. The second house, a crumbling two-bedroom dump, sat a quarter of a mile away on a little hill overlooking a desolate field. It provided the magazine's offices and home for the rest of the staff.

Although they shared some musical interests, new roommates Marsh and Lester were a study in contrasts, physically (Lester towered

over Marsh), personally (Lester was slovenly; Marsh fastidious), and politically. "Marsh tries to tell me that even though I call the New Left rank
I'm actually 'the most political writer around and don't even know it,' "
Lester wrote. "I generally hold to the opinion that the whole Movement
is a load of shit."

When Sinclair was finally released, Lester joked that they ought to
hold a concert to send John *back*. The war in Vietnam raged on despite
Henry Kissinger's announcement that peace was at hand, and Richard
M. Nixon was headed toward an easy reelection. Cynicism seemed to be
the only reasonable response to the times. "Marsh saw us as foot soldiers
in the counterculture revolution and Lester just saw us as bozos on the
bus," wrote *Creem* staffer Jaan Uhelszki. "We used to say *Creem* was a
cross between *Mad* magazine and *Esquire*. Marsh and Lester were largely
responsible for maintaining that delicate balance between the absurd
and the profane."

Never an easy balance to strike, it was especially difficult at Walled
Lake because the staff lived and worked together twenty-four/seven.
Marsh and Lester grew close without necessarily liking each other. "Part
of it was Lester was taking up a lot of space that used to be mine," Marsh
said. Wrote Lester: "Dave Marsh is so fucked-up I can hardly stand to be
around him half the time. He's such a morose know-it-all pompous little
over-intellectualized asshole. But I still love him like a brother."

There were no secrets in the tiny farm house. "We were so goddam
communal that I couldn't even go into the bathroom to jerk off to *Playboy* without having Marsh bust in on me just when I was trying to get
willie to rise to paper," Lester wrote. "He was at least polite about ducking out, but the point is *I couldn't even jerk off in peace*, no spuzz-spizz
forthcoming that nite."

The staffers had even less privacy at Walled Lake than they knew. In
the spring of 1999 the FBI responded to a Freedom of Information Act
request and declassified a thirty-page file on Barry Kramer and *Creem*.
According to these documents, in late 1971 two unnamed sources told
agents in the Detroit field office that they might find Kramer willing to
serve as an informant on activities of the White Panther Party. They
began to investigate and quickly pegged the publisher's true nature, writing, "The subject is not politically oriented but merely affiliated with the
New Left culture on a more or less continual basis through his business
contacts and interests in music. . . . If cooperative, subject could furnish
extremely valuable data regarding WPP and other related matters."

Ric Siegel; Lester and his pooch, Muffin; Marsh and his dog, Gloria;
Jaan Uhelszki; and Charles Auringer at Walled Lake, 1972.
PHOTO BY RICHARD LEE/*Detroit Free Press*

Around the same time another unnamed source fingered the *Creem* office as a potential "safe house" for members of the Weather Underground. The bureau began to monitor the magazine's phone records and subscription lists for contact with Weathermen and other radicals—the files don't say how agents obtained these records—and from March through July 1972 FBI operatives occasionally hid in the woods around Walled Lake, peering through binoculars as loud rock music wafted into the brush. Agents hoped to spy a stray subversive or catch Kramer alone for a friendly chat, but their hopes were dashed when they finally approached the publisher. "Pretext interviews and observation during surveillance resulted in the opinion that he would be somewhat less than cooperative," the feds wrote, "and might possibly display hostility which would lead to embarrassment of the Bureau." Translation: Kramer had told them to fuck themselves.

Unaware of this cloak-and-dagger intrigue, Lester lay awake at night listening to Marsh and his girlfriend, Robbie, making love. "Go, Dave, go!" Lester cheered. Not surprisingly, tensions mounted.

"Lester knew where all of Dave's buttons were, and he loved to push them," said fellow editor Ben Edmonds. "Dave is so earnest about whatever he happens to be earnest about at any point in time, and Lester was always looking to prick a balloon and blow something up." Lester and Marsh both had dogs, and even their canines were competitive. Marsh's dog, Gloria, was obedient and well heeled, while Lester's cockapoo pup ran wild. Her name was Muffin, but he called her Buttfuck, and she liked to shit under Marsh's desk. One day an enraged Marsh dumped a mound of dog crap in Lester's IBM Selectric. The editors wrestled, crashing through the house, out the door, and into the driveway. The brawl ended when Marsh gouged his head on the edge of an open car door.

The staff pronounced Lester the winner and branded him "Big Bully Bangs." He laughed at the irony when he wrote Roger Anderson. "When I was in high school I was wan and thin and faggy. Now I'm out here and most of the people I work with are midgets, so I end up having my mind blown when Barry Kramer comes to me with a jar of pickles: 'Here, Muscles, open this for me, will ya?' "

After the fight Lester and Marsh got along much better, but new battle lines were drawn between Lester and Kramer. In addition to providing food and lodging, the publisher paid everyone an egalitarian $22.75 a week, which they usually spent on noncommunal dope or beer. "Part of the commune idea was that Kramer was isolating people who had talent from the rest of the world," Marsh said. "It was a power trip, because he was the person who held the economic purse strings."

Lester augmented his meager allowance by writing for other outlets, including *Rolling Stone, Phonograph Record Magazine, Fusion,* and the odd combination of *Penthouse* and *Ms.* "I freelance more than anybody else at *Creem,* which has always irked Kramer because he figures it's making me rich as a bitch on HIS TIME," he wrote. "Yeah, sure. Most of this freelancing is done from the vortex of speed trips, on time which otherwise I'd just waste by sleeping, so Kramer can bite the wang."

One night Lester left his typewriter turned on, and the publisher pecked out a note.

Turn me off

Turn me off

Turn me off

Turn me off

Turn me off

You worthless Cretin Wimpoid <u>WRITER</u>!

"As Kramer himself will admit, he's jealous because he busts his balls for this mag and never gets no glory, all of which is hogged by us writers," Lester wrote. "Big deal." He refused to take the bait and duke it out, and that only made Kramer angrier.

⁘ ⁘ ⁘

The situation at Walled Lake might have been hellish for the staff, but the tensions resulted in an extraordinary magazine that embodied the spirit and energy of rock 'n' roll while refusing to take itself or anything else too seriously.

"*Creem* is a raspberry in the face of the culture," Lester told a visiting reporter, "and in a sense it's a raspberry in the face of itself." Yet it had a respect for its readership born of familiarity. Lester alternately called them "the counter-counterculture" and "Boone's Farmers," though he never declined when someone passed him a jug of the sickly sweet wine. *Creem* fostered a spirited dialogue with anyone who shared its enthusiasms, and for all its snotty attitude, it never talked down to anyone. It could be *stoopid*, but it was always smart, and just because an article was a gas to read didn't mean that it lacked ideas.

"Unlike *Rolling Stone*, which is a bastion of San Francisco counterculture rock-as-art orthodoxy, *Creem* is committed to a pop aesthetic," Ellen Willis wrote in *The New Yorker*. "It speaks to fans who consciously value rock as an expression of urban teenage culture."

The cornerstones of that culture were of course rock 'n' roll, drugs, and sex. Like a hungover reveler on New Year's Day, rock seemed to be suffering from a post-sixties malaise. The pop charts were dominated by the likes of "A Horse with No Name," "Joy to the World," and "Song Sung Blue," while the allegedly "progressive" FM radio stations lumbered under the weight of bloated, self-important *artistes*. James Taylor, Crosby, Stills & Nash, Jethro Tull, and Chicago were the enemy, and *Creem* happily ceded respectful coverage of them to *Rolling Stone*. It found its champions elsewhere: in Detroit via the Stooges, the MC5, Bob Seger, and Mitch Ryder; in the bargain bins with Lester's beloved garage bands; in maverick individualists such as Marc Bolan, Leon Russell, Dr. John, and Johnny Winter, and especially in the warped white blues of the nascent genre heavy metal.

The magazine was just as emphatic about its taste in drugs. It ran cover stories on "Sopor Nation," the new mass of kids hooked on Quaaludes and reds; "The Tobacco Companies and Dope"; and "A Luridly Complete Compendium of Street Drugs." Something of an expert in the area, Nick Tosches presented "Whiskey Is the Spirit of Christmas: Your De-Luxe Guide to Your Yuletide Econo-Hootch." After A-200 Pyrinate Liquid ("One shampoo kills lice and nits"), *Creem's* steadiest advertisers were Boone's Farm wine and the mail-order head shops hawking pipes, personalized roach clips, and something called the "grass mask" ("Shit, what a hit!").

Sex appeared in more subtle ways. There were the "come hither" expressions of the artists in the Creem Profile, a spoof of the Dewar's Profile ads that ran in more upscale magazines. Lester talked Grace Slick into baring a breast for her appearance. The movie column offered another excuse to feature a little T&A: a nude photo of Sylvia Miles and Joe Dallesandro from Andy Warhol's *Heat*, or a lascivious picture of Linda Lovelace accompanying Lester's review of *Deep Throat* ("It resembles such prior hotcha classics as *Tropic of Cancer* in that it's very funny, while its sexiness, not to mention sensuality, is entirely questionable"). Ladies' man art director Charlie Auringer also liked to use busty local girls as models for the house ads, especially those hawking *Creem* T-shirts displaying the cartoon mascot designed by R. Crumb.

The "notorious perverto cartoonist," as *Creem* dubbed him, visited in April 1969. Crumb drew the mascot and a cover illustration for forty bucks, but his imprimatur was worth much more. His presence in each issue symbolically marked the magazine as a successor to San Francisco's vaunted underground press. Crumb's mascot—a pudgy cartoon bottle—echoed an old Southern greeting by exclaiming, "Boy howdy!" The lil' fella soon became known as Boy Howdy himself—the personification of the *Creem* spirit. Subjects posed for the Creem Profile with dummy cans of Boy Howdy beer, and many readers thought Boy Howdy

R. Crumb pictured Boy Howdy! as an old-fashioned milk bottle.

was a beer bottle. But Crumb actually envisioned an old-fashioned bottle of milk or "cream."

The image on the artist's cover was a more obvious pun. A cartoon
spray can squirted a generous white "gloop" in the face of a big-breasted,
large-thighed, typically Crumb-style woman. "What's he doing to our
daughter?" a horrified mother asked. "Me next, Mr. Dream Whip!" another girl cried. The gal who was being creamed on simply said, "Wow!"
Creem's male editors never specifically addressed the lewder implications
of Crumb's ejaculatory fantasy, but Barry Kramer liked the cover so much
that he ran it twice, in black and white for the second issue and in color
in November 1971.

The men at *Creem* were no more sexist than their counterparts at
other counterculture institutions, but they frustrated the female staffers
nonetheless. The magazine's best women writers both started in nonedi-
torial roles. Kicked out of Catholic school for augmenting her uniform
with love beads, Robbie Cruger responded to a classified ad for a typist
who liked rock 'n' roll, and she was hired as Kramer's secretary. Her friend
Jaan Uhelszki opted out of secretarial school to sell sodas at the Grande
Ballroom, biding her time until Kramer hired her. "I always saw myself
doing what the boys at *Creem* were doing," she wrote. "I wanted to be the
Brenda Starr for rock."

Kramer liked Crumb's cover so much he ran it twice.

Uhelszki started as the "subscription kid," but Lester championed her writing and eventually convinced Kramer to make her an editor. After graduating from secretary to office manager, Cruger segued into writing the pseudonymous "Film Fox" movie column. "I always disagreed with Robbie about sexism at *Creem*," Uhelszki said. "I've always used my sex to my advantage. Otherwise it's just a rationale for failure." But two and a half decades later Cruger still objected to the hypocrisy. "When you're looking at that era, men definitely used the burgeoning feminism as an excuse to get whatever they wanted," she said. "It was like: 'Why won't you have sex with me? Aren't you sexually liberated?' There was a double standard, but there was lip service being given to feminism. Your average guy didn't get it. It was kind of a constant education, and it was exhausting."

In some ways Lester was one of the more enlightened men at *Creem*. He listened to the women complain about work and their boyfriends and advised them to stand up for themselves. In August 1972 the leading journal of the feminist movement published his attack on "cock rock" and a call for female equality. "Clearly we need an all-woman rock 'n' roll

Lester championed Jaan Uhelszki's rise from subscription kid to editor and writer.
Photo courtesy Jaan Uhelszki

band that can create the kind of loud, savage, mesmerizing music that challenges men on their own ground," he wrote in *Ms*. Of course, he was also known to call Cruger "Tits" or "the Midwest Milkmaid." She let him get away with it because he was "the good-natured dork from the sticks," and it was hard to stay really mad at him.

Lester complained constantly about his own love life, or the lack thereof. At first he and Andy wrote each other weekly and talked on the phone even more often, but communications slowly tapered off. Though neither of them was anxious to admit it, they knew that the break was inevitable. "We were still seeing each other, but it was really over before he went to *Creem*," Andy said. "We had that bond where we were afraid to say we weren't going to be together. But by then I was twenty-one and had finally gone out into the big world, and I was thrilled with it. For seven years I was baby-sitting Les, and then I had a drink and was like: 'Yeah! Why haven't I done this before? It's time for *me* to have some fun!' "

After Lester left, Andy sang in a lounge band, continued acting at college, took LSD for the first time, and moved out on her own. She kept her promise and visited Walled Lake for six weeks in late 1971, but she hated it. She decided the *Creem* commune wasn't for her when she went food shopping and watched one of the women shove packages of chopped meat under her blouse. She and her high-school sweetheart were also having trouble redefining their relationship as adults. "How can you start an intense sexual relationship after just petting for seven years?" Andy asked.

Although he was hurt, Lester took the split in stride. "I don't blame Andy for not wanting to be here because it's boring as hell and I wouldn't stay here for another minute if it wasn't for *Creem*," he wrote Roger Anderson in the spring of 1972. He had brief flings with a pretty young Canadian girl and a married woman who later told him that she was a lesbian, but these encounters did little to alleviate his growing loneliness. "I keep hoping something, uh, *meaningful* is gonna come along," he wrote. "Maybe it's just feeling sorry for myself, but if I can't find a good woman to love I figure I might as well be dead, or addicted at least. What a fucked-up attitude."

Increasingly Lester sought escape via a jug of Gallo port, a handful of Quaaludes, and the Dionysian roar of heavy metal. His two-part love letter to Black Sabbath has been credited with naming the sound that set millions of heads a-banging. "Bring Your Mother to the Gas Chamber: Are Black Sabbath Really the New Shamans?" began with a quote from

Nova Express—the Burroughs novel featuring the character the Heavy Metal Kid—but Lester's piece never used the words "heavy metal." The phrase actually appeared in *Creem* for the first time more than a year earlier in a May 1971 review by Mike Saunders of Sir Lord Baltimore's *Kingdom Come*. It had already appeared in the lyrics of Steppenwolf's "Born to Be Wild," of course, and it had been the name of the Fugs' publishing company, Heavy Metal Music. Saunders thinks he seized upon the term as a name for the emerging style based upon a conversation with Lester, but he isn't certain.

Wherever the genre's name originated, Lester certainly embraced its din. Black Sabbath was a band of working-class Birmingham toughs who merged horror-movie imagery with an equally ominous sound. Lester hailed them as "the John Miltons of rock 'n' roll." In the months that followed, he also championed the hammering rhythms, wailing guitars, and ululating vocals of Deep Purple, Dust, Black Pearl, and (with reservations) Grand Funk Railroad, all of whom were despised by other critics. "As its detractors have always claimed, heavy metal is nothing more than a bunch of noise," Lester wrote. "It is not music, it's distortion—and that is precisely why its adherents find it appealing."

Like his favorite metal albums, the Rolling Stones' murky new epic mirrored the ennui and the inarticulate energy of the times. "When you want to shout but can hardly speak it's mighty handy to have all them loud machines do it for you as you wham out, however sluggishly, your own nullasthenic frustration," Lester wrote of *Exile on Main Street*. Initially he hated the album, calling it "a mass of admittedly scalding gruel" and "the worst studio album the Stones have ever made." But by the time that review hit the newsstands in the summer of 1972, he'd reversed himself. "Hard to hear at first, the precision and fury behind the murk ensure that you'll come back, hearing more with each playing," he wrote in January 1973. "*Exile* is about casualties, and partying in the face of them. The party is obvious. The casualties are inevitable."

His second take on the album came in a piece on what the Stones had meant to Lester throughout his life, and it ran as part of a special issue on the group. He also contributed a chart detailing the eight layers of hangers-on separating the musicians from their fans as they made their first tour since Altamont. New York critic Robert Christgau submitted an essay analyzing the Stones' music to date, and a young writer named Patti Smith completed the package with a memorable piece about a key element of the band's appeal.

"I was scared silly," Smith wrote of the Stones' first appearance on *The Ed Sullivan Show*, continuing with little regard for capitalization. "the singer was showing his second layer of skin and more than a little milk. I felt thru his pants with optic x-ray. this was a bitch. five white boys sexy as any spade. their nerves were wired and their third leg was rising. in six minutes five lusty images gave me my first glob of gooie in my virgin panties."

Raised in suburban New Jersey, Smith was just beginning to earn a reputation in New York as a poet. She regularly sent poems and reviews to Lester and Marsh, and they were happy to print them in *Creem*. Her primary links to the rock world were through her boyfriend, Blue Öyster Cult guitarist Allen Lanier, and her pal, guitarist Lenny Kaye, but she had big plans, and in the summer of 1972 she traveled to Michigan to meet her editors. When she dropped by the *Creem* office, Lester started yammering excitedly. "Hi! I met you once before! It was at the Blue Öyster Cult party in Long Island. I was fucked up on Jack Daniel's and I walked up to you and said: 'Do you sing?' You said: 'No.' So I said: 'Well, don't worry about it, because all of us rock critics'll write that you *can* sing and got the greatest voice of all time, and then everybody'll believe it so *you'll* believe it and you *will* be the greatest singer of all time!'"

Marsh couldn't believe it. "You *didn't* say that," he groaned, but Smith thought Lester was a gas. They shared a similar background: As a kid she also went door to door selling *The Watchtower* with her Jehovah's Witness mom. Smith and a group from the magazine went to see Randy Newman in concert at Pine Knob. "First act is this dork named Jim Croce who looks like Frank Zappa and sings like James Taylor," Lester wrote his friend Roger Anderson. " 'You don't mess around with Jim . . .' Eat my wongo, Stupe! In separate parts of the audience both me and Patti are making ourselves thoroughly obnoxious yelling out things like 'Where's Bob Dylan?' and me braying like a jackass: 'I'VE SEEN FAHR AND I'VE SEEN RAAAAAAIIIN!'"

Embarrassed, Marsh stormed out of the show, but Smith and the rest of the *Creem* gang had a blast. Before returning to New York, Smith set Lester up with one of her best friends, Judy Linn, a photographer at one of the local suburban newspapers. For a while Lester thought it was true love. Linn sat next to him on the couch during a party at Walled Lake and announced that she'd heard him doing a stint as a guest DJ on WABX-FM. "The records you were playing—total trash—I just said to myself, 'Wow, this guy really *knows*,'" she said. "I was going to call you up and say: 'I'm yours, baby, take me,' but I chickened out.'" Lester couldn't believe his good fortune. "These kinda things don't happen to me every day!" he wrote. "At first we were together like every night and the only time we didn't see each other was when we were at work. That lasted for about a week. Then the second week we saw each other about every other night and I told her, without being sappy, that I loved her."

It was too much too soon. The relationship ended, and Lester returned to his usual routine. His roommates at Walled Lake often woke up in the middle of the night to find him sprawled in the old barber's chair in the living room, an empty bottle at his feet and Black Sabbath's *Master of Reality* spinning on the turntable. Even through the headphones, the volume was so loud that nobody else in the house could sleep, but for Lester the clatter was as soothing as a lullaby, and he smiled blissfully as he snored.

chapter six

Stay Alive
'Til '75

When Lester returned to California for Christmas, 1973, San Diego's own freeform rock station invited him downtown for an interview. Local native Cameron Crowe stood across Fifth Avenue from KPRI-FM's studio, listening on a transistor radio and watching through the plate-glass window as Lester jabbered at the DJ and spun wild, noisy records by Dust, Savage Rose, and Hawkwind. Crowe's mom dropped him off; he'd be taking the bus back home because he was still too young to drive.

"Your writing is damn good—for a San Diego boy," Lester wrote when Crowe sent his clips to *Creem*. The letter included an assignment for a feature on Humble Pie. Lester didn't know that his protégé was only fifteen, but Crowe snuck into the club and got the interview, and the feature ran in October 1972. When Lester emerged from the radio station a few months later, the younger writer ran across the street to introduce himself. The two went for a hamburger and chatted about music, writing, and romance.

"He was talking about a girl who still lived there who'd broken his heart," Crowe recalled. "Lester was still in love with her. My first reaction was that in person this guy seemed much more like a Left Banke song than a Stooges song. He was kind of melancholy about this girl and a real romantic. Seeing that in Lester validated for me that it's cool to have a heart, even if your front is all aggression."

Lester wore a Guess Who T-shirt and warned Crowe about the dangers of hype. "Don't be one of these guys that goes to all the parties, eats the free food, and drinks the free drinks," he said. Crowe hadn't had a drink in his life. "He said that I would go to L.A. and they would romance me—'They can corrupt you!'—and I should beware of that," Crowe said. "He was being a mentor, but it wasn't like a wise old professor. It was like I was Beaver Cleaver and he was Eddie Haskell mixed with Wally."

Crowe asked about *Rolling Stone*, and Lester told him to be careful. "They change what you write," he said.

For Lester the meeting was one of the only pleasant moments during his trip. His mother spent much of the time lecturing him about the coming apocalypse. The Jehovah's Witnesses had set yet another date for Armageddon, and it was rapidly approaching. Attendance at Kingdom Halls soared to a high of five million, and the faithful began selling their homes, quitting school, delaying marriages, and draining pension funds. They adopted a slogan that became ubiquitous as the date drew near: "Make do 'til '72. Stay alive 'til '75."

Lester tried reasoning with his mom—the church had been wrong about the end of the world twice in her lifetime—but she wouldn't be dissuaded. Finally he just tuned her out.

The visit with Andy was no more enjoyable. They rang in the new year at a party thrown by some of her friends. "Most everybody else there was a swinging single, or trying to be," Lester wrote. "I danced dirty with the hostess. It was right out of *Doctors' Wives*. My ex-galf'd got mad at me for rubbing up agin said hussy and huffed a bit. I bet Gore Vidal never came out with anything as deft as: 'Whatta you care? *You* won't fuck me!' She cried. Later in the car in savage ugly liquored sexual frustration I dug one of my nails into her wrist until it bled. She told me I was a sissy. I was." He returned to Michigan feeling more alone than ever.

High on speed, Lester wrote constantly at Walled Lake, churning out reams of copy for *Creem* in addition to dozens of poems, lyrics, and letters to his friends. He still tinkered with the old manuscripts for *Drug Punk* and *Journal of a Blob*, but the only new pieces he wrote along these lines were a funny autobiographical story called "John Coltrane Lives," about annoying his landlady in El Cajon by honking on a sax, and an unpublished piece about a kid who loved the Rolling Stones too much for his own good. He wanted to include the latter in a book about the band, which he initially envisioned as an anthology of everything he'd written on the group. Later, after he interviewed Mark

Shipper, author of the humorous Beatles novel *Paperback Writer*, he considered writing a fictional account of Mick Jagger and company. He had the opening line—"Dean Martin had a hard-on"—but his Stones book never went anywhere.

"I've probably never enjoyed writing about rock 'n' roll as much as I do now, but neither have I ever had as much time or felt as much like writing as I do now," Lester wrote to his first editor, Greil Marcus. "Rock 'n' roll is just not enough, either in volume or importance, to devote all my time to." He longed to focus on a novel—a "real book"—with a subject other than music.

According to the vaunted New Journalist Tom Wolfe, such an obsession with the novel was outdated. "It's hard to explain what an American dream the idea of writing a novel was in the 1940s, the 1950s, and right into the early 1960s," Wolfe wrote in his 1973 anthology *The New Journalism*. "The novel was no mere literary form. It was a psychological phenomenon." Starting in the mid-1960s writers such as Gay Talese, Norman Mailer, Joan Didion, George Plimpton, Truman Capote, Terry Southern, Hunter S. Thompson, and of course Wolfe himself began to merge the techniques of literature with old-fashioned reportage in the pages of *Esquire*, the *New York Herald Tribune*, and *New York* magazine. "This discovery, modest at first, humble, in fact, deferential, you might say, was that it just might be possible to write journalism that would . . . read like a novel," Wolfe wrote.

Before 1973 New Journalism had mostly danced around the edges of the rock scene. Wolfe had profiled producer Phil Spector in the *Herald Tribune* in 1965; three years later he chronicled the adventures of the Grateful Dead's pals the Merry Pranksters in *The Electric Kool-Aid Acid Test*. Robert Christgau appeared in Wolfe's anthology not with a piece of rock writing but with a feature about a girl who starved herself to death on a macrobiotic diet. In November 1971 *Rolling Stone* published Thompson's *Fear and Loathing in Las Vegas*, which rewrote *On the Road* substituting psychedelics for booze, but it made only tangential mention of music. The time was ripe for someone to give New Journalism a rock 'n' roll beat.

In *Creem* features such as "Jethro Tull in Vietnam," "Screwing the System with Dick Clark," and a funny demolition of Emerson, Lake & Palmer called "Blood Feast of Reddy Kilowatt!" Lester believed he had hit upon a style of critical journalism based on the sound and language of the music. Proving himself as adept as Wolfe at patting himself on the back, he noted in 1982 that these pieces and others "ended up influencing a whole generation of younger writers and perhaps musicians as well." But none of his articles were more influential than those chronicling his encounters with Lou Reed.

The first of these, "Deaf Mute in a Telephone Booth: A Perfect Day with Lou Reed," ran in the July 1973 *Creem* and related Lester's third conversation with the musician, following their initial meeting in Los Angeles in 1969 and an unrevealing phone interview in 1971.

Reed had made his solo debut in 1972 with a self-titled album produced by rock critic Richard Robinson and featuring backing from a group of British session hacks. The album "wasn't going to set the world on fire," Lester granted, but "when it comes to songwriters for our time, Lou Reed is the best." The artist followed with *Transformer*, a 1973 album produced by David Bowie. It scored a hit with the jazzy single "Walk on the Wild Side," but it reduced the Velvets' sophisticated portraits of the decadent Warhol crowd to caricatures. Meanwhile Reed remade himself as a gender-bending glam-rocker à la Bowie in his Ziggy Stardust phase.

The concept of alternative sexualities fascinated Lester, and he was forever quizzing his friend Donald Jennings, a bisexual poet from Detroit. "He was attracted to deviance of all kinds," Jennings said. "Junkies were deviant; homosexuals were deviant. That's what he loved in the first Velvet Underground album—that portrait of them." But Lester was appalled by the way glam reduced everything to a pose. "Will the real homosexuals please stand up?" he asked in *Creem*'s August 1973 cover story, "Androgyny in Rock."

Then as now the standard celebrity profile began with the writer meeting some fabulous personality. He basked in the star's presence, recorded his witticisms, and left after a few thousand words with the subject's prefabricated image shining brighter than ever. Lester took a different tack with Reed when they met in Detroit. "You walk into the dining room of the Holiday Inn filled with expectation at finally getting to meet one of the musical and psychological frontiersmen of our time," he wrote. "You sit yourself down and become aware pretty fast that there's this vaguely unpleasant fat man sitting over there with a table full of people including his blonde bride." Lester proceeded to introduce the "real" Reed, an artist whose face had a nursing-home pallor and whose hands shook constantly. Several handlers and his new wife, Betty, catered to his every whim, including an unquenchable thirst for Johnnie Walker Black.

British journalist Nick Kent sat in on the interview. "Reed was totally contemptuous towards him," Kent recalled. "This is going to be controversial to say, but I think that Reed, being at the very least bisexual, just found Lester unattractive to look at. If he'd been an effete limey with two scarves around his neck, dressed up like a glam-rocker like I was, then Reed could connect with that—a spurious connection based on style. This is the *Transformer* period, and Reed was selling that crap. But as has often been said, Lester looked like Rob Reiner with slightly longer hair. He had the mustache, he was drinking too much, and he had a slight body-odor problem."

Reed disliked Lester's reality, and Lester refused to buy Reed's new illusion. After the concert they came together for a second interview session in Reed's hotel suite. The writer matched the singer shot for shot. Then Lester started baiting Reed: "Hey Lou, doncha think Judy Garland was a piece of shit and better off dead?"

"No! She was a great lady," Reed said. "A wonderfully wise and witty lady . . ."

"Hey Lou, then doncha think David Bowie's a no-talent asshole?"

"No, he's a genius!" Reed said. "He's brilliant!"

"Ah, c'mon, what about all that outer 'Space Oddity' shit?" Lester prodded. "That's just Paul Kantner garbage!"

"It is *not*! It's a brilliant masterpiece! Oh, you are so full of *shit*!" Reed sputtered.

Lester pressed on, getting more personal and abusive. "Hey Lou, why doncha start shooting speed again? Then you could come up with something good!"

"I still do shoot it; my doctor gives it to me," Reed said. "Well, no, actually they're just shots of meth mixed with vitamins. . . . Well, no, actually they're just vitamin C . . ."

"It went on like that for a while," Lester wrote. "Finally the whole thing sort of flaked into silence, and a girl from his organization had to come and carry him off to his room. But I'll always carry that last picture of him, plopped in his chair like a sack of spuds, sucking on his eternal Scotch with his head hanging off into shadow, looking like a deaf mute in a telephone booth. (He's still pretty cool, though; I stole that last phrase from him.) If all this makes you feel sorry for him, then you can compliment yourself on being a real Lou Reed fan. Because that's exactly what he wants."

Round one of Bangs versus Reed went to Lester. Nick Kent had taken it all in from the sidelines, and he was astounded. He'd come to Detroit to meet his hero—Bangs, not Reed—and the writer didn't let him down.

Booted out of universities in Oxford and London, Kent started writing for the weekly *New Musical Express* in early 1972, inspired by Lester's work in *Creem* and *Rolling Stone*. "The guy was a poet," Kent said. "It wasn't some bullshit; he had a magic thing with words." The Englishman showed up unannounced on *Creem*'s doorstep in the spring of 1973. "I didn't make things easy for myself by taking two Quaaludes beforehand," he wrote, "so it's no small credit to the warmth of his enormous heart that when I mush-mouthedly asked Lester if, as the greatest writer of his day, he could, if not teach me, then at least indicate to me how to achieve some vague approximation of his creative intensity, he good-naturedly replied: 'Sure.' "

One morning Kent found his mentor sitting alone in the kitchen, crying. *Rolling Stone* had printed a story in which Carolyn Cassady described the pathetic reality of Jack Kerouac's life. "He was really upset about it, and it clearly meant something very, very strong to him," Kent said. After two months of trailing Lester around, the visitor returned to the U.K. with a new perspective. "I realized that I had to get my talent together," he said. "It couldn't just be bullshit anymore. Bangs showed me how to do it: Just be yourself. Be penetrating. And don't fuck around."

⁖ ⁖ ⁖

Seven years after the first examples of the form were published, most American rock writers could be placed into one of four general camps. Academics such as Robert Christgau, Jon Landau, Greil Marcus, and Ellen Willis wrote in a dense and sometimes unreadable style. Historians such as Lenny Kaye and Greg Shaw lauded obscure and unheralded artists, writing as enthusiastic fans and largely avoiding negative criticism. A third group wasn't critical at all; gossips such as Lillian Roxon and Lisa Robinson were the Hedda Hoppers of rock, peddling salacious information about the stars. Finally there was an unruly, contentious, and individually dissimilar group that James Wolcott later dubbed "the Noise Boys." Chief among them: John Mendelssohn, Richard Meltzer, Nick Tosches, and Lester.

The Noise Boys wrote everywhere, but they thrived in the pages of *Creem*. Though as court jesters they were loath to admit it, they viewed their writing as art—at least as important as the music. As with Dr. Gonzo, Hunter S. Thompson, their readers didn't always separate the individuals from the personas, and the writers sometimes had trouble with this themselves.

Based in Los Angeles, Mendelssohn was the odd man out and the most disliked by the others. A weird combination of raging egotist and jittery neurotic, he celebrated fey, stylish *artistes* such as the Kinks and David Bowie while skewering sweaty hard-rockers such as Led Zeppelin and Grand Funk Railroad. He described himself in his more manic moments as "the King of L.A.," and he became the first well-known rock critic to cross over to the other side, fronting a precious glam band called Christopher Milk. He didn't see a problem with hyping his own group while trying to destroy the careers of others, and he eventually fell out of favor as both a critic and a musician.

"Criticism to me was lashing out at someone powerful and making them tremble," Mendelssohn said in 1997. "I don't know that the writing for me was ever more than showing off and enjoying the glory of it. There were several types of rock critics in those days. There was the professorial school embodied by Marcus and Christgau; there was that whole school of East Coast anarchic drunken slobs, and then there was me. I stood out because I dressed like Rod Stewart. Plus I bathed and they didn't."

Admittedly a bit ripe on occasion (though never as odoriferous as Lester), Richard Meltzer became what he called "a minor New York celebrity" after *The Aesthetics of Rock* was published in 1970. He wrote for *Creem* and *Fusion* under his own name and a number of others, including Borneo Jimmy, (Not the) Audie Murphy, Jr., Fort Gray O' Hunky, and the Night Writer (Writes Only at Night). In any guise Meltzer wrote mostly about Meltzer, though sometimes he strayed from that subject long enough to address what he thought about various musical and cultural phenomena. Despite or perhaps because of his time at Yale, he came to despise academic discourse. By the mid-seventies he wrote in a style that read like the punk on the street corner talked, and it was widely imitated.

"The only rock critic I'd say I was influenced by was Meltzer, and I *was* influenced by him," Lester said in 1982. "In fact, he accused me once of ripping off my whole style from him, which I don't think was true."

The major difference between the two was that Lester never got over his love of the noise, while Meltzer maintained that rock 'n' roll as he loved it had pretty much died in 1968. "It certainly wasn't very 'alive' by '72, '73," he wrote, "by which time my pathetic insistence on keeping the (pre-megabuck) rock-roll 'faith' had pretty much rendered me persona nongrata with the mags, the record creeps, the promoters, the publicists, whomever. Operating under the premise that 'high mischief' was the basic, irreducible nub of any 'true' rock experience, and that if *I* didn't commit it with ongoing frequency no one else would (so, uh, BYE-BYE ROCK), I'd do things like jump in the fountain at a Rolling Stones press party, throw chicken bones at some annoying singer at the Bitter End, review (harshly) albums I'd obviously never listened to (or concerts I'd never attended), reverse the word sequence of a text to make it read backwards (or delete, for no particular reason, every fourth word)."

Always the romantic, Lester viewed Meltzer, Tosches, and himself as heirs to the Beats. He claimed the mantle of Jack Kerouac. Meltzer he named Neal Cassady, and Tosches became William S. Burroughs. Nobody wanted to be Allen Ginsberg.

Born in Newark, New Jersey, Tosches grew up in and around his father's bar on the west side of Jersey City. He skipped college and went to work as a paste-up artist for the Lovable Underwear Company across the Hudson River in Manhattan. One day in January 1972 he left for lunch and never returned. By then he had started writing—record reviews and essays mostly, but also his particular specialty, profiles of the unsung heroes of rock 'n' roll. These emulated the dramatic arcs of the Greek tragedies and the ornate prose of the Old Testament, both of which he invoked. He hoped to find an outlet for his fiction or poetry, but in the meantime rock writing brought in a few bucks, and it provided an audience. "I have come to realize I was fortunate to live at a particular moment in time where I could effectuate this," Tosches said years later. "I was this crazy fucked-up kid, there were other crazy fucked-up kids out there, and I could get away with writing the way I thought and wrote and somebody was going to dig it."

When Lester traveled east on assignment for *Creem*, he often crashed with Meltzer or Tosches rather than staying at the hotel provided by the record company. He hated to be alone. He didn't fit in the big city, and his New York pals considered him a hick. Once they were drinking at the White Rose Bar on Broadway when Tosches picked Lester's pocket, then loaned him his own money for cab fare. "I don't remember if he ever paid me back," Tosches said. Another time Lester rang Tosches's bell after waking up on the subway, uncertain where he'd been all night and with strands of hay sticking out of his hair. Tosches is still wondering where the hell one finds hay in New York City.

"We had a few things in common," Tosches wrote. "Neither of us had college degrees to fall back on, and we were both drunks. But, in more ways, we were oil and water. For the most part, we didn't like the same books, the same music, the same dope, or the same codependent cuties." Booze fueled the three-way friendship with Meltzer. "Lester was my friend, and my recollections of him have a lot more to do with that than with him as a writer," Meltzer said. "Nick and I have talked about this, and neither one of us had a strong sense of him as a writer back then. It was just that he was always wearing it around his neck—Lester Bangs, Writer—which to us seemed sort of fatuous. He was somebody we drank with."

Lester published Meltzer and Tosches in almost every issue of *Creem*, but their professional relationships did not lack friction. Through the early seventies Meltzer wrote a monthly column called "Dust My Pumice." In 1973 Lester wrote him urging him to do better: "As a fan and a friend I'm asking you to please GET YOUR ASS IN GEAR." An avid baseball fan, Meltzer submitted a new column parodying the *New York Times*'s list of the top two hundred batters based on two hundred or more at-bats. "I listed the first seven hundred members of the major leagues based on two or more syllables," he said, "but Lester didn't get the joke. He thought I was putting on the audience, and he didn't want to be doing that. He was angry with me by that point because I wasn't paying attention to the same bands he was." Meltzer's column came to an ignominious end.

In the spring of 1974 the three leading Noise Boys were among the writers who flew to Buffalo to appear at a college-sponsored "Rock Critics' Symposium" arranged by a group of young writers that included Gary Sperrazza, Joe Fernbacher, and Billy Altman. At Lester's urging, the organizers also invited former MC5 singer Rob Tyner, whose first meeting with Lester had been much like Wayne Kramer's. "So you're the asshole that nearly ruined my career!" Tyner said, but that was the beginning of a close friendship. "I came to know and respect Lester as a man of brilliance and incisive wit," Tyner wrote in 1990. "He had an enormous curiosity and a desire to get at the truth by any means necessary."

That weekend in Buffalo, Lester also had a considerable thirst. He and Tyner started drinking Wild Turkey at the airport and didn't stop until they got back on the plane three days later. The other critics paired up in rooms at the Hilton, but Lester and Tyner stayed at the Buffalo State College dorms. "Ah, home at last!" Lester said, surveying their closet-size quarters. The lavatory was empty when he staggered into the shower to prep for a night on the town. A little while later he stepped out with a face full of shaving cream and asked to borrow a razor. The coeds who'd filtered in got an unexpected eyeful and ran out shrieking. He hadn't realized he was staying in the girls' dorm.

Meltzer and Tosches came over and tried to get a party going, but the girls didn't seem very accommodating. It might have been their singing: "Buffalo gals, woncha come out tonight?" After a while the critics gave up and decided to hit a popular college dive called Mr. Goodbar. Despite a steady rain, a long line waited to get in. When the rock writers finally got to the door, the Elvis-look-alike bouncer told them they couldn't enter. "Why the fuck not?" Meltzer demanded. The doorman pointed to Lester, who stood snoring and gently swaying in the rain. "Because that guy's asleep!"

Bad vibes ran rampant by the time of the actual panel. Greg Shaw festered because the other writers had ditched him the night before. "You look like a fuckin' Mexican!" Lester said when he saw John Mendelssohn's Zorro mustache. "I guess I was supposed to take that as the prerogative of the genius," Mendelssohn said, "but I found it hurtful." Several of the other panelists had panned Mendelssohn's band. "I was going through a brief imbecilic macho moment and loudly talking about how I ought to punch Nick Tosches in the nose," Mendelssohn recalled. "I was assured by Lenny Kaye and Patti Smith that I would be signing my death warrant if I did that. Patti performed there, and I thought she was fucking dreadful. I still do."

Smith and Kaye had been gigging together since late 1973, performing songs such as "Piss Factory" and a cover of "Hey Joe" that incorporated a long monologue about Patty Hearst. Lester had developed a crush on Smith, and he chased her around campus all weekend. She spurned his affections with a mix of annoyance and playfulness. "Patti likes to have fun," Kaye said, "but Lester was so *not* Patti's type." Smith and Kaye opened the panel discussion by playing several songs. Afterward the writers sat at a dais that stretched across the stage like the table at the Last Supper. Nobody told them how to proceed, so Lester and Meltzer just started yelling.

"Hi, how are you?" Meltzer said. "Your mother sucks my dick!"

"Jim Morrison was going to be here, but he couldn't make it," Lester cracked. The Doors' singer had been dead for nearly three years.

Jeff Nesin taught a course about rock 'n' roll in the American Studies department at the University of Buffalo, and he acted as the moderator. "This is entropy at the beginning," he said. "What the hell. Lester, is it really true that you come from El Cajon?"

"Yes I come from El Cajon, a suburb of San Diego, California!" Lester said, speaking like a speed-crazed robot imitating Lenny Bruce and doing his best to insult all comers. "I came from a spic suburb full of Mexicans that eat tacos alla time! We used to cruise around in our Chevrolets! Then I went to Detroit! I worked in a shoe store before that! I got to look at a lot of pussy! Then I went up to Detroit to work at *Creeeeeem* magazine! I was living in the ghetto with all the niggers and winos and junkies!"

Meltzer interrupted—"His mother was a Gee-hovah's Witness!"—but Lester the amphetamine automaton didn't miss a beat. "My mother was a Jehovah's Witness, yes, thank you very much! I went out there to live in Detroit, and I thought it was the greatest thing I'd ever seen because I had lived in the suburbs in an apartment house!"

"How about the time you got gonorrhea in Tijuana?"—Meltzer again.

"I got gonorrhea in Tijuana, that's how I lost my virginity, so what!" Lester said. "We're here to talk about rock 'n' roll! Nobody gives a shit about rock 'n' roll! College students don't care about rock 'n' roll! They wanna make their grades! They're all studying for those finals tomorrow! Right?"

The crowd of a hundred or so hooted and hollered. Lenny Kaye quoted Lou Reed's rap from the Velvet Underground's *1969 Live*, asking whether anyone had a curfew. Tosches suggested that they run the discussion like *The Newlywed Game*, with participants answering questions from the crowd. "That's the only way you're gonna get your money's worth, because everybody up here including me is an asshole, and we're just gonna keep talking," he said. That elicited more applause.

Lester started chiding Mendelssohn, but Meltzer set him on a new course, ranking on a critic who wasn't present. "Lester, everyone at this table has no use for Robert Christgau," Meltzer said. "Let's dig into his ribs!"

"He's a pompous asshole!" Lester said. "He writes this column for *Creem* called the Christgau Consumer Guide! He gives an 'A-minus' to a soundtrack that Curtis Mayfield wrote for Gladys Knight that's only fucking nigger music!"

"Robert Christgau is thirty-one years old!" Meltzer shouted. "Thirty-one! He writes reviews of the New York Dolls and says they're good because they're 'teenage,' and he wishes he was a teenager himself, and he isn't anymore and never will be again! Christgau's a schmuck! He hasn't jerked off since he was nineteen; he told me that!"

"This all goes to prove—Christgau and the evidence in question—that rock critics are fixated asshole adolescents," Lester said, suddenly turning into a somber Perry Mason. Then he turned his attentions to *Rolling Stone*.

A year earlier Lester had written a viciously funny review of boogie merchants Canned Heat. Never his biggest fan, publisher Jann Wenner blew a gasket and ordered Lester banned for life. Record-reviews editor Jon Landau told Lester the news and chastised him for being "consistently disrespectful to musicians." For example, Landau asked, was that recent review of *Greetings from Asbury Park, N.J.* positive or negative? Lester told him it was obviously a positive review. "But you said his lyrics were idiotic!" Landau said, "Well, sure," Lester replied. "They *were*, and that was what was *good* about 'em!" Landau scoffed, "Well, Lester, I think *that's* the sort of criticism our readers can't follow."

Twenty-five years later—after he'd written the famous line "I saw rock 'n' roll future and its name is Bruce Springsteen" and become the Boss's

Lester shows Bruce Springsteen who's boss, New York City, 1975.
PHOTO BY CHUCK PULIN

manager—Landau didn't recall the conversation or banning Lester from *Rolling Stone*. "I did feel that that sort of diatribing about a band's personal characteristics—I didn't believe that that was good writing, and I would have told him so," he said. "Getting behind the typewriter and feeling that it was a license to vent at somebody—I had a problem with that."

"I always knew that *Rolling Stone* was a piece of shit," Lester said in 1982. "The reviews I did for them really stuck out like sore thumbs, and I never did get along with Jann, because he really likes the suck-up type of writing. He doesn't like people that are stylists, unless it's somebody he wants to suck up to himself, like Norman Mailer or Truman Capote or someone like that."

In 1974 Lester's indignation was still fresh, and he decided to entertain the crowd in Buffalo by reading the letter Canned Heat's manager had sent to the magazine. "Dear Sirs: Your review of Canned Heat's new album *The New Age* in the June 7 issue written by Lester Bangs is not only one of the shoddiest pieces of journalism ever to appear in your illustrious publication, it is an *outrage*! It is too bad that Mr. Bangs, whose name is so fitting, has nothing better to do with a column than to allocate his review—' "

Here Tosches ripped the screed from Lester's hands so the panel discussion (such as it was) could continue. Arthur Levy, editor of Florida's *Zoo World* magazine, made a game attempt to steer the symposium toward a serious examination of rock journalism, but Meltzer butted in to ask about Levy's favorite Jewish holiday.

"I'll tell you how I feel about rock 'n' roll journalism," Lenny Kaye said. "You're covering a field just like all those hot-rod magazines, and when you review records, it's like giving them a road test."

Eventually Patti Smith grabbed the mike. "I came to New York in 1966 to write rock 'n' roll articles because rock 'n' roll magazines in South Jersey kept me happy," she said in the frenzied rhythms common to her poetry. "All those pictures of all those guys, and I am so proud to have lived when the Rolling Stones lived, when Jim Morrison lived, when Jimi Hendrix—that was our generation, man! They were our fucking gods! I am proud to be living during then. Rock 'n' roll is not dead! I am not dead! And to me rock 'n' roll is anything that Richard Meltzer does. Richard!"

Meltzer had just ambled back to the table after standing to the side and pissing in his water glass. "I was born in Rockaway, New York," he said. "My mother was the handball champ of Far Rockaway High. . . . My father was a schmuck. Anyway my favorite song this week is from the

Something New album by the Beatles." He sang a few bars. "And now my co-author, Nick Tosches, the man who got Ed Sanders to write a book about Charles Manson."

"There's a party after this tonight," Tosches said dryly. "And, uh, anybody who came to this should go to the party. At least that should be interesting. Herewith I turn it over to a fellow known to speak at great lengths about boring topics, Lester Bangs."

"I used to be in college," Lester began. "I was going to be a college teacher until I discovered that I hated academic people and I couldn't stand college students because it's totally insular. And then I realized when I got into *this* bullshit that it's even more insular than that is! My feeling about rock 'n' roll is that it's a bunch of garbage! It's everything your parents ever said it was, it's in one ear and out the other, it's trash—here today and gone tomorrow—so what? The only people who are more unnecessary than rock musicians, who are totally interchangeable, is rock *critics*, because who gives a fuck, right? I think this whole thing is ridiculous, but I'm glad I'm here. I'm having a good time, and I hope *you* are!"

The session rambled on like a drunk in a strange city looking for his hotel room. Someone in the crowd wanted to know how the panelists defined rock 'n' roll. "Rock 'n' roll is the American art form," Lester said. "Eric Dolphy once said that music came out of his breath, went through the saxophone, and it was gone. That was a paraphrase, but it's true. It's evanescent. You can never capture it again. It's a moment in your life. It's your best fuck—"

"It's your worst fuck, too!" Meltzer shouted, stealing the ball. "Rock 'n' roll is nothing but chemistry, and sometimes you abandon it—you abandon it for years—and it will still come back and hit you, and you can't do nothing about it. It's a state of mind, a state of dick, a state of cunt, a state of hips, man, and it will hit you and what can you do? When you least expect it, rock 'n' roll is gonna grab you by the gonads."

Like a distaff Neal Cassady, Patti Smith yelled, "Yeah!" and with that, moderator Jeff Nesin ended the symposium. "We're all gonna go now, because that's all you asked for," he said. "Rock 'n' roll, like yourself, is what you make it."

*   *   *

"Ego? It may not be the greatest word of the twentieth century, but it's sure the driving poison in the vitals of every pop star," Lester wrote in

March 1975 in a piece he called "Let Us Now Praise Famous Death Dwarves, or How I Slugged It Out with Lou Reed and Stayed Awake." Everyone else at *Creem* simply called it "round two."

Reed was touring behind *Sally Can't Dance*, his fifth solo album and a slight pop effort that Lester considered an even more cynical cartoon than *Transformer*. The critic had praised Reed's previous studio album, *Berlin*, a lush but depressing song cycle about a masochistic heroin addict. Lester hailed it as "the most disgustingly brilliant record of 1973" and rock's answer to Tennessee Williams and Hubert Selby, Jr. He couldn't figure out which artist was the "real" one: the Reed of *Sally Can't Dance* and *Transformer* or the one who recorded *White Light/White Heat* and *Berlin*. He was determined to find out.

When Lester arrived at the Detroit Hilton, an angry Reed was pacing back and forth in the lobby. Trader Vic's, the hotel restaurant, had barred the artist from entering because the maître d' did not approve of Reed's black T-shirt and shades. Even Michigan's most notorious slob journalist had never been banned by that dump.

"Hi, Lou, I believe you remember me," Lester said, chuckling. "Unfortunately," Reed droned.

The interview ended a few minutes after it began when Reed bolted for a newspaper and didn't come back. His publicist promised to reschedule, and Lester returned to the hotel after the show. This time Reed lounged in bed in a dimly lit suite, surrounded by roadies, bandmates, and Rachel, the towering transsexual who'd replaced his first wife. "You simultaneously wanted to look away and sort of surreptitiously gawk," Lester wrote. "Purely strange, a mother lode of unholy awe. If the album *Berlin* was melted down in a vat and reshaped into human form, it would be this creature."

Lester had his own entourage, including his pal Esther Korinsky and his new girlfriend, Nancy Alexander. "I was this college girl from Detroit in a beige coat who had entered a den of iniquity," Nancy said. "I had never *seen* things like that." The next day the girls called Rachel "Thing," while Lester referred to her in his article as "the bearded lady." He felt guilty when he heard she'd been hurt by his words, but a furious Reed fired back. "He's just a big schlub from Detroit," the singer said of Lester in *Zig Zag* magazine. "He's fat and he's got a mustache. I wouldn't shit in Lester's nose."

As she watched Lester and Reed spar during the interview, Nancy became convinced that the two were obsessed with one another. "They just started screaming at each other and accusing each other of being frauds," she said. "It was extremely strange and theatrical." Drunk on Johnnie Walker Black—Lou's drink—Lester played the role of the noble savage, jiving and singing the Velvets' "I'm Waiting for the Man" in the style of Amos 'n' Andy. Reed struck the first blow. "You know, I basically like you in spite of myself," he said. "Common sense leads me to believe that you're an idiot, but somehow the epistemological things that you come out with sometimes betray the fact that you're kind of onomatopoetic in a subterranean reptilian way."

"Goddamn, Lou, you sound just like Allen Ginsberg!" Lester yelled.

"You sound like his father," Reed replied. "You should do like Peter Orlovsky and go have shock. You don't know any more than when you started. You just kind of chase your tail."

Lester laughed. "That's what I was gonna say to *you*!" he said. "Do you ever feel like a self-parody?"

"No," Reed said. "If I listened to you assholes, I would. You're comic strips."

"That's okay. I don't mind being a comic strip," Lester said. "*Transformer* was a comic strip that transcended itself." He asked Lou about the drug use and sexual experimentation of the glam movement. In his bored monotone Reed replied that it had nothing to do with him.

"Bullshit," Lester said. "You *started* it, singing about smack, drag queens, etc."

Reed stared at him. "What's decadent about that?"

"Okay, let's define decadence," Lester said. "You tell me what you think is decadence."

"You. Because you used to be able to write, and now you're just fulla shit." Reed started talking about his next album, which he promised would be a new extreme in heavy metal. "Most people can take maybe five minutes of it," he said. Lester cut him off and accused him of marketing pasteurized decadence.

"In your worst moments you could be considered like a bad imitation of Tennessee Williams," Lester said.

Reed paused for a second before delivering the knockout blow: "That's like saying in your worst moments *you* could be considered a bad imitation of *you*."

Prodded again by his wife, Barry Kramer moved *Creem* from Walled Lake in the fall of 1972. Seventeen miles northwest of Detroit, Birmingham was in the early stages of evolving from a middle-class suburb known for nice older homes and good schools into a yuppie enclave of condos, boutiques, and antique stores. As in El Cajon, realtors were suspected of redlining. Connie Kramer loved the new locale, but everyone else thought it was an odd home for America's Only Rock 'n' Roll Magazine.

For the first time the staff didn't have to live and work in the same space. The publisher rented a stately old home at 416 Brown Street that became known as "the Creem House." He secured office space a few blocks away, above a furrier in the Birmingham Theatre building. The magazine shared the second floor with a dentist and a pair of gay hairdressers. The stylists cut the journalists' hair for free, but the dentist was none too happy when a drunken Lester pissed through his mail slot one night. The editors did their best to eliminate the antiseptic vibe of the new digs, defacing the eggshell walls with posters and stains and heaping piles of record mailers, back issues, and garbage on the hardwood floors. Lester's desk sat beneath a mountain of Taco Bell wrappers, *Penthouse* magazines, Coke cans, ashtrays full of Winston butts, discarded press releases, band glossies, and unopened bottles of cough syrup—gifts from fans that he swore he never drank anymore (or at least hardly ever).

The move represented Kramer's desire to professionalize the operation. In early 1973 *Creem* sold 130,000 copies a month. The number wasn't huge—*Rolling Stone* reached 300,000 people every two weeks— but the publisher had plans for expanding his empire. The proposed *Creem* record label, radio hour, and British edition never got off the ground. Other projects fell far short of what they could have been. The *Rock Revolution* paperback was to have been a broad overview of rock history—*Creem*'s version of *Rolling Stone*'s rock encyclopedias—but it was churned out by an overworked staff during a long weekend fueled by speed.

Kramer remained committed. "What would we do with the money?" he asked when the trade magazine *Billboard* offered him $750,000 to sell. "We'd only start up another rock 'n' roll magazine." But *Creem* had come a long way from its origins on Cass Avenue. John Sinclair hardly recognized it anymore. "The local focus and the politics were gone," he said. "They supported the rougher-edged music, but it wasn't going anywhere—it was just another segment of the marketplace. By the time I got out of prison, *Creem* was championing stuff like KISS."

The changes partly reflected the times. Rock 'n' roll had become big business, another form of entertainment second only to Hollywood. In 1973 the music industry's gross annual sales topped $2 billion, more than three times what Americans spent on football, hockey, basketball, and baseball combined. By now many people were taking rock writing very seriously indeed. Once strictly the province of what Lester called "fanatical fans with fanatical opinions to inflict on people," rock criticism had become something you could do for a living—albeit a humble one—and a new group of careerists had emerged. This became obvious when some 140 critics gathered in Memphis on Memorial Day weekend, 1973, for the First Annual National Association of Rock Writers Convention.

The pretentiously titled event was actually the mother of all junkets, funded by the Ardent and Stax record labels to promote the bands Big Star and Black Oak Arkansas. The entire staff of *Creem* traveled from Birmingham, including a biker named Dirty Ed who posed as Barry Kramer's "bodyguard." The liquor flowed freely, and the writers mostly ignored the scheduled activities at the Rivermont Hotel. They did show up for a riverboat cruise on the Memphis Queen and a bus trip to Graceland, but when the King declined to meet them at the gate, Lester and Meltzer responded by pissing on his driveway.

The promotional aspect of the junket coupled with a plan to form a national rock writer's union under the auspices of the Teamsters, but the movement, led by Greg Shaw and Jon Tiven, only got as far as adopting a name: the Rock Writers of the World. Kramer had made up T-shirts with Boy Howdy! on the front and the words ROCK CRITIC on the back; he meant it as a joke, but plenty of others were claiming the appellation with pride. "Lester saw all these kids running around like kids in a candy store and he reacted very negatively," said his friend, *Creem* reviewer Andy McKaie. "They revered him like a god, but he turned to me and said: 'What did I spawn?'" Disgusted, Lester kept a low profile, though he did find time to tumble for New York writer Toby Goldstein. "He was the first person I cheated with on my marriage," she said.

Shortly after the Memphis trip Dave Marsh quit the magazine and moved to New York. "I thought *Creem* was fine with the comic-book aspect and a very serious aspect, but the tendency was to go just with the comic-book stuff," Marsh said. "Lester was a genius, so Lester could put the Magna Carta inside the comic book. But other people were not geniuses, and to me it came off mannered, labored, imitative of Lester, and not very good. It was difficult, but I don't think where I was going intellectually, journalistically, or literarily was conducive to staying with any of those people. I wanted to grow up, and they didn't."

Throughout his tenure Lester encouraged dozens of young critics. They sent their clips and ideas and received long, thoughtful letters in reply. Sometimes they also got late-night phone calls that lasted for hours. Lester's recurring message: Develop your own voice. Write from the heart. Don't try to write in the "*Creem* style." And don't imitate *me*.

"There were a lot of imitators because he freed up the language of writing about rock 'n' roll," said Robert "Robot" Hull, a Memphis native who started writing while at college in Rhode Island. "He would always call it into question and push you in another direction." Rick Johnson was muddling through school in western Illinois, washing dishes, and writing reviews in his spare time when his phone rang. "He was very encouraging, but I wondered, 'Why is this guy calling *me*?'" Johnson said. "He seemed lonely. It was ten o'clock at night, he was the only one in the office, and he sounded a little bit desperate."

Richard Riegel attended a Quaker school in Indiana, sat out the Vietnam War as a conscientious objector, and became one of Lester's favorite reviewers. In 1975 he wrote a bitingly funny critique of Mahogany Rush that included posthumous quotes from Jimi Hendrix, who complained about being ripped off. Not long after that, Lester ran his own interview with the deceased and disgruntled guitarist. Riegel felt flattered. "I don't think it was plagiarism," he said. "Because Lester was so much in tune with jazz, I think it was like a jazz musician taking a melody and improvising or expanding on it."

To many *Creem* subscribers Lester *was* the magazine. Every year he topped the readers' poll as their favorite critic. "Lester and I would stuff the ballot box," Jaan Uhelszki confessed, "but he didn't have to, because he always won anyway." In every issue half the letters either took Lester to task for some unconscionable slight or hailed him as an all-knowing sage. Musicians who could laugh at themselves were honored to be insulted by him, and many felt slighted if another writer was assigned to interview them. "After the Lou Reed interview, which I thought was wonderful, I was very upset if he *didn't* attack me," said Mott the Hoople's Ian Hunter.

In 1973 Lester flew to Atlanta to hear a new group called Lynyrd Skynyrd, produced by former Dylan sideman and Blood, Sweat & Tears keyboardist Al Kooper. "Lester was that rare breed of critic who could actually catch you with your pants down—that is, bust you *rightfully*," Kooper wrote. "Those that are being criticized *hate* that sort of criticism. I liked it, because mostly Lester didn't write about *me*." At the Skynyrd soirée Kooper watched as Lester ate the free food, drank the Jack Daniel's, and danced until well after the party ended—"the college Hunter S. Thompson."

Although it was slowing down, the record-company gravy train hadn't yet derailed. Every year Georgia-based Capricorn Records flew dozens of writers to the company barbecue in Macon. Owner Phil Walden was a millionaire good ol' boy and a buddy of Governor Jimmy Carter. He put on quite a spread, and Lester rubbed elbows with guests such as Bette Midler, Martin Mull, and Cher. "Lester and I got along really well," said label publicist Mike Hyland, "but I don't know if I'd want a room full of Lesters. When he and Nick Tosches were together, it was a bit much. They wanted everything for free: 'Gimme the records! Gimme the food! Where's the bar?' They weren't getting paid all that well, so the only time they were gonna have a big time was when it was on the record company, and they went for it."

While he and Lester were living it up at the Capricorn blowout in 1975, Cameron Crowe realized they were doing exactly what Lester told him not to do the first time they had met a year and a half earlier. Crowe

Lester, Gordon Fletcher, Cameron Crowe, Mike Hyland, Jaan Uhelszki,
and Neal Preston at the Capricorn Records barbecue, 1975.
Photo courtesy Mike Hyland

had also ignored Lester's advice about writing for *Rolling Stone*, and he was rapidly becoming one of its stars. "I remember feeling a twinge that I had crossed over into this other place that Lester didn't find as cool," he said.

Back in Detroit the post-interview food fight became a tradition, and Lester usually lobbed the first dinner roll. Once someone brought a cake backstage to celebrate Leslie West's birthday. Lester threw a fistful at him, and Mountain's guitarist gleefully joined in the fun. West had such a good time that he later agreed to be the pig-out model for Lester's epic "Consumer Guide to American Burger Stands," posing as a *Creem* centerfold surrounded by half-eaten hamburgers.

British bubblegum-rockers Slade were less receptive. The Warner Brothers label rep took everyone to eat at Trader Vic's. Lester started baiting the men who wrote "Mama Weer All Crazee Now," and chunks of pineapple, fish fillets, and shrimp were soon flying everywhere. "Noddy Holder and all those guys were aiming for real, because they couldn't believe anybody was saying this stuff to them," Jaan Uhelszki said. The *Creem* crew and the Warner's rep soon ditched the band and went upstairs in the Hilton to terrorize a Masons convention. Lester would amble up to a sixty-year-old couple in tuxedo and evening gown, smile unctuously, and politely announce, "Eat a bowl of fuck!" or "Slit yer mudder's tit, sir!"

Seconds before the fish fillets fly: Lester dines with Slade at Trader Vic's in Detroit, 1973.
PHOTO BY CHARLES AURINGER

Sometimes Lester's wisecracks backfired. He met Mitch Ryder in 1971 at the Detroit Wheels' Cass Avenue rehearsal loft, and they became friends after Ryder admitted he'd written phony letters to *Creem* trashing Lester just to get his goat. "Our relationship was going out to clubs together and getting shit-faced drunk and high," Ryder said. In December 1972 Lester wrote an enthusiastic overview of the Detroit rock scene for *Phonograph Record Magazine*. He claimed that Ryder's real name was "Bill Bradshinkel" and that the singer was "the supreme evidence of miscreant culture which results when Polacks take acid." Ryder thought that was pretty funny, but Lester went on to note that several throat operations had left the blues belter unable to sing. "It wasn't true, it was malicious, and I actually considered suing him for it," Ryder said. "I was at a point in my career where I didn't have management or booking, and any negative news about my singing ability was going to impact on me. He apologized, but that was it for me and Lester. I never saw him again."

"Fuck 'em if they can't take a joke," Lester maintained. He refused to treat rock stars different than anyone else, and he sprang into his abusive stance at the first sign of self-importance. "Basically I just started out to lead with the most insulting question I could think of," he said in 1982. "The whole thing of interviewing rock stars was just such a suck-up. It was groveling obeisance to people who weren't that special, really. It's just a guy, just another person, so what?"

During a mid-seventies visit to Los Angeles, Lester dragged his friend Michael Ochs on two very different interviews. "Linda Lovelace was wearing a see-through top," Ochs recalled. The star of *Deep Throat* was still years away from renouncing her porno past. "She had nice tits, and we were both in awe. Lester wasn't aggressive to her at all; he was like a little puppy dog. Then later that day with Charles Bukowski he was the exact opposite."

By 1974 Bukowski had joined Burroughs and Kerouac as one of Lester's favorite writers. The following year *Creem* would tap him to cover the Rolling Stones tour just as Jann Wenner turned to Truman Capote, but Lester also believed that Bukowski pandered to his cult by playing the belligerent barfly. The two put a serious dent in the poet's six-case stash of big-mouth beers and started screaming at each other at the top of their lungs. "It was like guerrilla warfare," Ochs said. "It sounded like they could come to blows, but they never did, and there was clearly a mutual respect." Finally Lester paused to go to the bathroom. "Is this guy all right?" Bukowski asked Ochs. "He really seems to be laying it on."

Lester thought a lot about the dangers of living up to an outrageous persona. "I didn't contrive an image for myself, although for a while in every story it seemed like, 'Lester Bangs Gets Drunk and Insults Another Pop Star,' " he told an interviewer in 1976. "But there's a danger in developing a persona. Part of the fun for me has been to say, 'The hell with subtlety!' But you can only go so far with that until it gets boring."

Yet it wasn't all an act. "Lester had a look about him," Mitch Ryder said, "and I saw that look once before in Jim Morrison's eyes."

John Cale recognized it, too. The former Velvet Underground bassist visited *Creem* in the winter of 1973. "Lester was a scary individual in a way," Cale said. "I was bouncing around the walls, but he bounced around his own walls. Every time I spoke to him, it was kind of a very easygoing conversation—a very rational sort of energetic conversation. But when it ended up on the page, it was another story. It had a completely different edge to it that was spectacular. That ability of being able to creep inside and squirm around your head on the written page was really extraordinary. It was almost like he was trying to be a collaborator."

With Paul and Linda McCartney backstage at Olympia Stadium in Detroit, 1976.
PHOTO BY ROBERT MATHEU

In the summer of 1975 Cale's former bandmate Lou Reed released an album called *Metal Machine Music* on RCA's Red Seal classical label. It was the extreme effort that he had promised during his last encounter with Lester, a step beyond "Sister Ray" that avoided any hint of melody, rhythm, vocals, or song structure. Instead it offered four vinyl album sides—each 16:01 long—of dense and disorienting feedback. Most critics considered it a hoax or a plot by Reed to get out of his contract. Lester loved it and played it constantly, driving co-workers from the office and roommates from the Creem House.

"One day in the summer of 1975 I awoke with a hangover and put on *Metal Machine Music* immediately," Lester wrote. "I played it all day and through a party which lasted all that night, in the course of which I got shitfaced again on cognac and beer, broke about half my record collection, punched out the front screen door in my house, physically molested one of my best friends' girlfriends of four or five years, told my friend who was a very talented poet that he couldn't write for shit, after getting thrown out of a restaurant for spilling beer all over his lap and myself and the table and creating a 'disturbance,' zoomed over to another friend's house where I physically assaulted her, repeating over and over in a curiously robotlike rant, 'I know you've got a bottle of Desoxyn in your dresser! Gimme, I want them, I want to take all of them at once!,' threw all the empty cognac bottles in the air as high as I could for the pleasure of watching them shatter in the street, ending up in a blackout coma stupor, which nevertheless never blacked me out quite enough to stop me from writhing on the couch, tearing at my hair and screaming at the top of my lungs, until the police came at seven a.m., whereupon I snapped to and told them that my friends, who were now out in the street breaking beer bottles and yelling 'MACHINE! MACHINE! MACHINE!' up at my bedroom window, had gotten a little rowdy and I would be responsible for them from here on out."

In February 1976 Lester interviewed Reed yet again. "This is not round three," he wrote, and this time the two chatted peacefully on the phone. Reed contended that *Metal Machine Music* contained symphonies hidden within its grooves. Lester told him he thought it was a giant "fuck you" that showed integrity—a sick, twisted integrity, but integrity nonetheless. "Hey, Lou, do you ever fuck to *Metal Machine Music*?" he asked.

"I never fuck," Reed replied. "I haven't had it up in so long I can't remember when the last time was."

"Listen," Lester said, "I was cruising in my car with *Metal Machine Music* blaring the other day when this beautiful girl crossing at a light smiled and winked at me!"

Reed cackled. "Are you sure it was a girl?" he asked.

With Lester's permission Jaan Uhelszki's younger sister listened in on another extension. JoAnn idolized Reed, but the interview disappointed her. It was *boring*, she said, just two guys chatting about an album that no one else in the world seemed to like. As one of the fringe benefits of working at *Creem,* Barry Kramer paid for his editors' therapy sessions. Lester's psychiatrist had suggested that *Metal Machine Music* represented his feelings about the fiery death of his father. Throughout the interview, Lester was effusive in listing most of the reasons he loved Reed's latest album, but he neglected to mention that one.

chapter seven

I Heard Her Call
My Name

When Lester tired of the grind at *Creem*, he often escaped across the filthy waters of the Detroit River to Windsor, Ontario. He first made the trek with Jaan Uhelszki on runs for "222's," codeine aspirins that *Creem* staffers gobbled by the handful during the deadline crunch. A bootlegging hub during prohibition, Windsor still retained a touch of frontier atmosphere in its many rowdy bars. Lumberjacks from the Upper Peninsula gathered to watch hockey with guys who worked at Chrysler's and GM's Canadian plants. They grumbled about "all the niggers" across the river and drank quart bottles of Molson and Labatts, which Lester declared the best beers in the world.

"I guess my claim to fame is that I introduced Lester to beer," said *Creem* contributor and Windsor native Alan Niester. The Golden House sold fifteen-cent drafts and hosted a band called the Blues Train that included several of Niester's buddies. He and Lester frequently climbed onstage to play cowbell and tambourine and sing backing vocals on "Honky Tonk Woman." Lester continued writing songs of his own, and he enjoyed rendering them at the top of his lungs during the drive back home. Niester's enduring image of his friend involves speeding through the night, wind rushing through the car, and Lester bellowing and waving a late-night burger and a Coke. "That was about as happy as I'd ever seen Lester," Niester said. "I think the *Creem* days were probably as good as it got for him."

One night at the Golden during the spring of 1973, Lester met a girl named Dori. Cute, blowsy, and buxom, the precocious high schooler snuck into the bars at night to smoke and drink sloe gin fizzes. She wore black leather and brushed the long black bangs from her eyes, and Lester fell for her hard. They spent passionate nights in his bedroom in Birmingham, and she didn't even complain about the mess. "I got a new baby," Lester wrote his friend Roger Anderson. "She's beautiful and I love her. She calls El Cajon 'Al Capone.' She's a cute Canuck. She said: 'What animals you got out there?' I said: 'Rattlesnakes, horny toads, gila monsters, and at the beach sharks and jellyfish.' She said: 'You come from a monster land!'"

Many of his friends told Lester that Dori was too young for him. When the *Creem* staff went to a party for Alice Cooper, Lester's co-workers suspected that she was just using him to get near the rock stars, but Lester was smitten. In the fall of 1973 she stunned him by announcing she was pregnant. He offered to marry her and care for the child, but she had other ideas.

"We had an abortion," Lester said in 1977. "Isn't that funny phraseology? She had an abortion. But I felt real fucked up about it for a long time, and I had to go to a shrink. It just felt like murder to me." He gave her the money for the procedure, and he cried when he drove her to the clinic. He still believed they had a future together, and he didn't understand why she kept pulling away. Finally she said she wanted nothing more to do with him, and he resumed his search for a soul mate.

Lester fell in love instantly, and his relationships unraveled just as quickly. He scared some women with his excesses, his poor hygiene, or his intensity. "He'd come on with these big bear hugs and try to get women in a clinch," Jaan Uhelszki said. "He was always trying to kiss people—like the kissing bandit." But Lester had little empathy when the tables were turned.

Like many who knew her, Richard Meltzer described Australian-born rock writer Lillian Roxon as "a saint." She flirted with Lester when he visited New York in 1973. "She gushed shameless *love* for the s.o.b.," Meltzer wrote, "ordering up a Lester button and leaving it in his hotel box. Response to this purest of offerings was: 'What's that fat cunt *want* from me?'" Roxon died of an asthma attack several months later. "When I say he was an asshole, well, I could be an asshole, too," Meltzer said. "But he was just so glaringly different people at different times."

The occasional macho bluster might have masked some deep-seated insecurities. During the 1974 trip to Buffalo, Lester visited the hotel room that Meltzer shared with Nick Tosches. "Do you ever get off better jerking off to pictures than fucking?" Lester asked while perusing a leg mag. "Sure," Tosches said. "Most of the time."

Seven years later Lester recalled his relief in an unpublished manuscript. "I didn't press the issue further but this did much to alleviate my anxieties in this department," he wrote. "I was still afraid I was a repressed queer, homosexual, closet case, whatever you want to call it. I fucked women at every available opportunity, even when they occasionally turned out to be so degraded or just beatdown that some aspect of their personalities physically repelled me, but I never could feel anything, only in masturbation and in brief gusts that flew through some of my frenetic fucks like summer showers and left me confused, wondering, sad, and afraid to confide in a soul in the world. Otherwise I was almost completely numb when in the presence of women, although I could and with the usual regularity did get a hard-on and in fact was afflicted with what's known as priapism, i.e. bangbangbangbang for hour upon hour, which naturally gave some of the women I contacted orgasms, and even led some of them to tell me I was the best lover they'd ever had, which made me even more sad."

In Birmingham, Lester built a trusted circle of friends in whom he could confide without playing the role of the great gonzo rock writer. He was equally willing to listen to their fears and concerns, talking for hours at any time of the day or night. "It was really important to him that he was a good friend," said his pal John Morthland. "Part of it was that you could say anything to Lester and he wouldn't be judgmental. We could just talk to each other forever about anything."

A year older than Lester, Morthland was also raised in Southern California near the edge of the Mojave Desert. In high school he wrote for the *San Bernardino Sun-Telegram*'s weekly teen section, and he scored an early interview with the Rolling Stones. In 1965 he enrolled in Berkeley, and through his roommate, Langdon Winner, he met Greil Marcus. He began writing for *Rolling Stone* in the same issue that featured Lester's attack on the MC5. Impressed by Morthland's Stones scoop, Jann Wenner hired him as an editor in late 1969. He started the week after Altamont and quit ten months later, when the job stopped being fun.

In 1974 Morthland was freelancing for *Creem* when Barry Kramer called with a job offer. The writer wanted to move from the Bay Area to

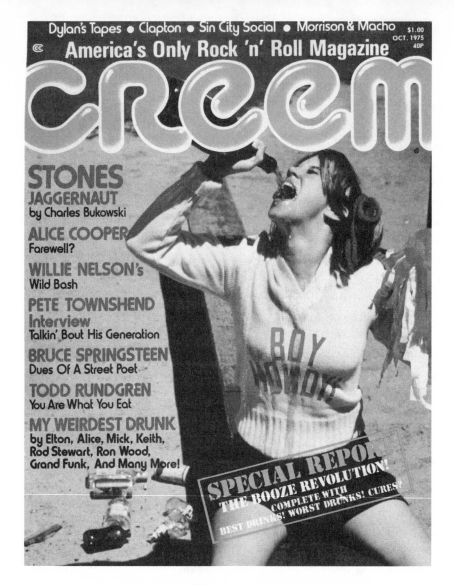

America's Only Rock 'n' Roll Magazine

creem

STONES
JAGGERNAUT
by Charles Bukowski

ALICE COOPER
Farewell?

WILLIE NELSON's
Wild Bash

PETE TOWNSHEND
Interview
Talkin' 'Bout His Generation

BRUCE SPRINGSTEEN
Dues Of A Street Poet

TODD RUNDGREN
You Are What You Eat

MY WEIRDEST DRUNK
by Elton, Alice, Mick, Keith,
Rod Stewart, Ron Wood,
Grand Funk, And Many More!

SPECIAL REPORT
THE BOOZE REVOLUTION!
COMPLETE WITH
BEST DRINKS! WORST DRUNKS! CURES?

Creem's special "booze issue," October 1975.
Leslie Alexander (née Brown) is the model lush.

the East Coast, and Birmingham lay in between. He agreed to edit *Creem* for six months and stayed for seven. "Kramer wanted to impose a certain amount of professionalism on the staff," Morthland said. In his low-key way he introduced more thorough editing and reinforced the sanctity of deadlines. Kramer had hired other editors to do the same, but Lester and the staff tortured them and drove them away. Morthland kept his cool and was liked by everyone. The only time anyone could tell that he was upset was when he smoked his unfiltered Luckies to the nubs.

A study in contrasts, Morthland and Lester became friends nonetheless. Morthland, as quiet and inscrutable as an extra in a Bergman film, was one of the handful of people who could tell Lester when he was being an asshole. For his part, Lester was one of a select few known to make Morthland laugh. "Lester was as funny in real life as he was in print," Morthland wrote, "and it was really funny ha-ha humor as often as it was black humor." Long after everyone else crashed, the two sat in the living room of the Creem House playing records and talking. They shared similar interests in music and literature and held the opinion that it was hard for nice guys like them to find true love. Of course, there was also the common bond of booze.

"John and Lester together drank more than any human beings I ever met in my life," said *Creem*'s associate publisher, Harvey Zuppke. "We'd go out to a bar and no one could even see anymore, but those two guys would still have another. They'd say and do things to provoke strangers, but they never felt any peril."

Richard C. Walls was another of Lester's drinking buddies. He had contributed jazz reviews to *Creem* in its infancy, and he met Lester in 1971 at the magazine's Cass Avenue loft. "Bangs and I hit it off immediately, having two things in common that would bond us like brothers," he wrote. "We were both unreasonably bugged about being born too late to be Beatniks—I mean, hippies were okay, sure, but Beatniks, man, they had *culture*—and we were both world-class lushes." A hairy, hulking presence, Walls would step out of the shadows, deliver his copy, then disappear—the Bigfoot of Cass Corridor. He was eventually diagnosed as having an anxiety disorder akin to agoraphobia.

Walls fell out of touch when the magazine moved to Walled Lake, but he bumped into Lester again in 1973 at a Cass Avenue dive called the Bronx Bar. "You oughta write for us!" Lester said. Walls happened to be carrying a couple of parody reviews, one of a movie called *I Eat Your Gore,* the other of an avant-garde jazz album by "the Black Badass Mystical Art Band." He gave them to Lester, they ran unedited, and Walls appeared in every issue of *Creem* after that.

On one of the rare occasions when they ventured out of his house, Walls watched Lester show off an expensive bottle of cognac that he'd received as a gift from a record company. Walls pocketed it and cracked the seal as he sat in the back of the 1969 Camaro that Lester had recently purchased for five hundred bucks. "My God, that's my bottle!" Lester yelled. "You stole it!" Walls nonchalantly replied that he had. "He seemed genuinely pissed," Walls recalled. "I thought, 'My God, he thinks I'm really a nice guy!' A lot of his humor and his edge came out of the fact that the world simply did not quite live up to what he wanted it to be."

To *Creem* typesetter Georgia Christgau, rock critic Robert's sister, Lester seemed to be gripped by a loneliness that intimates could not alleviate. Once he brought two businessmen home from the bar at the Detroit airport to listen to *Raw Power*, the Stooges' rampaging third album. They left the Creem House toting two of the thirty-five copies that he'd requested from Columbia for purposes of proselytizing. Another time a group of staffers were speeding down the highway when Lester leaned out the window and screamed "Fuckwad!" It was a new expression to the others, and they all cracked up. "The wonderful times were having him be that incredible daring and free spirit in a context where he was a regular guy as well," Christgau said. "He could make anything fun to do that was ordinary."

He was also unfailingly loyal and generous. "You could call Lester up at any time and he would meet you wherever you were if you needed someone to talk to," said his friend, Esther Korinsky. "I'd never met anybody like that. He would lend you his last penny, even if he only had five dollars in his pocket." Lester was heartbroken when Muffin/Buttfuck ran away, but the cockapoo eventually turned up with an old woman who lived in a trailer. When Lester went to retrieve it, he saw that the lady loved the dog so much that he tearfully insisted she keep it.

Lester felt especially close to the circle of friends around JoAnn Uhelszki, seven years her sister's junior. Several members of their high-school gang died in a car crash, and some of the survivors turned to drugs and alcohol. Others contemplated suicide. Mark Kogan's parents institutionalized him for shoplifting records, and Lester sent him a CARE package of tapes, a Hawkwind button, and his latest Lou Reed interview. "None of us were average kids," Kogan said. "We were freaks." Lester empathized but refused to let them feel sorry for themselves. "*Everybody* comes from a fucked-up family," he told JoAnn. "I'm the living example of not using that as an excuse."

At twenty-seven, Lester related to the teens of the seventies in many ways, but in others they seemed like aliens. They had no clue about history, politics, or religion. They could quote every line of dialogue from

Pink Flamingos or talk about why Evel Knievel failed to jump the Snake River Canyon, but they hardly took notice of the fall of Saigon or the Watergate hearings. They seemed to be alienated from every element of the culture except rock 'n' roll. "He felt that these were the neglected white suburban kids—a real out group," Morthland said. "He always thought of them as the children of the Velvets, even though at that point no else did because no one paid enough attention to the Velvet Underground to think about what their spiritual offspring might be like. But even back then Lester saw suburban kids as future shock."

JoAnn and her friends inspired Lester to write a proposal for a Studs Terkel–style book called *Lost Generation: American Kids Now in Their Own Words*. Once again the book went nowhere, despite an effective pitch. "What's really interesting about the whole generation of American youth that grew up in the seventies is that *they don't know they're alienated*," he wrote. "Where pop icons used to represent an ideal you would like to be, most of them today represent various avenues of escape from personhood and the painful necessity of emotion that goes with it. The stars are blanks, and blank is better because feeling has come to be automatically associated with pain. . . . I know these kids. In many ways, I'm still one of them myself."

∗ ∗ ∗

In the midst of a mid-seventies lull that had many fans questioning whether rock 'n' roll was dead, Lester continued to search for signs of life. He came up with several new heroes and heroines, but they were few and far between. In 1975 the newly formed Patti Smith Group signed to Arista and released its debut album, *Horses*. "What must be recognized is that Smith transcends bohemian cultism to be both positive and mainstream, even though her songs go past a mere flirtation with death and pathology," Lester wrote. He also continued to praise one of her future collaborators. "Bruce Springsteen reaches his stride at a time when the listening audience is not only desperate for a new idol but unprecedentedly suspicious of all pretenders to the throne," he wrote.

Lester raved about Roxy Music—"Just try to imagine a lead singer who sounds like a low-warbling cross between Bowie, Lou Reed and Elvis singing a wide crosscut of punk sneer overlaid with a broad swath of Victorian Romanticism and space noise"—and he championed the New York Dolls. "They gromp into 'Personality Crisis,' one of their primo big hits, and it's hotter 'n spic snatch in Guadalajara," he wrote. He also hailed the synthesized pop of the German band Kraftwerk, perceptively noting that they offered a glimpse of a techno future. But his favorite new sounds came from the island of Jamaica. "Reggae is not the laid-back, coconut-clonk, ricky-tick redundancy it might at first seem," he wrote. "It brims over with passion, love, rage, pain, anguish, and joy, just like the best of all music. And though most American listeners don't 'get' it at first exposure, perceiving it and even becoming addicted to it are not at all the artificial, hip-liberal-motivated processes you might think."

In February 1976 Lester spent a week in Jamaica courtesy of Island Records. One of the first American journalists to make the trip, he returned to describe the Rastafarian religion as a cross between John Sinclair and the Jehovah's Witnesses. Though he was ostensibly on a junket to hype Bob Marley, he decided to leave that to the reporter from *Rolling Stone*. When his story ran in *Creem* in the spring of 1976, it heralded lesser-known artists such as Burning Spear, Toots and the Maytals, and Lee "Scratch" Perry, though he did recount an interview with Marley as the singer leaned against the hood of his BMW. He transcribed the dialogue phonetically in an effort to convey the artist's patois.

"Would you like to see white kids in the U.S. with dreadlocks?" Lester asked.

"Yeah, mon!" Marley said, laughing. "Sure! Y'see, righteousness shall cover d'earth like da water cover d'sea, y'unnerstan'? So as far as we can go, we gonna live right. We're all jus' children on d'earth."

Marley talked about the day when he would return to Africa leading a group of Rastafarians numbering 144,000—a figure that registered with Lester from childhood Bible studies. "What will be the Rasta reaction if there's a lot of violence?" he asked.

"Dem guys not dealing with de twelve tribes of Israel," Marley said. "We not talking about govanment now; govanment wrong. We talkin' 'bout de twelve tribes of Israel. We wan' the unity, and the only unity we can get is troo Rasta. And the only way we can get the message troo right now is troo reggae."

Referring to an old Jamaican motor sport, Lester asked Marley whether he'd ever rammed a goat in his BMW. "No, no, no, don' think dat, man!" Marley replied. "People need live good purpose, man. When you see a goat, you are suppose to stop, communicate to de goat, and make de goat know de outcome."

"This guy's just a hippie," Lester declared. He related more to Perry.

The dub producer was no Rasta; he was an uptown cat, a regular hipster con artist. Escorted by Island owner Chris Blackwell, Lester visited Perry's Black Ark Studio. "A diminutive lion in his kingdom, he at length danced over to the corner where I was trying to be inconspicuous," Lester wrote.

"You wine man," Perry announced. "I *know* wine man." He handed Lester a plastic cup and a bottle of winecarnes, a local vintage fortified with meat extracts. "Now, dear reader, I know that this—one drunk recognizing another—is not the most profound or miraculous occurrence in the world," Lester wrote. "But here, in the middle of Herb Heaven, with every righteous Rasta and American hiplet in sight belittling the rum culture like it was 1967 all over again, it qualified as outright mind-reading."

As the second installment of the reggae epic hit the newsstands, Barry Kramer dispatched Lester to New York on a mission to recruit new writers to liven up the magazine. Lester stayed in the suite that Kramer kept at the St. Moritz Hotel and charged lavishly on *Creem*'s account, but he accomplished little besides partying with his usual East Coast pals, including the members of a band called the Dictators.

Lester had befriended the group when it stopped in Birmingham during its first tour, which was aborted before the band ever played a gig. With liner notes by Richard Meltzer and production by former rock critic Sandy Pearlman, the Dictators' debut album was a stark contrast to the prevailing sounds of 1975. *Go Girl Crazy!* sped by in a hyperactive blur of stolen Chuck Berry riffs, pro-wrestling machismo, and lyrics rife with sophomoric humor. "What the Dictators were about was a spirit still alive in America that was based on rock 'n' roll that was not about to be swallowed up by Led Zeppelin, the Allman Brothers, or the Eagles," guitarist Scott Kempner said. "It was a spirit that was alive in bands like the MC5, the Stooges, the Flamin' Groovies, and some of the Who's and the Rolling Stones' stuff, and Lester embodied the journalistic approach to that."

When Lester visited New York in the summer of 1976, the Dictators threw a party for him in the rehearsal loft they shared with Blue Öyster Cult. The writer strolled in, stripped down to his T-shirt, and grabbed singer Handsome Dick Manitoba in a half nelson. Documented by Roberta Bayley, the ensuing wrestling match ran as a photographic comic strip in the fourth issue of *Punk*. This snotty tribute to Lester almost equaled the magazine's homage to Lou Reed, who appeared as a cartoon Frankenstein on the cover of issue number one.

Inspired by the writing in *Creem* and the art in *Mad,* cartoonist

Lester, Patti Smith, and Lou Reed in New York City, 1975.
PHOTO BY KATE SIMON

John Holmstrom launched *Punk* in late 1975. His friend Legs McNeil suggested the name, drawing inspiration from the cover of *Go Girl Crazy!* "On the inside sleeve of the record was a picture of the Dictators hanging out in a White Castle hamburger stand, and they were dressed in black leather jackets," McNeil wrote. "Even though we didn't have black leather jackets, the picture seemed to describe us perfectly. . . . The word 'punk' seemed to sum up the thread that connected everything we liked—drunk, obnoxious, smart but not pretentious, absurd, funny, ironic, and things that appealed to the darker side."

Lester and Meltzer had long personified this attitude, but it was first dubbed "punk" and applied as a rock 'n' roll aesthetic by Nick Tosches in a July 1970 essay for *Fusion*. Tosches picked up the word from poet Ed Sanders, who was using it in the late sixties to describe his band, the Fugs. In "The Punk Muse: The True Story of Protopathic Spiff Including the Lowdown on the Trouble-Making Five-Percent of America's Youth," Tosches described an ideal "honky blues" that was a "visionary expiation, a cry into the abyss of one's own mordant bullshit." The punk motto: "Poetry is puked, not plotted."

In 1970 Lester appropriated the term for the title of *Drug Punk*. Like "heavy metal," he knew it from the writing of William S. Burroughs. In a scene in *Junky*, strung-out protagonists Will and Roy compete with "two young punks" to roll a drunk on the subway. The punks get the better of the junkies. "Fucking punks think it's a joke," Roy says. "They won't last long. They won't think it's so funny when they get out on the Island doing five-twenty-nine"—a six-month sentence at Riker's Island. Said Burroughs two decades later, "I always thought a punk was someone who took it up the ass."

Dave Marsh takes credit for using the phrase "punk rock" for the first time in the pages of *Creem*. In his Looney Tunes column in May 1971—the same issue that introduced the term "heavy metal" as a genre name—Marsh described an inspired set by sixties rockers Question Mark and the Mysterians five years after their hit, "96 Tears." Marsh was tired of hearing "punk" used as an epithet. "Culturally perverse from birth, I decided that this insult would be better construed as a compliment," he wrote, "especially given the alternative to such punkist behavior, which I figured was acting like a dignified asshole."

Through the mid-seventies, Lester, Marsh, Meltzer, Tosches, Greg Shaw, and Lenny Kaye were among the critics who celebrated music typifying the "punkist" attitude. In 1972 Kaye compiled the forgotten hits of psychedelic garage bands such as the Seeds and Lester's favorites, the Count Five, on a double album called *Nuggets*. The premise was that raw singles such as "Pushin' Too Hard" and "Psychotic Reaction" stood up as great rock 'n' roll even if the artists behind them were derivative, hadn't mastered their instruments, and were never heard from again. What Lester called the "proto-punk" bands joined groups such as the Velvet Underground, the Stooges, the MC5, the Modern Lovers, and the New York Dolls in what was emerging as an alternative canon.

"People read *Creem*—maybe they lived in Canada, maybe they lived in Chicago, maybe they lived in England—and they said, 'Wow! This is more interesting than Kansas and Yes, all those pompous bands,' " said the Dictators' Andy Shernoff. "It was just part of the cultural change in rock 'n' roll."

That change manifested itself most dramatically at CBGB-OMFUG, a derelict bar next to a flophouse on New York City's Bowery. Owner Hilly Kristal began booking rock in the dimly lit dive in March 1974. His original plan was to highlight "country, bluegrass, blues" and "other music for uplifting gourmandizers," the source of the acronyms on his canopy. A would-be music entrepreneur named Terry Ork convinced Kristal to showcase a band called Television, and soon groups such as the Ramones, Blondie, and the Talking Heads were performing regularly. The music at CBGB was first hailed in the pages of the *Soho Weekly News* and the *Village Voice,* New York's alternative weeklies, but word spread through *Creem* in November 1975 when Lisa Robinson devoted her "El- eganza" column to the bands that she called "the new Velvet Under- ground." By 1976 the new sounds needed a name, and Holmstrom's *Punk* arrived to provide one.

"*This* is punk?" Lester asked when he visited CBGB for the first time with his friend Billy Altman. Onstage three preppy nerds in sweater vests nervously imitated the Modern Lovers. After the Talking Heads finished, Television performed, and the group built to a climax with a long guitar jam called "Marquee Moon." It reminded Lester of the Grateful Dead. "This is just San Francisco all over again!" he railed.

"When Lester rolled into town there was a sense of, 'Here's Lester. The legend has arrived,'" said James Wolcott, who covered the scene for the *Village Voice*. "In the beginning he didn't like any of the music at CBGB. He eventually hooked onto it, but he went through this phase of, 'It's not Iggy. It's not the MC5. They're not taking the real risks.' Every- thing was filtered through Detroit, and that took a while to wear off."

∗ ∗ ∗

Nancy Alexander was midway through her senior year at Wayne State University when she met Lester in the winter of 1974. She was tall and graceful, with dark, curly hair and beautiful brown eyes. Her friends de- scribed her as "fashion-model pretty," but Nancy disdained trendiness. Lester called her "the most womanly pseudo-waif I ever saw." Before they started dating, she had rebelled against her strict Greek parents mostly by sneaking cigarettes and staying out late with the girls.

Like Andy, Lester's first love, Nancy preferred the theater to rock 'n' roll. She wanted to be an actress, but she had several links to the *Creem* crowd. She worked with JoAnn Uhelszki at a clothing store called Bizarre, and her friend Leslie Brown served as the magazine's new sub- scription kid. Leslie dated and eventually married Nancy's brother.

One night Nancy and Leslie went to the movies. The line stretched on forever, but Leslie saw Lester at the front near the cashier. Though they'd never met, Nancy strolled up to him in her cashmere sweater and beige coat, hugged him, and thanked him for saving her place. "I didn't know who Lester Bangs was—that he was this writer and that he was sort of famous—and I didn't care," Nancy said. "We hit it off right away."

A short time later Lester took Nancy to the movies for real. She tried to play it cool, hiding behind mirrored shades when they went for a burger after the show. Lester leaned over, knocked on her sunglasses, and said, "You don't fool me a bit. You're a *clown.*" Nancy took off her sunglasses and smiled. "He broke my little glass house," she said. "I always thought that he did that with everybody."

Nancy recalled her boyfriend's pulling up to her house in Southfield in his mufflerless red Camaro, shattering the suburban calm. "I would be locked in my bedroom and there would be this dread—I always felt like we lived in a bad Ingmar Bergman movie—and my father would go, 'Your *friend* is coming,'" Nancy said. Lester usually strolled to the door in his cowboy hat and black leather jacket. "Gosh, your daughter sure is *beautiful!*" he'd announce. "Got any cognac?" Nancy tried to stifle her laughter until they were outside. "Do my parents seem really strange to you?" she'd ask as Lester opened the rusted-out passenger door. "They're fucked up out of their minds!" he'd say, and they'd barrel off into the night, smoking cigars and swigging cognac.

In time the Alexander family welcomed Lester into their home. He ingratiated himself with Nancy's father by giving him an obscure Mingus record. Her mother got a favorite book, *Tales from the Dead,* and her brother received a shrunken head from Vietnam. Although she didn't understand English, Nancy's grandmother Yi-Ya loved Lester. "He will hold you in his hands forever," she told her granddaughter in Greek. When the couple left after Christmas dinner, Lester seemed ready to cry. "Family is something that he always yearned for," Nancy said, "as well as something that he rebelled against."

Sometimes the lovers tested each other's patience. Once Lester dumped a stack of jazz albums on Nancy, a big Led Zeppelin fan, and advised her to study up. "A few days later I told him I liked this wild Don Cherry piece, and he just went '*Rrrr!*' because he expected me to like

Nancy Alexander with Charlie Auringer at the Creem House, 1975.
PHOTO COURTESY LESLIE ALEXANDER

something really lame," she said. On vacation with her family in Virginia Beach, she saw a pet hermit crab that reminded her of Lester, and she bought it for him as a present. "Wow, thanks a lot," he said sarcastically, but he came to love the tiny crustacean. He named it Spud and filled one of the two bathtubs at the Creem House with sand so that it would feel at home.

"His extrovertedness brought me out," Nancy said, "and my soulfulness brought him in." But she didn't want to get too serious too soon, and insisted that they continue seeing other people. His lifestyle frightened her, and they shared a private joke for those occasions when Lester found himself slipping or being goaded into playing the notorious Noise Boy. "I would always say, '*Lester Bangs!*'" she said, "and that was the cue that he was becoming his persona."

"Nancy was totally unimpressed with the music biz, and that was really good for Lester," his friend John Morthland said. "She was a touchstone with reality. There were people she liked who were a part of the music scene, but by and large she really disliked that whole world and would say so all the time. There were always a lot of people around Lester who were attracted to the craziness of his writing. Nancy read those people. She really loved Lester as a person, not as this iconic figure, and she treated him that way."

Nancy didn't know much about alcoholism at the time, but several months into the relationship she began to suspect that her boyfriend had a problem. "There was a self-destructive thing in him that would not let him come to grips with all the chaos inside," she said. "There was the Lester Bangs who was the hit of the party—everywhere he went people related to him and he would kind of turn on and be funny as people pushed him to be that way. But I also saw the other side, the Lester who was seeing a psychiatrist. He had a tremendous amount of personal pain and absolute rage."

Lester saw a female therapist in Birmingham. He took the antidepressants she prescribed without telling her that he mixed them with his usual alcoholic and pharmaceutical intake. "You know you're bamboozling your shrink about your drinking," Morthland told him. "You're not telling the truth." It was one of the rare times when Lester wouldn't concede that his friend was right. Instead he raged at his psychiatrist, hurling furniture and calling her a "stupid kike." After that she refused to see him again.

Nancy and Lester split up and reunited several times in 1975, and he pushed her to make a commitment. In January 1976 she went to a party at the Creem House, and Lester chased her outside. The snow was two feet deep, and icicles hung from the trees. Her disregard for Lou Reed had always bothered him. Now he threw a copy of Reed's romantic new album at her feet. On the back of *Coney Island Baby* he scrawled a poetic love letter.

> Dear Nancy:
> I hate you! I hate your attitude (it sucks) (it's stupid).
> I hate your job, its hours, and the fact you prefer it that way.
> I hate your nervous breakdowns.
> I hate [your boyfriend] Dennis.
> I hate your slowness.
> I hate the melodramatic way you use your ambitions and their
>   frustration as an excuse for not seeing me when the
>   thing that really split us up was your curious "moral standards."
> I hate not seeing you.
> I hate the condescending way you say: "I know, I know" and
>   put me down when I tell you I hate not seeing you.
> I hate your house.
> I hate your car.
> I hate your little brother and his piano lessons.
> I hate your big brother. . . .
> I hate Yi-Ya.
> I hate Harold Pinter.
> I hate the Led (I hope their plane crashes en route to Detroit).
> I hate the way you start to intellectualize every time I tell you I
>   miss you.
> I hate missing you so fucking bad.
> Love, Lester

They could see their breath in the cold night air as they argued. They'd had this fight before, but this time Nancy rose to the occasion as an actress. "I can't really love anybody!" she said. "Don't you see I'm an ice queen? Leave me alone! Nobody is ever going to break through!"

Nancy started crying when he softly said, "Well, why can't you try?"

"He really broke through all my cynicism," Nancy said, and the two started talking about marriage.

By early 1976 Lester was the sole member of the *Creem* staff dating back to Walled Lake, let alone Cass Avenue. He was like the fifth-year college student reluctant to graduate. "The Birmingham Youth Club," Lester called the new crew, and they adopted an Italian restaurant on Woodward Avenue as their hangout. Pasquale's had surly waitresses, cheesy murals of Venice, rubbery meatball sandwiches, and—its saving grace— enormous bolos of cheap draft beer. Here Lester held court.

To "the boys"—Robert Duncan and Eric "Air Wreck" Genheimer— Lester dispensed wisdom about the art of pleasing a woman. "He gave Duncan some advice about how to eat pussy," Genheimer recalled. " 'If it smells bad, you just swig a beer and get right down there,' he said." To "the girls"—Susan Whitall, Leslie Brown, and Carol Schloner—Lester offered sympathetic counsel on the opposite sex. "All men are weasels," he said. "The only use they have for women is to get their rocks off, and half the time the only reason they wanna do that is to prove something."

Late nights at the office they played stupid phone games. Lester tried to interview Ugandan dictator Idi Amin via long distance and got as far as the palace operator. Once he placed a three-way call between

Nancy Alexander, Lester, and Robert Duncan spar with Gene Simmons of KISS, 1976.
Photo courtesy Jaan Uhelszki

short-tempered critics Ed Ward and Robert Christgau, listening in while the two yelled at each other about who called whom and why. "Duncan and I both looked up to Lester," Genheimer said. "We wanted to be like him, we wanted to write like him, we wanted to imitate him as much as we could." But Barry Kramer clamped down when they tried to keep Lester's 4 P.M.-to-3 A.M. hours. "*You* can't be Lester," the publisher said. "Only Lester is Lester."

In May 1975 Lester, Genheimer, and Whitall went to see longtime *Creem* favorites the Faces on their last tour before Rod Stewart quit the band. After the show they picked up guitarist Ron Wood, who invited them to a party at the house of former Temptations singer David Ruffin. Wood climbed in the back of the *Creem* cargo van and sat on a cinder block next to Lester. A black man tapped on the locked passenger door just as Genheimer started to pull away. "You always keep your doors locked in Detroit, and I was ignoring him," Genheimer said. "It was a typical Detroit thing."

"Hey, man, that's Bobby Womack!" Wood shouted. "Open up, let 'im in, he's comin' with us!"

They drove to a nice brick house on the east side of Detroit, where the party was going full tilt. "Everything was pristine, and everyone was really well dressed, and we were these scruffy white kids in blue jeans," Whitall recalled. Lester smelled bad and sported a dirty ABBA T-shirt. He grabbed a beer and slammed it down on a coffee table, and an attractive redhead ran over with a coaster. She was the only other white person at the party, and before she knew what was happening, Lester had her on the dance floor in an unwelcome clinch.

Genheimer and Whitall cringed as a guy the size of a professional linebacker approached them on the couch. "Do you know who your friend is messing with?" he asked. "Lester could *smell* it," Whitall said. "If he went to a party, it was always like: 'How am I gonna piss somebody off in the biggest way possible?' We go to David Ruffin's house, and he has to make a play for the host's girlfriend."

Eventually his colleagues pulled Lester into a back bedroom, where Wood and Womack were jamming. "I think someone had spiked us on acid, because the guitar neck seemed like it was made out of rubber," Wood recalled. Lester plopped down on the bed between them and started singing one of his originals: "Sho' wish ah wuz a nigger/Then mah dick'd be bigger!" Wood laughed. "I remember always gettin' on well with Lester," he said twenty years later. "Big guy with a mustache—he looked like Rob Reiner." But no one else at the party found Lester amusing.

"It took years before I realized what an asshole I'd been, not to mention how lucky I was to get out of there with my white hide intact," Lester wrote in 1979. The realization came in a controversial piece about racism called "The White Noise Supremacists," but it wasn't the first time he'd addressed the subject.

Back in El Cajon, Lester had probed the polite prejudices of his hometown in *Journal Of a Blob*, writing a chapter called "Drunk Punk Ofay Pretending He's a Nigger," inspired by social satirists Lenny Bruce and Paul Krassner. In the years that followed, he became increasingly scornful of what he called "pious pussyfooting by the counterculture on issues of race and sex." In 1975 he mulled over David Bowie's transformation into the soul singer the Thin White Duke. "Everybody has been walking around for the last year or so acting like faggots ruled the world," Lester wrote, "when in actuality it's the *niggers* who control and direct everything, just as it always has been and properly should be."

The word "nigger" appeared in the first draft of the piece a dozen times. John Morthland edited the story and cut out most of the usages. "It's like Lenny Bruce said: We just have to use the word over and over until it doesn't have any meaning anymore," Lester argued. If that were true, Morthland asked, why hadn't the word disappeared? "We weren't hostile, we were just talking about it," Morthland recalled. "I think Lester came to see that people weren't getting the point."

"Lester may have been racist or sexist by reflex, but not by heart," said his friend and fellow critic Richard Pinkston. The two met shortly after Lester arrived in Detroit. For years they double-dated and pursued shared passions for the Velvets, the Stooges, and the Beats. "I may have been his first and closest black friend, and I think his experience knowing me helped to open his eyes," Pinkston said. "Sometimes you have to let it hang out there. He took a chance on looking like an asshole because he was struggling with it, but at least he was honest about the struggle, and so many people aren't."

One day a hotheaded *Creem* staffer took offense to something Pinkston said and started choking the eighteen-year-old writer. Lester rushed to Pinkston's aid. "It was like Wally Cleaver stepping in to save me," Pinkston recalled. Lester clearly relished the role of protector. Another time he saw Susan Whitall fleeing Barry Kramer's office in tears. Without even knowing what had happened, Lester stormed in and decked the publisher, then followed Whitall into the ladies' room. "Safire, yo' ass is precious!" he said, lecturing her in the exaggerated dialect of Amos 'n' Andy. "Don' eben be *thinkin'* o' leaving heah!" She had to laugh, and Lester even succeeded in making Kramer apologize.

The publisher had always been mercurial, but through the mid-seventies he became increasingly paranoid and irrational. He bought an electronic eavesdropping system to monitor staffers' calls, and he often riffled through their mail. Sometimes he saw bugs on the pencil sharpener and refused to enter the office until somebody pretended to sweep them away.

Lester still had high hopes for *Creem*, and in February 1976 he wrote Kramer a ten-page memo addressing a wide range of topics. He declared the April issue "the best ever"—its contents included his posthumous interview with Jimi Hendrix and an attack on Bob Dylan for lionizing mobster Joey Gallo—and asked when employees would finally be getting health insurance. He informed Kramer that he and Nancy were considering a wedding date in the summer, announced that he had lost all interest in the subject of Lou Reed, and tried to clear up some muddled accounting. The publisher owed him $279.07 in expenses, but he owed *Creem* $100 for the time Harvey Zuppke bailed him out on a drunk-driving bust. The net came to $179.07, and he really needed the money *right now*.

Kramer never paid Lester. When the writer returned from his trip to New York that spring, the publisher erupted over the $1,600 room-service tab that Lester rang up at the St. Moritz. Kramer threatened to take it out of Lester's salary, and the two stopped speaking. The feud struck some as the inevitable collision between a stern father and a son struggling to assert his independence. "Barry and Lester got into a real personal thing," said associate publisher Harvey Zuppke. "It had nothing to do with rock 'n' roll and everything to do with Barry and Lester."

"There have been star editor/writers before Lester," Kramer told an interviewer in the summer of 1976, "and there will be star writer/editors after him. *Creem* is bigger than any one person."

A few years later Lester recalled his years at the magazine with undisguised bitterness. "It was basically a little fiefdom," he said in 1982. "You have a bunch of idealistic young people in the late era of hippiedom, and a guy comes in who sees that he can make a lot of money off of their idealism. So you'd hear things at the beginning like: 'In a year, we'll all be living in a big mansion. We'll all be rich.' All this bullshit. The guy got rich.

"Barry and Lester got into a real personal thing," Birmingham, 1976.
Photo by John Collier/*Detroit Free News*

He got his mansion and his country house, he drank Courvoisier VSOP, and he drove a Lincoln Continental, and when I quit after five years when I was senior editor—and I had contributed a lot to making the magazine whatever it was—I was still only taking home $175 a week."

Detroit had also started to grate on Lester. Coldly calculated revitalization projects such as the Renaissance Center clearly wouldn't restore the city to its former glory. Newspaper headlines told of kids from the ghetto climbing the embankments on the freeways to hurl bricks at oncoming cars, while the Detroit Police STRESS unit randomly cracked skulls in the black community. "I did five years in Detroit," Lester wrote. "That's how I always say it, too—'did' as in 'time.'" His friends and former co-workers Robert Duncan and John Morthland had both quit and moved to New York. The city had the only rock scene in America that seemed to be thriving, and of course it was home to the publishing houses and much of the music industry. Lester decided that the time had come for him to stop being a big fish in a little pond.

Late in the bicentennial summer Lester announced that he and Nancy were moving; they would marry as soon as they were settled in Manhattan. He sold his Camaro, stored many of his albums with Eric

Genheimer's parents, and made Susan Whitall promise she'd check in from time to time on the reclusive Richard C. Walls. The Birmingham Youth Club threw a going-away party in the backyard of Esther Korinsky's parents' house, and Lester got drunk and sang Stooges songs with a band called the Pontiac Punks. Afterward he made a pass at one of JoAnn Uhelszki's girlfriends, and she gave him a good hard shove into the gold-fish pond.

Whenever Nancy wasn't around, Lester's friend Carol Schloner kept a motherly eye on him. "People would often come to me to tell me Lester was in need of help, and I'd go and rescue him," she said. He gave her the nickname "Jah Woman." As the party wound down, she heard her brother shouting that Lester was drowning, and she ran over to find him facedown in the water. "Get up!" Schloner yelled, but Lester just rolled over in his back leather jacket, pretended to do the backstroke, and said, "Glub, glub."

Tender Vittles

While its rock scene was arguably more vital than ever, New York City itself was still struggling to come back from the brink of bankruptcy when
Lester and Nancy arrived. FORD TO CITY: DROP DEAD the headline of the
Daily News had declared a year earlier when the federal government refused a bail-out. A new President would take office in January 1977—
Jimmy Carter, who claimed to be a Bob Dylan fan, no less—but the perception remained of a city separated from the rest of America by politics
and culture as well as geography.

Lester and Nancy moved into a nine-unit apartment building over
Gum Joy Chinese Restaurant near the corner of Sixth Avenue and Fourteenth Street. As the boundary between Greenwich Village and Chelsea,
Fourteenth Street was a seedy non-neighborhood of junk stores, bode-
gas, and run-down bars. It reminded Lester of the Interzone in *Naked
Lunch*. Hookers and pill pushers operated relatively free from police ha-
rassment so long as they didn't stray into the tonier areas to the north
and south.

Robert Duncan was the first former *Creem* editor to find an apartment at 542 Sixth Avenue. He shared the unit at the rear of the fifth floor
with his new girlfriend, Roni Hoffman, previously Richard Meltzer's significant other. When Apartment 5F became available, Duncan called
Lester in Detroit and urged his friend to take it. He even wrote a check
fronting the first month's rent of $240.

"I always thought that Lester should be playing on a bigger stage,"

On Sixth Avenue, fall 1976.
<small>Photo by Roni Hoffman</small>

Duncan said. "He had outgrown *Creem*, but he was very nervous about coming to New York. He was scared. He worried he was too much the El Cajon hick—and he *was*; it was one of his endearing characteristics. For all of his swagger, I think he was very intimidated."

Nancy and Lester gave each other the moral support necessary to make the move. Nancy had never lived apart from her parents in suburban Detroit. Lester helped her escape, and in return she built his first real home since leaving California. She spent the first week painting the apartment while he made the rounds of editors, hustling work. They took the money they made from selling their cars in Detroit and went to Macy's at Herald Square, investing in a couch, some coffee tables, and a dinette set. They toasted their new life by sitting down to their first candlelight dinner, but they were horrified when they turned off the lights and saw dozens of roaches scurrying up the walls.

To Hoffman, the couple across the hall seemed to be playing house. She had witnessed Lester's slovenly ways when he visited her and Meltzer, and she was glad to see that Nancy hung a broom on a hook by the door. "People always got angry at Yoko Ono and Linda McCartney for changing their heroes," Hoffman said, "but I maintained that John and Paul finally found people who allowed them to be who they really wanted to be. Maybe there was that aspect in Lester—he wanted to be normal and settle down."

Lester's views on the give-and-take of relationships hadn't evolved much since his first long-term love affair. In his poem "Andy," he had scorned the idea of having a girlfriend who hailed his genius, then cleaned up the house. But in a new song called "Poo Pants," he envisioned Nancy performing an even more odious task.

> I wash his poo pants
> While he stands around and rants
> Living with an artist is aesthetic bliss
> But mama never told me there'd be days like this
>> Poo pants
>> Hangin' off his bottom
>> Oh, oh, oh poo pants
>> I'm so glad he's got 'em
>> Somehow they're endearing to me
> I wash his poo pants
> While he plays *Sally Can't Dance*
> But as he guzzles malt liquor and scoffs
> For five days he doesn't take 'em off
> He's a genius in the throes of ascension
> But I move in another dimension

Nancy thrived in New York, cherishing her newfound freedom. She felt she was making real progress in her therapy sessions and acting classes, and she didn't intend to be Lester's mother. "It started out good, but by the winter of 1977 it was getting hard," she said. Lester's drinking and drugging were getting out of hand. She had learned to tolerate his fascination with Lou Reed, but she hated most of the new punk rock he was playing. With a few exceptions such as John Morthland and Billy Altman, she also disliked most of his New York friends.

In April the couple threw a housewarming party. They invited every last person they knew in Manhattan and told them all to bring their friends. At 2 A.M. on Easter morning Lester stood in the doorway between the kitchen and the living room, surveying the scene as he pulled the tab on a fresh can of Rheingold. Morthland and musician Peter

Stampfel stood by the stereo playing the new Sex Pistols single, "Anarchy in the U.K." Three of the four Ramones leaned against the wall in their black leather jackets. Voidoids guitarist Robert Quine argued with Talking Heads bassist Tina Weymouth, Lenny Kaye and Billy Altman talked rock-critic shop, and Blondie's Chris Stein and Debbie Harry sat on the couch taking it all in. Jerry Harrison squeezed by on his way to the fridge.

"Hey! You know, I loved the Modern Lovers, but I never really liked the Talking Heads," Lester said. "I thought you guys were sort of lame compared to the rest of the punk scene, but now that I meet you, I think you're great!"

Old friends Ed Ward and Georgia Christgau helped with the food. Ward spent much of the night stirring a huge pot of gumbo, one of his specialties. "It sounds like a scene from a bad movie, but it really was a magical evening," he said. "It was like: 'Hi, we're the entire New York scene in Lester's apartment, and we're here to eat your gumbo!' If there'd been shellfish toxin in that stuff, that would have been it."

Nancy made her way through the crowd with a plate of chocolate-chip cookies, asking people if they needed a drink. She played the gracious hostess even though she was clearly hurting. A few days earlier some asshole had gotten carried away during an improvisation in acting class and hit her as hard as he could with a spiral notebook across the back of her neck. The chiropractor said this jerk had knocked one of her vertebrae out of place, and now she needed an X ray.

"That's how it's been, see—unbelievable ups and downs coming right on top of each other," Lester wrote his pal Richard C. Walls in Detroit. Take the party. "Nobody was an asshole, nobody got ugly drunk, hurt anybody, broke anything, we opened our house to complete strangers and the next day even all my rare rock 'n' roll records were still here. There was a sense of grace over the whole affair—people kept saying things like: 'This has something to do with Easter, doesn't it?' It was tremendous. Except that one exception I mentioned was—well, maybe I should just tell the story."

Shortly after he moved to Manhattan, Lester got a call from another new arrival. The guy used to work as a rack jobber stocking record stores in St. Louis, and he'd phone *Creem* late at night to talk jazz. Lester went record-shopping with him on St. Mark's Place. He was pleasant enough, except for the fact that he really seemed to dislike women. Lester invited him to the party. He came early and started pacing around, picking at the ass of his jeans and monopolizing the stereo. Then he sat down next to

Nancy. "I heard you're *sick*," he said. "Has Lester turned you on to *Romilar* yet?"

They launched into a deep discussion of good and evil. The rack jobber contended that you should use any means necessary to get what you want. Nancy disagreed and said you have to look for the redeeming factors in life. When he got up to change the record, Nancy turned to Lester on the other side of the couch. "Don't leave my side," she whispered. "This guy's up to something."

Lester told her she was just being paranoid. They had both been freaked out by stories making the rounds of sadomasochistic parties in Soho where a dozen people gathered at a table set with twelve drinks. One of the glasses contained poison, and the party supposedly ended when one of the guests dropped dead.

At exactly 11:30 P.M. the rack jobber went into the corner, took off his white shirt, and put on a black turtleneck. He sidled up to Nancy and slyly squirted something from a syringe into her glass of water. He didn't notice that he'd missed and shot the viscous liquid on her hand. Looking him straight in the eye, Nancy raised her glass, drained it, and strolled into the kitchen.

A little after midnight the rack jobber grabbed a tangerine from a tray of fruit and threw it at Nancy's feet. She picked it up and tossed it in the garbage. "I'll throw it away *for* you," she snapped. The guy started cackling. "I'm glad I don't take *poison*," he said. Nancy began poking him hard in the chest with her three middle fingers, backing him out the door. "You missed!" she said. "You got me on the hand!" The guy simpered like a wounded puppy. "Lester, I don't know what she's talking about," he said. "I didn't give her any poison!"

"The next day when I marveled that his whole personality could have changed in an instant, Nancy said that she thought he was playing the 'woman' for me, as opposed to the hateful aggressor with his phallic little poison squirter for her," Lester wrote. After Nancy kicked him out, he called from the corner asking for his jacket, and Lester threw it out the fifth-floor window.

"It was the most dangerous party I'd ever been to," Nancy said two decades later. "These people didn't think that way, but I did. That party for me was a defining moment."

"I'm not sure what all this means exactly except that for the first six months in New York we didn't even lock our apartment door when we went out," Lester wrote at the time. "We were totally oblivious to the evil, the clear and present dangers around us. Now we lock the door even when we're home. We have come to the conclusion that when you're confronted with the evil that exists in the world, with the Pit, the only possible response is total and immediate rejection, to turn your back on it and leave it to poison itself, or do like Nancy did and just sweep it out the door."

·°, ·°, ·°,

A year after his first visit to CBGB, Lester had become a convert to the sounds emanating from the Bowery. He decided that punk represented the children of the Velvets making the music of buzzing hazes and unconventional beauty that he'd been advocating since his letters to Greil Marcus in 1969. He threw himself into his new life as a freelancer, lauding the punk bands in publications ranging from *Circus* to the *Village Voice* and *Stereo Review* to *Screw.*

"Wouldn't you rather be run over by a berserk locomotive barreling downhill with a broken throttle, no brakes, and Bugs Bunny in the driver's seat?" Lester asked of the Ramones. The Talking Heads he branded "the most human of mutant groups . . . a marriage of diametrical opposites—abandon and inhibition, anxiety and ease, freedom and impingement unto paralysis." Television's flail he called "the compulsively insistent nerve-end that their demeanor denies, a twitch in the neighborhood of, but not sounding like, the Velvet Underground." And while Blondie blatantly imitated the old-fashioned sounds of the British Invasion, its members were "implicitly intelligent enough not to ram their understanding of earlier rock 'n' roll down your throat."

In the wake of the Beatles many first-generation rock critics differentiated between "rock 'n' roll"—the greasy kid stuff played by the likes of Chuck Berry and Little Richard—and "rock," the music of the sixties and bona fide art. To them, punk, like heavy metal before it, was simply one of myriad new genres that sprang up after that fundamental split. Lester ignored these distinctions; to him it was all rock 'n' roll. He charted the sound and attitude he loved from "La Bamba" by Ritchie Valens through "Louie Louie" by the Kingsmen, "You Really Got Me" by the Kinks, "No Fun" by the Stooges, right up to "Blitzkrieg Bop" by the Ramones. "There: twenty years of rock 'n' roll history in three chords, played more primitively each time they are recycled," he wrote.

Lester concluded that his own "career/life as a punk" had started ten years earlier when he forked over $3.50 for the Count Five album at Ratner's Records in San Diego. At the age of twenty-eight, he felt like a grand old man on the new rock scene, but as such he was perfectly positioned to chart the music's aesthetic and explain its impetus. "The point is that rock 'n' roll, as I see it, is the ultimate populist art form, democracy in action, because it's true: anybody *can* do it," he wrote. "For performing rock 'n' roll, or punk rock, or call it any damn thing you please, there's only one thing you need: NERVE. Rock 'n' roll is an *attitude*, and if you've got the attitude you can do it, no matter what anybody says. Because passion is what it's all about—what *all* music is about."

When he left Detroit, Lester had planned to continue freelancing for *Creem* from New York, but tensions with Barry Kramer soon made that untenable. Kramer still wanted Lester to pay the St. Moritz room-service bill. Lester refused, and Kramer threatened to garnish his freelance wages and block him from reprinting anything he wrote for the magazine. Lester's last article, a piece on the Jefferson Starship, appeared in March 1977. He considered it the worst thing he'd ever written, and a few months later he apologized to *Creem*'s readers in a letter to the editor. For the next few years the *Village Voice* would provide his most consistent outlet.

Founded in the fall of 1955 in the same scene that produced the Beats, the *Voice* claimed a place in the history of American journalism as the first newspaper to cover politics and art without restrictions on language. As underground papers proliferated in the sixties, it came to be considered stodgy in its content and conservative in its politics, though only in relation to the revolutionary blather of the times. In 1974, when Robert Christgau became music editor, the contentious and ever-evolving weekly was trying to strike a balance between what he called elitist bohemianism and popular consciousness. "As editor and writer my aim was reviewing more sharp-witted and intellectually unpredictable than the reverential auteurism-once-removed by then ensconced at *Rolling Stone*, preferably touched with the gonzoism of Lester Bangs's *Creem*," he wrote.

There was never much gonzo in Christgau's own style. The son of a fireman from Flushing, Queens, he attended Dartmouth on a scholarship and went on to work as a feature writer with a wire service in Newark, New Jersey. After stints as a music critic at *Esquire* and Long Island's *Newsday*, he settled in at the *Voice*. There he proudly claimed the title of "Dean of American rock critics," dispensing letter grades for albums in his Consumer Guide, which *Creem* reprinted through much of the seventies.

Christgau relished the role of the ex-hippie college professor too pre-occupied with great thoughts to trifle with everyday pleasantries. Lester talked about the time he went to Christgau's apartment and was greeted by the dean sans clothing. Christgau proceeded to edit Lester in the nude. At one point Christgau's upstairs neighbor Vince Aletti knocked on the door. Aletti often wrote about rock from a flamboyantly gay perspective—he came out in a column in *Creem*—and Christgau ran to put some clothes on before letting him in. "He didn't want to get the gay guy aroused," Lester said, "but it was fine to expose *me* to his flabby ass!"

"I would never claim that I was a close friend of Lester's," Christgau said, sitting fully clothed in the same apartment twenty years later. "He had a very, very different attitude toward life than I do. My relationship with him was primarily editorial. . . . Basically I think I was the best editor he ever had."

Lester often praised Christgau's editing, and during his first year in New York he wrote a series of extraordinary pieces for the *Voice*. He questioned why the brutal Stooges bootleg *Metallic K.O.* sounded "wrigglingly, obscenely alive" while the Iggy Pop singing on *The Idiot* "sounded like a dead man." He assessed the synthesizer drone of Tangerine Dream against a backdrop of Romilar-fueled hallucinations, and he approximated the sound of Big Youth's dub reggae in his prose. When Elvis Presley was found dead in his bathroom at Graceland, Lester eulogized him by pondering his real legacy. In 1969 he had dutifully taken Greil Marcus's advice and ordered the entire Presley catalog from RCA, but he had never been a huge fan of the music. In 1977 Presley's death said more to him about the state of American culture than it did about rock 'n' roll.

"If love truly is going out of fashion forever, which I do not believe, then along with our nurtured indifference to each other will be an even more contemptuous indifference to each other's objects of reverence," Lester wrote. "I thought it was Iggy Stooge, you thought it was Joni Mitchell or whoever else seemed to speak for your own private, entirely circumscribed situation's many pains and few ecstasies. We will continue to fragment in this manner, because solipsism holds all the cards at present; it is a king whose domain engulfs even Elvis's. But I can guarantee you one thing. We will never again agree on anything as we agreed on Elvis."

For the first time in his career, Lester struggled with his writing, doing numerous rewrites on some pieces and having others rejected by the *Voice* after days or weeks of work. "At *Creem* it was free rein, and he went from that to this intense editing," Nancy said. "It became a transitional time, and I don't know if he ever really came out of that."

Lester's old girlfriend Andy provided a bright spot that first winter when she spent two weeks visiting from California. Andy and Nancy hit it off well; they both loved the theater, laughter, and Lester. On his twenty-eighth birthday they dressed up and performed a goofy musical skit— "Onesies beats twosies, but nothing beats threes!"—much to the chagrin of Lester's new colleagues. "A lot of the people that Les hung out with in New York were extremely arrogant," Andy said. "Oh, God, the egos!"

Nancy remembered a torturous dinner with Christgau and his wife, Carola Dibbell. "Christgau accused Lester because he didn't go to college," she said. "He'd say, 'You're resting on ideas that we've all thought of!' Lester hated the way Christgau would write things like 'the joys of fucking in a monogamous relationship'—that he would even use the words like that without any sensitivity. The pomposity and the sense of arrogance and dominion aggravated Lester to no end." But Lester's biggest professional concern was that he was no longer connecting with readers. "Ever since I left *Creem* I don't have the close one to one contact with my audience that I enjoyed there," he wrote *Creem* contributor "Metal" Mike Saunders. "Especially putting reviews in places like the *Village Voice* and *Circus*, you wonder if anybody that thinks like you is reading them."

Whether or not they thought like him, many members of the New York punk scene celebrated Lester's arrival. As he and Nancy unpacked on their first night in town, eight young women wearing too much mascara and very little clothing gathered in front of the Gum Joy Chinese Restaurant and began screaming up at the fifth-floor window. The building didn't have doorbells, so visitors phoned from the corner or shouted from the sidewalk. Residents would jog downstairs or open the window and toss out the keys.

The girls intended to show the famous Lester Bangs around his new town, but when he plodded out in his sweat socks, he sheepishly apologized and explained that he couldn't go out with them. "I have to stay home with my girlfriend," he said. "We're playing *Barefoot in the Park*."

Lester didn't pass on these invitations for long. By his own account he spent nearly every night of 1977 at CBGB, "a haven where the meek have finally inherited a small portion of the earth armored in leather and dog collars." Here he was surrounded by young fans who considered it an honor to buy a drink or share a handful of pills with the man who'd named heavy metal, championed the punk aesthetic, and gone *mano a mano* with Lou Reed. "A lot of people used him to be *'Lester Bangs'*—this outrageous persona," Nancy said. "Sometimes I hated these people at CBGB. He would go there and they would all try to buy him drinks and egg him on to get him in his most destructive state where he'd just start lambasting. I really disliked that."

In the effort to reject bourgeois society, punk embraced the contrary, celebrating dirty instead of clean, ugly instead of beautiful, and ineptitude instead of accomplishment. Sometimes it went too far. Lester didn't have much use for the shock theatrics of razor-blade earrings, swastikas, and bondage gear, but he applauded the do-it-yourself ethic and the ideal of eliminating celebrity in rock. "If you don't need to know how to play your instrument to be a rock 'n' roll star, that means that theoretically everybody in the entire world can become a rock 'n' roll star," he wrote. Yet while the scene at least pretended to shun status and self-importance, it also elevated its own antiheroes.

Lou Reed, John Cale, Iggy Pop, and Patti Smith basked in what passed for admiration in the perverse world of punk whenever they entered the shadowy confines of CBGB. Perpetually slumped at the end of the bar, his stringy mustache hanging in his beer, Lester earned his place of honor as the last of the Noise Boys. Richard Meltzer had become increasingly disillusioned with music, journalism, and New York, and in the fall of 1975 he left for Los Angeles. Nick Tosches had also begun to distance himself from rock writing. He took off for Nashville for a time, and when he returned he favored the company at other bars to the kids at CBGB. "Lester never realized that they weren't actually idolizing him as much as he was like a sacrificial cow," Tosches said. "They would get fucked up and go back to their nice little suburban homes. Lester would get fucked up and stay fucked up."

It all took a toll on Lester and Nancy's relationship. They broke up and reunited several times after dramatic fights in the spring of 1977. One day Nancy stormed out of the apartment, announcing that she was never coming back. She got as far as the corner before she realized she had nowhere else to go. She returned an hour later and found Lester sitting at his IBM Selectric, typing something along the lines of, "She left me, slammed the door, and walked out."

"We both started laughing, because there was just so much love even at that point," Nancy said. "But it was all too much."

Nancy walked out again that summer, and this time she didn't return. Lester accepted that his behavior had driven her away, but he didn't understand why they had to break up when they loved each other so deeply. He tried to make sense of the split by writing Nancy a letter: "The biggest thing we did was create ourselves, and the next step is creating each other. It all comes down to control, and I realize that I am STILL not in control of my life, which is now what I long for even more than I long for your presence."

"When Nancy ended, everything changed for him," said his friend John Morthland. "She gave him a grounding that he didn't really have anywhere else. His excesses escalated after that, though in some ways it sort of wised him up, and he was trying to curb them. Certainly that breakup and that relationship had a huge impact on his life and a huge impact on what came next."

·ᴏ· ·ᴏ· ·ᴏ·

A few weeks after Nancy left, Lester leaned on the wall outside CBGB talking with Tish and Snooky Bellomo. The sisters ran a punk boutique called Manic Panic out of their apartment. They had sung backing vocals in an early incarnation of Blondie, and now they were fronting a group of their own called the Sic F*cks. They were also trying their hands at journalism, interviewing men on the scene for an article on "punk sex" in *New York Rocker*.

"I think punk sex is a bunch of fuckin' dog shit, like most things to do with punk," Lester began before they'd even asked him. "Most people are just doing what they think they're supposed to do, whether it's giving head in the bathroom or being asexual. It's shit. I'm not attracted to girls with green hair that wear garbage bags."

"Well, I beg your pardon!" Tish said in her thick Bronx accent.

Lester fumbled. "I mean, I'd be attracted to *you* if you were in a garbage bag, because you're so sexy," he drawled.

"*We* wore garbage bags onstage!" Snooky yelled.

"Oh, that's different," Lester said. "I'm not talking about *you*. I'm talkin' about *normal* people."

"Okay, Lester," Snooky said sarcastically. "Rate yourself." He didn't hesitate for a second. "I'm real tender," he said, and the girls cooed in unison. "I believe tenderness is where it's at," Lester continued. "It's like Tender Vittles. But a lot of people mistake certain things for sex that are not—like brutality for sex, coldness for warmth. If somebody kicked my face in, I wouldn't have an orgasm."

Dead Boys guitarist Cheetah Chrome bounded out the door of the club. Tish and Snooky had already interviewed him. "As soon as you find out how big Lester's pee-pee is, I have a beer waiting for him inside," he said, spying the tape recorder. "Hey, Bangs, while I'm here, how big *is* it?"

"I never measured," Lester said. "I used to read in all these books about how men would stand at these pissoirs and take a quick look at each other's dick to see who had the biggest one. I couldn't believe that anyone would do that. I read in these skin mags: 'My dick is ten inches long. How come I never get laid?' Maybe 'cause you never considered that it doesn't make any difference, and that even if you had ninety-three inches, if you're not tender and loving, if you don't act like a human being—like yesterday I was at the beach with my ex-girlfriend. These three jocks came along and one of them said, 'I'm in a really good mood today. I really wanna *rape* some girl!' That's accepted as not only normal, but something to be encouraged. That guy is a cool guy! I'm not trying to blow my own horn or say I'm such a great lover or anything, but I don't want to have anything to do with that. Punk sex sometimes encourages that, and I hate it."

The roar of half a dozen Harley-Davidsons storming down the Bowery momentarily drowned out the conversation. The New York chapter of the Hell's Angels was headquartered just down the block from CBGB, and some of the bikers occasionally wandered into the club. Owner Hilly Kristal let them drink for free, and in return they didn't hassle the punks. "Bye, boys!" Lester shouted as they sped off. "Say hello to Studio 54 for us! Tell Truman Capote and Bianca Jagger I said hello!"

The bikers were already at Cooper Square, so Lester returned to his lecture. He was on a roll. "I think a whole lot of the punk scene is based on sexual repression," he said. "Like the guys that are afraid they're fags, they come on with all this leather dog-collar bullshit and will not allow themselves to be vulnerable or human at all. And a lot of women put up with it. No man ever did anything that a woman didn't let him get away with. Punk women in general are full of shit, and so are the men. It's just posing. They don't even know what they are, and they don't want to find out. They're scared of what they might be. Why shouldn't a guy be sensitive sometimes? It's like armor. The punk thing is like: 'Oh, well, the world sucks and I'm an asshole. You suck, too. So who gives a shit.' Well, I'm sorry, but that's all a load of crap."

                       ❖ ❖ ❖

Cramps drummer Miriam Linna sauntered down Bleecker Street one night in the summer of 1977, laughing and joking with a friend when Lester came rushing toward her. She'd known him since she was a teenager in Cleveland and she and Charlotte Pressler wrote about Patti Smith for *Creem*. Pressler had been married to Lester's friend Peter Laughner, and Linna had managed the fan club for Laughner's old band, Rocket from the Tombs.

"How the fuck can you just laugh?" Lester screamed. She didn't know what he was talking about. "Peter Laughner had died, but I didn't know about it," Linna recalled. "He thought that I knew, and despite knowing, I could go out and have a wonderful time. But it was probably the most horrendous incident in my life."

As a bright, skinny twenty-year-old bored out of his mind in suburban Cleveland, Laughner had sent a letter to *Creem* that ran in April 1973. "I had a dream that I awoke from a terminal drunk on the floor of this strange room littered with album jackets and was greeted by a gorgeous redhead," he wrote. "She told me: 'Lester may not want you here, but you look O.K. I'll ask him when he gets back.' In the dream I think: 'Lester?' And then say: 'Where the hell am I?' She smiles warmly and says: 'Walled Lake, Michigan.' The rest of the dream involved horses."

More letters followed, and Lester soon invited Laughner to write for the magazine. They shared many of the same obsessions, including Lou Reed, William S. Burroughs, sex, booze, and speed. Laughner visited Birmingham several times in 1975 and 1976, and the two spent weekends drinking, drugging, and jamming on vocals and guitar. The visitor matched his Dylanesque melodies to Lester's lyrics. Late at night in the *Creem* office they recorded originals such as "Drug Store Cowboy" and "Bye-Bye Lou (Reed)," as well as covers of "Knockin' on Heaven's Door" and "Sister Ray."

One weekend Lester and Laughner wrote a torrid sexual fantasy about Marion Ross, who played Richie Cunningham's mom on *Happy Days*. Another time they co-authored a dark satire about the joys of having sex with babies—infants were nice and compact, so you could just stick them down your pants. They submitted the piece to *Screw*, but it was rejected as below even that magazine's sleazy standards.

Laughner looked up to Lester, and Lester admired Laughner's drive. "Peter had a pushy side to him," his widow, Charlotte Pressler, said. "That was part of his particular magic. If he visualized something, it was real. Lester was more reflective. They'd be pushing similarly, and they'd get to this point with a mutually constructed fantasy turning real. Lester would become slightly reflective with it, and Peter would want to push ahead."

They both dreamed of leading their own band, but Laughner did more than just talk about it: He joined his friend and fellow rock critic David Thomas in a jokey combo called Rocket from the Tombs. When the self-proclaimed "World's Only Dumb-Metal Mind-Death Rock 'n' Roll Band" broke up, Laughner and Thomas regrouped and recorded a powerful single as Pere Ubu. Released in December 1975 on Thomas's own label, "Heart of Darkness"/"Thirty Seconds Over Tokyo" was one of the first American punk records. Laughner's liner notes issued a call to arms for a new generation of bands: "Use your muscles, your brain, your tissues NOW! MAKE A MOVE!"

Lester considered Laughner's fiery solos the highlight of both the single and Pere Ubu's contribution of "Final Solution" to the live compilation album *Max's Kansas City 1976*, but the guitarist couldn't curb his urge toward self-destruction. In March 1976 Laughner wrote a review of Lou Reed's *Coney Island Baby* that echoed Lester's pieces on *Metal Machine Music*. "I ended up passing out stone cold after puking and pissing myself at a band rehearsal," he bragged, "had to be kicked awake by my lead singer, was driven home by my long-suffering best friend and force-fed by his old lady, who could still find it in the boundless reaches of her good heart to smile on my absolutely incorrigible state of dissolution."

Pere Ubu fired Laughner in mid-1976. He briefly played with Television, but that band canned him, too, further fueling his downward spiral. "By this time I was beginning to have reservations about a lot of aspects of our friendship, so before he hit town the next and last time, I laid it on the line," Lester wrote. "I told him I thought he was committing suicide, and that I couldn't subsidize it by getting high with him any longer."

In the spring of 1977 the two friends spent an afternoon jamming in Lester's apartment with fiddler Peter Stampfel, a veteran of the Fugs and the Holy Modal Rounders. When Stampfel left, Lester broke his promise and took some tranquilizers from his friend. "I just gave Lester some Dalmanes, so you better go up and check on him, because he may be dead!" Laughner told Nancy as he ran out the door. "I gotta go see Patti Smith!"

The Patti Smith Group performed during the first of a two-night benefit for *Punk* magazine, and Laughner tried to climb onstage and jam. Lenny Kaye and Patti's roadie brother, Todd, kicked him off the platform. For the rest of the night Laughner stood around glaring at everyone through crimson eyes. The next day he and Lester argued on Sixth Avenue, fighting over a five-dollar imitation black leather hat that Laughner had stolen from Lester's apartment. Lester sent him back to Cleveland empty-handed. Six weeks later Laughner was found dead in his parents' house at the age of twenty-four, a victim of acute pancreatitis and punk rock's first fatal casualty.

"There is more than a little of what killed Peter in me, as there may well be in you," Lester wrote in an obituary for *New York Rocker*. He did not insult his friend's memory by claiming that he'd never take drugs again himself. Instead he lashed out at those who could callously laugh at a wasted life. "Peter Laughner had his private pains and compulsions, but at least in part he died because he wanted to be Lou Reed," Lester wrote. "Today I would not walk across the street to spit on Lou Reed, not because of Peter but because Peter's death was the end of an era for me—an era of the most intense worship of nihilism and death-tripping in all marketable forms."

Richard Hell epitomized the pose that Lester railed against by wearing a notorious T-shirt: PLEASE KILL ME. Lester loved the driving rhythms, disjointed guitars, and soulful snarl of Hell's music, but he wrestled with the fact that the artist couldn't seem to transcend his self-hatred. "Who says it's good, good, good to be alive?" Hell sang. "It ain't no good, it's a perpetual dive."

Kentucky-born Richard Meyers arrived in New York during the Summer of Love with notions of becoming a poet in the tradition of the French symbolists. Inspired by the New York Dolls, he formed a band called the Neon Boys with a friend from boarding school named Tom Miller. The Neon Boys eventually evolved into Television, Miller became Tom Verlaine, and Meyers mutated into Richard Hell. "One thing I wanted to bring back to rock 'n' roll was the knowledge that you invent yourself," he said, hence his stage persona, a character that crossed Rimbaud with the dead-end kid in François Truffaut's *The 400 Blows*. In what became his signature song, Hell followed the Beats in coining a name for a new wave of writers, artists, and musicians: "I belong to the Blank Generation," he sang, "and I can take it or leave it each time."

Unwilling to share the spotlight, Verlaine kicked Hell out of Television in March 1975. Hell formed his own group, the Voidoids, a year and a half later. By then the major labels had descended on CBGB in search of the next big thing, and Hell signed to Sire, which released his debut album in mid-1977. Lester proclaimed *Blank Generation* the best record produced by the American punk scene. To celebrate its release he conducted a long interview with Hell for *Gig*, but in the resulting profile, he did most of the talking himself.

"Just for the record, I would like it known by anybody who cares that I don't think life is a perpetual dive," Lester wrote. "And even though it's genuinely frightening, I don't think Richard Hell's fascination with death is anything else but stupid. *I* suspect almost every day that I'm living for nothing, I get depressed and I feel self-destructive and a lot of the time I don't like myself. What's more, the proximity of other humans often fills me with overwhelming anxiety, but I also feel that this precarious sentience is all we've got and, simplistic as it may seem, it's a person's duty to the potentials of his own soul to make the best of it."

Although Hell later gained respect for the piece—as well as a subsequent fantasy in which Lester imagined him assuming John Lennon's place beside Yoko Ono—the artist hated the article the first time he read it. Lester just used him as an excuse to say what was on *his* mind, Hell thought. Afterward he did his best to avoid the writer, showing the kind of distaste that a junkie has for a lush. "When I think of Lester I see this big, swaying, cross-eyed, reeking drooler, smiling and smiling through his crummy stained mustache, trying to corner me with incessant babble somewhere in the dark at CBGB," Hell wrote two decades later. "He was sweet like a big clumsy puppy, but he was always drunk and the sincerity level was pretty near intolerable. All you could do was tease him and use him. He and Peter Laughner were very similar in these respects, though Laughner was harder and more self-destructive. In retrospect I realize of course that they were both better musicians than me, not to mention more decent people."

Invited to play for laughs, Lester made his musical debut at CBGB the night after his last jam session with Laughner. The Lester Bangs Conspiracy topped the bill on the second evening of the *Punk* benefit, May 5, 1977, headlining over the Cramps, Helen Wheels, the Dead Boys, Anya Phillips, Richard Hell and the Voidoids, and Blondie. Lester

At CBGB, June 1977.
PHOTO BY BOB GRUEN

screamed himself hoarse while fronting an all-star combo featuring Patti Smith Group drummer Jay Dee Daugherty, Television bassist Fred Smith, Andy Shernoff of the Dictators, and Blondie's Chris Stein, Jimmy Destri, and Clem Burke. The set consisted of covers such as "Mendocino" by the Sir Douglas Quintet, "Wild Thing" by the Troggs, and of course a long jam on the Velvet Underground's "Sister Ray."

During the set *Punk* magazine's Legs McNeil played maracas and did a drunken limbo between Lester's legs. Chris Stein threw something at McNeil, hitting him hard in the balls, and the audience cracked up as McNeil collapsed on the floor. Lester later berated him for detracting from the music. "I thought Lester was kidding around," McNeil said. "I didn't know how serious he was about his music. Everybody started laughing, and he got really upset. His music was awful; it wasn't fun at all. I always thought if Lester had his way, he'd put us all in a concentration camp and lecture to us like Jim Jones."

Bitten by the urge to perform, Lester decided to act on his long-standing desire to front a band of his own. "This is the era where everybody creates," Patti Smith had declared on *Horses*, and Lester had always said that the point was passion, not proficiency. "It all started when I got the Max's Kansas City album in the mail," he wrote his friend Richard C. Walls. "One day playing it and listening to all the shitty groups thereon while doing the dishes, I thought as we all do: 'Shit, these people haven't got any talent and neither do I, so why don't I make my own record?' "

Scenester Terry Ork offered to release a single on his independent Ork Records. Former Box Tops and Big Star bandleader Alex Chilton would produce. "My attitude about the whole thing is that I'm totally serious about doing it, but I don't take myself overly seriously, if you know what I mean," Lester wrote. "I figure at the very least I'll have something to toss my kids someday and say: 'See, I lived out my fantasies when I was young, now you go and do likewise.' "

Ork managed a movie buff's bookstore called Cinemabilia that employed both Richard Hell and Robert Quine, the Voidoids' lead guitarist. Lester needed to work with a musician who not only understood his noisy ambitions but was patient enough to transform his a cappella melodies into working arrangements. Ork suggested Quine. With his bald pate, frumpy suit jacket, and scruffy beard, Quine stood out at CBGB. Most people thought he looked like an insurance salesman. In fact, he had passed the bar in 1969 and spent several years practicing law before quitting to pursue his true passion.

Born in Akron, Ohio, in 1942, Quine fell in love with rock 'n' roll via Buddy Holly and Ritchie Valens. He learned to play guitar by strumming along to the sides that James Burton cut with Dale Hawkins and Elvis Presley. By college, he'd moved on to the blues and free jazz, but in 1968 the Velvet Underground rekindled his interest in rock. He strove to create a guitar style that combined the visceral kick of the Velvets, the hypnotic grit of bluesman Jimmy Reed, and the wild invention of Miles Davis's *On the Corner*. With the angular, strangled solos on *Blank Generation*, Lester thought he succeeded.

"Someday Quine will be recognized for the pivotal figure that he is on his instrument," Lester wrote. The admiration was mutual: Lester was the only rock critic that Quine had ever respected. One night the guitarist approached him at CBGB. Quine babbled on about the thirty-five hours of live Velvets tapes he'd collected, but Lester had heard it all before, and he yawned and walked away. They met again a month or two later while trawling through the ninety-nine-cents bin at Gramophone Records. The Voidoids had released an EP on Ork Records prior to signing with Sire, and Quine asked Lester if he liked it. Lester said it sucked.

"Yeah, it's pretty bad," Quine said. "We're doing an album that's going to be a lot better."

"That answer apparently impressed him," Quine said. "He'd had a lot of problems with people. He had championed the first Patti Smith album, and then *Radio Ethiopia* came out and he wasn't so enthusiastic about it. Patti and Lenny Kaye turned on him. This happened to him a lot, and he would always be sort of hurt and puzzled by it."

At their third meeting Lester asked Quine to play guitar on his single. Jay Dee Daugherty agreed to drum, and Quine recruited second guitarist Jody Harris and bassist Dave Hofstra from a band called the Loose Screws. They jammed on "Sister Ray" at a loft in the East Village, and Lester taped the session on his boom box. The next afternoon he called Quine and invited him for a walk.

"Wow, this guy is my hero, and I get to spend the day with him," Quine thought, but it didn't live up to his expectations. Lester ducked into a deli near Washington Square Park and bought two six-packs of sixteen-ounce Budweisers. They sat on a park bench surrounded by garbage, drug dealers, and mangy pigeons while Lester guzzled beer and blasted the rehearsal tape.

"You know, this is *not* my idea of fun," Quine said, but the two became friends nonetheless. Lester admired Quine's Sahara-dry sense of humor and sharp musical insights. Quine respected Lester's intelligence and passion, but he felt compelled to lay down some ground rules. "Basically when he drank, it was the worst thing in the world," Quine said. "Whatever was bothering him would come up, and I had some very harrowing, unpleasant experiences with him in public. At a certain point I said, 'What you do is your business, but don't call me if you're drunk. You're too unpleasant and out of control.' On cough syrup he was more placid. I could handle that."

In between gigs and rehearsals with their regular bands, the musicians got together with Lester and worked up a dozen of his originals. Quine led the way. On the song "Live" he suggested adding a bridge lifted from Otis Redding's "I've Been Loving You Too Long (To Stop Now)."

Dave Hofstra, Lester, Jay Dee Daugherty, Jody Harris, and Robert Quine at CBGB.
PHOTO BY BOB GRUEN

Lester looked at him in horror. "It's not like things like that haven't been done before or since," Quine said, assuming that Lester was shocked by the blatant thievery. Lester never mentioned that the song had provided the soundtrack for the Hell's Angels' gang bang in El Cajon.

Once, after the guitarist had improvised a particularly fiery solo, Lester asked him how he'd "written" it. "I just made it up!" Quine said. "What do you think, that James Williamson sight-read his solos on *Raw Power*?" Quine couldn't understand how Lester had been a critic for so long and remained so thoroughly mystified by the process of musicmaking.

In early May the group entered Big Apple Studios to record the strongest of Lester's songs, "Let It Blurt" and "Live." The band discarded the idea of having Alex Chilton produce, and Daugherty convinced Lester to let him oversee the sessions. Unfortunately the drummer ran roughshod over the others in an attempt to test all of his pet theories about recording. Quine and Harris played together with rare empathy, and they had worked out two dissonant, intertwining guitar parts for "Let It Blurt." Tensions erupted when Daugherty told them they'd have to come up with something more tuneful.

Midway through the project Ork Records ran out of money, and the tapes languished at the studio until a new label called Spy agreed to buy them. Spy was started by John Cale and Patti Smith's manager, Jane Friedman, and Cale stepped in to mix the recordings in order to avoid further squabbles between the musicians. As a former member of the Velvet Underground; the producer of the Stooges, Smith, and the Modern Lovers, and the man paying for the record, Cale's credentials were unassailable, but Quine still found reason to grumble. He and Harris planned to end "Let It Blurt" by fading out over dueling guitar solos, but Cale opted to use two tracks of Quine playing alone instead.

Destined for the A-side, "Let It Blurt" was powered by a surprisingly relaxed mid-tempo groove. The jaunty if skewed melody contrasted with bitter lyrics about Lester's relationship with Dori three years earlier. He was inspired to write the song when he ran into a musician from Windsor who breezily told him that Dori had gone around after the abortion bragging that the baby hadn't been his. Lester never told Nancy about the incident, and she heard the tune as a protest against the claustrophobia of the life he'd led with his mother. "That ranting—the part about 'bitch, bitch, bitch'—he would often plug into that when he was drinking," she said. "A lot of women manipulated and used him, but I always go back to the root—to the mother."

For the flip side of the single the band recorded a slow, warped ballad built around one of Quine's circular guitar riffs. Lester delivered another dramatic vocal as the verses built up to the one-word chorus and title. The sustained scream of "Live!" could be heard as a command to a premature corpse or a plea from a lifeless body.

"This is the one I'm most proud of," Lester wrote, "although nobody but Nancy seems to agree with me." In fact, Cale was a fan of both songs. "It was a ballsy move," the musician said. "It was like Lester relished the idea of putting his head in the lion's mouth, and I think that he pulled it off. It was funny as hell, and it was all Lester."

Designed by Lester, the front cover featured a photo of him flashing the look of the wild-eyed visionary that he'd perfected back in high school. It was printed in two-color contrast à la the cover of Lou Reed's *Transformer*. He incorporated a joke about his first girlfriend in the name of his fictitious publishing company—Andrea Virgin Music—and completed the package with a back-cover photo of himself at age five, marching with his mother at a convention of the Jehovah's Witnesses in San Diego. He and Norma both carried signs posing the question: WHAT IS YOUR DESTINY? In the background another poster announced: NO BAND CONCERT TO-DAY.

The cover of "Let It Blurt"/"Live."

The band celebrated the end of the recording sessions with a three-night stand at CBGB on the weekend of June 10–12, 1977. The quintet never did manage to come up with a suitable moniker. Quine wanted to call it The Lester Bangs Memorial Band, but Lester didn't take kindly to that. He suggested Tender Vittles after the dry cat food that had recently been introduced on the market, but everyone else balked, and the band remained nameless.

The ten-song set included covers such as Little Milton's "I Feel So Bad," the Stooges' "TV Eye," and the Doors' "Five to One," as well as originals such as "I Ain't Pouting" ("I'm thirty years old and I don't give a damn/Pop-star blues is just Kentucky ham") and "I Sold My Body/Flesh For Sale," a multilayered tune that included a dig at Barry Kramer ("Sat down and wrote ten million words/Sent them off like flocks of birds/I didn't care about copyrights/Now some sick sucker owns my flights").

"You suck!" a heckler shouted midway through Sunday's show.

"Who cares?" Lester bellowed back. "I ain't doin' nothing you can't do! Get up here and do it yourself if you don't like it!"

The band headlined over the Cramps and the Ramones on the first two nights, and the crowd packed CBGB to capacity. Alex Chilton replaced those groups as the opener on the final night, and the crowds thinned out. By then Lester had gotten over his nervousness and loosened up, and the musicians thought it was their best performance. Afterward they joined Lester in a booth by the pool tables to settle up. The hangdog look on his face reminded Quine of Walt Disney's Pluto: The bar tab had wiped out their earnings.

"I think he ended up owing *them*," Quine said. "He had morals—he knew this was wrong. After that I flat-out refused to play with him anymore. Lester approached me a few times about doing it again, and I said, 'Listen, you do really good stuff, and you're really writing good songs, and if you want to, you should do it. But you'll have to do it without me. And whatever you do, don't sell your typewriter and buy an electric guitar.'"

Review copies of new albums continued to arrive on Lester's doorstep daily, but the paychecks gracing his mailbox came to be fewer and further in between as he concentrated on making music instead of writing. In September 1977 James Grauerholz sent him a note scolding him for forgetting to keep his agent apprised of important pieces. "Right now I have no assignments outstanding," Lester wrote back, "a condition which will have to be remedied this week or I'll be eating Twinkies in November."

Lester first met Grauerholz in his role as William S. Burroughs's secretary. After years of self-imposed exile in Tangier, Paris, and London, Burroughs had returned to New York just in time to be hailed as a godfather of punk. He settled three blocks south of CBGB in a former gymnasium that he called "the Bunker."

In late 1975 Lester had flown to New York to interview Patti Smith for *Creem*, and photographer Kate Simon encouraged them to drop in on Burroughs, whom the two writers had never met. Grauerholz watched as Simon shot photos and Lester and Smith tried to impress their idol. "Patti was aloof and girlish and happy all at the same time," Grauerholz said. "Lester was manic. He really was kind of goin' and blowin', as we say out here in Lawrence [Kansas]."

Adopting a Christ-like stance against the Bunker's stark white walls, Lester posed while flashing a T-shirt proclaiming himself the LAST OF THE WHITE NIGGERS. It was a crudely reworded nod to Norman Mailer's famous Beat-era essay, "The White Negro." Smith first explored the idea

In the Bunker, 1975.
PHOTO BY KATE SIMON

that an artist is by nature a "nigger" in her poem "neo." She took the concept further in the liner notes to her second album, *Radio Ethiopia*, and on her third effort, *Easter*, she recorded a song called "Rock 'n' Roll Nigger."

Lester, Smith, and Burroughs had a spirited discussion about the notion of the artist as the ultimate outsider while passing around a fifth of Jack Daniel's that Lester cheerfully charged to *Creem*. After forty-five minutes the visitors bid their host a respectful farewell. "William didn't have any strongly negative reactions or anything strongly positive," Grauerholz said. "It was like: 'That was another adventure. Now, where are we going out for dinner?' "

Two years later Grauerholz was prodding Burroughs to finish his novel *Cities of the Red Night*, and attempting to build a hip literary agency with clients Ed Sanders, Kathy Acker, Martin A. Lee, Smith, and Lester. Among his most daunting tasks: trying to come to terms with Barry Kramer over the rights to Lester's pieces for *Creem*. With typical overkill, the publisher had made all of his employees sign an agreement stating that he owned the rights to their work in perpetuity in exchange for their paychecks "and other good and valuable considerations"—i.e., the rent at the Creem House and the bratwurst in the refrigerator. At the time copyright law held that the magazine owned all the rights anyway.

"Barry Kramer owns every word I ever wrote for him and I'll almost certainly have to fight tooth and nail when I get ready to put out a collection in book form," Lester wrote his friend Richard C. Walls.

In early 1977 Lester completed a proposal for a book on punk culture. He hoped for a quick sell to pay the rent while he wrote fiction and made music. The plan for his untitled tome included some of what he called his "greatest hits"— "John Coltrane Lives," "Psychotic Reactions and Carburetor Dung: A Tale of These Times," "San Francisco on Two Cents a Day," and "Consumer Guide to American Burger Stands"—as well as pieces by Richard Meltzer, Legs McNeil, and Andy Shernoff. Grauerholz started exchanging letters with Kramer in January 1978 in an effort to resolve the rights issue. The publisher seemed reluctant to grant Lester free use of his own material, but the question of what Kramer wanted in return was never resolved, because Grauerholz couldn't find an imprint that wanted the book.

Lester resigned himself to continuing the freelance grind. Sensing his desperation in sporadic letters and phone calls, his mother and his half sister, Ann, started sending him ten-dollar bills when they mailed him the usual copies of the *Watchtower* magazine. Things were beginning to look dire when he received an unexpected invitation to write for *Rolling Stone*. The "ban for life" had lasted one month short of five years.

"When Paul Nelson got the job of record-reviews editor, he told Jann Wenner, 'There's certain people I want to write for the magazine,'" Lester said in 1982. "Wenner said, 'Like who?' And Nelson said, 'Well, like Lester Bangs.' Wenner said, 'No way!' Nelson said, 'Well, if you don't take him, you can't have me.' That's what kind of a friend Paul Nelson is. He has integrity, which Jon Landau didn't have."

Raised in Northern Minnesota, Nelson was renowned among fellow rock writers for playing Robert Zimmerman his first Jack Elliott and Woody Guthrie records back when the young folk musician was still singing Harry Belafonte songs in the coffeehouses of Minneapolis's Dinkytown. For several years in the late 1950s and early '60s Nelson wrote about the folk scene in his fanzine *The Little Sandy Review*. When Zimmerman—now calling himself Bob Dylan—plugged in and went electric, so did Nelson, and he went on to write some of the most informed and erudite prose of any of the early rock critics.

In 1970 Nelson accepted a job as a publicist at Mercury Records. Always happy to take a hungry writer to lunch, he befriended Lester during junkets and publicity parties. In time he graduated from publicity to A&R, working closely with the Small Faces and Rod Stewart and signing punk progenitors the New York Dolls. "It was the best thing I ever did and the worst in that it got me fired," Nelson said. He appreciated Lester's support of the band, and it was one of the reasons they became friends.

The plaid cap Nelson wore to cover a thinning hairline made him look like a suburban dad during an afternoon on the golf course, and his manner was quiet and thoughtful. "Somebody once said that Lester and I had absolutely nothing in common except for the fact that we both thought that music was everything," Nelson said. "We were so completely opposite, but I think we both had that romantic thing about us—that naive romance."

Nelson continued writing reviews for *Rolling Stone* throughout his tenure at Mercury. Shortly after the magazine moved to New York in 1976, Jon Landau left and his friend Dave Marsh became the fourth record-reviews editor. When Marsh quit in 1978 to write books, Jann Wenner offered Nelson the job. A short time later Lester reappeared in the magazine's pages with a review of Bob Marley's *Kaya*. As with his MC5 review nine years earlier, he raged against what he perceived as a hype.

Billy Altman, Richard Robinson, Lester, and Paul Nelson, 1978.
PHOTO BY BOB GRUEN

"For my money, Toots and the Maytals, who never got promoted properly, are the real heat waves from a Stax/Volt kitchen," Lester wrote, "whereas Marley always struck me as so laid-back that he seemed almost MOR. *Rastaman Vibration* was the last straw: an LP obviously calculated to break Disco Bob into the American Kleenex radio market full force, complete with chicklet vocal backups chirping 'Pos-i-*tive!*' and an opulent, palm-thatch Tarzan-like press kit that would have made serviceable shelter for Gilligan and the Captain."

Island Records responded by running an ad quoting numerous positive reviews of *Kaya* on one side and one line from Lester's slam on the other. Luckily Jann Wenner was not a reggae fan. Lester went on to take potshots at art-rockers Styx (their "narcissistic slop" was "tight as a tissue") and disco heroes the Village People ("they prove that gay people can be as stupid and banal as anybody else"), but these were safe targets as well. "He knew that if he wrote a totally wild review, there was no way in hell I was gonna get it in," Nelson said. "You don't win fights with Jann if he makes a federal case of it, so Lester never turned anything like that in." The magazine paid more than any other music publication—a whopping quarter per word to everyone else's dime—and Lester needed the work.

Between the ups and downs of his career, the lows in his relationship with Nancy, and the high of making music, the summer of 1977 was already the most memorable of Lester's life. Topping it off, New York City suffered the biggest blackout in its history on July 13. Con Edison's northern power lines were struck by lightning on a sweltering Wednesday night, and the electricity cut off for twenty-five hours. Looting broke out in the streets, resulting in 850 fires and 3,400 arrests. For some reason one square block of the city at Seventy-seventh Street and Lexington Avenue had its power restored after only a few hours. Nelson lived in the middle of this lucky neighborhood, and Lester hiked uptown to take advantage of his friend's good fortune.

Nelson had always been a "stone cutter," journalists' slang for an extremely slow and methodical writer. At one point during the blackout, Lester had a thought about relationships, borrowed Nelson's typewriter, and hammered out sixteen pages in an hour. "Jesus hell!" Nelson thought as he watched his friend connecting with the muse. "I don't write unless I have to, and even then I fucking hate it!"

Lester played the Sex Pistols' new single "God Save the Queen" over and over again until Nelson cued up a copy of *The Pretender*. Lester protested that he hated Jackson Browne, but his friend persisted. "This record is all about love and loss—all this stuff we've been talking about—and some of this is just about as heartrending as it gets," Nelson said. Lester finally agreed to listen, and the album became one of his favorites.

After a while Lester and Nelson climbed up to the roof. They could see the fires in the Bronx, and Lester grew increasingly worried: Nancy was living there with a friend from acting class, but the phones were out and there was no way to check on her. The two men lay on their backs staring up at the night sky and talking about life and love as the apocalyptic glow of the flames illuminated the darkened city below.

There's a Man
in There

Lester stomped into the Bells of Hell at four-thirty one afternoon wearing his typical uniform of cowboy boots, dirty jeans, Carpenters T-shirt, and black leather jacket. He skipped the customary pleasantries and slammed his hand on the bar. Nonchagrined as always, co-owner Peter Myers calmly asked what he was having.

"I'm in a black mood," Lester announced with a hint of menace. "I mean a really *black* mood. What *should* I have?"

Myers suggested a Black Russian. That sounded fine, and Lester downed it. He proceeded to run through the gamut of every black elixir that he and Myers could think of, including shots of Johnnie Walker Black, Black & White, Black Bush, Black Velvet, and blackberry brandy, as well as a Black & Tan, a Blackthorn (Irish whiskey, dry vermouth, Pernod, and bitters), a Blackwatch (scotch, curaçao, brandy, lemon slice, and a mint sprig), and a Black Licorice (Sambuca and Kahlúa).

At 8 P.M., still early for the usual crowd at the Bells, a girl rang up on the phone. "Is Lester Bangs there?" she asked. Myers said yes. "May I speak to him?" she asked. "That would be impossible," the bartender replied in his thick northern-English accent. She was losing her patience. "I thought you said he was there!" Myers explained that Mr. Bangs was indisposed; Lester lay passed out on a bench, a puddle of drool collecting beneath his chin.

"Lester was one of the best," Myers said. "He could really put it away. How he wasn't sick that black night—I was waiting for him to throw up, but it didn't happen."

The Bells of Hell originally opened at 105 West Thirteenth Street under the ownership of raconteur-turned-memoirist Malachy McCourt. Myers started tending bar there when he came to the States on holiday, and he never left. Business flagged and McCourt closed the place, but Myers and a partner bought it and reopened. They kept the old name, which McCourt had taken from a line in a song in the stage version of Brendan Behan's *Borstal Boy*: "The Bells of Hell go ding-a-ling-a-ling for you but not for me."

In addition to a coterie of West Village eccentrics and neighborhood alcoholics, the Bells drew many of the Australian and British journalists who had started flooding into New York when Rupert Murdoch bought the *Post* in 1976 and turned it into a right-leaning scandal sheet. The other gang labored for a variety of publications, some of even more dubious merit. These habitués were too young and too hip for the traditional newspaperman's hangout, the Lion's Head, and though they were all rock fans, they had decided to seek a slightly calmer alternative to CBGB as they approached the median age of thirty. They included *National Lampoon* contributors Dean Latimer, Ted Mann, and Doug Kenny (who eventually wrote the screenplay for *Animal House*); *Monster Times* correspondent Joe Kane; prolific freelancers Nancy Naglin and Nancy Duggan; and former Yippie Rex Weiner, who was working on a humorous book called *Woodstock Census* with his then-girlfriend, Deanne Stillman.

Some of the writers and cast from *Saturday Night Live* used to stop by as well, but most of the other regulars were rock critics. Lester and Robert Duncan lived just around the corner, a short stumble away. The writers fueled and fed off each other, sitting with one ear on the current conversation and the other cocked to pick up any interesting ideas or turns of phrase. Here Lester found a perfect forum for his monologues. Rants were encouraged, though the ranter understood the risk of being shot down by the brutal zingers of his peers.

"Bangs was sort of like a clown for everybody, and he hated that role," Rex Weiner said. "He wasn't a very talented clown; it was basically just: 'Watch me self-destruct! Watch me offend everybody! Let me insult the host!' It wasn't all that witty or clever, but it was a time when things were pretty much laid waste, so anybody who could rise up and stir the muck a bit was well appreciated."

Despite the nonstop ribbing, the writers were generally willing to front each other a couple of bucks, pass along the name of a sympathetic editor, or make sure that someone who'd been overserved made it home safely. One night Duncan got into a drunken fight with a boxer, and Lester and Nancy came to his rescue. "They were buying me beers—I was in terrible pain—and Lester said, 'Take these,'" Duncan recalled. "I don't know what they were, but the next thing I know it's the next morning and I'm in Lester's apartment in Lester's bed. I looked next to me and I saw Lester's girlfriend. I thought, 'Oh, my God, what the fuck happened?' Then I realized that Lester was on the other side of me and I was fully clothed. I was just so fucked up that they couldn't let me go anywhere."

More often Duncan wound up carrying Lester home, a formidable task given the 205 pounds on his six-foot-one-inch frame. The Bells never stopped serving a thirsty soul before closing time or unconsciousness. Once Nick Tosches got a call from bartender Nick Brown saying that Lester wanted to drink on Tosches's tab. "Everybody had a tab at this joint," Tosches said. "You'd look down the bar and there was never any money." He asked Brown what Lester was drinking. "Blackberry brandy," Brown said. Tosches gave the okay, but asked Brown to hold him to ten.

"You could go into the Bells with no money, get drunk, get doped up, get laid, and walk out of there with money because there was this guy named Al Fields who'd play dice with you, and he never won," Tosches said. "It was that type of place."

Thanks to the critics, the jukebox in the front room was the coolest in New York City. They stocked it with prerelease copies of the Sex Pistols' singles, Ork Records test pressings, and raunchy blues, country, and rock sides dating back to the fifties. Everyone's favorite rarity was a strange single cut by a group of L.A. studio musicians under the moniker the Executives. "Stickball" started out innocently enough, with the echoed voice of a young boy asking a woman if Johnny could come out to play. Then the singer flew into a torrent of profanity guaranteed to make Richard Pryor blush. Ted Mann would amble over to the jukebox and play the song whenever some unsuspecting ladies happened into the bar.

"The scene was almost all men," Nancy Naglin said. "I was there once when a couple of women came to the window and thought about coming in. Nick Tosches organized this whole group of men to run to the window, make faces, and chase them away. The guys sat down and they were thrilled. There was a thread of misogyny in the place, and there were some very raw, pornographic jokes that just wouldn't go today."

The Bells' back room held a few tables and chairs and a small stage that hosted bands on the weekends. The walls were decorated with paintings of the flags of Afghanistan, India, Pakistan, and Colombia—all of the world's biggest dope exporters—but most of the drug action actually took place downstairs in a small room in the basement. "We were doing a lot of crystal meth in those days," said Michael Simmons, the son of *National Lampoon*'s publisher. "Mostly snorting it, mostly the critics and musicians. The speed dealers would grab a stool and lay out lines of crystal meth, and there'd be an orderly line to get your line. Then you'd go back upstairs and keep drinking as the whole bar was methed out of their minds."

Simmons led a country band called Slewfoot that regularly performed in the flag room. He'd leap off the stage and walk through the crowd with an extra-long guitar cord, swooping from table to table and downing people's drinks. A band called King Rude also played on occasion, and it featured several of the regulars, including Rex Weiner, Joe Kane, and Deanne Stillman's sister, Nancy. Lester sometimes added harmonica, and everyone cheered for a song called "The Rock Critics Roll." Weiner would name the writers in attendance—"And then I saw Billy Altman starting to dance!"—and shine a flashlight on them until they strutted their stuff.

Other talents that graced the Bells' stage included the Irish duo Turner and Kerwin, who later formed Black 47, and a pair of comedian/magicians named Penn and Teller. "They'd get up during the intervals, and I couldn't stand them," Myers said. "They did this dummy routine with the little guy sitting on the big guy's knee. I never paid them." Then of course there was "the Reverend" Al Fields, a.k.a. "the Village Legend."

A silver-haired black gentleman who worked as a waiter at a midtown burger joint, Fields played piano and drank what he called "kerosene," a vodka concoction in a pint-size beer mug. He'd come in around two in the morning, play dice until he lost that night's tips, then set his mug on the old upright piano and sing show tunes and strange originals such as "The Happy Birthday Concerto," an intricate instrumental that inexplicably broke into "Happy Birthday." Discerning listeners loved him. Nick Lowe and Elvis Costello stopped by to cheer him on after they played the Bottom Line, and a post–New York Dolls, pre–Buster Poindexter David Johansen joined him to sing "Give My Regards to Broadway."

In 1978 English punks the Clash came to New York to record their second album *Give 'Em Enough Rope* with Sandy Pearlman, the former rock critic turned Svengali/producer of Blue Öyster Cult and the Dictators. Pearlman brought Joe Strummer and his bandmates to the Bells, and they recruited Fields to play on a song called "Julie's in the Drug Squad." Fields wasn't impressed with the tune—it had only three chords!—but the Brits paid him union scale, and he bought a round for everyone in the bar. Billy Altman took him backstage the next time the Clash played New York, and the musicians swarmed around him. "Al Fields! The Village Legend!" That night's other distinguished visitor was perplexed. "*Who* is Al Fields?" Andy Warhol asked.

Regulars at the Bells held several running debates about the state of popular culture, but the biggest concerned the growing obsession with celebrity. Time-Life, Inc., introduced *People* magazine in 1974, but the circulation boomed between 1976 and 1978. Daily newspapers across the country imitated its success by adding gossipy "people" pages, and the rock critics began to hear the death knell of more substantive criticism and reportage. "*People* magazine changed the nature of the whole thing," said John Swenson, the record-reviews editor at *Circus*. "Suddenly *Crawdaddy!* and *Rolling Stone* were trying to mimic *this*."

Reviews became shorter, more superficial, and preferably positive, while the emphasis in features shifted from the music to the personalities. "To me the vital part of rock writing died when these legitimate straight magazines started covering rock 'n' roll on a regular basis, not understanding the phenomenon," Tosches said. "Places like *People* and *Time*, and then the writing in *Rolling Stone* became more like that, and it just became an adjunct of the industry like any other form of show business. That's when I realized that the avenues I was fortunate enough to have open to me in the early part of my career were now gone. It happened anew with punk, with a younger generation. There was a lot of fun going on there. But in the early seventies it was spontaneous, natural fun, where with punk it almost became enforced fun."

Many of the rock critics considered punk the most exciting movement in rock since the sixties, but in 1978 it had yet to capture the imagination of the American public. Instead people were buying music that the would-be tastemakers despised even more than earlier insipid phenomena such as B. J. Thomas and Three Dog Night. Released in December 1977, the double-album soundtrack *Saturday Night Fever* eventually sold more than 20 million copies. Adding to the insult was the fact that the movie was based on a piece of New Journalism written by one of the critics' own. Dublin-born rock writer Nik Cohn later admitted that he'd fabricated his story for *New York* magazine, inventing characters such as the one who inspired John Travolta's Tony Manero.

As disco swept the charts, the record industry changed the way it did business. The number of expense-paid junkets and lavishly catered listening parties dwindled to the point where they were almost nonexistent. The major labels finally realized that the print media don't sell records nearly as effectively as radio or TV. A new breed of career publicists emerged along with the rising class of careerist rock writers, and they posed a practical question: Why submit artists to the aggressive grillings and adolescent antics of Lester Bangs or Richard Meltzer when well-placed people items and fawning profiles written by cooperative young scribes made everyone so much happier?

Before she moved to the Bronx and stopped coming around the Bells, Lester's girlfriend, Nancy, grew all too familiar with the ongoing debate over that question and the looming menace of *People* magazine. "Lester and John Morthland and all of them had big discussions about it," she recalled. "They said, 'We will no longer be able to write what we want; it's all demographics.' Lester called it the beginning of the end of journalism. He was always so antagonistic, searching for a greater truth. To me it marked the beginning of a time when maybe a Lester Bangs wouldn't fit in so well."

∗ ∗ ∗

After Nancy's departure Lester began dating in earnest. He felt like a teenager again, and he hated it. "I was very romantic, a real gushomatic," he wrote. "I wanted desperately to be in a successful long-term relationship with a woman whom I could also be madly, passionately in love with and wildly attracted to sexually. That's not so much to ask, is it? Of course not. Consequently, I went around falling in love all the time, scaring the hell out of prospective girlfriends, or at least bed partners."

Young punks from CBGB followed Lester home and sat on the couch until dawn, doing speed and talking about their troubled upbringings and inability to show warmth to other human beings. He vowed never to repeat the experience after one girl showed him the freshly razored scars on her wrists. Sometimes he woke up beside more mature female peers from the Bells after evenings of drunken revelry. Unfortunately these women often suggested that he consider bathing, or inquired when he was going to grow out of all this juvenile rock 'n' roll. "These were women of refinement and urbane cachet," Lester wrote. "Some of them took cabs everywhere they went! The first one I engaged even had a doorman, who thought I was a hoodlum and hated my guts because no thirty-year-old man walks around jobless in a black leather jacket alla time."

After several months of flirting with painter and part-time bartender Jean Holabird, Lester enlisted her help on an article that he envisioned as a cover story for the *Village Voice*. He called the piece "Street Hassling," a title borrowed from Lou Reed's latest album. "Lester had decided to become a feminist," Holabird said, "so he cooked up this plan where I was gonna walk down the street first in normal clothes and then in so-called sexy clothes. He was going to chronicle how the guys hooted at me, but nobody paid attention to me at all, and we walked for like an hour."

The *Voice* rejected the story, but Lester and Holabird started dating. "He was very sweet," she said. "We'd go to Italian restaurants for dinner and hold hands walking down the street. These were times when he didn't have to be 'on.'" But when it came to music, Lester had grown even less tolerant. "I remember when I fell asleep at a concert by Captain Bearheart at the Bottom Line," Holabird said, referring to Captain Beefheart. "This was tantamount to treachery: 'How could you? What kind of a woman are you? Don't you understand?' He was very didactic. You could either go along with it or not."

Lester was in a quandary. He'd met another woman, writer Cynthia Heimel, who approached him at a new rock club called Hurrah. "I just took half a Quaalude and drank three scotches, and I'm not responsible for anything I do," she said. He fell for her instantly. "Her body was *zaftig* in just exactly the way I love 'em best," he wrote. "She was a writer for all kinds of chic magazines that the kind of people I hate drool over. I just thought she had the wildest personality! And sense of humor, *whoo-ee*! I was looking for someone who could keep up with me, you see."

Through early 1978 Lester attempted to juggle both relationships, literally shuttling from one bed to the other. "After about a week of this I got so confused I came down with primary impotence: couldn't even get it up to jerk off," he wrote. "My dick was smarter than I was." He broke up with Holabird, though as with many of his lovers, they remained friends and she continued to think of him fondly.

Like Holabird, Heimel discovered that Lester could play the role of the courtly boyfriend. He took her to Rumplemeyer's for an ice cream sundae after a painful trip to the dentist, and they played word games and read each other's works in progress. When she ran out to the store for a break from a difficult column, he finished it for her in typical Bangsian style. "Of course I left it in," she said. On top of all that, the sex was great. Nineteen years later Heimel proudly revealed that she was the unnamed "Primal Earth Goddess in a frowzy black slip" described by Lester in a steamy piece first published in *Psychotic Reactions and Carburetor Dung*.

"Of course I told her I loved her," Lester wrote. "Almost immediately she began to warn me that she was very neurotic and I really didn't know her that well yet."

"His self-awareness was nil," Heimel said. "He did not realize he could talk for sixteen hours about 'Lou Reed, Lou Reed, Lou Reed, Lou Reed.' The thing about Lester—I thought he was very cute, very cuddly, and when I would snuggle with him, he'd put his arms around me and I felt very safe. Which is of course insane. I remember when I did that horrible girl thing of breaking up with him by just kind of avoiding him. He came over to my house and started throwing everything. He decided: 'Now I am going to have a temper tantrum,' and then he had one. He just threw things—nothing breakable—and went into this whirling dervish routine. Then he left. He was not in any way frightening. It was just sort of cute and sort of sad at the same time."

Standing at exactly the same spot in Hurrah where he first encountered Heimel, Lester met fellow rock critic Debra Rae Cohen. They dated for several months, and he tried to be more responsive to her needs. His friend Kathy Miller gave him some advice about pampering a woman, so he rented a hotel room and stocked it with roses, bubble bath, and scented candles. Cohen welcomed it as an alternative to his trashed apartment. "It was this lovely, sweet, romantic thing," she said. "But while the relationship went on, it just reached the point of suffocation very quickly. It was just like living in a closet, or living under a spotlight, or some bizarre combination of the two. He loved so intensely that he ended up being very smothering."

Cohen tried to avoid a confrontation and simply withdrew. A frustrated Lester hurled his typewriter at the wall and spent the next few weeks submitting articles without any E's. "Blam- it on D-bra Ra-," he wrote one editor. "B-tt-r y-t, s-nd h-r th- r-pair bill; sh-'s a wr-tch-d cunt who's gonna grow up to b- Fay- Dunaway in *N-twork* anyway."

In the notes he'd begun keeping for his oft-delayed novel, Lester decided that he had a hazardous attraction to Jewish-American Princesses.

"It's a fate worse than death as anyone knows," he wrote, "except I didn't because I grew up in a part of California so homogenized I didn't even know what a Jew was 'til I moved to Detroit."

In between Heimel and Cohen, Lester dated freelance journalist Susan Toepfer and singer Galen Brandt, who collaborated with him on a profile of Brian Eno, a hero because of his championing of the nonmusician. Toepfer thought Lester had serious problems with women stemming from his childhood. "It was just very, very emotionally complicated," she said. Brandt believed that he was fragile and easily hurt, and that many women dated him because they wanted to take a walk on the wild side. "We were all sort of nice, upper-middle-class white girls," she said. "We wanted a genius, we wanted a bad boy because those were the times, and we wanted a good boy who would love us true—all of that, plus there was a little reflected glory in hanging around with Lester."

As always, Lester believed he'd found true love. "I have deep feelings for Galen," he gushed in a letter to his old girlfriend Nancy, "not only protective of intellectual respect or physical desire (sometimes that's the last thing), but also a primal sort of spiritual bond which does not need to be spoken—perhaps could not BE spoken. You'll see when you meet her." But once again his drinking and drugging derailed the relationship. "I felt that he was going to die," Brandt said. "I loved him, but I could either spend the majority of my life energy trying to rescue him or I could remand him to his own care and move on."

After bonding at the Memphis and Buffalo rock-critic gatherings, Billy Altman became one of Lester's closest friends, as well as his chosen successor as *Creem*'s record reviews editor. Altman scoffed when Lester told him that he wanted all of his girlfriends to see him at his absolute worst. "But this is *me*!" Lester said. "This is the way I *am*! They can take it or leave it, but at least I'm straight with them!"

The two friends were both single and feeling sorry for themselves when Nancy took pity and invited them for dinner on Thanksgiving, 1977. She had a new boyfriend and seemed to be in love, but Lester couldn't let go. "Our bond is strong / Somehow the others never seem to apply," he wrote in a song called "Nancy Two."

Waiting for the subway home from the Bronx, Lester drunkenly declared that Nancy was his soul mate and they'd ultimately reunite. "Lester, she's making another life for herself," Altman said. "Wake up!" Lester threw a punch at him, and the fight escalated until the two were flailing away just inches from the edge of the platform.

When the subway arrived, they stumbled onboard, barely harnessing their anger. A couple of older black passengers whispered about the spectacle these foolish white boys had made, and finally Lester and Altman started laughing. They shook hands and hung on the straps, trying to keep their footing as the train lurched toward home.

• • •

Lester had been to the U.K. several times through the seventies to profile the likes of Slade and David "Rock On" Essex for *Creem.* He appreciated the codeine-enhanced aspirin and Night Nurse, England's answer to Romilar. But with scattered exceptions, he found the music dreadful and the rock criticism worse.

The country's best-read rock publication, the *New Musical Express,* sold a quarter of a million copies weekly through much of the sixties, but like its competitor *Melody Maker,* it fell into a post-hippie slump in the early seventies. Circulation plummeted to sixty thousand as readers skipped long and ponderous interviews with wankers such as Alvin Lee, Rick Wakeman, and Keith Emerson.

In 1972 Nick Logan assumed the editorship and began steering the paper away from progressive-rock dinosaurs toward rising glam acts such as David Bowie and Roxy Music. He struck an agreement with *Creem* that allowed him to reprint its articles, and Lester began to appear in the paper regularly. Logan also gave free rein to a new cast of flamboyant English writers that included Nick Kent, Charles Shaar Murray, and Mick Farren, all of whom admired Lester's style. "We were all championing Lester because he was the one who was breaking ground," Farren said. "There's no question about it: In the field of journalism—forget about *rock* journalism—he broke ground that has now been concreted over."

As a rock fan and *NME* contributor who moved to London from her native Ohio, Chrissie Hynde was uniquely positioned to assess Lester's influence. "Lester had this iconlike status with these English guys," she said. "As far as Iggy Pop and the New York Dolls, some of the greats from that period, there's no question that it was Lester who brought them to any kind of media attention. No one at all was interested in those guys. He was the first to write about them, and he had a big influence on the writers over here."

Whenever he traveled to the U.K., Lester was surprised to find that the top rock writers were as well known as the musicians. "Visited our sister publication, *New Musical Express*, where the journalists are pop stars," he wrote for *Creem* in 1975. "To wit, Nick Kent, who looked just like the Stooges' Scott Asheton, and Charles Shaar Murray, who came to the *office* dressed as Lou Reed. Not only do they get to dude up like this, they get their pix in the mag so all the young kids in England can see them and get the hots." He was even more shocked when he realized that English audiences allowed writers to wear more than one hat.

Rock critics moonlighting as musicians had never made much of an impact in America. Greil Marcus and Langdon Winner's Masked Marauders were notable only as a prank; the band parodied the super sessions of the late sixties by releasing a record that was supposed to be a bootleg of Bob Dylan, Paul McCartney, and Mick Jagger jamming, and it sold thousands of copies before the hoax was exposed. Peers thought John Mendelsohn had crossed a line in hyping Christopher Milk, but most listeners just ignored the group. *New York Times* rock critic Robert Palmer had a strong reputation as a clarinet player, but that was in the world of avant-garde jazz. Though the Dictators and Pere Ubu made important albums, relatively few people read Andy Shernoff's fanzine *Teenage Wasteland Gazette* or David Thomas's columns in the Cleveland weekly *Scene*.

In the U.K., things were different. Mick Farren had a colorful history as a performer dating back to the Deviants in the sixties. Nick Kent spent several months playing with Sex Pistols Steve Jones, Paul Cook, and Glenn Matlock before their manager tossed him out for having too many ideas of his own. Chrissie Hynde went on to form the Pretenders, and *NME* writer Bob Geldof led the Boomtown Rats.

On a junket in November 1975, Lester still found the English music scene lacking. "England is a suckshit country that deserves to sink into the ocean like California has been threatening to all these years," he wrote. "I've never seen a place where more people concealed more hidden rage behind the blandest facade this side of Donny and Marie." But things were about to change.

Inspired by the New York Dolls, whom he managed late in their career, self-styled provocateur Malcolm McLaren encouraged the Sex Pistols to be as outrageous as possible. "We're not into music, we're into chaos," guitarist Steve Jones told the *NME*. Punk polarized recession-torn England as disenfranchised teens embraced the angry and energetic new sounds. The Pistols released "Anarchy in the U.K." in November 1976 and made their infamous obscenity-laced appearance on Britain's

Today show shortly thereafter. From that point on, they seemed to make headlines daily for the next two years.

"If you think it's presumptuous for a Yank to butt his two-cents' worth into the already sky-high reams of blather concerning the Sex Pistols, you're right," Lester wrote in the *NME*. He nevertheless felt compelled to pronounce the group's first single one of the greatest records ever made. "Johnny Rotten, furthermore, is the most enraged vocalist I've ever heard. He's even more pissed off than Iggy used to be, and you know that's saying something."

Twenty years after abandoning his *nom de rock*, John Lydon returned the compliment. "Lester was a madman, and I used to really like his writing," the singer said. "Although it could be perceived as nasty, there was always a sense of fun in it. This is why British music journalism adopted that style, but they got it wrong. It just turned into something nasty. Lester questioned things, and you'll find the majority of people don't like to question what they just take for granted."

While the Sex Pistols' subsequent singles confirmed his unrestrained fandom, Lester warmed slowly to the other English punk bands. "That Clash record is garbage," he wrote of the "White Riot"/"1977" single, but he eventually came to love the band. He celebrated its mix of red-hot garage rock and cooled-out reggae as "the missing link between black music and white noise." The group shared a view of rock history similar to his own. "It ain't punk and it ain't New Wave," guitarist Mick Jones said of his music in the *NME*. "Call it what you want; all the terms stink. Just call it rock 'n' roll."

In November 1977 CBS International sprang for a now-rare junket, flying Lester to London to accompany the Clash on its Get Out of Control tour. The company hoped his coverage would convince a reluctant U.S. branch to release the band's self-titled debut in the States, but it would be more than a year and a half before that finally happened. Prompted by a reading of Margaret Drabble's novel, *The Ice Age*, which he loved, Lester expected to find a U.K. so troubled by economic collapse that people actually welcomed depression as a relief from anxiety. He was surprised to discover that English punk was more political and motivating than punk as practiced in New York.

Lester spent six days on the road with the Clash, filing an unprecedented epic that filled nine broadsheet pages over three consecutive issues of the *NME*. "Everybody in the office was like: 'Who's gonna edit *this*?'" Farren recalled. "It was the biggest article the paper had ever run."

The piece began with Lester sitting in the airport in New York, reading *The War Against the Jews 1933–1945*, and encountering a young British girl in a wheelchair. He was ashamed to admit that he couldn't meet her gaze. The theme of people struggling to treat each other with basic human decency ran through the entire article.

At first Lester thought that the Clash was different—the Clash seemed to be "righteous." The group wasn't even pretentious about it. The band members regularly let fans crash in their hotel rooms, and they expected him to do the same. When he tried to quiz Mick Jones about politics and his relationship to the audience, the guitarist just laughed at him. "Oh, so is that gonna be the hook for your story, then?" Jones asked.

"The fact that Mick would make a joke out of it only shows how far they're going towards the realization of all the hopes we ever had about rock 'n' roll as utopian dream," Lester wrote. "Because if rock 'n' roll *is* truly the democratic art form, then democracy has got to begin at home; that is, the everlasting and totally disgusting walls between artists and audience must come down, elitism must perish, the 'stars' have got to be humanized, demythologized, and the audience has got to be treated with more respect. Otherwise it's all a shuck, a rip-off, and the music is as dead as the Stones' and Led Zep's has become."

By the end of the week and part three of the story, disillusionment had set in. The trouble crept up unexpectedly with the customary tour high jinks. One night Lester strolled into a hotel lobby and found yet another food fight in progress. After a while he noticed that the band's driver had stopped horsing around and started brutally beating a young fan as members of the Clash stood by and laughed. Lester spent the night with the bruised boy, hashing over the incident and the way it conflicted with the image the band projected. It wasn't until the next morning that he realized that he himself had sat there reading *The War Against the Jews* while failing to help the kid. Righteousness did not come easily.

"If anything more than fashion and what usually amount to poses is going to finally come of all this, then everybody listening is going to have to pick up the possibilities with both hands and fulfill 'em themselves," Lester wrote. "Either that or end up with a new set of surrogate mommies and daddies, just like the hippies did, because in spite of whatever they set in motion that's exactly what Charles Manson and John Sinclair were."

The editors of the *NME* were proud of the piece, but they didn't think it demystified the Clash or taught the group's fans anything new. "I

With Topper Headon, Paul Simonon, and Joe Strummer, 1977.

think the kids sort of knew all this," Farren said. "Only Lester didn't. That was the fascinating thing—to see him be so taken by this thing and not be able to accept that it was just business as usual. The way Lou Reed could be nice to him one day and curse him out the next, the Clash were exactly the same. I was always surprised that he wasn't aware of this."

Disenchanted, Lester returned to America and started to scrutinize the movement he'd championed so enthusiastically. In particular he grappled with the issues of racism and sexism, which were as prevalent in his musical utopia as in society at large—and indeed within himself.

Richard Hell and the Voidoids opened for the Clash throughout the Get Out of Control tour. One night Lester stormed into the New Yorkers' dressing room. The set had been lackluster compared to their usual performances because they hadn't adjusted to the English punks' habit of "gobbing" or spitting on them. Lester tried to get a rise out of them by shouting, "Nigger!" The Voidoids' black rhythm guitarist threw a beer at him. "Not in my dressing room!" Ivan Julian yelled. "Get the fuck out!" Lester padded off sheepishly; he and Julian had always been friends.

Back in the United States, Lester called Julian and told him he wanted to interview him for an article in the *Village Voice*. "He came on the phone and started asking me questions like 'Has anyone ever discriminated against you on the punk scene?' " the musician recalled. "I said, 'Yeah, a few people, and I know who *they* are. So what?' That's what didn't come through in the article: that this happens, but that's life. You deal with it and you go on. When I read the article, it was almost like he was trying to cleanse himself of guilt. He was trying to make a point, and the point just wasn't there."

One of the most controversial music pieces the *Voice* ever published, "The White Noise Supremacists" started on the front page of the paper on December 17, 1979. The article called out several punk scenemakers and questioned their words and actions. Lester wondered what had prompted Miriam Linna to pose for a photo in front of the headquarters of the United White People's Party; asked how Andy Shernoff could joke in *Punk* magazine about Camp Runamuck, "where Puerto Ricans are kept until they learn to be human"; and pondered how *Punk*'s John Holmstrom and Legs McNeil could dismiss as "nigger disco shit" the Otis Redding records that Lester had played at his Easter party.

"When he wrote the punk racism piece, it was sort of a mea culpa on some levels," John Morthland said. "He was sort of chastising himself for the error of his own ways, which he had come to see and hadn't before. I think in his mind and in his heart he hoped that other people in the article—whether named or not—might have a similar reaction. But of course none of them did."

"I knew I wasn't a racist; I was just making a tasteless joke," Shernoff said years later. "I was a little freer then, and this was totally before political correctness." Linna called Lester in a fury when the article came out: He'd used a photo that had been intended as a joke to paint her as a racist. "I was devastated when the *Voice* article came out," she said. "I got right on the horn and said, 'You know it's totally untrue.' He apologized profusely. He said, 'If you write a response, I'll make sure the *Voice* prints it,' and they did print it. But by that time the forces of PC had done their damage."

Twenty years later, Linna still had mixed feelings about the whole episode. "It put me up against the wall for quite a while, and even now people still take verbatim what Lester was plowing at," she said. "I don't bother to answer them. I just sort of look toward the heavens, smile, and say: 'I'll get you one of these days!' "

Many at CBGB believed that "The White Noise Supremacists" had been influenced by Lester's editor, Robert Christgau, who had always been scornful of the punk scene. "Lester was affected by the political tone of New York and the *Village Voice,* but I don't think it was me particularly," Christgau maintained in 1997. "Like any other rock 'n' roller who gets politics, it wasn't a perfect fit. But I personally think that's a completely successful—well, probably not completely—but a ninety-five-percent successful and extremely powerful piece. Sometimes moral awkwardness is powerful because it's a sign of sincerity, and sometimes it's just a sign of ineptness, but not in this case."

Following the October 1978 murder of Sex Pistols groupie Nancy Spungen and the subsequent overdose of bassist Sid Vicious—both of which he covered for the *Voice*—Lester began to withdraw from the punk scene. "The White Noise Supremacists" drove the wedge deeper, and the publication of his first book, *Blondie,* made the split permanent.

In 1979 James Grauerholz and William S. Burroughs moved to Lawrence, Kansas. For a while Grauerholz persisted in his efforts to run a hip literary agency, but he eventually gave up without having sold any of Lester's ideas. Lester had written proposals for ten different books, including the punk-culture tome; his greatest hits collection; his oral history of kids in the seventies; the Rolling Stones novel; *Rock Through the Looking Glass: A Book of Fantasies*, which would have rounded up his fictional writings about John Lennon, Rod Stewart, Barry White, and others; *Beyond the Law: Four Rock 'n' Roll Extremists*, a rock version of A. B. Spellman's *Four Lives in the Bebop Business* focusing on Marianne Faithfull, Brian Eno, Danny Fields, and Screamin' Jay Hawkins; a critical examination of the Beatles called *They Invented It (You Took It Under)*; a book on noise-rock called *A Reasonable Guide to Horrible Noise*; and *Women on Top: Ten Post-Lib Role Models for the Eighties,* profiles of various "postfeminists," such as Lydia Lunch. Grauerholz shopped many of these ideas around, but most of his calls went unreturned.

Lester did contribute to several other books, writing five chapters for *The Rolling Stone Illustrated History of Rock & Roll* and submitting an essay on the one album he would take to a desert island to Greil Marcus's 1979 anthology, *Stranded*. He chose Van Morrison's *Astral Weeks*, one of the records that helped him through the difficult period that followed the Hell's Angels' gang bang. "What *Astral Weeks* deals in are not facts but truths," he wrote. "It is a record about people stunned by life, completely overwhelmed, stalled in their skins, their ages, and selves, paralyzed by the enormity of what in one moment of vision they can comprehend." The essence of Morrison's philosophy: "a knowledge of the miracle of life." If he was aware of it, Lester did not mention that the singer's mother had been a Jehovah's Witness who dragged her son along as she preached a very different sort of spiritual message.

While Lester searched for a new agent to shop his other projects, he stumbled into a deal to write a lavishly illustrated fan book about Blondie. The group had released three albums since he hailed its debut in the *Village Voice,* and it became the first and only CBGB band to achieve a number-one hit with the glossy disco single "Heart of Glass." Delilah Communications was a small New York company that "packaged" rock books, delivering the finished text and photographs to other publishers. "Nobody did rock 'n' roll books in the late seventies and early eighties," editor Karen Moline said, "and that didn't change until [Delilah founder Stephanie Bennett] published Dave Marsh's *Born to Run*." Now Bennett wanted to capitalize on Blondie's success, and Moline tapped Lester.

A self-professed "club slut," Moline was a familiar presence on the downtown rock scene. "The most indefatigable and possibly most physically beautiful woman in New York City, and my pal," Lester called her. "I think Lester was just happy to be given a platform," Moline said, "and nobody was in charge of it except me, this twenty-five-year-old moron. I

With Karen Moline during a book signing for *Blondie*, 1980.
PHOTO COURTESY KAREN MOLINE

thought, 'I'm gonna try to let him get away with it.' I was in such awe of Lester's talent."

What Lester tried to get away with was writing a fan book with critical insights as well as pretty pictures. "I told the people at Delilah, 'The fan-book thing has been misunderstood,'" he said in 1982. "When you write a fan book, you don't have to kiss ass. They say, 'Oh, we want a book for the fans,' and they think all the kids can take is that stupid bland shit. But I know that's not true from many years of experience. Basically these book companies are like the record companies. They'd rather have that than something that has some vitality to the writing. So you just fight to get that in."

The rumor on the punk scene was that Lester took Delilah's $6,000 advance—half his annual income for 1979—and wrote the Blondie book in forty-eight hours on speed. John Morthland believes he might actually have taken as long as seventy-two hours—"ninety-six at the absolute most"—but he noted that much of Lester's best work was done this way. Blondie singer Debbie Harry and her partner, Chris Stein, did not cooperate, but Lester included lots of history for the fans, as well as a chapter putting the group in context of the entire New York punk movement.

More interesting were prescient discussions of Blondie's ironic pose and the issue of who is really in control when a smart woman decides to market her sexuality. Three years later these topics would be endlessly pondered by critics in connection with another blonde named Madonna, but in 1979 Lester was already considering why he wasn't turned on by the infamous poster of a seminude Harry under the slogan RIP HER TO SHREDS. "I think if most guys in America could somehow get their fave-rave poster girl in bed and have total license to do whatever they wanted with this legendary body for one afternoon, at least seventy-five percent of the guys in the country would elect to beat her up," he wrote. Elsewhere he anticipated a new critical buzzword. "The Blondies are hip to postmodernism, and postmodernism is hip to them, which is why even their most bland-out lyrics get quoted in *Village Voice* articles on the subject," he wrote. "It's a marriage of convenience. And convenience is the name of the game, otherwise why bother with anything? Make it spare and clean and fast. Above all, don't expect. Because it isn't there. I'm not there. I say what I mean: Nothing. Cathode trance is perfect orgone isolation, fixed beyond Burroughs, goes on long as Con Ed holds out. But the lines are fixed, too. No cheap sentiment or jackoff rage: Passion in this context is useless as a luxury liner in the middle of the Sahara. . . . These people are beyond in-jokes, beyond coy, beyond their own beyondness. Nada chucks Dada out the window, bye-bye clutter."

Reviewing *Blondie* for *Rolling Stone*, Greil Marcus called it "an antipostmodernist manifesto." Debbie Harry and Chris Stein called it much worse. "Every time Chris and Debbie did an interview for the next year and a half, it was 'Blah, Lester's book is a piece of shit,' " Lester said in 1982. "I was at the point of writing them a letter and thanking them for selling so many copies." Harry and Stein seethed and set out to record their version of history with Victor Bockris in the 1982 book *Making*

Tracks: The Rise of Blondie. They tried to paint Lester as a hypocrite by including part of *Punk* magazine's photo comic "Mutant Monster Beach Party." The strip featured Lester portraying a Hell's Angel carrying a screaming Harry on his shoulder and lasciviously pawing her ass.

Two decades later the artists' bitter feelings hadn't ebbed. "It was a nasty book," Harry said. "He really stabbed us in the back. Lester was losing his mind by then. He went on to become a lead singer of his own band, and that was horrific in itself. Then he verbally retracted everything that he had written, telling us, 'I never realized how hard it was!' He went on and on, sort of crawling on the floor of CBGB, which was kind of enjoyable, but it didn't really mean anything to the world." Stein agreed. "In the long run history has proven him totally inane for the shit he wrote," the guitarist said. "I mean, he spent twenty pages talking about Debbie's underwear. He was one of these guys who thought he was a purist and Mr. Honesty, but he was a jerk. At least Charles Bukowski *knew* he was a jerk. Lester had a tendency to think he was God."

As with many of the women in his life, Lester was often disappointed when his musical heroes failed to live up to his ideals. Lou Reed was the most obvious example, but there were many others. Captain Beefheart had invited him to spend some time in the studio during the

Portraying a Hell's Angel harassing Debbie Harry, 1977.
PHOTO BY CHRIS STEIN FOR *PUNK* MAGAZINE

recording of *The Spotlight Kid* in 1973. They sat up until 7 A.M. drinking grenadine. "For the first two or three hours I thought it was the most brilliant conversation I'd ever heard, then decided he was just like any other ugly dogged self-assertive drunk," Lester wrote Greil Marcus. "I think it's Langdon [Winner]'s fault, too. Well, really *Rolling Stone*'s and all of our faults. We were the ones who kept hammering away at what a genius he was. Pretty soon he started to believe all that shit and shifted full elbow jut from off the wall genius to just another podunk oracular twit."

By the time *Radio Ethiopia* was released in late 1976, Lester had also become skeptical of Patti Smith. Musically he protested that the band didn't go far enough in its pretensions toward a merger of rock and free jazz. "I think Patti should make her *Metal Machine Music*, and *Radio Ethiopia* didn't even come close," he wrote. But he was even more critical of what he perceived as Smith's self-mythologizing "Holy Crusade." He wrote a harsh review of her second album for the *Village Voice*, but Robert Christgau rejected it. "He thought it was because I was in Patti Smith's pocket, and he got very mad," Christgau said. "He said, 'This is a great piece!' Well, it wasn't; it was just him being mean. I felt that it was too personal and not Lester's best side. It was resentment, and that's not a pretty thing in anybody."

Even though the article was never published, Smith and guitarist Lenny Kaye felt betrayed. "Lester turned against us because he felt we sold out with *Radio Ethiopia*," Smith told interviewer Thurston Moore in 1995. "Everybody thought we turned into heavy metal, and meanwhile that record sold 30,000 copies 'cause nobody would rack it 'cause it said 'Pissing in the River' on it."

Kaye thought his peers should have been more understanding. "We were so closely aligned with the rock-writer thing—these people were our friends!—that my feeling was 'Hey, man, you may not like our record, but at least try to understand what we're doing,'" he said. The guitarist believes that Lester looked at Smith, knew she didn't have anything he didn't have in terms of musical ability, and resented the fact that she succeeded as a musician. "There was some jealousy that we were able to get past the conceptuals of rock 'n' roll and into its grit," he said. "Lester never moved beyond writing about rock 'n' roll. He never wrote his novel. Is someone who's a critic or someone commenting upon art—are they equal to that art?"

For his part Lester was insulted that his friends couldn't accept his criticism. "You turned it into a classic case of You're Either On the Bus or

Off the Bus," he wrote in an open letter to Smith. "You and I had only known each other for five fucking years, plus I used to go out with your best friend, you even set us up together in the first place, plus I was your editor at *Creem* but we were always closer friends than that, in fact I treasured your friendship and when your first album came out I was one thousandfolk sold and souled too. Everything was just peachy keen 'til I committed my own unpardonable sin of just for some reason not happening to think *Radio Ethiopia* was the greatest avant-garde masterpiece since Ornette Coleman and Jackson Pollock were weaned in the same cradle, but what I had not yet realized when I first received a copy of it in the mail was that you were in the throes of a rather eerily messianic power-trip of such total proportions you became even more of a Phenomenon than you'd been when you were a great artist but still a human being."

Hype was the number-one enemy, Lester concluded. It could pervert everything an artist stood for—especially when he or she started to believe it.

On June 27, 1980, John Lydon appeared on the *Tomorrow* show to talk about his new group, Public Image, Ltd., but host Tom Snyder couldn't get beyond his sensational notions of Lydon's Sex Pistols past. Disgusted, Lester phoned his friend Rob Tyner in Detroit and told him to switch to the spectacle on NBC. "Shit, man, how would you like to end up getting called the 'leader' of a whole big fad espoused by assholes around the world in terms having nothing to do with anything you ever said or did?" Lester asked. The former MC5 singer laughed. "Hey, pal, I was in *that exact same position!*" Tyner said.

"Ever get the feeling you've been cheated?" Lydon had asked during the Sex Pistols' last concert at San Francisco's Winterland. In 1980 Lester answered the question in an unpublished manuscript. "Yep, I'm bitter, because I've gone full circle maybe one too many times," he wrote. "This makes the third myth bought in on by me if you count the Beatniks who were really before my time, one self-con job a decade, guess that's not really so bad. But it is all pretty obviously futile in terms of anything whatsoever beyond a good record here, a good record there, big deal, you got a hobby. It seems to me I've reached the inevitable impasse, the place where all that's left for me to do (all I *can* do) is rant and rave ineffectually. Which means I've now got to find something else. And I guess the bottom line, for me at least, is that I have never been able to convince myself that people in any appreciable numbers getting together to create or accomplish something actually *works*. And that really the only kind of fixed group, organization, or club I could ever imagine myself joining was a rock 'n' roll band."

٭ ٭ ٭

"Enjoy the aeronautical sound of Lester Bangs's new band Birdland, coming to your town and vinyl soon," read a note on the cover of the "Let It Blurt" single. Shortly after performing at CBGB with the group he would have named Tender Vittles, Lester started a new band with Mickey Leigh, a.k.a. Mitch Hyman, best known on the punk scene as Joey Ramone's kid brother.

Lester and Leigh met through Joey's girlfriend at the time, Robin Rothman. She and Lester used to compare poems at the bar at CBGB. "I couldn't call myself a pot dealer, so I called myself a writer," Rothman said. She accompanied the Ramones on their first trip to England and sold T-shirts at their shows. Leigh went along as a roadie. He had played in bands since his teens and was technically a better musician than any of the Ramones. They leaned on him to notate their music so they could copyright their songs, and part of him resented their success. Rothman listened to Lester and Leigh whining about their separate musical frustrations, and she brought them together.

The pair clicked when they realized that they'd both been listening to Gunther Schuller's *Jazz Abstractions*. Lester already had a name for the group, based on New York's famous jazz club and the song from Patti Smith's *Horses*. His vision of Birdland combined the wild experimentation of free jazz, the transcendent quality of Van Morrison's *Astral Weeks*, and the good-time hooks of bubblegum rock. It was a tall order, and he and Leigh spent a year putting music to lyrics and burning through a succession of drummers and bassists. "We were trying to bridge those gaps as best we could, but it was hard," Leigh said. "Lester wasn't a great musician."

Birdland's eventual drummer put it more succinctly: "Lester sounded like a baying walrus." A former percussion major at Brooklyn College, Matthew Posnick acquired the nickname "Matty Quick" because of his propensity for speed. Birdland finally gelled when he joined in the fall of 1978, taking his place beside bassist David Merrill, the son of opera singer Robert Merrill. The four bandmates spent several months rehearsing for three or four hours a day at Quick's loft on Spring Street.

Lester had started to study with a vocal coach, and he often came to practice straight from singing lessons.

"Certain people that are friends of mine think that me being in a band is like, 'Oh, you're regressing to your adolescence, why don't you grow up?' " Lester said. "What they don't realize is that this goddamn band is the most responsibility I've ever had in my life to date!"

The band members were all committed to the project, but they had some basic musical and philosophical differences. "I just want you to tell me what you think of this guitar solo," Lester said to Leigh at practice one night. He proceeded to blast "I Heard Her Call My Name" by the Velvet Underground on the stereo as the musicians wandered into the kitchen for a beer. "Who was that guy?" Leigh asked when the song ended. "He's the greatest guitarist I've ever heard in my life!"

Lester beamed. "Then I caught this little gleam in his eye, and everything crumbled," he wrote. "I am a purdee gullible sucker from the word go. He started laughing—hell, they *all* did, *my* fellow musicians in *my* band, laughing contemptuously at me—slapped me on the back and said: 'Listen, Lester, I couldn't play that solo. David couldn't play that solo. But *you* could play that solo in three days and I'll show you how!' Harde-harhar. Mickey couldn't play that solo because it's just not in him. He told me once: 'That solo is just like somebody grabbing up huge globs of paint and throwing 'em at a canvas.' I told this to Brian Eno and we both had the same response: 'What's wrong with that?' "

From December 1978 through the spring of 1979, Birdland played a dozen gigs, ranging from dive bars on the Jersey shore to opening for the Ramones at the Palladium. Billy Altman often mixed the sound. Some of the best shows were before the most hostile audiences. When a crowd at CBGB kept shouting for headliners the Dead Boys, Lester baited them with taunts of "Name three words that rhyme with de-evolution!" At first he vehemently protested his bandmates' suggestions that he dress a bit flashier. He usually walked onstage in whatever he'd been wearing that week, but people responded positively when he began sporting white overalls à la the thugs in Stanley Kubrick's *A Clockwork Orange*, so he took it a step further. He donned oversized railroad workers' gloves that emphasized his gestures and made him look like a big cartoon character.

Though he often performed while drunk or tripping on Romilar, Lester attacked his bandmates for indulging before shows. Once he yelled at Quick for giving Leigh some speed, then turned to the drummer and asked if he could borrow a Quaalude. "Here he was cruising one end of the ozone while I was cruising the other, and he was criticizing *me*," Quick said. "He was sort of a lonely guy, but at the time I had a good thing going with lots of young girls. Lester used to say that I was a chauvinist. 'What, 'cause I'm having sex, you fucking asshole? Go get laid, Lester!' I used to give it to him pretty good. I'd be orbiting around the whole band like Sputnik, and he'd be like the planet earth."

Bassist David Merrill worked part-time at Electric Lady, the recording studio Jimi Hendrix built on Eighth Street, and in the spring of 1979 the band crept in for some after-hours sessions. The group laid down eight originals and a cover of Bobby Fuller's "I Fought the Law," but Lester thought the tedious process of multitracking killed the energy of the songs. "Hey, do ya think Sam Phillips might rent us a barn?" he cracked. He preferred the first demo the band recorded on a four-track in the loft one hungover Sunday morning. But while they were far from *Astral Weeks*, the tapes captured a tight and spirited garage band with the noteworthy element of Lester's lyrics.

Birdland: Matty Quick, Mickey Leigh, Dave Merrill, and Lester, 1979.
PHOTO BY ROBERTA BAYLEY

Over the hyperactive Bo Diddley groove of "I'm in Love with My Walls," Lester sang about abandoning the nightlife to live like a hermit in his apartment. Some of his old *Creem* pals wondered if the title was a punning homage to his agoraphobic friend Richard C. Walls. In the spirit of the cult film *Freaks*—which gave the Ramones their pinhead mascot and chant of "Gabba gabba hey!"—Lester's "Accidents of God" chronicled the plight of a sensitive sideshow freak. He dusted off his trusty harmonica for a wild intro to the raging antilove song, "Fade Away," while "Kill Him Again" found him assuming opposing roles in a poignant minidrama. In the hard-driving verses he portrayed a member of a blood-hungry mob bent on vengeance, while the melodic bridge found him jumping into the role of the victim. He said the song was inspired by the recent Son of Sam killings, but lines about the elders denying absolution also recalled his experience being disfellowshipped by the Jehovah's Witnesses.

The most striking of all the Birdland songs was "There's a Man in There." Lester told Billy Altman he wrote the lyrics without realizing what they were about. Later he showed them to his therapist, Phil Sapienza, who praised them as an artful depiction of the death of his father. "Lester said it was one of those moments where he just kind of shuddered and went, '*Oooh*,'" Altman recalled. Two decades later Sapienza still remembered the song's imagery. "That was the most haunting episode in Lester's entire life," he said. "He came back to it over and over again—death by fire, and of all people his own father."

Sapienza had been recommended by his stepsons, Mickey Leigh and Joey Ramone, and Lester started seeing him in early 1978. "He just plopped himself down on my couch and said, 'Okay, let's go to work,'" the psychiatrist recalled. Sapienza scaled down his fees to accommodate Lester and treated him for about a year and a half. They also became friends outside the therapy room, and Lester sometimes joined Sapienza, his wife, Charlotte Lesher, and her two sons for family dinners and weekends at their country home in Massachusetts. One weekend a drunken Lester stumbled on a rock in the woods and cut a deep gash on the bridge of his nose. Sapienza bandaged the wound.

"I had the feeling that I was sitting with a little boy," Sapienza recalled. "Lester was never indulged emotionally in his life—no mother, no father. Whenever he got angry, I had the feeling it was for that reason. He didn't know how to ask for affection and love and indulgence. It was easy just then because he was sitting there on the toilet bleeding; he didn't have to ask for anything. I never forgot that moment in the bathroom with him. In those ten minutes I was in fact his mother, his father, his nephew Ben. He was an infant—infantile."

In the therapy room, Sapienza and Lester addressed his drinking and drugging, his upbringing, his relationships with women, and his work. "His creativity was a very important part of this," Sapienza said. "He was a critic, that was his profession, but he aspired to his own creativity. He didn't really know which direction to go with that. For a period he was part of a musical group, and it didn't work out. He also wanted to write a novel, but he didn't know how to do it."

Searching for the key, Lester had begun reading Dostoyevsky and Tolstoy, obsessing that he'd never measure up to the great novelists.

At Phil Sapienza's country place, 1979.
PHOTO COURTESY PHIL SAPIENZA

Sapienza told him to forget about writing the *ultimate* novel and just write *his* novel. "He did that with everything," the therapist said. "Not only the ultimate novel, but the ultimate romance, the ultimate performance, the ultimate work of art. This is the way he approached everything."

His bandmates in Birdland appreciated the power of Lester's words. " 'There's a Man in There' is a fantastic song—the hackles on my neck still rise when I think about it," Quick said. Leigh spent hours with Lester trying to marry his lyrics to melodies. "He would give me things that were more stories than lyrics," he said. "Everybody knew that Lester was a great writer, that he could do great things with words. There were some people that appreciated the performances, too, but things could get very raw onstage."

Artists whom Lester had praised or panned now found themselves in the odd position of judging his music. "The last time I saw Lester, he got me to go down to Max's Kansas City to see his band," Ian Hunter recalled. "It struck me that this guy had amazing taste as a critic, but when he was in a band, it was like the worst band I've ever seen in my life. I didn't know what to say to him because it was so bloody awful."

Birdland shared several bills with the Talking Heads, and the opinion of keyboardist Jerry Harrison was typical of the musicians at CBGB. "We all admired his writing," Harrison said, "but I don't think he had the impact as a musician that he had as a writer, obviously."

In fact, Lester didn't distinguish between writing a song such as "There's a Man in There" and an article like his Clash epic. "In both cases he had something important to say and he wanted people to hear it," John Morthland said. "It was really just different mediums." But his bandmates came to believe that Lester's notoriety as a writer—which they'd initially seen as an asset—was beginning to hold them back.

Birdland broke up in April 1979. Tensions had been building ever since the band hired a manager, Rick Schneider, a low-level record-company executive who packaged music for films. He prodded the musicians to try to convince Lester to become a behind-the-scenes figure like Brian Wilson, who wrote songs but did not perform with the Beach Boys. Schneider thought they needed a "more professional" singer. "It's more important to reach Middle America than the underground rock scene," he told *New York Rocker*.

Lester painted the conflict in more classical terms. He embodied the Dionysian spirit, he said, while his bandmates were Appollonians. "For him everything always had to be broken down; it had to be crumbled; it couldn't be pristine, nothing could be right," Leigh said. "If it was all right, then something was wrong with it. Except in these other circumstances where he praised bands like ABBA. They were okay; they were perfect. I never quite got it."

Things came to a head during a rehearsal when the group was running through a powerful song called "Give Up the Ghost." The lyrics stemmed from an ongoing debate between Lester and his friend Robert Quine. An ever more liberal Lester opposed long prison sentences and the death penalty, but Quine was hard-core. "I always told him that he reminded me of the guy in the R. Crumb comic having the shit beat out of him by the Black Panthers and saying, 'I *understand* why you are doing this,' " Quine said.

Leigh told Lester that the song was too wordy, and Lester exploded. "I write the lyrics and this is *my* band!" he roared. The group tried to play the tune. "You want to punish what you won't understand/Electrocutions on TV/You want your little shots of death on demand / Well, baby, don't come lookin' at me," Lester sang. He inched forward with every word, backing Leigh into the corner.

"It was a scary moment because Lester was losing it," Quick said. "It was very emotional, and he was singing his heart out in a way, but at the same time he was pushing us away. It was frightening, because I didn't know if he was gonna hit Mickey or if Mickey was gonna have to bang him over the head with the guitar. And it was clear that this was how the band was gonna end."

That night manager Schneider offered Lester the Brian Wilson deal, and Lester told him to fuck himself. For a long time afterward he was bitter about the Birdland experience, but he eventually turned philosophical, concluding that the other members of the band had done him a favor. "Not because of masochism, but because I don't like to *think*," he wrote. "That was undoubtedly the whole reason I ever let myself get the least bit conned re this 'rock star' business that the other guys were all so starry-eyed about. As stated, I'm lazy, and becoming any variant of the genus 'rock star'—even an also-ran, a Richard Hell or a James Chance—is ensuring that you will never have to think, ever, for a very long period of time."

chapter ten

Jook Savage on the Brazos

The towering black transvestite stared at Lester with the scornful look that doormen at New York nightclubs hone like a knife. "Have you got an invitation?" he sneered.

Newly opened on lower Broadway, Berlin was the hot New Wave dance club in the summer of 1980. Lester had learned to avoid these temples of hipster fascism after several unpleasant incidents at the Mudd Club. "You're not Lester Bangs, you're Porky Pig," a bouncer cracked one night when Lester said that his name was on the guest list. This process of passing muster before being granted admittance had started uptown, of course; only the beautiful people were welcome at Studio 54. The door policy at CBGB still stood as an egalitarian contrast—there was none—but punk had mutated into New Wave, the lines with disco had blurred, and the odious disco door policies had spread to the newer rock clubs.

To Lester it was all the logical result of the celebrity elitism that had been festering in rock 'n' roll since the Rolling Stones toured after Altamont, surrounded by phalanxes of hangers-on that isolated them from their fans. These days he mostly avoided the clubs and stayed home, but several members of Joe "King" Carrasco and the Crowns were visiting from Austin, Texas, and the musicians wanted to sample the vaunted New York nightlife. Like so many others, the band's manager, rock critic

Joe Nick Patoski, had first contacted Lester at *Creem*, and their friendship blossomed during the late-night phone calls that followed.

The band's roadie, Tim Hamblin, had a friend who worked at Berlin
and was supposedly having a party there, but the doorman wouldn't
budge when they couldn't produce an invitation. Finally a shadowy figure in an expensive suit whispered something in the bouncer's ear, and
the velvet rope parted. John Morthland led the way up the stairs to another door and another bouncer. This one sported two buttons on his
black leather jacket, one bearing the face of Sid Vicious, the other with
the two-word creed PISSED OFF. He made them wait ten minutes before
letting them through.

Inside they saw a throng of people dressed like members of the Ad-
dams Family dancing under green neon lights. Bad British bands mixed
American funk bass lines, Teutonic synthesizers, and wimpy Anglo vocals. The Texans asked what it all meant. "Oh, the end of the world or
some shit like that," Morthland deadpanned.

They wandered over to another queue waiting for admittance to the
VIP room. A Bryan Ferry look-alike escorted them down a passageway to
yet another door, this one guarded by a New Romantic goon dressed like
Robin Hood minus the bow and arrows. After making them endure another humbling wait, this guy let them into the inner sanctum. Big deal,
Lester thought. The same music blared as outside, but in here everyone
sat silently on plush velvet couches, sipping champagne and practicing
looking elegantly wasted.

Once again the Texans were puzzled. "What's the point of all this?"
asked Kris Cummings, Joe Nick Patoski's girlfriend and the Crowns' keyboard player.

"For the people inside each room to think they're better than the
people in the one just before it," Lester explained. "But I'm happy."
Patoski asked why. "Because we went through five Checkpoint Charlies
tonight, which is a new record for me," Lester said. "They only used to
have one or two at the Mudd Club. And because I can get into a place
where Billy Idol can't!"

Patoski hadn't heard "Dancing with Myself," Idol's big hit. "Billy
who?" he asked. Lester laughed. "He's famous," the critic said, "but as of
now I'm famouser." Just then Idol strolled across the room sporting a
shoddy green raincoat and his trademark bleached-blond hairdo. He was
trailed by a succubus in python-green eye shadow and a black leather
corset.

"I didn't have a date and it was Saturday night," Lester wrote. "To cover my embarrassment I started making a speech about equality, elitism, and all that garbage, but somebody cut me off with: 'Yeah, but you're still hangin' around in here.' I didn't have anything to say to that."

Lester had been living in New York for almost four years. Like every New Yorker, he had begun to hate the city the moment he arrived, but he maintained that there was nowhere else he'd rather live. "I'm more comfortable with my mutanthood here than I would be in, say, San Diego where I grew up, or even Detroit where I did time," he wrote. He told Patoski that Manhattan was just the biggest small town in the world. "Here he was in New York—he finally arrived, as it were—and what he saw was: 'This is a crummy little burg, basically. Everywhere I go, I run into the same twenty people,' " Patoski said. "It was because he ran in music circles, and he was sick of the same people who ran in music circles with him."

Patoski began traveling to New York with the Crowns in late 1979. Bandleader Joe "King" Carrasco was a whirling dervish who played a hyperactive mix of rockabilly, polka, Tex-Mex border music, and garage rock, and he took to the stage wearing a ridiculous cape and crown in an homage to James Brown. Lester introduced the group whenever it performed. "This was at a time in New York when everybody was wearing black, and here we were a bunch of goofy Texans," Patoski said. "Joe 'King' Carrasco was the anti-person-in-black. Lester liked that, and he was instrumental in launching the band's career—or at least giving them their fifteen minutes of fame in New York."

Midway through a series of gigs in the spring of 1980, Lester wrote a cover story praising Carrasco in the *Soho Weekly News*. The initial shows drew only a handful of people, but the gigs after Lester's article hit the stands had lines stretching around the block. Karen Moline threw a big loft party for the band, and a drunken Lester spent the evening hurling insults at the other guests. An anonymous pair from Athens, Georgia, crashed the festivities in search of a meal; Peter Buck and Michael Stipe planned to start a band of their own, and they drove to New York following their friends in Pylon to check out the scene. They were hungry, they barely had the gas money to get back home, and they were disappointed that Moline had nothing to eat but cheesecake and jelly beans.

"I had read all of Lester Bangs's stuff in *Creem* and thought he was the greatest thing in the world," Buck said fifteen years later. "Now here we were at this party, filling up on birthday cake and jelly beans. Lester was standing there, and every time someone walked by—it was like a mantra—he'd have some word to say to them. He called me a rotten cocksucker. I didn't take it personally because everybody else got it, too. I was like: 'That's Lester Bangs! That's so cool! I was cursed at by my idol!' "

"I liked Lester because he was like me," Carrasco said. "I knew who he was and stuff, but I wasn't reading *Creem* magazine—that's not where my head was at. I liked Lester for the person he was. When we were together, we talked about women problems mostly. That was the predominant thing in our lives: Women couldn't make sense out of us. He was totally burned out on romance and music and pretty much everything else."

The Crowns released their first single on Gee Bee Records, an independent label started by an Austin fan named Gretchen Barber. Her then-boyfriend Billy Gibbons bankrolled the project. In the mid-sixties Gibbons fronted a psychedelic garage band called the Moving Sidewalks; in the eighties he was better known as the leader of ZZ Top. Beneath the image of a burly, bearded boogie monster he was an erudite aesthete who owned one of Houston's finest art collections.

Lester and other critics had long dismissed ZZ Top as music for beer-swilling bikers, but Gibbons had a plan to rectify that. "Billy had his agenda, and his agenda was that [their breakthrough album] *Deguello* was almost out," said Ed Ward, then the rock critic at the *Austin American-Statesman*. "He basically hitched a credibility ride—I don't want to put him down for that, but that's what he did—and he got into the New Wave scene and the credible critics with that album and Joe 'King' Carrasco."

Gibbons and Barber flew to New York whenever Carrasco performed, and the night usually ended with a big dinner at Un Deux Trois. Lester and Gibbons bonded by trying to outdo each other with tales of music-industry outrage. By the time ZZ Top released *Deguello* in the spring of 1980, Lester had become a fan. "What makes ZZ Top a kitchen-slinger, party-time band from here to the Brazos is that, like Austin's Fabulous Thunderbirds, it's saved white blues from being yesterday's conceit," he raved in *Rolling Stone*. "Punks used to wear razor blades, but these guys play 'em, lividly. It's fun, like eating tequila backward."

Lester penned a flattering profile of the trio for *Musician*, and Gibbons showed his appreciation by inviting the critic to visit him in Texas. "Billy was always doing things like that," Barber said. "He was really very generous that way." If his hosts were willing to have him for a while,

Lester thought he could do some serious writing in Texas—maybe even start his novel. He'd always been curious about the state where his father was born, and he was intrigued by what his friends told him about Austin. He was also anxious to record the album of songs that had been percolating since Birdland, and he thought that Gibbons and Barber might pay for it.

"I didn't mean to lead him on; I just did this one single to help Joe Nick Patoski and the band," Barber said. "I had to say, 'Lester, I'm *not* going to do your record.' I didn't want to break his heart because I loved him so much as a friend, but we cleared that up before he ever came down here." Undaunted, Lester figured that if Austin was really the musical mecca that Patoski, Carrasco, and Ward described, he'd find some way to record.

While making the rounds to say his good-byes, Lester ran into Glenn Morrow, an editor at *New York Rocker*. Morrow had been kicked out of his place and was sleeping on the office couch. Lester's invitation to

Lester in his apartment, 1980.
PHOTO BY CHRISTINA PATOSKI

house-sit seemed like a godsend, but Morrow got more than he bargained for. He had to spend several days clearing out the debris just to make the place habitable. Dishes piled up in the sink from meals that seem to have been cooked two years earlier. Rotting newspapers and porno mags covered the brass bed, which had collapsed so that the mattress lay on the floor atop empty bottles of orange juice and half-eaten containers of Chinese food.

"The token emblem which I thought said it all was a bottle in the bathroom of Johnson and Johnson baby shampoo," Morrow said. "Cockroaches had climbed in and fallen into the shampoo, so it was kind of like the La Brea tar pits. After I cleaned up the place and wanted to show someone what it had been like, I'd bring out the shampoo bottle. Living in that environment, you could totally see why Lester was fed up with New York. His own personal chaos was literally and physically choking him."

Accompanied by his girlfriend and his stockbroker, Billy Gibbons pulled into Houston's William Hobby Airport in his red Cadillac convertible. An inebriated Lester stumbled off the plane wearing his usual Chuck Taylors, dirty jeans, and ABBA T-shirt. In lieu of luggage he carried an old portable typewriter, a stack of notebooks, some albums, and a paper bag with a change of underwear.

"We had volunteered to be the host and hostess, and brother, it wasn't with the mostest," Gibbons said. " 'Escorted' would be an understatement; he was literally being held up by the stewardesses and the captain. His head was waving and nodding, and I said, 'Oh, my God, look at this disheveled wreck. This is gonna be great!' "

Lester left a trail of notebooks behind as he walked through the airport, but Gretchen Barber followed behind and picked them up. "Man, I haven't been out of New York City in years," he said. "You don't know what this means to me." When Gibbons realized that his guest hadn't brought any clothes, he told Barber to take Lester to Neiman Marcus and set him up Texas-style. She outfitted him from head to toe with new cowboy boots, a couple of pairs of khaki pants, and a selection of Izod Lacoste polo shirts.

Gibbons put Lester up at a comfortable hotel downtown, but Houston was a bore, so Lester and Barber soon set off for Austin. He lasted only a couple of days at Barber's house before being relocated again. "I would come back and he would be passed out on the couch or walking around in his underwear," Barber recalled. "I would go, 'God, Lester, put something on! I can't take this!' I was a young girl, and it was not my scene. That's how the Alamo Hotel came up."

Located on the corner of Sixth and Guadalupe streets six blocks from the capital building, the Alamo was a grand and stately old place fallen on hard times. It was best known for housing LBJ's brother Sam Houston Johnson while he drank himself to death. In the early eighties the lounge off the art-deco lobby was also home to Austin's burgeoning nouveau country scene, and it hosted regular performances by Nancy Griffith, Joe Ely, and Butch Hancock. These artists weren't exactly Lester's bottle of Romilar, but he was closer to being in his element.

Barber watched him set his typewriter on the rickety old desk in his room. This was the sort of place where Hemingway would write, Lester said. "He said no one had ever done anything so nice for him before," Barber recalled. "He held court there, and the rest of the story was he had groupies and parties and was just a cool dude around town. I didn't really see a lot more of him during the time he was in Austin."

Long an oasis of creative freethinkers, Austin was just starting to be recognized as one of the country's strongest regional music scenes. The beer and the cover charges were cheap, and there was live music everywhere. Country, blues, rock, jazz, and Mexican conjunto and mariachi music competed for an audience at some forty clubs, many of them little more than a tent thrown up over a small wooden platform for a stage.

The New Wave scene revolved around Raul's north of the Alamo Hotel near the University of Texas campus. The club hosted touring stars such as Patti Smith and Elvis Costello as well as local groups such as the Big Boys, the Huns, and the Standing Waves. "There was this kind of buzz going around—'Lester Bangs is coming to town!'—and everybody was waiting for him to show up," said Standing Waves manager Roland Swenson. "I went down to Raul's and I was talking to some friends. Somebody said, 'Did Lester Bangs ever show?' And somebody else said, 'Yeah, that's him over there.' And there he was, puking in the parking lot."

Carrasco and the Crowns were out of town when Lester arrived, but he had no trouble finding other willing tour guides. Margaret Moser managed several bands, led a gang of groupies called the Texas Blondes, and penned the ubiquitous rock-club graffiti, "Margaret Loves John Cale." Under the pseudonym Babs Modern, E. A. Srere wrote an acerbic gossip column for the punk fanzine *Sluggo!* Kathleen Barbaro was a smart and pretty freelance writer. "I had worshipped Lester from afar as a rock critic, and one day Ed Ward called me up and said, 'I have Lester Bangs here,'" Moser recalled. She and Srere picked Lester up at Ward's house, then hit Barbaro's place in search of speed.

"Kathleen and Lester and I packed ourselves off into her bathroom," Moser said, "and within about four hours of meeting one of the rock critics that I had worshipped and admired, I was shooting him up with speed, looking into his sweaty face, and thinking, 'This is a moment I'll remember forever.' You know, it's kind of a dubious thing, but that was the way it was back then."

"Margaret brought Lester over to my house, and we did drugs," Barbaro said. "That was like a two-day extravaganza, and then I went over to the Alamo and picked him up to hang out. He talked endlessly, a million miles a minute. He just spilled his guts about his mother and everything from the day that I met him—'We may as well start with the day I was born'—and he was like that the whole time. I remember when I picked him up, he'd been with a hooker the night before, and he was very remorseful about that."

True to form, Lester fell in love with Barbaro. She gently discouraged him, and he settled for friendship. "The stories of Lester in Austin are that he was rampaging, but I just didn't see it," Barbaro said. "He was pretty much an extremist when it came to drugs: If he started doing them, he would do them. But it seems to me that he was always more or less trying *not* to do them. He seemed more and more to be moving away from it."

To Lester, the Austin music scene was devoid of the jaded cynicism that infested the scene back home. "Even though everybody keeps telling me it's stagnant I knew as soon as I hit town that Austin has plenty more vitality re New Wave music and the attendant scene than New York," he wrote in an account of his trip. "Walked into Raul's the first night and there were all these kids dancing, having (especially for New Wave) relatively unself-conscious fun in the old style. Nobody trying to look or be sleazy. Nobody on junk. Didn't see all that many who even looked like *Rocky Horror Picture Show* alumni. Relatively little posing. Just kids out looking for kicks, and not so all-fired worried about how hip they look in the process."

The first time he called John Morthland, he was ecstatic. "It had an unreal quality to it because Lester was saying, 'Everything's different now,' but he'd only been gone a few days," Morthland said. "Really everything wasn't different. He was just in a different place."

In Austin,1980.
PHOTO BY ELLEN GIBBS

After about a week Lester checked out of the Alamo. He hadn't been an ideal guest—there were noise complaints stemming from the cheap guitar and amp that Billy Gibbons gave him—and a story circulated that he had been kicked out. "It was really something when you were too low-down for the low-down Alamo," Margaret Moser said. Actually Lester left because he was lonely. He had always preferred crashing with friends to staying at a hotel, and he gladly accepted an offer to move into what everybody called the Contempo House.

Contempo Culture was a photocopied fanzine that incorporated music, art, politics, and humor. In one issue a photo montage of Barbie demonstrating methods of birth control followed a satirical dig at Ronald Reagan and a question-and-answer interview with Joe "King" Carrasco. Editor Stewart Wise and three friends shared a three-bedroom bungalow on Eighteenth Street near the University of Texas. Wise read about Lester's arrival in Ed Ward's column in the *Austin American-Statesman*, and he told his roommates that he'd love to meet him.

Cheryl Gant wasn't familiar with Lester's work, but she bumped into him at Raul's and invited him home. Lester enthusiastically followed, unaware that Gant was a lesbian. "I came home and I was astonished because Lester Bangs was in my living room," Wise said. "I was also kind of heartbroken, because he looked like he was really sick. He smelled horrible and he was sweating like crazy, even though we had the AC on."

The roommates invited Lester to stay. He claimed the living-room couch as his own, piled his clothes in the dormant fireplace, and adopted *Contempo Culture* as a pet project. He contributed drawings, a story about noise-rockers DNA, and a stream-of-consciousness rant called "Trapped by the Mormons" to the fanzine's fourth issue, and he guest-edited issue number five, soliciting contributions from his friends Richard C. Walls, Rex Weiner, Joey Ramone, and Mary Harron. "He was writing stories and editing my stuff, and it was like a dream come true," Wise said. Unfortunately he was also charging hundreds of dollars in long-distance phone calls and drawing a nonstop parade of visitors to the house. "It was fun at first—a party for the first week or two—but then it got to become pretty horrible," Wise said.

Lester showered only three or four times during a ten-week stay, but his hosts conned him into skinny-dipping in the pool next door whenever he got too ripe. When he went off for a weekend of fishing and hunting with Billy Gibbons, they hauled his clothes to the Laundromat, making a big show of carrying his socks with a pair of barbecue tongs.

Gibbons thought up the weekend excursion near the Mexican border to give Lester a taste of "the real Texas." They set out accompanied by Gretchen Barber and music-store-owner Mark Erlewine, who built guitars for ZZ Top, the Eagles, and the Rolling Stones. They started with a foray to Matamoros, where everyone loaded up on cheap sombreros and bottles of tequila in the shape of guitars, guns, and horseshoes. Lester also scored a handful of black-market Darvon.

Crossing back into the United States, they boarded a small boat to try their luck in South Bay before hitting the Gulf of Mexico. Lester wore a pair of plaid Bermuda shorts and a *Punk* magazine T-shirt. As soon as they dropped their lines, he started blasting a mix tape that Robert Quine had given him. "We might do a little better if we hold off on the music until we hit shore," the guide suggested. Lester turned off the tape player, and within seconds he had a strike.

"This line was going for it," Gibbons said. "Lester could barely see, much less reel it in, so we had to put our arms around him and clamp onto this bay rod. Normally you don't find great fighting fish in the bay, but there was a big, feisty, God-knows-what on the end of the line, and it gave us a run for our money. He boated the damn thing, and Gretchen still has a picture of Lester with this shit-eating grin holding his catch in one hand and a bottle of tequila in the other. We called it 'Punk Fish.' "

The group checked into two condo units at an exclusive country club on South Padre Island. Barber and Gibbons took one suite, while Erlewine paired off with Lester in the other. Lester promptly phoned room service and ordered a hammer. A befuddled bellhop brought the tool to the door, and Erlewine watched as Lester used it to crack open the plastic shells of a half dozen nasal inhalers. He swallowed the ephedrine-coated wicks and stayed up speeding all night, flipping channels on the TV, cranking music on his Walkman, and chowing down on corn chips and bean dip.

Erlewine tried to ignore the ruckus and get some sleep, but when Lester started flicking bean dip at him, he decided he'd had enough. He got up and punched the noisy son of a bitch. "He didn't think anything of it," Erlewine said. "I really couldn't tell if he was trying to get a rise out of me or if he was just that screwed up."

The next morning everybody donned matching Gibbons-issued hunting fatigues—"One of Billy's things is that the group always has to look good," Barber said—climbed into a four-wheel-drive truck, and headed into Brazos Island State Park. They lined up behind a crowd of hunters at the height of dove season. A group of somber game wardens checked their licenses. The guide had all their paperwork in order, but Lester didn't look right, and the wardens thought they smelled tequila on his breath.

"Y'ever seen a gun before, suh?" one of them asked. Lester smiled. "Maybe not this long, but I'm from New York," he said. "I see a lot of guns!"

"Man, that cracked them up," Gibbons said. "The game guy said, 'Well, it's maybe a little different than what you see up there in Manhattan, but that'll do. Next!' "

Out in the field the guide loaded Lester's rifle. "When these birds start flying, it's gonna get wild, and I want you to be ready," he said. "Fire off a few rounds just so you get the feel of the kick on this damn thing." As the guide turned to load another gun, Lester shouldered his and took aim at a beer bottle sitting near a row of bushes in the distance. There was a faint muttering from that direction, and the guide turned back to see Lester taking dead aim at a blind. He slammed the barrel to the ground a split second before Lester shot another hunter in the back.

The resulting tension took a while to dissipate, but the mood lightened when everybody started bagging some birds. Lester imitated a hound, running through the tall grass with a dove between his teeth. That night they grilled their catch using the guide's special barbecue sauce, and they polished off what was left of the tequila. "I had a blast," Gibbons said. "Can't speak for Erlewine. The guide, he was kind of removed from it—we were gonna be out of his hair in twenty-four hours—so he just rolled with it. Gretchen had already had her introduction to Lester up in New York, so she was just laughing. But from my perspective, my time with Lester was a gift."

Lester started searching for musical collaborators the moment he arrived in Austin. His experience with Birdland had convinced him to recruit guests specifically for the project, as he had done for his single. "This thing of having a band and you play together and play together and then you go in to record and you hate the songs—I just don't want to do that," he said in 1982. He began auditioning musicians during jam sessions in Margaret Moser's living room, but then he heard a group called the Delinquents.

The Delinquents were a New Wave garage band with hints of surf and country influences. Their initial claim to fame was a DIY release called "Alien Beach Party" that had been selected as a Single of the Week by the *New Musical Express*. Singer Layna Pogue, the daughter of Skylab astronaut Bill Pogue, quit shortly thereafter. When Lester got to town, a reconfigured quintet led by bassist Brian Curley was playing a Thursday-night residency at Duke's Royal Coach Inn on Congress Street. The group was midway through its set one night when Curley looked down and saw a drunk hauling a table onto the middle of the dance floor. The guy proceeded to drink pitcher after pitcher of beer, hooting and hollering in between every song. By the end of the night he was dancing on top of the table.

"After our second set I was standing at the bar and I saw this guy coming toward me," Curley said. "I was like: 'Oh, God, another fucking drunken fart to deal with.' He came up to me and went, 'I'm Lester Bangs. Do you know who I am?'" A devoted Deadhead, Curley remembered a 1971 article in which Lester declared that he didn't merely dislike the Grateful Dead, he *hated* them. "Yeah, I know who you are," Curley told him. "I think you're a fucking asshole!" Lester put his arm around the musician's shoulder. "You and I are going to be great friends," he said.

Curley had been trying to make it as a musician ever since he ran away from home in New Mexico at the age of fourteen. The Delinquents had never been the most popular group in Austin, but Lester loved them and decided to make them his backing band. The move caused resentment among many of the musicians who'd jammed with him and hoped to play on his record. As he had with Mickey Leigh, Lester sang his lyrics a cappella to Curley and Delinquents guitarist Andy Fuertsch, and the musicians matched them to chord patterns and arrangements. The group tightened the songs onstage, ushering Lester out after its regular set with a James Brown–style vamp called "You Can't Sing." The band played about a dozen gigs in October and November 1980, making road trips to Dallas, Fort Worth, and San Antonio, as well as performing around Austin.

On Halloween Lester and the Delinquents played a party at a University of Texas frat house. While the band did its usual opening set, Lester swallowed the wicks from several nasal inhalers and washed them down with a bottle of cough medicine. "When they finally called me up onstage to start singing my songs, I of course was in no condition," he wrote, "but through some transference of memory and association was seeing traumatic rooms of my childhood and came on or at least felt like this tragic stricken gloomy poetic young soul who obviously was just too sensitive to live. The whole Byronic romantic-agony shtick, with palpable overlay of skid row. Cute, eh? The frats didn't care. They loved us, and why shouldn't they? We were the geek show."

The night ended with a chaotic version of "Louie Louie," which had been enshrined as the ultimate frat-party anthem by *Animal House*. As Lester sang, he fancied himself part Van Morrison and part Iggy Stooge, playing with the phrasing and twisting the famously garbled lyrics on every pass: "I sailed a ship across the sea/A fine little girl waiting for me / On the ship I dreamed she there / Smelled aroma . . . the roses . . . the Romilar . . . down in her hair." He had no delusions about the quality of his performance. "No doubt I sucked," he wrote. "Nobody cared. In fact they were in ecstasy. So who knows, maybe I didn't suck. Which just might be the essence of Frat Existence and Philosophy: Hey, you, World—I DON'T SUCK, GODDAMMIT!!!!!"

With the Delinquents at Club Foot: Mindy Curley, Lester,
Rebecca Bickham, Halsey Taylor, Andy Fuertsch, Brian Curley.
PHOTO BY MICHELLE LEVINAS, COURTESY BRIAN CURLEY

On November 21 the band played a more prestigious show opening for the Talking Heads at the Armadillo World Headquarters, Austin's version of the famous Fillmore West. Every New Wave band in town wanted the gig, but Lester landed it with one phone call to the Heads' manager, Gary Kurfurst. Unfortunately November 21 was also the night that *Dallas* revealed who shot J.R., one of the most widely watched episodes in TV history. Even his friends Kathleen Barbaro and Stewart Wise stayed home in front of the tube. The handful that made it to the show on time were less than enthusiastic. "The Delinquents were never any good, and now they were the Delinquents with Lester in front of them," Ed Ward said. "I remember that it was fairly horrible." Many of the punks thought Lester was trying to antagonize them by wearing an Izod polo shirt, a symbol of the frats who often tormented them, and some of them booed and gave the finger.

Two weeks later the Delinquents entered Austin's Earth and Sky Studios. Lester recorded eleven songs in sixteen hours, in between sessions for the band's own album. Curley paid for and oversaw the recordings, but after his experience with Jay Dee Daugherty on "Let It Blurt," Lester was wary of the word "producer." The album credits would read,

"Produced by Lester Bangs and Brian Curley (according to Brian). Produced by nobody. Producers suck (according to Lester)."

Several songs on the album dated from the Birdland era. Lester gave Mickey Leigh co-writing credit for "I'm in Love with My Walls" and "Accidents of God," but "Fade Away" and "Kill Him Again" had become completely different tunes. The latter was particularly powerful in its new incarnation, thanks to Fuertsch's edgy, Quine–like guitar. Of the newer songs, "Life Is Not Worth Living (But Suicide's a Waste of Time)" was an exercise in what Lester dubbed "No-Wave country," with lyrics attacking the Richard Hell philosophy of punk ("You call yourself a nihilist / Because you've read Céline / Put cigarettes out on your wrist / You still won't be James Dean"). "Legless Bird" was a party tune that rewrote the immortal "Surfin' Bird," while "Nuclear War" chronicled the travails of members of the JoAnn Uhelszki crowd over a rollicking Farfisa-driven groove.

Lester took special pride in his butter-knife slide guitar on "I Just Want to Be a Movie Star," a country blues about a pathetic drunk. "I'm so tired of sleeping under this bar / I just wanna be a movie star," he howled. At Quine's suggestion the Delinquents covered "Grandma's House" by Dale Hawkins, but Lester added new lyrics that turned the song from a woodsy idyll into a sinister story of a serial killer. The album ended with the song that led to Lester's ouster from Birdland, "Give Up the Ghost," but the penultimate track was by far the most striking tune. Over a Velvets-style musical backing, "Day of the Dead" explored Lester's relationship with his mother, how it affected his dealings with women, and how he was still haunted twenty-three years later by the day she turned to him in the car and told him of his father's death.

The lyrics are one of the few times Lester directly addressed his relationship with his mother in print; in conversation, he was often ambiguous about his feelings for her. "He was always talking about his mother and values and morals and the lack thereof," said Delinquents' guitarist Rebecca Bickham. "It was a sick kind of a relationship, but at the same time I think it was very loving. I think she was a very strong figure in his life. He would just kind of change when we talked about her and the Jehovah's Witnesses. The album cover—the Jesus Christ woman with the thorns—that's Lester to me, suffering and taking the passion to the extreme."

Curley decided to release both Lester's album and the Delinquents' own on the band's Live Wire Records label; for cover art Lester chose a haunting charcoal sketch titled "Woman in Anguish" by a Spanish artist named Annantes that he'd seen hanging in the apartment of a friend who

Cover art for *Jook Savages on the Brazos*.

was a prostitute. During the recording Lester compiled a list of potential album titles, including *Executions on TV, Ghosts Don't Know No Better, Adoration of the Miscreant, How to Spit on Eden, Jook Savages of Fourteenth Street,* and *Jook Savages on the Brazos*. The latter won out.

At Lester's request Nick Tosches contributed the liner notes. Tosches had written some notes for country outlaw Delbert McClinton which had never been used. He substituted Lester's name and hometown of El Cajon for McClinton's name and hometown of Fort Worth and handed them to his pal. Lester told him they suited him perfectly and Tosches really understood what he was all about.

On the last day of mixing, Lester sat in the studio with the Delinquents and listened to the finished album. Flushed with pride, he grinned broadly. "I'm gonna go back to New York and kill myself so you guys can become rich and famous rock stars," he said.

· · ·

In between the excitement of the recording sessions Lester followed the headlines, ranting at the news as it unfolded in late 1980. In a landslide win that November, Ronald Reagan was elected fortieth President of the

United States. When the Moral Majority claimed victory on the evening news, Lester hurled obscenities at the television. Reagan reminded him of the character Andy Griffith played in Elia Kazan's 1957 film, *A Face in the Crowd*—a malevolent demagogue "who through the usual ministrations of mighty media gets 'discovered' twangin' on a geetar and singin' his folksy ole noble savage heart out."

A few weeks later, on December 8, Mark David Chapman shot John Lennon five times outside the Dakota Apartments in New York. Spurred by radio's constant playings of "Imagine" and commentators' characterizations of the former Beatle as "a rock 'n' roll martyr," Lester sat down the next morning and pounded out a piece for the Opinion section of the *Los Angeles Times*, one of the few articles he wrote while in Texas. "I don't know which is more pathetic," he railed, "the people of my generation who refuse to let their 1960s adolescence die a natural death, or the younger ones who will snatch and gobble any shred, any scrap of a dream that someone declared over ten years ago."

Lennon was just "a guy," Lester argued—one who despised cheap sentiment—and his fans' refusal to accept that was ultimately as deadly as the assassin's bullets.

Oddly enough, the incident contributed to Lester's growing homesickness. "I'd open up *The New Yorker* and see what's going on at the Thalia and all this," he said. He had begun to sour on Austin midway through his stay when a three-day binge landed him in the drunk tank. He emerged from jail to tell everyone within shouting distance that Texas was a fascist police state. A short time later, he was asked to move out of the Contempo House. "Everyone felt real protective of Lester," Stewart Wise said, "and that's why it was real hard for us to ask him to leave, but it was either that or all of the roommates would wind up hating each other."

Lester crashed with Brian Curley for a while before linking up with a fun-loving divorcée named Veronica Sullivan. Her white nurse's uniform struck him as the sexiest thing he'd ever seen. "Lester liked me because I wasn't real impressionable and I didn't know who he was," she said. "He kept asking me, 'Don't you know who I am?' And I'd say, 'No, why don't you tell me?'" Lester fell in love, but once again it wasn't reciprocated. "He truly loved me," Sullivan said. "We never slept with each other, although we did sleep in the same bed because my house was so cold. He was a little bit too chubby for me, but I could tell that if I wanted anything more, he'd be up for it. Mainly I enjoyed his company and he enjoyed mine. I think he knew I had more of a sense of stability, even though I was flaky. He was not wanting to do drugs anymore, but he would say it was hard to not do them. He knew that it wasn't good for him. He would just talk about stuff and I would listen: 'Women don't love me enough; people don't love me enough; I'm so good.' He'd say, 'People suck the life out of me. They take everything. I have nothing left!' Then he'd talk about people he did business with: 'I can't do anything more for them. They want me to give them my blood. I feel like Jesus Christ!' "

By Thanksgiving, 1980, *Jook Savages on the Brazos* was finished. Lester was flat broke, and he'd worn out his welcome in many corners of Austin. "Everybody was fed up with him," Sullivan said. "He'd made some enemies in town." Tapes in hand, he flew home shortly before Christmas and headed straight from the airport to John Morthland's place. The only thing his friend had to drink was a bottle of cheap cooking wine, and Lester downed it. "He was definitely not in real good shape," Morthland said. "His hands were shaking, and I don't remember ever seeing his hands shake before."

All My Friends
Are Hermits

"Hi, my name is Lester Bangs," he said, shifting his weight nervously from one foot to the other. "I'm a drug addict and an alcoholic." They were right—saying it felt good. Only later, over stale danish, cigarettes, and Styrofoam cups of coffee, did someone approach and gingerly explain that *here* he was only Lester, not *"Lester Bangs."*

Through the first few weeks of 1981 Lester raged out of control. "When he came back to New York, that was the worst I had ever seen him," said Robert Quine, echoing the comments of many of Lester's friends. Ma Bell cut off his phone because he couldn't pay the long-distance bills from Texas, so the familiar late-night calls to his buddies became history. CBGB had lost its allure, and the Bells of Hell had closed in late 1979, victim in part to the tabs that its owners never collected. Increasingly Lester did his drinking and drugging while sitting home alone.

Lester's insomnia was the worst since the Romilar funk of 1968, and when he did sleep, he was troubled by a recurring nightmare. "I can take a nightmare with bodies getting hacked up and the world getting blown to bits," he said, "but my worst nightmare is I'm back in El Cajon. I'm back in school. I'm never going to graduate, and I'm living in my mother's house. I want to get back to New York, but I have no money. I'm stranded. There's a 7-Eleven and nothin' else, and it just goes on and on in dull nothingness. Those are the worst nightmares—stranded back there and *not writing*."

Two incidents seem to have convinced Lester that he needed help. One morning he woke up on the sidewalk around the corner from his apartment. "He had been sleeping in the street like a bum," said his friend Kathy Miller. "He told me, 'This is it. I'm not drinking anymore.'" A short time later his next-door neighbor, Robert Duncan, brought him some troubling news. Lester and Duncan had stopped speaking—tired of his excessive behavior, Duncan was no longer willing to carry him up the stairs or otherwise abet his self-destruction—but when he got the call from Detroit, he felt compelled to tell his old friend and co-worker that *Creem* publisher Barry Kramer had died. "Lester was shocked and saddened," Duncan said. "I remember thinking to myself, 'All the shit he rants and raves about Kramer . . . ,' but his mouth fell open and he just sort of sighed."

For the past year Kramer had been struggling through a bitter divorce. The publisher of America's second-largest rock magazine was living in the Birmingham House Motel, not far from *Creem*'s offices. Early on the morning of January 29, 1981, he called a female friend and asked her to bring him a pack of cigarettes. She arrived to find his body slumped in a sitting position on the floor, a plastic bag on his head and notes for future covers scattered nearby. Paramedics pronounced him dead on the scene at the age of thirty-seven. Four days later the coroner ruled it an accidental suicide. Police had found several vials of prescription pills in addition to the canister of nitrous oxide that Kramer was inhaling through the plastic bag.

"When Barry was alive and the magazine was extremely viable, people could have had a wonderful life," Kramer's friend Harvey Zuppke said in 1997. "We envisioned that there would be a publishing house, and maybe we'd be doing today's *Wired* magazine. We all saw it as the beginning of a unique opportunity for a group of people who could maybe see the future better than other people." In 1981 *Creem*'s former associate publisher sat shivah with Kramer's family. Zuppke asked Connie Kramer what he could do to help, and the widow asked him to return to the magazine. He quit his job at New York's *Guitar World* and moved back to Birmingham. Connie became the titular publisher in trust for her son J. J., but Zuppke and ever-reliable art director Charlie Auringer spent the next few years actually running the magazine.

Creem did not founder commercially or editorially after Lester's departure. The circulation hovered around two hundred thousand, and though letter-writers bemoaned the loss of the former star, his influence continued to infuse the features and record reviews. Editors Susan Whitall and Billy Altman published many of the writers Lester had mentored, while the core of the staff in the early to mid-eighties—Dave DiMartino, Bill Holdship, and John Kordosh—grew up reading Lester's *Creem* as if it were the Bible. Irreverent as ever, the magazine's humor changed with the times, becoming more glib and ironic. Staff writer Rick Johnson became "the new Lester," and he garnered almost as much mail. The secret of his sarcastic and funny prose was that he walked around with a stack of index cards, jotting down weird phrases and quips whenever he heard them, then shuffling through the deck while writing his reviews until he found the appropriate one-liners.

The impact of Barry Kramer's death on Lester is hard to gauge. He did not write about it, and after the conversation with Duncan, he didn't discuss it with any of his friends, including *Creem* veteran John Morthland. But two things happened shortly thereafter. The magazine reappeared on the lists of freelance markets that he kept in his notebooks under the heading "Asse(t)s," and he began to attend Alcoholics Anonymous.

Lester had tried to clean up on his own many times during the past fourteen years. Some of his efforts lasted months, and some didn't make it through the end of the day. He had addressed his substance abuse with his therapist in Birmingham and again with Phil Sapienza, but he heard only what he wanted to hear. Lester told his friend Richard Meltzer that Sapienza actually *encouraged* him to drink because he wouldn't be as good a writer if he stopped. "Both my shrinks, especially this guy, they had real great humanist compassion and empathy and all that, but I know what both of 'em did, and in the long run in essence they were no good for me, because they were getting off on me being there," Lester said. "It's like they're so bored, one housewife after another: 'I don't love my husband; I don't know why.' Then they get someone like you or I that's actually interesting, that has ideas, and so it's fun time for 'em. I mean, if I hadda follow this guy's advice, I'd be *dead* pretty soon."

Sapienza said he advised Lester to stop drinking in the same manner that he suggested his patient approach his relationships with women and his desire to write a novel: Be realistic and abandon the usual all-or-nothing assault. But Lester seemed unable to do anything in moderation.

Nick Tosches recalled an evening at an Indian restaurant on Carmine Street. "During dinner, we began talking about drinking," Tosches wrote. "Lester was on the wagon. He began interrogating our companion, who was sipping a glass of wine, asking her how she could possibly be satisfied by that mere glass of wine. 'Don't you want oblivion?' he asked in all sincerity and earnest."

In the spring of 1981 Lester called Jim Fouratt. An impish Irishman with a shaggy blond mane, Fouratt had grown up in Rhode Island, joined and left the priesthood in the sixties, and became an actor, a Yippie, a gay-rights activist, and a perpetual player in the music business. He and Lester met in Detroit when Fouratt came out to caucus with John Sinclair's Rainbow People's Party. They continued to run into each other through the years when Fouratt worked as a publicist at Columbia Records, then again when he managed the New Wave discos Hurrah and Danceteria. Since 1979 he had succeeded in staying sober and active in the rock world, and he became Lester's sponsor at AA.

"I don't think there was much support around him," Fouratt said. "There was that ethic of rock 'n' roll and wild living, and he had his own reputation to live up to. He was '*Lester fuckin' Bangs*.' People who are not addicts can take a little of this, a little of that, but addicts can't. He was having a real hard time admitting that. That's what happens, and people die. I'm not romantic about it. I just couldn't get through my stupid little head why we people *have* to die. I said that I wasn't going to take control of Lester's recovery, I was just going to be there for him."

Though he tried hard to stay straight, Lester sometimes slipped. For the next year he could appear to be Mr. Rogers one day and Johnny Thunders the next. "During those last few months, if I didn't hear from him for three or four days, I knew that he was on a bender," Morthland said. "When he would get off it, he would call and he would be even more remorseful than the last time: 'Oh, God, I can't believe I did this. I feel so terrible.' Then he would go for like a month being really clean. It's real common for people to not succeed at quitting on their first try, or even sometimes on their tenth try." But Morthland took it as a positive sign that Lester picked himself up and kept trying.

The second of AA's twelve steps is that the alcoholic believe in a power greater than himself to restore him to sobriety. This aspect of the program disturbed Lester. He had escaped the shackles of religious dogma once, and he didn't want to be imprisoned again. "People have a hard time when they see all that God crap," Fouratt said. Many return to

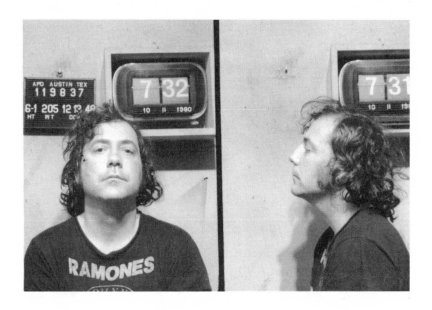

Bottoming out: Lester's Austin mug shot.
PHOTO COURTESY MARGARET MOSER

the religion of their youth, but AA literature allows the individual to determine how "God" is defined. While Lester was opposed to organized religion, he was also deeply spiritual, and he could have decided that music or literature was his higher power. "There is something spiritual about an art museum or a symphony," reads a testimonial written by a Jesuit in the so-called big book. "There is something spiritual about AA, too."

In the mid-1980s the wake-up call of AIDs and the ravages of cocaine addiction would prompt a wave of musicians, artists, and writers joining twelve-step programs, but there were already several special AA meetings geared toward New York's hip subcultures in 1981. Fouratt took Lester to the Village for the "rock 'n' roll meeting," which happened to be the same one that Lou Reed attended.

Reed had released his thirteenth solo album, *Growing Up in Public*, in 1980. It boasted a snide song called "The Power of Positive Drinking," but a short time later the musician launched his own attempt to change his life and shake his old persona. On Valentine's Day, 1980, he married Sylvia Morales, a punk scenester he met at CBGB. In 1981 he joined Narcotics and Alcoholics Anonymous. He began chronicling the difficult battle to sober up in harrowing new tunes such as "Underneath the

Bottle" and "Waves of Fear," and he formed a new group centered on his fan and Lester's friend, guitarist Robert Quine. Many critics considered it his best band since the Velvet Underground, but even at New York's rock 'n' roll AA meeting, Reed could still be too hip for the room.

"How dare you be here—you're the reason I took heroin!" a fellow addict once charged. Lester didn't think that was fair, but he and Reed did not speak. What was there to say? In Peter Laughner's obituary Lester vowed never to write about Reed again. He broke that promise only once over the course of five years and five albums, reviewing *The Bells* for *Rolling Stone* in June 1979, and dedicating the critique to Laughner.

"Everybody always talks about the poor homeless orphan waifs, but what about the homeless fathers? The time has come to call the fathers home from the stale curbstone shores," Lester wrote. "Lou Reed is a prick and a jerkoff who frequently commits the ultimate sin of treating his audience with contempt. He's also a person with deep compassion for a great many other people about whom almost nobody else gives a shit. I won't say who they are, because I don't want to get too schmaltzy, except to emphasize that there's always been more to this than drugs and fashionable kicks, and to point out that suffering, loneliness, and psychic/spiritual exile are great levelers."

Through 1981 and into 1982 AA was part of an overall effort by Lester to change his life. He spoke more often and more empathetically of his mother, he decided to open himself up to the blues (which he'd never much cared for), and he made a concerted effort to try to live healthier. Things like the Christmas tree decorated with Romilar bottles didn't seem quite so funny anymore.

For the last few years he had suffered from chronic bronchial infections—friends such as Kathy Miller and Fran Pelzman were forever running over with chicken soup and herbal tea—and now he demanded that his landlord fix the heat. Other ideas were more misguided. In lieu of booze he started drinking Ramblin' root beer; he loved the name as well as the taste and could guzzle two sixty-four-ounce bottles at a sitting. The other staples of his new "healthy" diet were Stouffer's spinach soufflés and frozen yogurt. "Lester, the only thing good about yogurt is that it has living organisms in it that help you," Quine told him. "If it's frozen, you've *killed* them all."

Lester started talking about the idea that age is cooler than youth, a radical notion in rock 'n' roll. "While not as old as I'd like to be (though I

pass sometimes) I've been hep to this primacy of age business for years,"
he wrote, "ever since I first realized that Uncle Scrooge, Charles
Bukowski, and Malcolm Muggeridge were all cooler than almost any
rock star I could think of." Of course, in order to grow old you had to take
care of yourself. Pelzman was always stuffing the pockets of his rotting
cashmere coat with cans of tuna and boxes of raisins so he'd have something in his apartment to eat. In a letter in January 1981 he thanked her
for the gesture but chastised himself for necessitating it.

"Dammit, I'm thirty-two fucking years old and shouldn't need a
bunch of baby-sitters to see that I stay healthy, wealthy, and creative if
not wise just because I'm a 'genius' or some such shit as that," Lester
wrote. "I hate that kind of shit, that whole 'ze great artiste genius idiot savant who must be taken care of so he can create his masterworks un-
bothered by the paltry concerns of the everyday peons' bullshit. I've seen
it a million times in people with boundless talent and no-talent poseurs,
in Lou Reed and Patti Smith and Captain Beefheart and Chrissie Hynde
and Charles Bukowski and Hunter Thompson and Jack Kerouac and all
the Ramones and just about every musician as well as most of the writers I've ever met. . . . Of course such a state of being inevitably culmi-
nates in literal physical death, usually at an early age. So FUCK IT.
Everybody believes it because they think it's romantic but it's not romantic, it's a bunch of cheap bullshit and it'd be a much better world with
more and better art if we got rid of it forever."

By 1981 the company that packaged *Blondie* had become an actual publisher, Delilah Books, an imprint of G. P. Putnam's Sons. Lester encouraged his friend Paul Nelson to pitch a project to editor Karen Moline.
She rejected his idea for a book on Jackson Browne but encouraged him
to write about Rod Stewart, whom Nelson had come to know during his
days at Mercury. The singer had recently abandoned the gutsy R&B of
the Faces and his early solo career to score vapid hits such as "Hot Legs"
and "D'Ya Think I'm Sexy?" Nelson had panned these sounds in *Rolling
Stone*, but he agreed to write the book.

Stewart refused to cooperate, and Nelson hit the worst writer's block
of his career. "The Nelson book was not a happy time, because Mr. Nelson had a deadline problem—he couldn't meet one," Moline said. The
publishers weren't sympathetic. The book had to be done while Stewart

was hot, and if Nelson couldn't deliver it, someone else would fill the space between the photos.

"Lester bailed me out on it basically," Nelson said. Signing on as co-author, Lester wrote eighty-eight pages in one weekend compared to Nelson's five. When it was published in the fall of 1981, *Rod Stewart* included two chapters by Nelson and five chapters, a preface, and an epilogue by Lester, but Lester nevertheless insisted that Nelson's name precede his own.

For the most part the two men worked separately, though Nelson thought they ought to collaborate on one chapter. Lester disliked writing with other people; "You can't think because you're always talking," he said. Nelson suggested that they simply chat for the benefit of the tape recorder. "I don't think either one of us thought we did much of anything, but that chapter's one of my favorite things I've ever been involved in," Nelson said. The conversation ran verbatim under the title "Two Jewish Mothers Pose as Rock Critics," and it was indeed the highlight of the book, a freewheeling, wide-ranging look into two sharp and funny critical minds.

Lester also had a contract with Delilah for another collaboration with his old friend Michael Ochs. The project originated in 1978, shortly after Ochs left record-company publicity to start a rock 'n' roll photo service. Based in Venice Beach, California, the Michael Ochs Archives licensed rare publicity shots and album covers to magazines, publishers, advertising agencies, and anyone else who'd pay for the images. Whenever he dealt with a publisher, Ochs pitched an idea for a photo book featuring the highlights of his collection. A company that compiled mail-order cassettes bought the project for $10,000, and Ochs gave half of it to Lester to write the text.

"Every time we talked, we'd say, 'We've got to do that book someday,' " Ochs said, "and it was always: 'When things slow down' or 'When I get off alcohol.' "

In 1980 Lester wrote a new book proposal with the hope of scoring a more lucrative contract. The title *Rock Gomorrah* nodded to Kenneth Anger's underground classic, *Hollywood Babylon*, and Lester described the tome as a collection of "every verifiable incidence of pig-fucking in the twenty-five-year history of rock 'n' roll." The oral history would compile in one place all of the best tales of bad behavior and dirty deeds from three decades of rock history, as told by its foremost raconteurs. "We are not ashamed to claim that it might be the world's ultimate bathroom reading," Lester wrote. His new agent, Keith Korman of Raines & Raines, convinced Delilah to buy the book for $25,000. Lester and Ochs repaid the original advance, split the rest of the money, and put off work for another year and a half.

In the summer of 1981 the two friends finally met in Chicago to begin doing interviews. They traveled cross-country in a rental car, sleeping on friends' couches and trying to arrange interviews on the fly. More often than not they failed to connect with their subjects. Other times they found that the outrageous stories they first heard after recording sessions or at hotel bars were repeated in a much less entertaining manner once they turned on the tape recorder. In Chicago they interviewed former Chess producer Ralph Bass and soul man Syl Johnson; in Nashville, Brenda Lee; in Memphis, producer Jim Dickinson and rockabilly guitarist Paul Burlison; and in Alabama, the famous Muscle Shoals rhythm section. Lester hadn't had a driver's license since he was arrested for drunk driving in Detroit, so Ochs spent all the time at the wheel. Lester blasted *Metal Machine Music*, Ochs played the Jaggerz, and the two interacted like lemon juice and a paper cut.

"I'm never going to be in the same car with you, the same plane with you, or the same city with you again!" Lester railed. By the time they got to New Orleans, Ochs was suffering from cluster headaches. They sat in a hotel room trying to reach Bobby Marchan, a female impersonator and the singer with Huey "Piano" Smith and the Clowns. (He was most famous for being erased from the 1959 hit "Sea Cruise" and replaced by Frankie Ford.) "We kept calling every day, and his boyfriend was like, 'He didn't come home *again* last night,'" Ochs recalled. "It was one disaster after another, and we were getting more and more frustrated, because we thought New Orleans would be the killer."

Sober throughout the trip, Lester hit the drugstore and fell off the wagon after first concocting a cure for his friend. "I always thought he missed his true calling as a pharmacist," Ochs said.

After the road trip the project took another turn for the worse when Ochs shipped Lester the interview tapes and the post office lost half of them in the mail. Lester exploded, and Ochs flew to New York so they could figure out what to do next. They divided a list of additional interviews to be done separately: Ochs with Sonny Bono, Kim Fowley, and Flo and Eddie on the West Coast, and Lester with Screamin' Jay Hawkins, Ronnie Spector, and *Astral Weeks* producer Lewis Merenstein in New York. As they hashed out their salvage plan at a diner on Fourteenth

Street, a bum at the next table keeled over and hit the floor, dead. Lester was nonplused. "It happens all the time," he said.

Work on the book dragged into 1982. Delilah grew increasingly frustrated, but the company still believed in Lester enough to discuss a collection of his articles, tentatively titled *New Wave Scrapbook*. Although he was anxious to compile his greatest hits, Lester hoped he could do better than Delilah. He had written his first proposal for an anthology in 1977, copping the title *All the Things You Could Be by Now If Iggy Pop's Wife Was Your Mother: A Book of Jive 'n' Verities* from the name of a piece by Charles Mingus. (The bassist had used "Sigmund Freud" in place of "Iggy Pop.") In February 1982 Lester completed a second proposal with an updated table of contents and a new title, *Psychotic Reactions and Carburetor Dung: Lester Bangs's Greatest Hits*.

"I edited this collection the same way I used to edit a monthly record review section: purely for style and readability," Lester wrote in a preface dated February 27, 1982. "If any kind of 'aesthetic' emerges it's due more to monomania than design. Unlike most rock books crammed with 'facts' or theoretical axes to grind, I just wanted this one to be as much fun as listening to the music." He also penned the dedication: "To Nancy, with all the love in the world."

Lester discussed this book in a letter to Greil Marcus. "You know, I've always looked up to you as a sort of father figure, all that aw shucks business," he wrote. Marcus didn't know exactly what Lester wanted him to do—"Maybe he thought I could help get it published, which I probably could have," he said—but he agreed to help in whatever capacity he was needed.

While his book projects inched forward, Lester continued freelancing to pay the rent. He rarely sought work, preferring to wait until editors approached him; then he accepted any assignment they offered, regardless of how poorly it paid. He had never had much skill at handling money, and in the spring of 1981 he wrote his friend JoAnn Uhelszki complaining that he'd been locked out of his apartment for four days because he couldn't pay the rent.

Because Lester no longer had a phone, Robert Christgau had to bike over when it came time to edit his pieces for the *Voice*. When Christgau took a sabbatical, Jon Pareles filled in, and he was amazed at how little work Lester's copy needed. "You didn't have to change a comma," Pareles said. But other editors had problems with aspects of Lester's professionalism. Ira Robbins paid double the usual fee when Lester agreed to profile the

Ramones for *Trouser Press*, but the writer sold the piece to the *New Musical Express*, and it appeared there first, scooping the magazine that had made the assignment.

Lester disliked both *Trouser Press* and *New York Rocker*, and he wrote for each of the leading New Wave journals only once. He considered them havens for the young careerists and shills for the industry, lauding bad music just because it was new or obscure. In a letter to the *Voice,* one of the *Rocker*'s editors castigated him for becoming like those crotchety old critics who disdained the innovations of Ornette Coleman's *Free Jazz.* "Unfortunately, all that cowplop you tell your readers to run out and buy every month is not some ineluctable avant-garde that threatens everybody," Lester replied. "It's a bunch of nothing that challenges no one."

So-called players' mags such as *Musician, Gig,* and *International Musician and Recording World* provided Lester with steady if unsexy work. In between the ads for synthesizers, bass strings, and fuzz boxes, he expounded on "Rock's Top Ten Guitarists" and examined the posthumous career of Jim Morrison. Jean-Charles Costa recalled Lester's coming to his office and nervously asking if he could write for *Gig.* "I wanted to get down on my knees: 'Could you write for me? What, are you shitting me?'" Costa said. "I was editing this second-rate publication! He said, 'One thing—don't make me write about Lou Reed. I'm burned out on him.' I said, 'Write about whatever the fuck you want!'"

Though several publications offered him one, Lester seemed unable to produce a regular column, which would have given him a sorely needed base income. He delivered one installment of a proposed television column for *Gig* and turned out only a handful of "Back In the U.S.A." columns for the *NME*. In late 1980 he finally fell into a regular groove with the unambitiously titled "Music" column for *Music and Sound Output,* a slick bimonthly that was part players' mag and part *Rolling Stone.* Drawing on a decade's observations and his own experiences as a musician, Lester not only deconstructed the music industry, he attempted to demolish it.

"As soon as he realized that I wasn't going to check him, Lester just seemed to let loose, and he was getting progressively angrier," editor Bill Stephen recalled. Various columns argued that touring was a nonglamorous "road to nowhere," that the old-fashioned "all-for-one, one-for-all" rock band should be rejected in favor of juxtaposing different players and songwriters, that low-tech and "less is more" were the ways to go in recording, and that the most exciting music in the future would come from local scenes far removed from music-industry hubs—he cited Austin and the Pacific Northwest as examples. The Top Forty hit "Bette Davis Eyes" prompted a rant against the insidious evils of mindless hooks, while an interview with an unnamed record-company executive illuminated how independent promoters or "hit men" influenced radio play.

"The music business was always cynical," Lester wrote in late 1981, "but the cynicism of the music business as it stands today is awesome, surreal."

His growing bitterness toward the industry didn't dampen Lester's love of musicmaking. He jammed with his friend Nancy Stillman whenever they could get together, and he sat in with anyone else who invited him. One night in late 1981 he drank a bottle of Romilar and started fooling around with a Casio keyboard. He wasn't a huge fan of Grandmaster Flash, but he thought rap music had potential. In the spirit of the South Bronx as well as his own teenage Beatnik role-playing, he filled a sixty-minute tape with improvised freestyling over the machine's preset rhythms. He also collaborated with downtown performance artist Laurie Anderson, spending hours recording long, tangled rave-ups on "Hey Joe." One day Anderson played him a song of her own called "O Superman," but Lester told her it was no good because there weren't any people in it.

Released in late 1981, *Jook Savages on the Brazos* slowly filtered into record stores via the independent distributor JEM. Brian Curley had been able to press only a thousand copies. Of those he sent fifty to Lester and about a hundred to reviewers. Robert Christgau gave it a "B+," the same grade he awarded *Blank Generation* by Richard Hell, *The Bells* by Lou Reed, *Wave* by Patti Smith, and *End of the Century* by the Ramones.

"I'm real proud of it, but it's funny getting all these reviews now," Lester wrote his friend Richard Riegel in February 1982. "Except for a couple of them it feels the same reading the reviews that say it's great ('masterpiece,' one said), the reviews that say it's dog shit (*NME*, etc.), and the reviews in between." Quine gave a copy of the album to Lou Reed, and it made Lester's month when he heard that Reed liked it. But his favorite comment came from a review by Rick Johnson: "This album features a type of songwriting which, if it were a prison or an insane asylum, would be classified as *seriously understaffed.*"

One night in the spring of 1981 Lester, Kathy Miller, and five or six other women sat around the living room of an apartment in a midtown high-rise. The phones were dead. As usual the conversation turned to work, so Lester switched on his tape recorder. From the beginning the women had been incredibly receptive to his project. Usually he didn't even have to ask a question before they took off running about their experiences as hookers.

"People these days have these ideals like everything is perfect about sex or perfect about your partner," Lester said. "So as a result you're totally unsatisfied all the time."

"How long does it take them to wise up?" asked Vera, a forty-year-old Communist who became a prostitute to pay the medical bills when her husband had a stroke.

"I don't know, but *Charlie's Angels* is on TV, this totally plastic ideal of sexuality," Lester said. "Because of things like that I think a lot of people think something is happening somewhere—some wonderful sexual ideal—and it doesn't include them." He changed the subject. "You were talking about guys who were jerks," he said. "I've heard you girls say that a john is a john is a john. Sooner or later do they all act like this? Do they get trickified?"

"A john is a man is a person," said Gail, a big-boned girl from Ohio whom the others ribbed for being a sex change (she wasn't). "A trick is a trick is a trick. On one level, it's just an extreme of capitalism—the power of money."

"I've had guys say, 'Are you hungry, do you want a sandwich or something?'" said Holly, a ringer for a young Joan Collins. "Just little things like that can make a difference, but most of 'em haven't accepted the fact that they've dialed a hooker on the phone, so they take it out on you. There's lots of guys I feel sorry for. I feel sorry for Jerry, because he's so hung up about the lost leg. But he's a gentleman, he's always nice, a sweet man. He's someone you can feel sorry for, or some guy who's lost his wife and he's lonely. . . ."

"Oh, God, some of them guys make me cry!" said Elaine, a forty-five-year-old Greek woman from Brooklyn.

"I had a guy tonight, his back hurt, so I gave him a massage," Holly continued. "We fucked, we frenched, we talked; it was nice. Okay, he's a trick, but I gotta treat him nice because he treats me nice. But most of these johns don't even have fantasies. They have no creativity! They want something new, wild, freaky, a fantasy, but they don't know what it is. You get lines like 'What's a nice girl like you doing in this business? By the way, honey, *get the balls.*'"

Everyone laughed. "Remember the night I called you up?" Lester asked Miller. "I called the agency one night. I was so fed up with dating and being in fucked-up relationships. I just felt so alienated from trying to relate to anyone, so I was drunk and one night I called here. I've known Kathy for like—what, eight years now? And I said, 'I wanna be a *john.*' It's like four A.M. 'I wanna be a *john.*' She says, 'It's peak hours now, Lester. Call me back in a half hour!' She knew I'd be asleep."

"No, that wasn't it at all," Miller said. "I'd have sent you somebody. I had three people available, and I wouldn't send Chris because you know her. I wouldn't send Ginger, because I was like: 'I can't do this to a friend of mine.' And I had Gracie. She's very sympathetic and easygoing. The real reason you were booking wasn't sexual. You were alienated, you were lonely, your relationship was going kaput. So I said, 'Lester, call me back in forty-five minutes.'"

"How do you think you would have done?" Vera asked.

"Oh, horribly, of course," Lester said. "I was drunk. Are you kidding?"

"You were drowning your sorrows," said the motherly Elaine.

"Maybe I wanted even the illusion that a woman was attracted to me," Lester said. "Maybe some of these jerks you were talking about become enraged and they manifest that because they know that's not true. I don't know. Maybe I'm perfect john material. Except I think too much, so sooner or later it probably wouldn't work."

Sharp and sassy with a cutting sense of humor, Kathy Miller had been Lester's entrée into the world of the working girls, and she ranked among his closest friends in New York. Encouraged by Lillian Roxon, she had started writing about rock 'n' roll as a teenager in Long Island City, Queens. Roxon told her to contact Lester, so in 1972 she wrote a 25,000-word review of Jefferson Airplane's *Long John Silver.* Lester rejected it, but she sent his letter back with a note rejecting his rejection. "Lester thought that was such a ballsy move," she said. Soon she was writing for *Creem*, immersing herself in the New York rock scene, and managing the fan club for the New York Dolls.

Their friendship blossomed via four-hour phone calls and twenty-page letters. Lester and Miller finally met in person when he came to New York for his ill-fated stay at the St. Moritz. One night they went barhopping with a group that included Dictators singer Handsome Dick Manitoba and Lester's old colleague Dave Marsh. They kept getting thrown out of places because Lester carried a boom box blasting a tape of the dialogue from *Taxi Driver*. "Marsh was there with a girlfriend, but he was terribly embarrassed and left us all behind," Miller said. Lester never saw much of Marsh in New York after that.

Shortly before Lester moved to town, Miller began working as a self-described "hooker booker" for one of the biggest escort agencies in New York. "I heard about this opportunity from a friend, and as a writer I said, 'How can you say no to this?'" she recalled. For twelve hours a night, five nights a week, she manned a large desk in the apartment of a doorman building where a dozen women waited to cab out to calls. "Kathy handles the bookings with all the finesse and crucial attention to detail of an air traffic controller," Lester wrote. The women passed the time by watching TV, gossiping, smoking, and drinking countless cans of Tab. They welcomed Lester as comic relief and a pleasant diversion. "Basically he was a sponge," Miller said. "He wasn't the focus of attention, he was just always around."

"There's something airless and timeless about the environment that's both stultifyingly boring and addictive," Lester wrote. "The hours go on and on, and the longer a visitor stays the harder and more arbitrary it is to finally decide to pick your ass up and get back out in the real world."

Lester didn't talk much about the women with his other friends. "It was a place completely outside his normal circle," John Morthland said, "and he'd go there and then he'd come back to the normal circle." He already had the opening line for his book—"The girls are a part of my life now, and I never even fucked any of them"—as well as a possible title, *Catholic School Girls in Trouble.* "Almost everything ever written on the subject of prostitution is bullshit, either designed to titillate or another 'Ain't it a shame' story," Lester wrote in yet another unsuccessful proposal. He would tell it straight, and in so doing he might even shed some light on the sorry state of romance.

"He had various running themes, one of which was how bad things were turning between men and women during the seventies," Morthland said. "He used to talk about how many people were turning to homosexuality that probably weren't homosexuals, and about how the poses of women in these skin magazines were being perceived as real erotic, but they were really saying, 'Fuck you, asshole.' The thing with the prostitutes that always got to me was that he always talked about how these women were basically happy—they were making good money, they took care of themselves, they liked their job—but they never seemed happy to me. They were always drinking a lot and taking Quaaludes and what-have-you with liquor."

Miller maintains that if Lester romanticized prostitutes, he was no different from most men. "Most guys do think it's a lot more glamorous than it really is," she said. "Yes, the women are beautiful, but it's a job, and it's really boring just like any other job. Initially, Lester— Well, look, he got the clap when he was seventeen, he went to Tijuana, and he had these ambivalent feelings about hookers in general. As he came to know the girls better, he began to realize that he was wrong about the sex industry, and he began to form this perverse pride in the fact that he was one of the gang."

"I really want a woman like you," Lester often told Miller, but she would remind him that she was a lesbian. They tried sleeping together a few times over the years, but it was mostly out of curiosity. "I was like, 'I love this man; I've never felt this way toward any other man before, I'll sleep with him,' " she said. "Then from my point of view it was like, 'Is that all there is?' I realized the love I felt for him was a lot deeper. It wasn't a sexual love, and I don't think it was for him either." Mostly they leaned on each other for support, advice, or a kick in the ass.

Feeling beaten down at the end of an awful week, Miller called Lester late one night and casually remarked that she felt like killing herself. Ten minutes later he kicked down the door to her apartment. "What are you doing here?" she asked. "You were gonna kill yourself!" he panted. "I wasn't really gonna do it," she said. "And why did you kick the door down? It wasn't even locked!"

Whenever he started a new relationship, Lester turned to Miller for advice; when it ended, he expected her to help pick him up. "He was always going out with the wrong women," she said. In the winter of 1981 he once again found himself torn between two relationships. He had started dating a woman who worked at his bank. "She's real nice but too normal if y'know what I mean," he wrote his friend JoAnn Uhelszki in Detroit. Meanwhile he was also smitten with Marcia Resnick, a downtown photographer who'd dated Johnny Thunders. "She's really nice except for one thing: She's a junkie," Lester wrote. "Just like everything else in my life these days it seems these two women represent certain polarities I've gotta figure out some way to resolve."

Resnick recognized Lester's dichotomy. "He was hanging out with earthy, punky, dirty me and this banker person at the same time, but I think his life was ordered more to the dirty, punky, earthy thing," she said. Lester thought otherwise. When he finally realized that Resnick wasn't about to stop shooting heroin, he refused to see her again.

Lester was wandering through the Village feeling sorry for himself on December 13, 1981, when he ran into Pam Brown, a petite brunette who had written for *Punk* magazine. They went to dinner at a Greek restaurant and spent the rest of the night talking in his apartment. "He seemed sad—he had this big bump on his head—and he was just foundering, ungrounded," Brown said. "He seemed so down on himself and lonely. Here he was, Lester Bangs, it was his thirty-third birthday, he was alone, and nobody cared."

You could talk about "options" and "lifestyle choices" all you pleased, Lester wrote, but nobody wanted to be alone. "When did New York become a city of perfectly healthy single men and women who just absolutely cannot find each other?" he asked in a piece for the *Village Voice*. He was fascinated by the burgeoning phenomenon of "salon-events" where men and women came together to "network." He attended an evening at the Underground sponsored by Yippie agitator–turned–yuppie matchmaker Jerry Rubin. The resulting article provided an insightful snapshot of the eighties singles scene, but the *Voice* rejected it. The editor said they'd already done enough pieces about Rubin.

New Year's Eve, 1981–82, was spent watching TV with Robert Quine and his girlfriend, Alice Sherman, in their studio apartment on St. Mark's Place. Lester had become a player in a love triangle with writer James Wolcott and a blond Southern belle named Judith Wilmot. She was a freelance writer who aspired to be a novelist. That night Lester was the odd man out and feeling miserable, but by the spring of 1982 he had prevailed. "People hated Lester and me dating because I broke up with Jim Wolcott to start dating Lester," Wilmot said. "It was like: 'You're dating too many writers!' or something."

Early in the new year the *Voice* ran an article entitled "Yecch! An Interview with a Slob." It opened, "One day not long ago, a bum/derelict wandered into our offices. I was on the verge of calling 911 when someone greeted this monstrosity with 'Lester Bangs—glad to see you!'" Fashion writer Stephanie Hill went on to query "this walking dirt bomb" about why he dressed as he did. "I'd rather buy records than clothes," Lester said. "If I could I would make myself more nondescript. I would just like to blend." He played along with the piece, posing for photos and contributing a sidebar on the life of a slob, but several of his friends thought that the paper was despicable for portraying one of its best writers in such a light, especially when Lester had come so far in cleaning up.

A week after the article ran, Lester and Wilmot went out to dinner with Kathy Miller and Vera from the escort agency. Lester sported a fresh haircut, a crewneck sweater, and a new tweed sports coat, and Miller thought he'd never looked better. *Reds* had recently opened, and she joked that he was sporting his "Warren Beatty/John Reed look." He proudly announced that he had been sober for two months, and he and Wilmot talked a lot about a trip to Mexico, where he would finally begin working on his novel. "He seemed resolved to [quit drinking]," Miller said, "and he was on the brink of getting to where he wanted to be as a writer and as a person. He was sick of being a rock critic, and he really wanted to take that next step toward being a serious author."

One day in early 1982 Robert Quine sat on the couch in Lester's apartment and watched him throw album after album on the discard pile. Lester said that he tried not to break the shrink wrap on the review copies because he got more money when he sold them unopened.

"Lester, you're an asshole; there might be something good in there," Quine said. Lester scowled at him—"Believe me, man, it's all garbage"—but Quine persisted.

"Okay, Bob, let's *listen* to them," Lester said as he smiled maliciously. By the fifth or sixth record Quine was getting shaky; by the seventh or eighth he was begging for mercy. Lester was right: It was truly dire crap. Quine grabbed the stack and led the way to Second Hand Rose.

Every January since 1973 Robert Christgau had polled rock critics across the country on the ten best albums of the year just past, soliciting ballots from *Rolling Stone* editors, daily newspaper writers, lowly fanzine scribes, and everyone in between. Early in the new year he printed the results as the *Village Voice* Pazz & Jop Critics' Poll and wrote a long introductory essay about the state of popular music. For 1981 his most celebrated contributor filed a protest ballot.

"Almost all current music is worthless," Lester wrote. "Very simply, it has no soul. It is fraudulent, and so are the mechanisms which perpetuate the lie that anybody else finds it vital enough to do more than consume and file or 'collect' (be the first on *your* block). New Wave has terminated in thudding hollow Xeroxes of poses that aren't even annoying anymore. Rap is nothing, or not enough. Jazz does not exist as a musical form with anything new to say. And the rest of rock is recycling various formulae forever. I don't know what I am going to write about—

music is the only thing in the world I really care about—but I simply cannot pretend to find anything compelling in the choice between pap and mud."

Christgau published Lester's diatribe, calling it "inspired, provocative, funny, and dead wrong." The dean dissented—"with special emphasis, of course"—from Lester's contention that nobody else found new music vital. The critics had voted, and 1981's top ten were printed on the preceding page: *Sandinista!* by the Clash, *Wild Gift* by X, *Trust* by Elvis Costello and the Attractions, *Tattoo You* by the Rolling Stones, *Pirates* by Rickie Lee Jones, *East Side Story* by Squeeze, *Dreamtime* by Tom Verlaine, *Controversy* by Prince, *Street Songs* by Rick James, and *Beauty and the Beat* by the Go-Go's.

According to Christgau, Lester's problem was that he wanted to "transform the thrill-seeking impulses of adolescence into a workable aesthetic, if not philosophy, if not way of life." Lester couldn't see anything wrong with that. Buffeted by dreadful new sounds, he found solace in old music. This wasn't living in the past, he wrote; no one in their right minds would want to go back to the fifties or sixties. "But preferring Hank Williams or Charlie Parker or the Sun Sessions or the Velvet Underground to Squeeze and Rickie Lee Jones and the Go-Go's and the Psychedelic Furs is not nostalgia. It's good taste."

He had effectively stopped writing about the music industry's new product. So what? The one line in his *Voice* diatribe that was disingenuous was his assertion that he didn't know what he would write about next.

"I feel like I gotta write a book that's mine alone and exists for no other reason than I need to get something off my chest," Lester wrote his friend Richard Riegel in February 1982. " 'I wanna be an artist,' he said, flinging his block with the letter 'R' on it into the bowl of coagulant Maypo and adding 'WAAAAAA!' for good measure. So I figure I'll go down to Mexico—my brother told me about this village called Zacatapec, which is where Emiliano Zapata's from and hardly anybody now lives there, which is the kind of environment I need population-wise—and get it written, then come back, write another more commercial book, then make my second album." (Lester hoped to talk Quine into recording with him again; if that failed, he would try to do an album in England.)

The notion of creating great literature at a Mexican hideaway had been planted when Lester read the Beats back in El Cajon. Some of his peers scoffed at the romantic vision of Lester huddled in a hacienda over a hot typewriter. "It seems like a bad place to start, giving yourself this condition: 'I'm going to go to Mexico in order to write a book,' " Nick Tosches said. John Morthland didn't really believe he'd go, but Lester went as far as calling the airlines to find the cheapest flights, diligently logging the fares in his notebook along with a reminder to pay his taxes and a schedule of various AA meetings.

There could have been another reason for the trip: Part of the recovery process in AA is to separate oneself from the people and places that present the temptation to drink. Once removed, the alcoholic is encouraged to conduct a personal inventory. "I had almost gotten him to that place where he would just go away and think about his relationships," said his sponsor, Jim Fouratt.

Although he produced a few hundred pages of notes and early drafts, Lester never wrote a book proposal for his novel. He did have a title—*All My Friends Are Hermits*—and a concept that crystallized with a piece he wrote for the *Village Voice* in December 1979. Former *Creem* artist Wes Goodwin was living in New York and doing paste-up for the paper at the time. He protested to section editor Guy Trebay that the *Voice* could do better at the start of a new decade than the traditional New Year's Eve bar guide. "I said, 'You oughta get somebody like Lester to do a real piece,' " Goodwin recalled, "and on short notice Lester brought this manuscript that was like a ream of paper. He saw it as pointing the way for him."

The article recounted the events of every New Year's Eve that Lester had spent since 1967. He used his personal recollections as a framework for considering how the sexes interacted at the start of what he feared would be an increasingly antisocial decade. "I suppose you think I'm being negative," Lester wrote. "All right, if I'm being negative you go tell *Mother* there's something wrong with the womb. Ha, gotcha! Besides which, as the '80s loom I suspect that my antisocial minority will soon become a majority. . . . There are two directions in which extants can go: (a) stasis or (b) decay. And New Year's Eve is the biggest bummer yet, because we all go out with these expectations and get totally soused just so we can stand to be around each other. . . . Go ahead and feel distaste for my antics with the lush, call me misogynous, misanthrope, Mr. Rogers. Just don't call me late for my Zoom 'n' Locker Room! Every single one of you has acted every bit as oafishly base some New Year's or other or several or all of them. And you're gonna do it again this year."

Whenever someone pressed him on the subject of the novel, Lester would offer only a thumbnail description: "It's about life in New York City and people's relationships—how people's relationships fuck them up."

Although Nancy Alexander had moved to Florida, Lester and his old love remained close. "I considered Lester my soul mate," she said, "and even when I got married, I dreamed I had two rings on and one was his." She encouraged him to follow his vision for the novel, and he kept her posted on its evolution. "I'm beginning to think that my real strength might lie in some crossbred form of my own," he wrote her in the summer of 1980. "A mix of reportage and poetry and dreams and fiction and fancies and associations and jokes and just about everything else—you know, like I talk."

Nancy believed that Lester would write his book, and that despite his self-doubts it would be the "Great American Saga" that he jokingly called it. "He had the vision," she said. "I think he was very aware of that, but I think there was too much in his way. He was in emotional pain. I think many people focus on the drinking, but he would take Valium to cover the pain. He'd wake up in dread and anxiety. It was like the fire coming up."

In November 1981 Lester made his first trip back to California in almost five years. He couldn't bring himself to go straight to San Diego, where his mother was living with his nephew, Ben Catching III. He girded himself for the inevitable family reunion by spending a couple of days partying in San Francisco first.

Lester had a brief but passionate fling with Joan Goodwin, who was in the process of splitting from her husband, Michael, the former *Rolling Stone* film critic. "It only lasted twenty-four hours, sorry to say, but it was sort of quintessentially Bangsian," she wrote. "It was just the natural extension of a hug. I think every woman who could stand Lester whatsoever wanted to hug him. He was like some big sweet Labrador retriever mutt who'd join you sitting on your front steps and just lean against you until you scratched him behind the ears. When he wasn't too out of control on drugs and booze, he was very comfortable to be with. He wasn't 'sexy,' but his body was so connected with/expressive of his feelings, there wasn't a hard line between an emotional connection and a physical connection." Lester fell asleep in the middle of their lovemaking, but they resumed when he woke at dawn.

Howie Klein was a former schoolmate of Richard Meltzer and Sandy Pearlman who had started a record label called 415. He didn't drink, but he escorted Lester on a drunken club crawl. Lester passed out at the Mabuhay Gardens, but only after encouraging Klein to sign the band that was sound-checking when they stumbled in. The group was fronted by a rotund but sexy frontwoman named Deborah Iyall. Klein took Lester's advice, and Romeo Void established 415 with its hit "Never Say Never."

After a week in San Francisco, Lester finally headed down the coast. "My mother is aging and ailing and endeavored to manipulate me into feeling guilty for those facts," he wrote. Despite his new short haircut Norma told him he looked like an overgrown hippie. She kept asking if he wanted a tuna-fish sandwich. "Sometimes I said yes; sometimes I said no," he wrote. "Conversation was intermittently enjoyable, as long as she didn't start in again with that wheedling tone." He tried to get his mother to talk about his father, but she spoke only haltingly of the past. Lester told her she had a heck of a story and ought to write it down. "Writing is *your* thing," she said, and he considered it one of the nicest things she'd ever said to him.

Whenever Norma got on his nerves, Lester went down to the basement to play Public Image, Ltd.'s *Metal Box* on Ben's stereo. "Albatross" seemed like the theme song for the entire trip. His nephew had followed his work in *Creem*, and he used to ask his grandmother how her son was faring. "Everything's fine," she'd say. "Les is working very hard, and he's considering coming back to the church." Ben always knew that was a lie. Now that he'd reconnected with his uncle, he realized that Norma had lied to him, too. Lester had believed her, however, when she said that Ben had become a devout Jehovah's Witness, and that was the reason he'd never called or written.

The two childhood companions picked up where they'd left off. Lester tried to turn Ben onto Public Image, Ltd., but his nephew wasn't interested. "I'd say some stupid thing like 'I'm still mad at you for making me buy all those Grand Funk Railroad records!'" Ben recalled. "'And besides, at least Kenny Loggins can play an F-sharp seventh!' We'd have an argument, and then he'd come back at me later and say, 'You know, you're right.' I didn't know what was happening in music at that point at all, but I wasn't going to back down from an argument with him."

After a few days Lester returned to New York, but Norma's health continued to fail. Fearing the worst, he came back to California four months later in February 1982. At age seventy-six Norma had been admitted to a Witness hospital in San Diego. Her middle child, Lester's half brother Bill Catching, lived ninety minutes north in a mobile home in

Studio City, close to the Hollywood lots where he worked as a stuntman. Lester stayed with him for a week—the only extended period they ever spent together—and the two black sheep of the Catching and Bangs clans drove down to visit their mother daily.

On one trip Lester astounded Bill by ducking into a Salvation Army Thrift Store near the hospital. He traded his relatively new sports coat for a tattered secondhand suit jacket. "He wanted to look 'depressed' or whatever the word is," Bill said. "He came out looking worse than he had when he went in. When he went in to see Mom in the hospital, he had on this ragged jacket with the elbows missing. Now, I'm probably the most conservative guy that ever lived besides a John Wayne or a Ronald Reagan. When he came out of this place, I thought, 'Well, I'm not gonna say nothing to this kid.' I didn't know him very well, but I figured he was into drugs, and I thought, 'What a waste.' I didn't call him on it, because he was like me, and you don't call me on nothin'. But anybody that gets into that stuff is kind of weak in the mind."

Richard Meltzer saw Lester several times during the trip, and he was surprised to find that his old friend remained clean and sober, even when they traded rants for the tape recorder or played poker with members of the Blasters, the kinds of occasions that would have prompted outrageous behavior in the past.

"It also warmed my cockles, considering his record in the mere civility dept., to see him relate (graciously) to his half-brother's wife, this unaffectedly pretty twenty-year-old rural Mexican the macho blusterer, a stuntman by trade, had recently acquired, maritally, while on location Down South," Meltzer wrote. "Though she knew purt near zero English, my first sight of her she was watching some random English-language crap, while hubby rested for a shoot of the *Fall Guy* series, on the tiny TV in her fussily suburban kitchen; materially cozy for the first time in her life, she seemed lonely, disoriented, far from home. Silent and solemn, she visibly stiffened—shyly? menially?—at the intrusion of Lester, my girlfriend Irene, and me, only to be put at ease by Lester *introducing us*, without missing a beat, as, well, *friends of the family*. Like it mattered to him that she feel *like* family—and thus shared in all aspects of etc.—and for a moment the loneliness left her face; she smiled broadly, shook (or at least took) our hands, went back to her tube."

Meltzer watched as Lester packed for the trip back to New York. His mother seemed to be recovering, and she was about to check out of the hospital to stay with her eldest son, Ben Catching, Jr., at his home in

Earp, California. Lester called her before he left for the airport. "Look, don't get worse just to make me come down here again," he said sweetly. "I'll come anyway."

Four weeks later, early on the morning of March 13, 1982, Ben Jr. peeked into Norma's bedroom and saw that her bed had already been made. The dog ran in and found her body on the floor between the bed and the window. "She loved to sit there because that front bedroom looked over the river," he said. "Evidently she was sitting there and her aorta burst, and she just fell over dead."

Lester borrowed the money from John Morthland to return for the funeral. It was a typically emotionless Jehovah's Witness ceremony. Afterward Norma's four children gathered together for the first time that any of them could remember. Lester wasn't drinking, but he had a cassette of *Jook Savages on the Brazos* with him, and he played it for his family. "It didn't go over," said his nephew Ben. "He probably took it much more seriously than we did."

Ben invited Lester to stay for a few days. On a trip to Tower Records in San Diego, Lester bought his nephew a copy of Lou Reed's new album, *The Blue Mask*, while his great-niece Karen, a sophomore in high school, got a pressing of *London Calling* by the Clash. He ducked out to see some of his old friends from El Cajon, checking in with Rob Houghton and Gary Rachac, and they were surprised to learn that he wasn't drinking.

One night Ben came home and found Lester scanning the bookshelves in his bedroom. He couldn't believe that his nephew had read all of these authors. "Jesus, *I* should read Faulkner!" he said. "He's talking about families and generations and things that are happening!" His own family and its interactions with the Jehovah's Witnesses might be a better tale than anything he'd ever written, he added. "The older Les got, the more he realized that that might be the bigger story than rock 'n' roll," Ben said. "He saw Faulkner and I think he was clawing towards that. It was catching up with him, and he didn't want to be thought of as just a rock 'n' roll writer."

Saying it was high time he got back to work, Lester left for New York. He would have stayed to help scatter his mother's ashes, but his half brother Ben Jr. found that it wasn't as simple as just climbing in his boat and tossing them in the Pacific Ocean. He had to get a permit.

When the paperwork arrived a few weeks later, Ben III, his wife, Midge, and their daughter, Karen, joined Norma's eldest son and set sail with the urn carrying her remains. Per her wishes, her great-grand-daughter Karen read a long and meandering letter about the role the Je-hovah's Witnesses had played in her life. As his father held the boat steady, Ben III tried to open the urn, but it wasn't easy. "We pushed and we pulled and we twisted, and all of a sudden it just gave way," he said. Ashes and bits of bone matter scattered in the wind, blowing into the hair and clothing of everyone on board. "It was awful," Ben said, "but we just looked at each other and said, 'Well, now Grandma's *really* with us.'"

chapter twelve

Ignore That Door

On April 14, 1982, Lester was close to completing the text for *Rock Gomorrah*, a project that had been kicking around for more than four years. He was angry that a writer named Gary Herman had done a quickie book called *Rock and Roll Babylon* that seemed to nick his title and concept. He planned to rename his tome with Michael Ochs *Tales from Beyond the Grooves*, printing the title in EC Comics–style lettering. "It'll be coming out before Christmas, I guess—for the holidays," he told me when I interviewed him. "We're turning it in next week, if I can just get off my ass and finish it."

After that, Lester maintained that he was heading to Mexico to write his novel. "I've got to do something that has nothing to do with music," he said. "I don't have a deal to sell this book or anything, I just hope that somebody will want it. If nobody wants the novel, well—it's something that I really want to do, and I figure that that's the most important thing. It's been percolating around inside for a while." Writing the book in New York City was unthinkable. "The city's been really irritating me," he said. "Last summer was so bad, and this summer's going to be even worse. The quality of life here is just getting worse and worse. The problem is you get out into America and it's like everybody out there is depressed, so it's sort of like *no life*. And here there's life, but everybody is desperate, so it's really abrasive, hostile, unpleasant life. I don't know which is worse. Which do *you* prefer, anxiety or depression?"

Not everyone shared his opinion of Manhattan, and during the next two weeks Lester hosted several enthusiastic visitors from Detroit. Carol Schloner arrived on Easter weekend, and they had a good time seeing the sights. The friend he used to call "Jah Woman" worried about him. "I didn't think he looked really healthy," she said. "But he was going to AA, and he kept saying that everything was going really well."

The week after Schloner left, former MC5 singer Rob Tyner came to town with his roadie Gil Clark to record some tracks for a solo album. The finished manuscript of *Rock Gomorrah/Tales From Beyond the Grooves* sat in a box in the corner. "Who do you wanna read about?" Lester asked. He riffled through the pages as his houseguests tossed out names like Little Richard, Johnny Rivers, and Eddie Cochran. Lester sported a T-shirt promoting former Stooge Ron Asheton's new band, Destroy All Monsters, but he wasn't raising any hell. "Me and Rob were both really on the wild during that trip," Clark recalled. "We offered Lester stuff, but it was always 'Nah, none for me.' I thought he had reformed. I was definitely *not* reformed. I was having the time of my life."

Lester and the author, April 14, 1982.
PHOTO BY RAYMOND ZOLTOWSKI

The two rockers returned to Detroit on Thursday, April 29. Robert Quine came over that night and shouted up at Lester's window. He carried a tape of *Destiny Street*, the long-delayed but recently completed second album by Richard Hell and the Voidoids. Lester's girlfriend, Judith Wilmot, left the apartment as Quine entered. Lester emerged from the bathroom and swallowed a handful of pills. "Valium," he said when Quine inquired. They listened to the album in silence. "It looked to me like he was sleeping, but once in a while—like at the end of 'Ignore That Door'—he would give a little smile," Quine said. "Judy had left, and he was in a pretty negative frame of mind—hostile and a little surly."

Lester suggested a walk, but it didn't improve his mood. "This is going to be a really bad summer," he kept saying. They stopped in front of a Middle Eastern place called Eva's on Eighth Street; Lester loved their frozen yogurt. Quine was hungry but wary of his friend's foul humor, so he declined the invitation to get a bite, and they parted ways at Fifth Avenue.

Several hours later Lester called Nancy Alexander in Florida, presumably from a pay phone. He still hadn't made amends with the phone company. "Lester, it's three in the morning!" Nancy said. "Call me tomorrow." She worried about him all day on Friday when he didn't call back. The last time they had spoken, her old boyfriend had told her about a dream. He stood facing three doors. He opened the first and saw his mother lying dead in her sleep. Behind the second he found the flames that consumed his father. He woke up in a cold sweat, unable to open the third.

Late on the morning of Friday, April 30, Lester stopped by the offices of Delilah Communications and delivered the finished manuscript for *Rock Gomorrah/Tales From Beyond the Grooves*. From there he went to see John Morthland, who was having a hard time finishing his own book, *The Best of Country Music*. They spent several hours talking about Morthland's writer's block and the books that Lester planned next. He was enthusiastic about his novel, *All My Friends Are Hermits*, and his planned anthology, *Psychotic Reactions and Carburetor Dung*, but he wasn't feeling well. "He had the flu," Morthland said. "Not like a little bug—he was really sick, just narcoleptic. He was fine spiritually—he was talking a lot about all these projects he wanted to do—but when you're sick, you feel down and you talk that way. There was not a lot of expression in his voice."

On the way home Lester dropped by Second Hand Rose and bought a copy of *Dare* by the Human League, an English synth-pop band that Wilmot liked. Before climbing the stairs to his apartment, he made some calls from his favorite pay phone on the corner of Fourteenth Street and Sixth Avenue. At about 6 P.M. he rang Billy Altman to ask what time they were having dinner. Altman chided him for getting things screwed up; the plan had been set for Saturday. Next he called Wilmot, who thought he was in a bad mood because of problems with Ochs on the book. "The last thing I said to Lester was 'I love you more every day,' and I think that helped a little bit," she said. He phoned Robert Christgau to extend a deadline for the *Village Voice*, and finally he called his friend Nancy Stillman and invited her over to jam.

Stillman was always excited when she got a call from Lester. She hadn't heard from him all winter, and now it was as if he were coming out of hibernation. A relatively sober person, she thought she recognized the higher pitch that Lester's voice assumed when he took Valium, and she asked him what he was on. "Don't be my fucking mother," he snapped.

Around 8 P.M. Abel Shafer heard Lester bouncing between the railing and the wall as he climbed the stairs to his apartment. The genial old man lived in the unit below Lester's, and despite the sometimes unbearably loud music, he was fond of his upstairs neighbor. He opened the door and asked Lester how he was feeling. "Fine," Lester replied. Shafer heard him make the last flight, throw open his door, and plop down on the couch as he had countless times before.

A half hour later Stillman arrived and started yelling up at the window. Lester didn't hear her, and she thought he must have been asleep or blasting the stereo. She kept hollering until Shafer came down at about eight forty-five.

"I saw him and he looked really gray," Shafer said. "That's a bad color. I've seen Lester not well, but I've never seen him look this bad." He let her into the building, and she ran upstairs to find Lester lying on his back on the couch, his eyes open and his left arm dangling to the floor. *Dare* was spinning on the turntable, and the needle was stuck in the end groove.

"He looked like he was sleeping," Stillman said. "It's not like in the movies where you think, 'Oh, my God, he's dead!' " She ran downstairs and asked Shafer to call for help. Lester's old friend and next-door neighbor heard the commotion. "I went in and I had a bad feeling right away," Robert Duncan said. "Roni [Hoffman] came in behind me and just said, 'Oh, shit.' " Duncan grabbed Lester's wrist to feel for a pulse but realized that he didn't even know where to look. Ten minutes later the paramedics arrived, but they seemed reluctant to do anything. "He's a young man, put the paddles on him!" Duncan screamed. "We heard him just a half hour ago. We've got time to recover him here!" One of the emergency medical technicians lost his cool and hissed that even if they *did* get a heartbeat, the guy would be brain dead; he could tell by the way the pupils were fixed.

According to the police report two officers from the Thirteenth Precinct arrived at five minutes after nine. One was a seasoned black beat cop, the other a rookie policewoman. "She was a real Brunhilde type," Stillman said, but she'd never seen a corpse before, and she had to leave the apartment. The other cop waited for what he called the "meat wagon." He started picking through the stacks of albums, and asked if he could take a rare Miles Davis side. "It reminded me of the scene in *Zorba the Greek* where all the old ladies come while the person is dying and start taking things out of the house," Duncan said. "But then I thought, 'Shit, Lester would have *wanted* this guy to have the record. He would have been proud that this guy was interested in his jazz collection.'" Duncan told him to help himself, and he went next door to call John Morthland.

The New York City medical investigator finally showed up at 11:40 P.M. It took him only ten minutes to compile his report. "The deceased is a thirty-three-year-old musician who lives alone," he wrote. Lester might have smiled at that—"musician," not "writer"—as well as at another no-tation: "No history of drug abuse." The scene: "a filthy two-room apart-ment without evidence of struggle." Circumstances of death: "possible O.D.; Valium and other meds found."

Shortly after Morthland arrived, Judith Wilmot wandered in, un-aware of what had happened. She was devastated. Morthland found Lester's address book, and early on the morning of May 1 he began mak-ing calls. He'd spend much of the next two weeks on the phone. "People were calling me from around the world—just some kid in Finland who heard Lester died and traced it to me," he said. "I don't know how they all got my number. A lot of them were people from his past that maybe I had met once and they saw a newspaper or wire-service article." He also experienced a ghoulish New York tradition as realtors and used-book dealers called to ask about Lester's apartment and book collection.

When Ben Catching III got the call, he couldn't believe that his uncle had died so soon after Norma. Only six weeks earlier they'd stood in the bedroom talking about Faulkner. Ben wasn't the closest relative, but someone had to settle Lester's affairs, and he couldn't imagine any of the Jehovah's Witnesses doing it. He and his wife, Midge, borrowed the money from her boss and flew to New York.

On May 1 a New York medical examiner began Lester's autopsy at the Manhattan Mortuary. External examination indicated that the body was unremarkable. The only odd characteristic: "A circular contusion in the mid-line of the forehead at the hairline measuring one-half-inch in diameter." A lump. The internal organs were all healthy and of normal size, though the examiner noted some congestion in the lungs. She finished her work and dictated her report at 12:45 P.M.

The director of toxicology would not complete his analysis of the bodily fluids and liver until May 27. The laboratory findings he reported included a "concentration greater than two milligrams percent" of propoxyphene and a trace amount of diazepam in the liver, unspecified amounts of propoxyphene in the stomach fluid and urine, and an unspecified amount of diazepam in the bile. Propoxyphene is the centrally acting narcotic agent in Darvon; diazepam is the chemical breakdown of Valium. From the lab report, it appears that the toxicologist didn't test the blood for either substance, but he did look for alcohol, barbiturates, methaqualone, and opiates (which would include dextromethorphan, the key ingredient of Romilar), and he found no trace of any of them.

On June 25 the medical examiner amended her report with a cause of death. "Acute propoxyphene poisoning," she wrote. "Circumstances undetermined." Darvon did it, she concluded.

A combination of narcotic and analgesic, manufactured by Eli Lilly and Company, Darvon was one of the many pills that Lester had taken on and off for kicks since 1967. "Darvons are the 'biggies,'" he wrote in his adolescent novel *Drug Punk*, referring to the size of the large pink capsules. Doctors had begun to steer clear of the drug in the late seventies because of the dangers of overdose. A 1975 survey of Darvon-related fatalities cited in *The Physicians' Desk Reference* noted that 20 percent of the deaths occurred within the first hour of overdose, 5 percent within five minutes. It added, "Many of the propoxyphene-related deaths have occurred in patients with previous histories of emotional disturbances or suicidal ideation, or attempts as well as histories of misuse of tranquilizers, alcohol, and other CNS [central nervous system]-active drugs."

No one will ever know for certain whether Lester took two Darvons or twenty-two. In 1998 the autopsy report was reviewed by Dr. Robert Kirschner, the former medical examiner of Cook County, Illinois, head of the pathology department at the University of Chicago Medical School, and one of the country's preeminent forensics experts. He characterized it as "primitive, even for 1982" and "pretty much worthless." The New York toxicologist stopped his analysis as soon as he found an indication of propoxyphene, Kirschner said; standards in Chicago at the time would have required much more thorough testing. The measure "greater than two milligrams percent" does not indicate how much of the drug Lester ingested. The literature notes that the average fatal level in the liver is *six* milligrams percent.

"Lester Bangs probably did die of an overdose of Darvon, and probably Valium as well," Kirschner said. "But in order to determine whether it's an overdose, you need some quantitation, and there's none here. If I were going to court and somebody asked me, 'Did this man die of a drug overdose?' I'd have to say, 'I don't know.' "

Lester's body was cremated in Hillside, New Jersey, on the evening of May 2. Traffic in the Holland Tunnel delayed the arrival of the ashes at Redden's Funeral Home on Fourteenth Street the following morning, when attendance at the wake was limited to about a dozen close friends. Nancy Alexander heard the news from Morthland, and she flew to New York from Florida. "I just ran out of the house and threw myself to the ground sobbing," she said. "I was enraged and screaming at God."

Andrea di Guglielmo, Lester's first love, was working for a pharmaceutical company in Connecticut, and she also attended. "I always thought it was extremely telling that Les died only six weeks after his mother," she said. "I just couldn't believe it. He loved his mother very much, and in a weird way she gave him a lot of stability. I think part of Les just died with her. She was his ultimate lifeline."

Andy was the only person at the wake that Ben and Midge Catching knew. Throughout the service and the lunch that followed, Ben was consistently surprised by the depth of the feelings for his uncle displayed by friends such as Morthland, Kathy Miller, Georgia Christgau, Paul Nelson, and Billy Altman. Years later many of Lester's intimates still expressed their loss in terms similar to something Nick Tosches said: Sometimes he will be at a party and he'll sense a physical hole—the space that Lester should be filling.

After the wake Ben took the remains back to California. For eight years they sat unobtrusively in a corner of a house near the Pacific Ocean. One day in 1990—"There was no special reason; it was just one of those kinds of days"—he carried them to the water's edge. The container was much easier to open than the one that had held the remains of Norma Belle Bangs. "It was just like some old coffee can—they do things right in New York," Ben said, letting loose a big, goofy laugh that many have compared to Lester's. With no thought of obtaining a permit or reading some sanctimonious letter, he scattered his uncle to the waves, and then he turned and went home.

PHOTO BY CHRISTINA PATOSKI

Afterword

While not nearly as ubiquitous as Dead Elvis, Lester has nonetheless had an active career since his demise. In recent years he has been the subject of various readings and panel discussions: at the Poetry Project in New York, the South by Southwest Music and Media Conference in Austin, and the Music Journalism Awards and Conference in Los Angeles. As the Rolling Stones brought Muddy Waters onstage to jam and to bask in his aura, other rock critics regularly cite Lester's name. In the style of his chat with Jimi Hendrix, several magazines have published interviews with him from beyond the grave. He's been invoked in the monikers of at least two underground rock bands, listed as an inspiration in the liner notes of many others (including Mick Jones's post-Clash effort, Big Audio Dynamite), sampled by the Mekons ("One Horse Town" on the EP *F.U.N. '90*), and pictured on the cover of an EP by alternative folkie Mary Lou Lord, a former girlfriend of Kurt Cobain who says that Lester frequents her sexual fantasies.

He also appears in lyrics by artists ranging from Bob Seger ("Lester Knew") to the Ramones ("It's Not My Place [In the 9 to 5 World]) and from Red Dark Sweet ("Lester Bangs Is Going to Hell") to R.E.M. Years after the party that Karen Moline threw for Joe "King" Carrasco and the Crowns, R.E.M. singer Michael Stipe had a dream about a soirée where everybody had the initials L.B. and they all took part in a spirited food fight. In "It's the End of the World as We Know It (And I Feel Fine)" Stipe sings, "Leonard Bernstein, Leonid Brezhnev, Lenny Bruce, and Lester

Bangs/Birthday party, cheesecake, jellybeans, boom!" The song is one of the group's biggest hits, but fanzines and Web sites often have to identify the names that are mentioned, for the benefit of younger listeners.

By the early eighties the punk and heavy-metal aesthetics that Lester championed had become accepted not only by the rock underground but in some cases by the mainstream. His three-chord history of rock 'n' roll can now be extended from "La Bamba" through "Blitzkrieg Bop" up to "Smells Like Teen Spirit" by Nirvana. The second album that his favorites, the Count Five, made only in his imagination—a work "so grungy that on most of the songs you could barely distinguish anything except an undifferentiated wall of grinding noise and intermittent punctuation of glottal sow-like gruntings"—has arguably been realized many times over, in grunge, industrial dance music, noise-rock, hard-core rap, and many other genres.

Some of the artists Lester lauded are now considered icons, their careers commemorated in a ludicrous glass pyramid in Cleveland. (Jann Wenner is a driving force behind the Rock and Roll Hall of Fame and Museum, and *Rolling Stone* is hailed in a large exhibit, while the now-defunct *Creem* and the rest of the history of rock journalism gets a small glass case in the basement.) In 1998 Lou Reed performed at the White House for President Clinton and Czech President Václav Havel, who cited Reed's most famous band as an inspiration for the so-called Velvet Revolution. "His oft-stated ambition is to become a great writer in the literary sense," Lester noted the last time he wrote about Reed. In the 1990s Reed issued a hardcover collection of his lyrics and spread his words before him like notes on a lectern while performing material from *Set the Twilight Reeling*, an album of love songs inspired by his new companion and Lester's former collaborator, Laurie Anderson.

Interviewed circa the release of his 1991 album *Magic and Loss*, a tribute to dead friends, Reed paused for a long time when I asked him about Lester. "Sometimes when people get obsessed with your work, it's really dangerous for both of you," he said. "You can disappoint someone like that so easily when they find out just how human you are."

Of Lester's own music, only his posthumous album with Birdland is currently available. After he left the group, the other members soldiered on without him as the Rattlers. Following Lester's death Mickey Leigh paid tribute by scraping together the money for an independent release of the Electric Lady recordings. The album, *Birdland with Lester Bangs*, was reissued on CD by Dionysus Records in 1998.

Paul Kolderie and Sean Slade, the producers of alternative-rock bands such as Hole and Dinosaur Jr., hoped to rerelease *Jook Savages on the Brazos* in 1997, but their deal with MCA Records fell through. They hear Lester's album with the Delinquents as a predecessor of so-called alternative-country bands such as Wilco and Son Volt. "We were the guys who produced Uncle Tupelo's first two albums, and a lot of that was informed by Lester's album," Kolderie told me. "His album was the way that I came into country music, and I think people who appreciate the No Depression stuff would really get into it."

The two perverse fan books published in Lester's lifetime, *Blondie* and *Rod Stewart*, are both out of print in America, and his finished manuscript for *Rock Gomorrah/Tales from Beyond the Grooves* was never published. Karen Moline had left Delilah but was set to edit the book on a freelance basis when Lester died. When I interviewed her in 1997, she blamed Michael Ochs for derailing the project. "Lester worked really hard on this book, and I can't believe it wasn't what he wanted," she said. "Michael was always difficult, let's just put it that way." Then and now such talk makes Ochs furious. "After Lester died, Delilah started putting stuff out on the street that I was ready to kill them for," he told me. "I took the book back from them and said, 'Fuck you! This book is not yours. Sue me over the damn thing!'"

Ochs tried to find a new publisher, but none was interested. In a memo to Delilah dated July 2, 1982, Robert Devereux, an editor with the book's prospective English publishers, Virgin Books, Ltd., characterized the manuscript as "unbelievably dull" and completely unsuitable for publication. "The quality of the writing is extremely poor and seems to contain little of the talent we know Lester Bangs had," Devereux wrote. Having read the three hundred anecdotes and snippets of oral history originally intended to serve as photo captions, I have to admit that I agree.

Several months after Lester's death his first editor, Greil Marcus, began compiling the collection of his "greatest hits." Marcus secured a $15,000 contract with Alfred A. Knopf, and friendly editors helped amass many of Lester's far-flung writings. John Morthland and Billy Altman also salvaged a small mountain of unpublished material from Lester's apartment. But while he took the title and some cues from Lester's own book proposals, Marcus told me in 1997 that he ultimately followed his own vision. "I thought, 'This is the only book there's ever gonna be. This is the book that has to tell the story. It's gonna be distorted, because it's gonna be my version of it. It'll be what I value. A lot's gonna be left out, but it's also gonna be a long book, and everything that I love is gonna be in there.'"

Psychotic Reactions and Carburetor Dung received almost universally positive reviews when it was published in 1987, and it remains in print in the United States, England, Germany, and France. But some critics believe that it suffers from Marcus's attempt to tell a story and from the influence of his friend Robert Christgau, who pressed for the inclusion of "The White Noise Supremacists" and other *Village Voice* articles at the expense of work that Lester preferred. The book ignored his many lyrics and poems, included none of his writing about heavy metal, and side-stepped the memorable essays in which he mocked the music industry and the business of rock criticism. "I felt that Marcus's collection was an attempt to enshrine Lester but also to sabotage him," *Vanity Fair* media critic James Wolcott told me in 1997. "There's a jealousy with both Christgau and Marcus, because Lester really reached readers. Bob and Greil have their followers, but they don't have the kind of intense fandom that Lester had. You felt connected to him. You can't imagine, like: 'Jeez, I wanna hang out with Greil Marcus.' What Lester had was really rare."

The charisma that comes through on the page is one of the two reasons Lester lives on. Like his favorite artists, he was larger than life, updating the romantic tradition of the madman as truth-teller via a manic indulgence in Romilar and rock 'n' roll. Once he was dead, this act could be emulated without the risk of his puking on the carpet. The surviving Noise Boys and a handful of heirs have long found themselves unwelcome in the Big Boys' salon. In an essay published in 1999, Richard Meltzer lashed out at Marcus and Christgau in their self-appointed roles as intellectual overseers of the rock-critic academy. "At a crucial juncture they blocked my progress to wider (um) recognition, effectively consigning me to marginality, and in the long run denying me any significant role in official—'authorized'—'accredited' rockwrite (as opposed to rock) history," he wrote. "The annals—the archive—the fugsucking 'pantheon'! Oh yes—another pathetic house-o-cards for sure, but these two clowns act like they fucking OWN it."

Lester is safely enshrined because he is conveniently dead. Many of those who invoke his name do so as a deterrence machine against charges that their own work is academic, joyless, imperious, and oh so politically correct. They are the anti-Lesters. "Intense emotionalism is not a valid criterion for judging music," Christgau told Lester, but for Lester it was always the primary one.

"When I wrote somewhere that one of the things which helped kill Lester Bangs was WRITING, [Marcus and Christgau] accused me of romanticism," Meltzer wrote. "How can writing *kill*?, they questioned. Well, guys, it doesn't always kill, but it certainly comes closest when you're doing it right. Only when it makes active use of your blood, your heart, your nerves, glands, sex fluids, vertebrae and whatall, and don't forget your stink, in a word: your body. In a word: your life. They were more annoyed, I would guess, that I considered it a pity *rock*-writing was the genre that gored Lester, that a diet of rock and nothing but had rendered him too dumb to get out of the way."

The other reason for the canonization of St. Lester is, of course, the writing, though it is impossible to separate the personality from the prose. Arriving in rock criticism's second wave, he did not invent the form, he perfected it. A fair number of practitioners attempt to mimic his style, but they generally ignore the outrageous metaphors, the playful torrent of words, and the eye for telling detail in favor of the first-person confessions. Devoid of Lester's insights, honesty, and intellectual content, theirs is an empty noise, and attacking Lester for encouraging it is like blaming Little Richard for Pat Boone.

Like his heroes the Beats, Lester was a modernist. Though his most innovative writing challenged the accepted structures, he was hot, never cool, and the word "passion" appeared in his critiques more than almost any other. Nick Tosches likes to tell the story of how Lester rushed into the street in his underwear the night an apartment in his building caught fire. "He's gotta save something, right?" Tosches said when I first interviewed him in 1990. "All he comes out with is that British record in a film can [Public Image, Ltd.'s *Metal Box*]. Forget about the two hundred dollars on the dresser; forget about the clothes, the shoes. That's what he saves. That's indicative of Lester's love for rock 'n' roll."

"When I look back on it, it was obvious that I was gonna end up doing this, because my two big obsessions were always music and writing," Lester told me in 1982. "It's an outgrowth of being a fanatical record collector and a fanatical listener: You have fanatical opinions that you want to inflict on people."

He saw little of that fire in those who professed to emulate him. "It's dismal," Lester said when I asked about the state of rock criticism. "It's people who were going to journalism school and they realized that being a rock critic was an easy way to get a foothold in a journalistic career. They don't have the passion for the music that somebody who gets into

it because they really love music has. I've seen their record collections—
a few Bonnie Raitt albums and that's it. The next thing they go out and
buy the Public Image, Ltd., because that's the thing they're supposed to
do. I hate that kind of shit—people who are being trendies or oppor-
tunistic."

The careerists have continued to thrive since Lester's death, earning
a lucrative living unthinkable in the days of poetic fifteen-dollar record
reviews. They succeed by placing a long list of people—the artist, the
record company, the publicist, the publisher, the editor—ahead of the
person for whom they're allegedly writing. Like the literary critic Lionel
Trilling, Lester often employed the first-person plural in his reviews, addressing his readers as fellow appreciators instead of mere consumers.
When he was at his best, his "we" spoke not for his friends and fellow
hermits but for a sensibility attuned to the rhythms of the Zeitgeist, and
he expected his readers to do their fair share in picking up the beat.

"Critical journalism is an epigrammatic shorthand awaiting comple-
tion by the reader," scholar Morris Dickstein wrote in *The Critic & Society*. Many of Lester's readers obliged him. They also tolerated his flip-
flops on albums such as *Kick Out the Jams, Exile on Main Street*, and
Radio Ethiopia, accepting that passion isn't always neatly constrained by
reason. Why should Lester have been hobbled by that hobgoblin of little
minds?

Nearly all of his peers agree that Lester would have a hard time finding a forum in the media today. The current flood of product and pro-
motion overwhelms critics in every field, and they are reduced to offering mere opinion—what *New Yorker* film critic David Denby calls "the
whooshing of thumbs, up and down." By no means is this a recent problem. In a 1946 essay entitled "Confessions of a Book Reviewer," George
Orwell noted that "the prolonged, indiscriminate reviewing of books is
a quite exceptionally thankless, irritating, and exhausting job. It not
only involves praising trash but constantly *inventing* reactions toward
books about which one has no spontaneous feelings whatever. . . .
[The reviewer] is pouring his immortal spirit down the drain, half a pint
at a time."

What *is* new in this age of irony is that criticism has been stripped
of whatever shred of sincerity remained. Corporate irony ridicules not
only the thing that it is selling but the very act of selling it, Denby observed. In the process it disarms critics by making anyone who goes
against the flow of commerce seem clueless. "Irony is a low-lead brand

of gasoline that may be ecosound and gov't approved but it sure won't put a tiger in your tank, nor take you as far as either moxie or rage or conscience (even that crap!) or even crassness," Lester wrote in 1972. He had seen rock 'n' roll future, and its name was Hype.

"I was out west not long ago, and I was stuck in Yuma, Arizona, where my sister lives," Lester told me less than a year after MTV's debut. "I had nothing to do but sit in a trailer all day and watch this *Music-on-TV*, this music station on cable. I sat there, and there's Elvis Costello and Styx and Echo and the Bunnymen and Pat Benatar—all the New Wave stuff mixed in with all the Styx and REO Speedwagon–type stuff—and it all sucked dogs equally. NO GOOD! There's something about videotape that's intrinsically cold. It lends itself to soap operas and *Mary Hartman, Mary Hartman*, and that's sort of anti–rock 'n' roll right there. . . . Even right now it's like rock 'n' roll doesn't exist. It's getting like jazz used to be—big in Europe. Those kids out there, they're concerned with getting good jobs and stuff. They'll go see Styx, and it's like spectacle. It's very much leisure-time activity right now. It's just something to consume."

This leads to one of the two questions that people often posed as I conducted the interviews for this book: Would Lester have stopped writing about rock 'n' roll?

Though he seemed committed to reinventing himself in a forum outside rock journalism, to some extent Lester was trapped by the need to pay the rent and keep himself supplied with spinach soufflés and frozen yogurt. In his song "I Sold My Body/Flesh for Sale," he equated his career as a rock critic with that of the prostitutes who worked at the escort agency. "I think there's not the slightest chance he would have stopped writing about music," Robert Christgau said when I interviewed him in 1997. "One of the reasons I think it's inconceivable is that economically it's what he would have had to do."

On the other hand, Meltzer and Tosches provide two of many possible models that Lester might have followed had he lived. Tosches lives alone in Manhattan, where he has written successful biographies of Dean Martin, the Sicilian financier Michele Sindona, and boxer Sonny Liston, in addition to novels such as *Trinities*. Meltzer lives with his companion, Irene Forrest, in Portland, Oregon. Though he is still a primarily underground phenom, he is held in high esteem by the readers of books such as *The Night (Alone)*, a novel, and *L.A. Is the Capital of Kansas: Painful Lessons in Post–New York Living*, a cultural diatribe. Both men also write poetry, but they hardly ever write about rock 'n' roll.

In 1989 the acclaimed science-fiction author Bruce Sterling published a short story called "Dori Bangs" that imagined another possible future for Lester. In real life, underground cartoonist Dori Seda died in 1988, and she and Lester never met. (She was not the Dori from Canada.) In his story Sterling fantasized that they lived and married. Lester wrote a Hollywood screenplay about a fictional heavy-metal band, published a book called *A Reasonable Guide to Horrible Noise* with an introduction by a French semiotician, taught Rock and Popular Culture at a state college in Kansas, finally completed his novel shortly after the turn of the century, when it seemed quaint and dated, and died of a heart attack in 2015 while shoveling snow. He was survived by Dori, who learned the meaning of life from a vision of the child they never had.

Anything is possible for Lester in the afterlife, but one thing he definitely did not do was write the letters from heaven that appeared at the beginning and end of *Psychotic Reactions and Carburetor Dung*. Those were penned by Mark Shipper, whose Beatles novel, *Paperback Writer*, inspired Lester to start a similar book about the Stones. Shipper intended the missives as dadaist tributes, and he never imagined that they would end up in Marcus's anthology.

The other question that came up in many interviews: Did Lester intend to die?

Though Lester often spoke of being depressed, his therapist Phil Sapienza does not believe that Lester suffered from clinical depression. "I saw very few signs of depression in Lester either as a therapist or as a friend, and I'm trained to know about those things," Sapienza told me in 1997. "Lester loved life. There was a vitality about him that was real and genuine. He was always searching, but what does that mean? If you stop searching, you are depressed, by definition. And he never stopped searching."

"What happened almost instantly was that the contingent that wanted to keep Lester as this out-of-control rock hero wanted to have him die as an out-of-control rock hero," said his friend, Kathy Miller, who graduated from hooker booker to corporate executive at one of the country's largest health-maintenance organizations. "I found that whenever I was in the context of someone who wanted to talk about Lester, they wanted to hear 'famous Lester stories' about the fucked-up, outrageous Lester, and that was not who I remembered. God knows I was the recipient of some of those stories, but that was not the person I loved. Then there was the opposite, which was 'Lester was a saint and he was getting ready to bump Mother Teresa and this cruel act of fate intervened.' Lester was no saint. He was a man who was always going to struggle with demons, was always going to struggle with trying to put right for him emotionally these huge issues like family, having children, women, and ambivalent feelings almost bordering on hostility toward gays. He was always a guy grappling with huge issues and trying to understand."

In the process of writing this book I probably came to know the many sides of Lester Bangs better than many of his intimates or even Lester himself, and I still don't feel qualified to answer the question of whether his death was intentional, an unfortunate error, or something at neither of these extremes. For that matter I have no confidence in speculating whether he was great despite his excesses or because of them. St. Lester has become a rock 'n' roll icon, and people read into him the myths that they need. In the end these questions aren't really relevant to the legacy that inspired this project, and here Lester deserves the last word. Writing for *Musician* in 1981, he considered the career of Jim Morrison, whom he called "Bozo Dionysus."

"Perhaps what we finally conclude is that it's not really necessary to separate the clown from the poet," Lester wrote, "that they were in fact inextricably linked, and that even as we were lucky not to have been around any more than our fair share of Dionysian infants, so we were lucky to get all the great music on these albums, which is going to set rock 'n' roll standards for a long time to come."

How to Be a Rock Critic

A Megatonic Journey with Lester Bangs

Lately I've noticed a new wrinkle on the American landscape: It seems as if there's a whole generation of kids, each one younger than the last, all of whom live, breathe, and dream of but one desire: "I want to be a *rock critic* when I grow up!"

If that sounds condescending let it be known that I was once just like them; the only difference was that when I held such aspirations, the field was relatively uncluttered—it was practically nothing to barge right in and commence the slaughter—whereas now, of course, it's so glutted that the last thing anybody should ever consider doing is entering this racket. In the first place, it doesn't pay much and doesn't lead anywhere in particular, so no matter how successful you are at it, you'll eventually have to decide what you're going to do with your life anyway. In the second place, it's basically just a racket in the first place, and not a particularly glorious one at that.

It almost certainly won't get you laid. (Rock critics *are* beginning to get groupies of a sort now, but most of them are the younger, aspiring rock critics—like the kind on *Shakin' Street*—of one sex or another.) It won't make you rich: The highest-paying magazine in the rock press still only pays thirty bucks a review, and most of the other magazines fall way below that. So you'll never be able to make a living off of it. Nobody will come up to you in the street and say, "Hey, I recognize you! You're Jon Landau! Man, that last review was really far out!" A lot of people, in fact, will hate you and think you're a pompous asshole just for expressing your opinions, and tell you so to your face.

On the other side of the slug, though, are the benefits. Which are okay, if you don't get taken in by them. The first big one is that if you stay at this stuff long enough you'll start to get free records in the mail, and if you persevere even longer you may wind up on the promotional mailing lists of every company in the nation, which will not only save you a lot of money on pay day and ensure that you'll get to hear everything and anything you want, but help to pay the rent on occasion when you sell the albums spilling into your bathroom to local used records stores, at prices ranging from five cents to over a dollar apiece. Plus on Christmas you don't have to buy anybody any presents if you don't want to: Just give your mother the new Barbra Streisand album Columbia sent you because Barbra's trying to relate, your big sister one of the three copies of the new Carole King that you got in the mail, your little sister that Osmonds double live LP you never even opened because you're too hip. . . . all down the line, leaving you with enough money saved to stay fucked-up on *good* whiskey over the holidays this year.

Another fringe benefit which will sooner or later accrue if you hew steadily on this jive-ass scrawl is that you will be invited to press parties for the opening of new acts in town. It helps to live in places like L.A. and New York, because they have more of them there; I know some people, in fact, who have almost literally kept themselves from starving for months at a time by eating dinner at a different press party every night. (I know other people who have made entire careers out of *attending* these things, but that's a different story.) The food's usually pretty good to magnificent, unless it's some blue-jeaned folkie and the company's trying to be with-it by serving organic slop unfit for the innards of a sow; even in such an extreme case as that, though, you can content yourself with sopping up the booze, which is plentiful and usually of high quality. So even if you live at home or haven't had any trouble lately keeping the wolf from the door, you can get drunk free a lot and that's always a pleasure, even if you do usually have to sit through some shit like John Prine or Osibisa just for a few glasses of gin. Sure you're prostituting yourself in a way, but so are they, and what are most modern business, social, or sexual relationships if not a process of symbiotic exploitation? It's the same tub of shit no matter where it perches, so you might as well kick back and enjoy yourself while you can.

The next big step up after press parties is that you'll start receiving invitations to concerts, events, and record company conventions in distant cities. Free vacations! The record companies will pay your plane fare, put you up in a swank hotel with room service (usually), and wine and dine you like mad for the duration of your stay, all just because they want you to write about some act they're trying to break. This is where things get a little cooler and less of a hustle, because once you've had enough stuff published that they're willing to drop a few hundred smackeroos to get you to do a story on somebody in their stable, you can pretty much pick and choose who you want to write about. Well, not totally, but everybody finds their own level, and it finds them. Like if you're a red-hot flaming-eared heavy metal fanatic, they'll call you up one day and offer to fly you to Chicago or New York to see, oh, the Stooges, maybe. Or at least Jukin' Bone.

The final benefit (and for some people, the biggest) is that during most of these stages and at an increasingly casual level as time goes on, you'll get to hobnob with the Stars. Backstage at concerts, in the dressing room drinking their wine, rapping casually with the famous, the talented, the rich, and the beautiful. Most of 'em are just jerks like everybody else, and you probably won't really get to meet any real Biggies very often since the record companies don't need publicity on them so why should they inflict you on 'em, but you will become friends with a lot of Stars of the Future. Or at least also-rans.

Okay, so that's the rosy vista. I painted it for true, and if you want it, it's yours, becuz after almost five years in this racket I finally decided I'm gonna break down and tell the whole world how to break in. I could get a lotta dough for this if I wanted to—some of us have talked for years about starting a Famous Rock Critics' School—but fuck it, I'm too lazy to take the time to set up some shit like that, and besides it's about time everybody got wind of the True Fax of Rock 'n' Roll Criticism. Listen well, and decide for yourself whether you wanna bother with it.

The first thing to understand and bear in mind at all times is that the whole thing is just a big ruse from the word go, it don't mean shit except exploitatively and in the zealotic terms of wanting to inflict your tastes on other people. Most people start writing record reviews because they want other people to like the same kind of stuff they do, and there's nothing wrong with that, it's a very honest impulse. I used to be a Jehovah's Witness when I was a kid so I had it in my blood already, a head start. But don't worry. All you gotta do is just keep bashin' away, and sooner or later people will start saying things to you like, "How do you fit the Kinks into your overall aesthetic perspective?"

Well, they won't really talk that jive-ass, but damn close if you travel in the right (or wrong, as the case may be) circles. Because that old saw is true: most rock critics *are* pompous assholes. Maybe most *critics* are pompous assholes, but rock critics are especially—because they're working in virgin territory, where there's absolutely no recognized, generally agreed on authority or standards. Nor should there be. Anything goes, so fake 'em out every chance you get. Rock 'n' roll's basically just a bunch of garbage in the first place, it's noise, it's here today and gone tomorrow, so the only thing that can possibly trip you up is if you begin to reflect that if the *music's* that trivial, can you imagine how trivial what *you're* doing is?

Which actually is a good attitude to operate from, because it helps keep the pomposity factor in check. Half the rock critics in the country, no, 90% of the rock critics in the world have some grand theory they're trying to lay on each other and everybody else, which they insist explains everything in musical history and ties up all the loose ends. Every last one of 'em has a different theory and every last one of the theories is total bullshit, but you might as well have one as part of your baggage if you're going to pass. Try this: ALL ROCK 'N' ROLL CULTURES PLA-GIARIZE EACH OTHER. THAT IS INHERENT IN THEIR NATURE. SO MAYBE, SINCE WHAT ROCK 'N' ROLL'S ALL ABOUT IS PLAGIARISM ANYWAY, THE MOST OUT-AND-OUT PLAGIARISTS, THE IMITATORS OF THE PRIME MOVING GENIUSES, ARE GREATER AND MORE VALID THAN THOSE GENIUSES! JUST CHECK THIS OUT: THE ROLLING STONES ARE BETTER THAN CHUCK BERRY! THE SHADOWS OF KNIGHT WERE BETTER THAN THE YARDBIRDS! P. F. SLOAN'S FIRST ALBUM WAS A MASTER-PIECE, WAY BETTER THAN *BLONDE ON BLONDE* (I know one prominent rock critic in Texas who actually believes this; he's a real reactionary, but so are most of 'em!)!

Pretty pompous, huh? Well, that just happens to be one of my basic theories, although I don't really believe all the stuff I said in there (not that that makes a diddley damn bit of difference), and you can have it if you want it to bend or mutate as you please. Or come up with your own crock of shit; anyway, it's good to have one for those late-nite furious discussions leading absolutely nowhere. See, the whole thing's just a big waste of time, but the trappings can be fun and you always liked to whack off anyway. Like, look, you can impress people you wanna fuck by saying impressive things like, "John Stuart Mill couldn't write rock 'n' roll, but Dylan could have written 'An Essay on Human Understanding.' Only he would have called it 'Like a Rolling Stone!' " (Dave Marsh of *Creem* magazine actually said that to me, and everybody else who lived with us, and everybody he talked to on the phone for the next month, once.) Just imagine laying that on some fine little honey—she'd flip out! She'd think you were a genius! Either that or a pompous asshole. But in this business, like any other, you win some and you lose some. Persevere, kid.

Where were we? Ah yes, you should also know that most of your colleagues are some of the biggest neurotics in the country, so you might as well get used right now to the way they're gonna be writing you five- and ten-page single-spaced inflammatory letters reviling you for knocking some group that they have proved is the next Stones. It's all very incestuous, like this great big sickoid club full of people who were probably usually the funny-looking kid in class, with the acne and the big horn-rims, all introverted, and just sat home every night through high school and played his records while the other kids yukked and balled it up. Tough luck, genius is pain. Or frustrated pop stars—*all* rock critics are frustrated pop stars and you should see 'em singing to themselves when nobody else is around. Boy, do they get corny! Melodramatic? Whooo!! Some of them actually go so far as to invest their entire life savings in trendy pop-star wardrobes, and others are so monomaniacal as to go beyond that to the actual steps of *forming a band of their own*. And you can rest assured that all of them write songs, and have constant daytime and nightdaze fantasies of big contracts with ESP Disk at least.

Speaking of investing your life savings, another good way of letting on to everybody on the block that you're a rock critic is to go out and waste a lot of money buying old albums in bargain bins. They have these turd-dumps in most drugstores or supermarkets, full of last year's crap and older stuff at prices ranging from as low as a quarter all the way up to $2.50 and more. If you patronize these scumholes regularly, you will soon begin to build a Definitive Rock 'n' Roll Albums Collection, which is of course a must for anybody who's into this way of life really seriously. The object is simple: you gotta have EVERYTHING, no matter how arcane or shitty it is, because it all fits into the grand bulwark of Rock. So just go out there and throw all your money away, it's a good investment. You'll be filling your room with mung, but so what: How many *other* people do you know who have the Battered Ornaments album? Right. They don't know what they're missing.

I know one rock critic who actually drew out his life's savings and drove from St. Louis, where he lived, to New York and back, by way of Chicago, Detroit and New Jersey, AND STOPPED AT EVERY BARGAIN BIN ALONG THE WAY. That was the entire purpose of the trip, to visit bargain bins. Now this guy is obviously a real doofus and totally out of his mind, but you can see where this business can lead you if you're lucky and apply yourself: *down blind alleys.*

Speaking of this same doofus reminds me of another riff that is essential to have if you're gonna be a hotshit rock critic. You gotta find some band somewhere that's maybe even got two or three albums out and might even be halfway good, but the important thing is the more arcane it is the better, it's gotta be something that absolutely nobody in the world but you and two other people (the group's manager and one member's mother) knows or cares about, and what you wanna do is TALK ABOUT THIS BUNCH OF OBSCURE NONENTITIES AND THEIR RECORD(S) LIKE THEY'RE THE HOTTEST THING IN THE HISTORY OF MUSIC! You gotta build 'em up real big, they're your babies, only you alone can perceive their true greatness, so you gotta go around telling everybody that they're better than the Rolling Stones, they beat the Beatles black and blue, they murtelyze the Dead, they're the most significant and profound musical force in the world. And someday their true greatness will be recognized and you will be vindicated as a seer far ahead of your time.

Sometimes this scheme can really pay off, like if you happen to pick a Captain Beefheart or Velvet Underground way before they get widely known, although they're not really eligible because this group has gotta be so obscure that they can put out all kindsa albums and nobody pays any attention to 'em but you, they're just off moldering in a cutout rack somewhere if not for your devoted efforts.

Doofus (of the preceding paragraph) came up with a lulu in this department, couple of 'em in fact: All he ever talks about is Amon Düül II,

Bang, and Budgie. Ever heard of any of 'em? That's what I thought. And you probably never will except if he's around to pester you about them. Amon Düül II are this psychedelic experimental avant-garde chance music free jazz electronic synthesizer space rock group from Germany. They got all kinds of albums out over there, there's even two groups with the same name, Amon Düül I and Amon Düül II, but they only got three albums out here and hardly anybody ever heard of 'em, although a whole shitload of people sure will if Doofus keeps up his one-man propaganda campaign on their behalf! They happen to be real good, but that's beside the point. And Bang and Budgie, his other two pet monomanias, are a couple of Black Sabbath imitations, one from Florida and one from England, one pretty good and one not so hot. So he and this other critic from Texas (also previously mentioned) send big long hate letters back and forth to each other telling each other what morons they are, because the Texan don't like Budgie or something like that. Get the idea?

Also I turned Doofus onto Can, another German psychedelic schnozz-ball that has lotsa 17-minute electro-raga jams, and he listens to one side of their album one time and sez to me: "Don't you think Can are better than the Stooges?" See what I mean? When all week he's been asking me things like, "Don't you think Amon Düül II are the greatest group in history?" and "Don't you think *Dance of the Lemmings* (one of their albums, featuring such standards as "Dehypnotized Toothpaste," "Landing in a Ditch," and "A Short Stop at the Transylvanian Brain Surgery") is the greatest album of all time?" and I keep saying no, but he won't take no for an answer, he's a man with a Plan! A crusader on behalf of Neglected Genius. So you see the key: *persistence*. Make a total nuisance of yourself, and people will begin to take you seriously. Or at least stop regarding you as not there. And if he wants to continue on this obscuro roller-coaster ride, there are zillions of German bands: Take Guru Guru or Floh de Cologne, for example—these qualify as two of the finest choices in the Arcane Masterpiece department in history, indeed they do, because both are imports and you can't even find a single Floh de Cologne or Guru Guru album anywhere in the United States except by ordering it special from Germany! *Nobody* knows what it sounds like, so they gotta listen to Doofus. As you can see Doofus copped himself a real hot item, but chances like that come only once in a lifetime.

That pretty much takes care of the qualifications. Like what you see? Wanna give it a try? Well, get ready, because the big time is just around the corner. The only thing left to mention before you embark on your career as a rock critic is that talent has absolutely nothing to do with it, so don't worry if you don't know how to write. Don't even worry if you can't put a simple declarative sentence together. Don't worry if you can only sign your name with an X. Anybody can do this shit, all it takes is a high level of unconsciousness (and you just got done reading an unconsciousness-expanding session) and some ability to sling bullshit around. Also the bullshit is ready-made, you don't even have to think it up, all you gotta do is invest in a slingshot. All the word-type stuff you need has already been written anyway, it's in old yellow issues of *Shakin' Street*, *Rolling Stone*, *Creem*, and all the rest; just sit around reading and re-reading the damn things all day and pretty soon you'll have whole paragraphs of old record reviews memorized, which is not only a good way to impress people at parties and girls you're trying to pick up with your erudition, but allows you to plagiarize at will. And don't worry about getting caught, because nobody in this business has any memory and besides they're all plagiarists too and besides that all record reviews read the same. I learned to write 'em outta *Down Beat*, and it's the same shit in *Rolling Stone*; it's the same shit all over. Just stir and rearrange it every once in a while. Take one riff and staple it to another; and if you get tired of thinking about how you're a rock critic, remember William Burroughs and the cut-up method and think about being avant-garde. I do it all the time.

Okay, now it's time for you to write YOUR VERY FIRST ORIGINAL RECORD REVIEW. It's easy, all you gotta do is point. First, pick a title for the album:

A. *Oranges in Exile*
B. *Outer City Blues & Heavy Dues*
C. *Cajun Sitar Dance Party*
D. *Hungry Children of Babylon*
E. *Eat Your Coldcream*

Got it? Okay, the next part's just as easy. Just fill in the blanks:
This latest offering from_____

A. Harmonica Dan and His Red Light District
B. The Armored Highchair
C. Ducks in Winter
D. The Four Fat Guys
E. Arturo de Cordova

is_____

A. a clear consolidation of the artistic moves first tentatively ventured in his/her/their/its last album.
B. a real letdown after the masterpiece album and single that carried
   us all the way through the summer and warmed us over in the fall.
C. important only insofar as it will delineate the contours of the
   current malaise for future rock historians, if there *are* any with
   all the pollution around now.
D. definitely the album of the year.
E. a heap of pig shit.

(How you doin' so far? See how easy it is!) Onward! Choose one of
the following for the next sentence:

A. In dealing with such a record, the time has come at last to talk
   about the responsibilities, if any, which any artist making rock 'n'
   roll bears to his audience, and specifically how those responsibilities relate to the political situation which we, all of us, and
   perforce rock 'n' roll, are compelled to come to terms with by dint
   of living in the United States of America today.
B. I don't really think these guys/this dude/the chick in question/a
   singing dog can defend musical output which has proven increasingly shoddy by referring to such old handles as "personal
   expression," "experimentalism," "a new kind of artistic freedom,"
   or any other such lame cop-out.
C. It's such a thrill that this album finally came, that I am finally actually holding it in my hands, looking at the fantastically beautiful M. C. Escher drawing on the cover whilst trembling all over
   to the incredible strains of the music on the record from inside
   it which even now are wafting from the old Victrola, that I really
   don't know if I am going to come or cry.
D. It's so goddam fucking boring to have to open all these pieces of
   shit every day, you waste your time, you break your fingernails,
   half the time it's just a repeat of an album that came yesterday,
   that I can hardly bring myself to slit open the shrink wrap once
   I get 'em outta the cardboard (which piles up in a big mess all
   over the house after it gets dragged outta the corner by all my
   asshole friends!), and I really can just barely stand to put the

goddam things on the turntable after that. I wish it would break anyway so I wouldn't have to listen to 'em anymore. (Good one, huh, more than one sentence in this one!) But anyway, I put this piece of shit on just like all the others except the ones I never get around to, and right now I'm listening to it and you know what? I was right. It *is* a piece of shit!

E. I don't remember how I got here, whose house this is, or where this typewriter came from, but anyway this new album is by the greatest fucking rock 'n' roll band in the whole wide world/most talented, sensitive balladeer of his generation whom many of us are already calling the New Dylan/sweetest songbird this side of the Thames has saved my life again just like all the others did, so I don't even care where I am, I don't care if I got rolled last night, I don't care if this place gets busted right now, I don't care if the world comes to an end because the cosmic message of truth and unity which this music is bringing to me has made me feel complete for the first time since 1968.

(Well, that wasn't hard at all, was it? A whole paragraph written already! But this is no place to stop: the most fun's yet to come. Tally ho!)

The first song on side one_____

A. "Catalina Sky"
B. "Death Rays in Your Eyes"
C. "I Wish I Was a Rusty Nail"
D. "Lady of Whitewater"
E. "Nixon Eats"

(choose again)_____

A. is a rousingly high spirited opener in march tempo.
B. starts things off at an extremely high energy level.
C. sets the pace and mood of the album most atmospherically.
D. won't win any Grammies this year.
E. reminds me of my Grandmother puking up her sherry into the bathtub the night we had fish that had gone bad for dinner when I was three years old.

The first thing you notice is_____

A. the vicious, slashing guitar solo.
B. the deep, throbbing bass lines.
C. how mellowly the sensitive, almost painfully fragile vocal is integrated with the mesmerizing Spanish chords from those four fine hollow-body Gibson guitars.
D. the cymbals aren't miked right.
E. that the entire mix is a washout and this album has what is probably the worst production of the year.

The full impact of what's going on in this cut may not reach you the first time, but if you keep listening a couple of times a day for a week or two, especially through headphones, it will come to you in a final flash of revelation that_____

A. you were wasting your time.
B. you are listening to such a masterpiece of rock which so far transcends "rock" as we have known it that most people probably won't recognize its true worth for at least ten years.
C. the instruments are out of tune.
D. you should have bought The Band instead.
E. you're deaf in one ear.

Cut two is_____

A. a nice change of pace
B. more of the same phlegm
C. a definite picker-upper
D. interesting, at least
E. insulting to the human ear (my dog didn't like it either)

by virtue of the fact that_____

A. it was produced by Phil Spector's cousin from Jersey.
B. it's only two seconds long.
C. the lyrics say more, and more concisely, about what we have done to our natural environment than anything else written in the past decade.

   D. Bobby Keyes, Jim Price and Boots Randolph sit in for a real old-
      time "blowing session."
   E. I spilled Gallo Port in the grooves and it made it sound better.

In spite of that, I feel that the true significance of its rather dense
and muted lyrics can only be apprehended by _____

   A. the purchase of a hearing aid.
   B. reading the sheet enclosed with the record.
   C. going back and listening to "Memphis Blues Again," *then* come
      back to this and see if it doesn't blow you out the door!
   D. taking a course in German.
   E. throwing the incoherent piece of pig shit in the trash and going
      out for a beer, where something good is probably on the jukebox.

(Time for paragraph three already! Smooth sailing, bunky! You're
almost there.) This record has inspired such _____

   A. ambivalent feelings
   B. helpless adoration
   C. bile and venom
   D. total indifference
   E. a powerful thirst

in me that I can't bring myself to describe the rest of the cuts. Track-
by-track reviews are a bore anyway, and the album only costs $4.97
at the right stores, so go down and get it and find out for yourself
whether you'll like it or not. Who am I, who is any critic or any other
sentient being on the face of the earth, to tell you what a piece of
music sounds like? Only your ears can hear it as only your ears can
hear it. Am I right or am I wrong? Of course I am. I do know that I
will_____

   A. go on listening to this album till I drop dead of cancer.
   B. walk out into the backyard and toss this offense unto mine eyes
      into the incinerator soon as I finish typing this spew.
   C. never forget the wonderful chance I've had here in the pages of
      Fusion to share this very special record, and my own deepest
      dredged sentiments about it, with you, who whether you know

it or not are a very special person whom I love without qualifi-
cation even if we've never seen each other, I don't even know
your name, and am so righteous that I don't even care if you look
like a sow.
  D. break this elpee over the head of the very next Jesus Freak or
     Hare Krishna creep I see in the street, just for thrills!
  E. go to sleep now and awaken upon a new morning in which I may
     be able to appreciate this unabridged poetic outpouring with
     fresh ears.

So before I sign my name at the bottom of this page and pick up the
check from the cheap kikes that run this rag that will never pay me anyway, I would like to leave you with one thought:_____

  A. Today is the first day of the rest of your life.
  B. There are many here among us who feel that life is but a joke.
  C. The red man lost this land to you and me.
  D. Rock 'n' roll is dead. Long live rock 'n' roll.
  E. Since these assholes that're stupid enough to print this stuff
     don't pay me anything, why don't you? I've probably turned you
     on to a lot of good records over the years, and what do I get out
     of it? Nothing but a lot of grief! A lot of abuse from cretins who
     can't understand that rock 'n' roll IS the Revolution! A lot of
     cheap bloodsuckers like hell hounds on my trail! I got "Yer
     Blues"! I've paid my body and soul! So send me some $$$, god-
     dammit, or I'll never write a word again as long as I live!

    Your faithful correspondent, _____

    You did it! You really did it! There, you see, that wasn't so hard, was
it? Now YOU TOO are an officially ordained and fully qualified rock
critic, with publication under your belt and everything. Just cut out the
review, if you're finished filling in all the blanks, and send it to the rock
magazine of your choice with a stamped, self-addressed envelope! If they
send it back, send it to another one! Be persistent! Be a "go-getter"! Do
you think Jon Landau ever let rejection slips get him down? No! And if
you send it to all the rock mags in America, one of them is bound to print
it sooner or later because most of them will print the worst off the wall
shit in the world if they think it'll make 'em avant-garde! You could send

'em the instruction booklet on how to repair your lawn mower, just write the name of a current popular album by a famous artist at the top of the cover, sign your name at the bottom of the last page, and they'll print it! They'll think you're a genius!

And you are! And when all the money you asked for in this review starts pouring in from your fans, you'll be rich! David Geffen will invite you out to his house in the Catskills for the weekend! Miles Davis will step aside when you walk down the street! Seals of Seals & Crofts will tip his hat to you and sing "Bah'aii!" as you walk down the street! David Peel will write songs about you! So will John Lennon! So will everybody! Andy Warhol will put you in his movies! You'll tour with David Bowie, Leon Russell, and Atomic Rooster, reading your most famous reviews to vast arenas full of rabid fans! You'll be an international celebrity and die at 33! You made the grade! You are now a rock critic, and by tomorrow you will be one of the most important critics in America! You'll make *Esquire's* Heavy Hundred in 1974!

Congratulations, and welcome to the club!

Your pal,
R. J. Gleason

Selected Lyrics by Lester Bangs

"Let It Blurt"

Had a Quaalude romance
A real modern affair
Fucking for hours to *Raw Power*
A whole lifetime we shared
She was my teenage dream
But I was twenty-five
After the abortion only rancor left alive
But that's O.K., baby
I just told her what I had to say:
"Bitch! Bitch! Bitch! Bitch!
I wish your ass was dead!"
    And if it hurts
    Just let it blurt
Vitriol all down your bib
You know you can always leave
If you don't like what's-s-s happenin'

Sittin' by the dock of the bay
Later on the same ol' D-Day
Drinkin' port wine and singing "Sister Ray"
Wonderin' why I wasn't born gay
Makes you feel just like an ofay
But that's cool too, baby
Just say what you've gotta say:
"Bitch! Bitch! Bitch! Bitch!
The baby wasn't mine!"
    You know it hurts
    Just let it blurt
I know it ain't funny
It ain't funny at all, baby
That's why I'm laughing
To keep from crying
That's why I'm crying
Because I'm laughing
Haw! Haw! And fuck you!
I'll see you in hell, baby
I'll see you in hell, baby
I'll see you in hell

"There's a Man in There"

The night was awful but the food was good
We all stood just where we should
Everybody comin' in the congregation
Come to watch the conflagration
It was the finest fire that I ever seen
Don't mistake just what I mean
A real eighth wonder of a manmade pit
Till I saw a hand wave so deep in it
    I said there's a man in there
    He's peeling near shapeless bubbling fat
    They took a glance and just laughed, "Where?"
    Stoked the furnace and that was that
So I crept a little closer just to check my wits
Saw two eyes pleading from an iron spit
Shot right between 'em with a smell most foul
That was when he began to howl
    I cried there's a man in there
    Not pretty to look at but he's not all gone
    Give him, give him, give him some air
    They refilled my drink and smiled, "Welcome home"

    It's just kindling from that same old bin
    Civilized folk don't go burnin' men
    We all can tell sport from sin
    Sometimes, I said, kindling is kin

It blazed and razed till it was sated
I could not turn away though the fire faded
The folks went home but I was caught
By such deep dread and knew not what I sought
    There's still a man in there
    I screamed and fell to tear the ashes
    While janitors just stared and stared
    My heart burned ten thousand lashes
    There's a man in there

"Day of the Dead"

I sleep in torment
Dream while I'm awake
If love is dormant
I'd only love you for my own sake
  Ooh mama, take me away
  From that terrible, terrible day
  A car of death and the cask enclosing
  You've lost yourself and everyone knows it
I want you more than life itself
But life seems such a paltry thing
That doesn't mean I need your help
And just what are you offering?
  Ooh mama, take me away
  From that terrible, terrible day
  A car of death and the cask enclosing
  You've lost yourself and everyone knows it

  I want it all
  I want it all
  I want it all
  I cry when you call

Kindness of strangers should not be disdained
I don't want the rest of my life
To feel so defiled, defiled and stained
What could I possibly think of my wife?
  Ooh mama, take me away
  From that terrible, terrible day
  A car of death and the cask enclosing
  You've lost yourself and everyone knows it

"Live"

People in the cemetery
They're not all alone
Some buried in each others' arms
And some got telephones
They don't mind dyin'
They got a message to give
And they ain't lyin'
When they say:
    LIVE!

Death is only temporary
But life rolls on and on
There's a lotta folks walkin' around
Who've turned to stone
And if they don't mind dyin'
'fore it's time to give in
I'm not tryin' to cop no attitude
Just trying to say one thing:
    LIVE!

Don't mean to be didactic
There's plenty 'nuff static around already
It's just that stealin' from yourself
It's such an odd kinda stealth
So forgive me before you forget
That the dead are talkin' straight at you, baby
And they're takin' such sorrowful bets
That you won't
    LIVE!

Notes

Introduction

Bangs's performance, pp. xix–xx: Bangs, "My Night of Ecstasy with the J. Geils Band," and interviews, Auringer, Niester, Schloner, Jaan Uhelszki, and Wolf.

I.   The Closed Circle

Family history, pp. 3–6: Interviews, Imogene Bangs; Ann, Ben Jr., Ben III, and Bill Catching; and Steve and John St. Clair. Dates were verified by the birth and death certificates of Conway, Norma, and Leslie Bangs, and additional information was culled from Leslie's birth announcement in the *Escondido Daily Times-Advocate*. Robert Christgau's *Village Voice* obituary and Greil Marcus's introduction to *Psychotic Reactions and Carburetor Dung* both state an incorrect birth date.

History of the Jehovah's Witnesses, p. 7: Penton, *Apocalypse Delayed*; The Watchtower Bible and Tract Society of New York, *Mankind's Search for God*; Rosten, *Religions of America*, and Miller, *America's Alternative Religions*.

Bangs on "a fluctuating fanaticism," p. 12: "Psychotic Reactions and Carburetor Dung: A Tale of These Times"; **Bangs on his "library" system and brother Bill, p. 14:** *Drug Punk*.

The Fire, p. 16: *Escondido Daily Times-Advocate*, "Man Dies in Flaming House Here"; **sharing his mother's bed and seeing the flames, p. 17:** interviews, Nancy Alexander, Miller, and Sapienza.

II.   Birth of the Cool

Bangs on Escondido, pp. 18–19: *Drug Punk* (the Witnesses and collecting), "A Reasonable Guide to Horrible Noise" (the cat), and "Slow Times In Detroit" (the fight); **sexual abuse, p. 19:** interviews, Anderson, Jennings, Miller, Pelzman, and Sapienza; **Bangs on his "dark, distorted childhood mythology," p. 19:** *Drug Punk*.

Bangs on his childhood fantasy and his records, pp. 20–21: "Psychotic Reactions and Carburetor Dung"; **Bangs on Davis, p. 21:** letter to John Sinclair; **Bangs on Mingus, p. 22:** "Notes on Mingus"; **Bangs on Kerouac, p. 22:** book review, *Doctor Sax / Mexico City Blues / Lonesome Traveler*; **Bangs on his "saints," p. 22:** letter to Sinclair.

Bascom on Bangs, p. 25: Kriner, "Ex-Inlander and Rock Music Critic Dies in N.Y."; **Bangs on his ideal review, his "books," and his "eternal critic," pp. 25–26:** *Drug Punk*; **Bangs on his early sexual experiences, p. 26:** "Street Hassling" (the cheap feel), "Psychotic Reactions and Carburetor Dung" (playing footsie), and letter to Sinclair (the teacher's daughter); **Bangs on the "speckled wombat," p. 27:** *Drug Punk*.

Bangs on the Stones, p. 29: album review: *Get Yer Ya-Ya's Out*; **Bangs on burning his manuscripts and his "Sound aborning," p. 30:** *Drug Punk*.

Bangs on life with Norma, p. 30: *Journal of a Blob*; **Bangs on his half brother Ben, p. 32:** letter to the editor, *Teenage Wasteland Gazette*; **disfellowshipment, p. 33:** Penton, *Apocalypse Delayed*, and the Watchtower Bible and Tract Society, "Family Responsibilities in Keeping Jehovah's Witnesses Pure"; **Bangs on the Witnesses, p. 33:** "Big Youth Go Home."

III.   Drug Punk

Bangs's letter to Burroughs Wellcome, p. 35: *Drug Punk*; **Bangs on the psychedelic subculture, p. 37:** *Drug Punk*; **Bangs on Romilar, p. 37:** "I Saw God in a Bottle of Romilar"; **Bangs on the effects of dextromethorphan, pp. 37–38:** *Drug Punk*.

Bangs on his music lessons, p. 38: "John Coltrane Lives" and "Rock Critics Rule! And Other Startling Musical Revelations"; **Bangs on "Psychotic Reaction," p. 39:** "The Count Five."

Bangs on Darvon, p. 40: *Journal of a Blob*; **Bangs on his music and his roommates, p. 41:** "Untitled Notes, 1981," from *Psychotic Reactions and*

Carburetor Dung; **Bangs on Silly Willie, p. 41:** *Drug Punk*; **Bangs on cop-hating and his arrest, p. 42:** *Journal of a Blob;* **the Hell's Angels gang bang, pp. 43–44:** Bangs, *Drug Punk*; and interviews, Anderson, Butler, Ben Catching III, and di Guglielmo.

Anderson on Bangs, p. 45: "Growing Up with Lester"; **Bangs on the fall of 1968, p. 45:** "Astral Weeks" from *Stranded*; **Bangs on records as therapy, p. 45:** *Journal of a Blob;* **Bangs on his "spazzouts," p. 45:** "Sexual History"; **the fight with Andy, pp. 45–46:** Bangs, *Drug Punk*, and interview, di Guglielmo; **Bangs on "the kind of woman," p. 46:** "Andy"; **Bangs on the doctor, p. 46:** *Journal of a Blob.*

IV.   Make It or Break It

Bangs on waking from "the funk," p. 47: *Drug Punk.*

Marcus on Meltzer, p. 50: introduction to *The Aesthetics of Rock*, Da Capo edition; **Bangs on critics, p. 51:** letter to Marcus, July 1969; **Bangs on the literature of the counterculture, p. 51:** *Journal of A Blob.*

Sinclair on the riots, p. 52: *Guitar Army*; **Bangs on the MC5, p. 52:** Ironically, Lester's *Rolling Stone* review earned a stern rebuke in the pages of a new Detroit rock magazine called *Creem.* "Thanks for revealing your undying ignorance of most matters which would appertain to the reviewing of any powerful and sincere rock 'n' roll music," wrote founding editor Tony Reay.

Bangs on Julie Driscoll, p. 55: letter to Marcus, late November 1969; **the letter from Maureen Tucker, p. 55:** interview, Anderson. Tucker did not recall the letter or meeting Bangs. **Bangs on meeting the Velvets, p. 55:** *"Dead Lie the Velvets Underground"* and letter to Marcus, November 4, 1969; **Jac Holzman and Clive Davis were angry, p. 57:** Draper, *Rolling Stone Magazine: The Uncensored History*; **Miles was pissed off, p. 57:** Bangs, *Rock Gomorrah / Tales From Beyond the Grooves,* and Draper, *Rolling Stone Magazine: The Uncensored History*; **Bangs on the Kerouac dream, p. 57:** "Elegy for a Desolation Angel"; **Bangs on the Mingus piece, p. 57:** letter to Marcus, July 1969; **Bangs on Gleason and Wenner's reaction to *Drug Punk*, p. 58:** letter to Marcus, November 9, 1969. **Altamont, pp. 59–61:** Andersen, *Jagger Unauthorized*; Anderson, "The Last Anniversary: An Altamont Memoir"; Bangs, "Five Hundred Mile Pilgrimage to a Hell's Angel Death Festival," "I Only Get My Rocks Off When I'm Dreaming," and "1973 Nervous Breakdown: The Ol' Fey Outlaws Ain't What They Used To Be—Are You?";

Booth, *The True Adventures of the Rolling Stones*; Draper, *Rolling Stone Magazine: The Uncensored History*; various authors, "Let It Bleed" (the *Rolling Stone* cover story); and interviews, Anderson, Bovee, Marcus, Morthland, and Winner. Often overlooked in the many accounts about Altamont is the fact that only one of Hunter's Angel assailants was ever identified and indicted. The biker's lawyer argued self-defense, and a jury of his peers acquitted him.

Marcus on Altamont, p. 61: Goldberg, "Greil Marcus, World's Greatest Rock Critic"; **Marcus was fired, p. 61:** Through his publicist, Wenner declined to be interviewed on this point and others. In the interest of disclosure, I should note that I, too, was fired by Wenner in 1996 after eight months as a senior editor of *Rolling Stone*'s music section. **Rolling Stone's loans from CBS and Elektra, p. 61:** Anson, *Gone Crazy and Back Again*, and Draper, *Rolling Stone Magazine*.

V.   Boy Howdy!

Bangs and Ginsberg, p. 63: interview, Rachac. Ginsberg's note appears on the cover sheet of Lester's copy of *Journal of a Blob*. **The Grunt party, p. 64:** Meltzer, "Jack Bonus Stole the Show: Grunt, What a Lovely Sound"; interviews, di Guglielmo and Meltzer; and Willis, e-mail to the author. **Bangs on the draft, p. 65:** *Drug Punk*. His Selective Service record indicates that he never reported for his physical, and his local draft board seems to have lost track of him when he moved to Detroit. **Bangs on his car accident, p. 65:** "Street Hassling."

Bangs on Detroit, p. 68: "Slow Times in Detroit"; **Lennon's apathy quote, p. 68:** Goldman, *The Lives of John Lennon*; **Barry Kramer's background, p. 68:** interviews, Auringer, Marsh, Ryder, and Jaan Uhelszki; **"Deday" LaRene, p. 69:** Ingersoll, *"The Rise and Fall of Deday LaRene,"* and Lengel, "Giacalone Lawyer Gets Year in Prison"; **Marsh on his epiphany, p. 70:** *Fortunate Son*; **Bangs on the New Left, p. 72:** *Journal of a Blob*; **Jaan Uhelszki on Bangs and Marsh, p. 72:** "Twenty-Five Years of *Creem*, Part Three"; **Bangs on Marsh, p. 72:** letter to the editor, *Teenage Wasteland Gazette*, and "Admit It: You Like to Kick Cripples, Too."

Bangs on *Creem* as a "raspberry," p. 75: Trbovich, "Where *Creem* Is At"; **Willis on *Creem*, p. 75:** "My Grand Funk Problem—And Ours"; **Jaan Uhelszki on Brenda Starr, p. 77:** "Twenty-Five Years of *Creem*, Part Three: Look Back in Anger"; **Bangs on heavy metal, p. 81:** "Admit It:

You Like to Kick Cripples, Too"; **Bangs's second take on *Exile on Main Street*, p. 81:** "I Can Only Get My Rocks Off When I'm Dreaming"; **Smith on the Stones, p. 82:** "The monkey man swings home for a snort of Cognac with his pals, Bianca and Boy. He may top it off with a Cold Italian Pizza. Ook, ook." **Bangs on meeting Smith and dating Judy Linn, p. 82:** letter to Anderson, winter 1972.

VI.   Stay Alive 'Til '75

Bangs on Andy, p. 85: "New Year's Eve"; **Bangs on writing, p. 86:** letter to Marcus, early 1972; **Wolfe on the novel, p. 86:** *The New Journalism;* **Bangs on "critical journalism," p. 86:** unpublished author's bio quoted in *Psychotic Reactions and Carburetor Dung;* **Bangs and Reed, p. 87:** Bangs, "Deaf Mute in a Telephone Booth"; and interview, Kent; **Kent on the visit, p. 88:** *The Dark Stuff.*

Meltzer on rock circa 1973, p. 91: introduction, Da Capo edition of *The Aesthetics of Rock;* **Tosches on Bangs, pp. 91–92:** *Lester;* **Tyner on Bangs, p. 92:** "Lester & Me"; **Rock Critics' Symposium, pp. 92–95:** An audiotape of the session was provided by Richard Pachter. **Bangs on being banned from *Rolling Stone*, p. 95:** "Getting Bids on the Albatross: Or, How Does It Feel to Be Frank Zappa?"; **Tosches ripped the letter from Bangs's hands, p. 96:** Meltzer and Tosches had been banned from *Rolling Stone* several months earlier after they reviewed the first album by Commander Cody and His Lost Planet Airmen under each other's bylines and using each other's signature styles. Tosches got the better deal: Meltzer sent the "Tosches" review to *Rolling Stone,* and Tosches pocketed $75. Tosches sent the "Meltzer" review to Fusion, and Meltzer got fifteen bucks.

Bangs and Reed, pp. 98–99: Bangs, "Let Us Now Praise Famous Death Dwarves"; and interviews, Nancy Alexander and Korinsky.

***Creem*'s 1973 circulation, p. 100:** Curtis Circulation Company, "The Wild & Wacky Story of a Music Magazine"; ***Rolling Stone*'s circulation, p. 100:** Anson, *Gone Crazy and Back Again;* **Kramer on selling *Creem*, p. 100:** Macrae, "Rock's New *Creem* of the Crop"; **music industry sales in 1973, p. 101:** Anson, *Gone Crazy and Back Again;* **Lester encouraged dozens of young critics, p. 102:** In addition to Hull, Johnson, and Riegel, those he published while at *Creem* included Billy Altman, Lauren Agnelli (a.k.a. Trixie A. Balm), Cary Baker, Cameron Crowe, Joe

Fernbacher, Toby Goldstein, Gerritt Graham, Donald Jennings, Peter Laughner, Miriam Linna, Andy McKaie, Kathy Miller, Alan Niester, Joe Nick Patoski, Richard Pinkston, Charlotte Pressler, "Metal" Mike Saunders, Gene Sculatti, Kathy Stein, Michael Weldon, James Wolcott, and Howard Wuelfing, among others. **Kooper on Bangs, p. 102–103:** e-mail to the author, 1997; **the food fight with Slade, p. 104**: Bangs, album review: *Sladest*; and interviews, Auringer and Jaan Uhelszki; **Bangs on his image, p. 106:** Macrae, "Rock's New *Creem* of the Crop."

Bangs on *Metal Machine Music*, p. 107: concert review, Mars and the Contortions; **Bangs and Reed, pp. 107–108:** Bangs, "How to Succeed in Torture Without Really Trying," and interview, JoAnn Uhelszki; **Bangs's therapist on *Metal Machine Music*, p. 108:** interview, Jennings.

VII.   I Heard Her Call My Name

Bangs on Canadian beer, p. 109: "This Beer Belly Thinks Canadian Brew's Best"; **Niester on Bangs's singing, p. 109:** album review: Christopher Milk, *Some People Will Drink Anything*; **Bangs on Dori, p. 110:** letter to Anderson, April 1973; **the abortion, p. 110:** Bangs, interview tape with Richard "DNV" Sohl, 1977; and interviews, Georgia Christgau, Kent, Niester, Schloner, and Jaan Uhelszki; **Meltzer on Bangs and Roxon, p. 110:** "Lester Recollected in Tranquility"; **Bangs on his priapism, p. 111:** "Sexual History"; **Morthland on Bangs's humor, p. 113:** e-mail to the author, 1999; **Walls on Bangs, p. 113:** "Twenty-Five Years of *Creem*, Part Two."

Bangs on Springsteen, p. 115: album review: *Born to Run*; **Bangs on Roxy Music, p. 115:** album review: *Stranded*; **Bangs on the Dolls, pp. 115–116:** concert review: Mott the Hoople, the New York Dolls, and Dr. Hook and the Medicine Show; **Bangs on reggae, p. 116:** "How to Learn to Love Reggae"; **Bangs on the trip to Jamaica, pp. 116–117:** "Innocents in Babylon"; **Kempner on the Dictators and Bangs, p. 117:** audiotape of the Lester Bangs panel, South by Southwest Music and Media Conference, March 12, 1992; **Holmstrom launched *Punk* in late 1975, p. 118:** This was actually the second magazine with the name. Billy Altman and Joe Fernbacher had published an earlier *Punk* in Buffalo that printed a piece by Lester. **McNeil on the Dictators, p. 118:** *Please Kill Me*; **Marsh on punk, p. 119:** *Fortunate Son*.

Bangs on Nancy, p. 120: letter to Nancy Alexander, mid-1974; **the fight with the therapist, p. 122:** interviews, Nancy Alexander, Duncan, Jennings, and Morthland.

Kramer on Bangs, p. 127: Macrae, "Rock's New *Creem* of the Crop." In the same article Lester announced that he'd be leaving the *Creem* staff but would continue working as a consulting editor while editing Larry Flynt's *Hustler* spin-off, *Chic*. "Flynt wants to buy class," Lester said, "and it's gonna be interesting." The job offer apparently evaporated shortly thereafter, because nobody remembered his talking about it again. **Bangs on Detroit, p. 128:** "Slow Times in Detroit."

VIII.   Tender Vittles

The Easter party, pp. 132–135: Bangs, letter to Walls; and interviews, Nancy Alexander, Harrison, Morthland, Quine, Stampfel, and Ward.

Bangs on the Ramones, p. 135: album review: *Ramones Leave Home;* **Bangs on the Talking Heads, p. 135:** "David Byrne Says 'Boo!'"; **Bangs on Television, p. 135:** album review: *Marquee Moon*: **Bangs on Blondie, p. 135:** "Blondie is more Fun"; **Bangs on twenty years of rock history, p. 135:** "Protopunk: The Garage Bands" in *The Rolling Stone Illustrated History of Rock & Roll;* **Bangs on passion, p. 135:** *Blondie;* **Christgau on his goals for the *Voice*, p. 136:** *Grown Up All Wrong;* **Bangs on Iggy Pop, p. 137:** "Iggy Pop: Blowtorch in Bondage"; **Bangs on Presley, p. 137:** "Where Were You When Elvis Died?"; **Bangs on his audience, p. 138:** letter to Saunders, February 9, 1977; **Bangs on CBGB, pp. 138–139:** "Peter Tork at CBGB?"; **Bangs on not knowing how to play, p. 139:** concert review: Mars and the Contortions.

The Bellomo sisters interview Bangs, pp. 140–141: interview tape, summer 1977, and Tish & Snooky Bellomo, "Sex and the Single Forkhead."

Hell on inventing yourself, p. 144: Heylin, *From the Velvets to the Voidoids;* **Hell on Bangs, p. 145:** e-mail to the author, 1997; **Bangs on Quine, p. 147:** "The Clash: Lester Bangs Falls in Love"; **Bangs at CBGB, pp. 151–152:** performance tape, June 12, 1977.

Bangs and Smith meet Burroughs, pp. 153–154: interviews, Grauerholz and Simon. Smith writes of the meeting in *Patti Smith Complete* but does not mention Bangs. **Bangs on Styx, p. 156:** album review: **Pieces of Eight: Bangs on the Village People, p. 156:** album review: *Cruisin'.*

IX.   There's a Man in There

Cohn fabricated his article, p. 163: Cohn, "Disco's Homeboy Turns Hitman."

Bangs on romance, p. 163: *All My Friends Are Hermits*; **Bangs on women of refinement, p. 164:** "New Year's Eve"; **Bangs on Holabird and Heimel, pp. 164–165:** *All My Friends Are Hermits*; **Bangs on Cohen, p. 165:** "Getting Rid of the Albatross: Or, How Does It Feel to Be Frank Zappa?"; **Bangs on "JAPs," pp. 165–166:** *All My Friends Are Hermits*; **Bangs on Altman, p. 166:** *All My Friends Are Hermits*.

***NME*'s circulation, p. 167:** Kent, *The Dark Stuff*; **Bangs on the *NME*, p. 168:** "Letter from Britain"; **Bangs on England, p. 168:** "Hey Johnny— There's a Geezer Out Here Says He's Got the Answer to All Your Problems"; **Steve Jones on the Sex Pistols' music, p. 168:** Gimarc, *Punk Diary*; **Bangs on the Sex Pistols, p. 169:** "Hey Johnny"; **Lydon on Bangs, p. 169:** Lydon interview by Jaan Uhelszki, June 1997; **Mick Jones on the Clash's music, p. 169:** Gimarc, *Punk Diary*; **Smith on Bangs to Moore, p. 178:** quoted in Johnstone, *Patti Smith: A Biography*. Smith declined to be interviewed. **Bangs on *Radio Ethiopia*, p. 178:** "Patti Smith's Top Forty Insurrection"; **Bangs's open letter to Smith, pp. 178–179:** unpublished excerpt from *Rod Stewart*; **Bangs on the conversation with Tyner, p. 179:** "Notes on Austin."

Bangs on Birdland, p. 180: audiotape, Bangs watching *Hec Ramsey* and talking on the phone; **Bangs on playing the Velvets, p. 181:** "DNA: A Nation of Sheep"; **Bangs on the Electric Lady sessions, p. 182:** "Recording: Less Is More"; **Birdland breaks up, pp. 185–186:** Presley, "Birdland: The Flight . . . and the Fall," and interviews, Leigh and Quick; **Bangs on Birdland, p. 186:** "Sexual History."

X.   Jook Savage on the Brazos

Bangs on Berlin, p. 187: *All My Friends Are Hermits*; **Bangs on the Mudd Club, p. 187:** "Sexual History"; **Bangs on New York, p. 189:** "Everything Above Fourteenth Street Is Gila Bend, Arizona."

Bangs on Austin, p. 194: "Notes on Austin." A much-truncated version of Lester's travelogue eventually ran as a scene report in *Musician*.

Bangs on having a band, p. 198: interview with the author, 1982; **the frat party, p. 199:** Bangs, "Notes on Austin"; and interview, Curley; **Bangs on being homesick, p. 203:** interview with the author, 1982.

XI.   All My Friends Are Hermits

Bangs at AA, p. 205: interviews, Fouratt, Miller, Morthland, and Wilmot; **Bangs on his nightmare, pp. 205–206:** jam tape with Rex Weiner, March 27, 1981; ***Creem' circulation,* p. 207:** Berman, "The Queen of *Creem*"; **Bangs on his therapists, p. 207:** Meltzer's "Lester Recollected In Tranquility" features this quote as part of a transcription of a taped conversation between the two friends. **Tosches on Bangs, p. 208:** "Lester"; **Reed joined NA and AA, p. 209:** Bockris, *Transformer*; **Reed was attacked at AA, p. 210:** interview, Fouratt; **Bangs on old age, pp. 210–211:** "Ian Hunter: The Coots Are All Right."

Bangs on collaborating, p. 212: interview with the author, 1982; **Bangs on "cowplop," p. 215:** "Bad Taste Is Timeless"; **Bangs on the music business, p. 216:** "Every Song a Hooker"; **Anderson and Bangs, p. 216:** fax to the author from Laurie Anderson, September 30, 1998; **Christgau on *Jook Savages* and similar grades, p. 216:** *Christgau's Record Guide: The '80s.*

Dialogue at the escort agency, pp. 217–218: Bangs, interview tape. The participants in the recording were identified in a partial transcript that appeared in a working draft of the book on prostitutes. It was augmented by an interview with Miller. **Bangs and Brown, p. 221:** interview, Brown. She was painting and raising a daughter in California when we talked in 1997. She died from breast cancer a year later.

Bangs on nostalgia, p. 223: "Bad Taste Is Timeless."

Goodwin on Bangs, p. 225: e-mail to the author, 1997; **Bangs on his mother, p. 226:** "The Problem With California." **Bangs encouraged Norma to write, p. 226:** When it was published, he gave her a copy of *Blondie* inscribed, "I hope this will make you proud of me. At least now you know all those years of horrible noise weren't totally in vain. Now you should write *your* book." Norma did indeed begin a memoir shortly thereafter, but she produced only a few pages, and her son never read them. **Meltzer on Bangs, p. 227:** "Lester Recollected in Tranquility."

XII.   Ignore That Door

Tyner's visit, p. 231: interviews, Clark and Becky Tyner. In 1990 Rob Tyner paid tribute to his friend in a special issue of *Throat Culture* fanzine. "Lester has come to me in my dreams & has told me how much he hates

being dead," Tyner wrote. "He told me not to try it. It's dull & horribly boring & dreary. So far I've been able to take his advice, but that can't last forever. So be it. . . . Some day I'll hear that old rattletrap Camaro pull up
in the driveway & honk the horn. It'll be Lester. The muffler will need to
be fixed again. No sweat. I'll throw the bag in the back seat & jump in."
Tyner died of a heart attack a year later on September 18, 1991. **Bangs's
death, pp. 233–237:** In addition to interviews with the people on the
scene, I drew from the reports listed in the bibliography under "Public
Documents."

Afterword

Meltzer on Marcus and Christgau and on writing, p. 241: "Vinyl
Reckoning"; **Denby on criticism, p. 243:** "The Moviegoers: Why Don't
People Love the Right Movies Anymore?" **Bangs on irony, pp. 243–244:**
album review; Randy Newman, *Sail Away*/Nilsson, *Son of Schmilsson*.

Sources

Interviews

*Throughout the book all direct quotes have been taken from interviews con-
ducted by the author between June 1996 and January 1999, unless another
source has been cited in the text or the endnotes.*

Primary sources (subjects interviewed numerous times): Kate (formerly
Nancy) Alexander, Billy Altman, Roger Anderson, Charlie Auringer, Ann
Bowman (née Catching), Jack Butler, Ben Catching, Jr., Ben Catching
III, Bill Catching, Brian Curley, Andrea DeLucia (née di Guglielmo),
Robert Ducan, Jim Fouratt, Eric Genheimer, Rob Houghton, Donald
Jennings, Lenny Kaye, Nick Kent, Mickey Leigh, Dave Marsh, Richard
Meltzer, Kathy Miller, John Morthland, Paul Nelson, Alan Niester,
Michael Ochs, Joe Nick Patoski, Richard Pinkston, Robert Quine, Gary
Rachac, Marcia Resnick, John St. Clair, Steve St. Clair, Nancy Stillman,
Carol Swanson (née Schloner), Nick Tosches, Jaan Uhelszki, JoAnn
Uhelszki, Richard C. Walls, Ed Ward, Susan Whitall, Judith Wilmot,
Esther Woodward (née Korinksy).

Secondary sources: Lauren Agnelli, Veronica Albright (née
Sullivan), Leslie Alexander, Bob Alford, Joyce Altman, Laurie Anderson,
Debbie Arnold (née Rachac), Ron Asheton, Cary Baker, Gretchen
Barber, Snooky Bellomo, Tish Bellomo, Rebecca Bickham, Victor

Bockris, Stanley Booth, Jim Bovee, Galen Brandt, Karen Brown, Peter Buck, John Burks, John Cale, Joe "King" Carrasco, Tom Carson, Midge Catching, Stephanie Chernikowski, Georgia Christgau, Robert Christgau, Gil Clark, Debra Rae Cohen, Alice Cooper, Jean-Charles Costa, Cameron Crowe, Roberta Cruger, Jay Dee Daugherty, Imogene DeWitt (née Bangs), Buck Dharma, Carola Dibbell, Dave Dixon, Ben Edmonds, Brian Eno, Mark Erlewine, Alejandro Escovedo, Mick Farren, Joe Fernbacher, Danny Fields, Brad First, Kim Fowley, Simon Frith, Deborah Frost, Andy Fuertsch, Ina Galyean, Cheryl Gant, Gail Gant, Vic Garbarini, Billy Gibbons, Ellen Gibbs, Tony Glover, Toby Goldstein, Joan Goodwin, Mike Goodwin, Wes Goodwin, James Grauerholz, Tim Hamblin, Jody Harris, Jerry Harrison, Mary Harron, Debbie Harry, Cynthia Heimel, Richard Hell, Karen Hildebrandt (née Catching), Roni Hoffman, Jean Holabird, John Holmstrom, Robert Hull, Ian Hunter, Mike Hyland, Chrissie Hynde, Tony Iommi, David Johansen, Kevin Johnson, Rick Johnson, Ivan Julian, Joe Kane, Gary Kenton, Robert Kirschner, Howie Klein, Mark Kogan, Paul Kolderie, Al Kooper, Keith Korman, Connie Kramer, Wayne Kramer, Harvey Kubernick, Jon Landau, Ronnie Lane, Jon Langford, John Laycock, Charlotte Lesher, Judy Linn, Miriam Linna, Lydia Lunch, John Lydon, Kathleen Maher (neé Barbaro), Toby Mamis, Handsome Dick Manitoba, Greil Marcus, Jim Marshall, Andy McKaie, Legs McNeil, John Mendelssohn, Jim Miller, Karen Moline, Glenn Morrow, Margaret Moser, Peter Myers, Nancy Naglin, Colin Newman, Niagra, Glenn O'Brien, Ozzy Osbourne, Richard Pachter, Jon Pareles, Gail Parenteau, Mark Parenteau, Abe Peck, Fran Pelzman-Liscio, Charles Perry, Matthew Posnick, Charlotte Pressler, Neal Preston, Bobby Radcliff, Joey Ramone, Jerry Raney, Lou Reed, Richard Riegel, Pam Roberts (née Brown), Ira Robbins, Wayne Robins, Lisa Robinson, Richard Robinson, Robin Rothman, Mitch Ryder, Phil Sapienza, Mike Saunders, Andy Schwartz, Greg Shaw, Suzy Shaw, Andy Shernoff, Mark Shipper, Ric Siegel, Michael Simmons, Kate Simon, John Sinclair, Tom Sinclair, Gary Sperrazza, E. A. Srere, Peter Stampfel, Chris Stein, Kathy Stein, Bill Stephen, Deanne Stillman, Danny Sugerman, John Swenson, Roland Swenson, Susan Toepfer, Roy Trakin, Maureen Tucker, Becky Tyner, Rex Weiner, Michael Weldon, Timothy White, Jeff Whittington, Paul Williams, Ellen Willis, Langdon Winner, Stewart Wise, James Wolcott, Peter Wolf, Ron Wood, Howard Wuelfing, Milton Wyatt, Dave Wyndorf, Chuck Young, Harvey Zuppke.

Bibliography

Lester Bangs,
Articles and Reviews

Entries are arranged in chronological order with the intent of illustrating the unfolding soundtrack of Lester's life. Short reviews in *Creem* are denoted by their section headings: Off the Wall (books), Rock-a-Rama (albums), and Short Takes (movies). Bylines are noted for collaborative efforts, and I have included pseudonymous entries that *Creem* staffers have credited to Lester.

CD after an entry indicates that the piece was included in *Psychotic Reactions and Carburetor Dung*. Lester wrote two book proposals for versions of his own "greatest hits" collection; **LB1** indicates that the piece was included in the 1977 proposal, while **LB2** indicates that it appeared in the proposal completed shortly before his death.

Every effort has been made to find all of Lester's far-flung writings, but because he was so prolific, there are almost certainly pieces missing. If you are aware of any, please contact me at jimdero@earthlink.net or P.O. Box 577010, Chicago, IL 60657.

Poem: "Bartók Images." *Thought* (El Cajon Valley High School literary magazine), winter 1963–64.
Poem: "Idioms, Timeless & Prelude to Burning Rain, or, Asleep, Poem of Dreams." *Thought*, winter 1963–64.

"Two Excerpts from 'Death's Head Ragas.'" *Thought,* spring 1965.

Sounds of the Scene column: Bob Dylan, the Pretty Things, and the Kinks. *Smoke Signal* (El Cajon Valley High School newspaper), October 15, 1965.

Sounds of the Scene column: the Yardbirds. *Smoke Signal,* November 12, 1965.

Sounds of the Scene column: the future of music. *Smoke Signal,* May 1, 1966.

Short story: "Between Light and Shade." *Thought,* January, 1967.

Album review: The MC5, *Kick Out the Jams. Rolling Stone,* April 5, 1969.

Album review: *The Illinois Speed Press/Black Pearl. Rolling Stone,* May 3, 1969.

Album review: *The Velvet Underground. Rolling Stone,* May 17, 1969.

Album review: Alice Cooper, *Pretties for You. Rolling Stone,* July 12, 1969.

Album review: The Youngbloods, *Elephant Mountain. Rolling Stone,* July 12, 1969.

Album review: *It's a Beautiful Day. Rolling Stone,* July 26, 1969.

Album review: Captain Beefheart, *Trout Mask Replica. Rolling Stone,* July 26, 1969.

Album review: Cat Mother and the All-Night Newsboys, *The Street Giveth and the Street Taketh Away.* Rolling Stone, August 9, 1969.

Album review: Chuck Berry, *Concerto in B Goode.* Rolling Stone, August 9, 1969.

Album review: *Blind Faith. Rolling Stone,* September 6, 1969.

Album review: *Bread. Rolling Stone,* September 6, 1969.

Album review: Julie Driscoll, Brian Auger, and the Trinity, *Streetnoise. Rolling Stone,* September 6, 1969.

Album review: The McCoys, *Human Ball. Rolling Stone,* September 20, 1969.

Album review: The Byrds, *Preflyte. Rolling Stone,* October 10, 1969.

Album review: Savage Rose, *In the Plain. Rolling Stone,* October 10, 1969.

Album review: Miles Davis, *In a Silent Way. Rolling Stone,* November 15, 1969.

Album review: The Electric Prunes, *Just Good Old Rock and Roll*/Vanilla Fudge, *Rock and Roll. Rolling Stone,* November 15, 1969.

Album review: The Tony Williams Lifetime, *Emergency. Rolling Stone,* November 15, 1969.

"Elegy for a Desolation Angel" (Jack Kerouac obituary). *Rolling Stone,* November 29, 1969.

Album review: *Alice Faye in Hollywood (1934–1937). Rolling Stone,* December 13, 1969.

Album review: The Bonzo Dog Band, *Tadpoles. Rolling Stone,* December 13, 1969.

Album review: The Box Tops, *Dimensions/Nonstop/Superhits*. *Rolling Stone*, December 13, 1969.

Album review: The Flamin' Groovies, *Supersnazz*. *Rolling Stone*, December 13, 1969.

Album review: The Bar-Kays, *Gotta Groove*/The Watts 103rd Street Rhythm Band, *In the Jungle, Babe*. *Rolling Stone*, December 13, 1969.

Album review: Gladys Knight and the Pips, *Silk 'n' Soul/Feelin' Bluesy/Nitty Gritty*. *Rolling Stone*, December 27, 1969.

Album review: Johnny Winter, *Second Winter/The Johnny Winter Story*. *Rolling Stone*, December 27, 1969.

"Let It Bleed" (Altamont report), by Lester Bangs, Reny Brown, John Burks, Sammy Egan, Michael Goodwin, Geoffrey Link, Greil Marcus, John Morthland, Eugene Schoenfeld, Patrick Thomas, and Langdon Winner. *Rolling Stone*, January 21, 1970.

"Five Hundred Mile Pilgrimage to a Hell's Angel Death Festival" (Altamont report). *IT*, January 28, 1970.

Album review: *Roxy*/the Guess Who, *Canned Wheat/Valhalla*. *Rolling Stone*, February 7, 1970.

Album review: The Pretty Things, *S. F. Sorrow/ Yes*. *Rolling Stone*, February 7, 1970.

Album review: The Temptations, *Puzzle People/Cloud Nine*. *Rolling Stone*, February 7, 1970.

Album review: Aurora, *Stained Glass/Bodine/Locomotive*. *Rolling Stone*, February 7, 1970.

Album review: *Methuselah*/SRC, *Milestones*/The Frost, *Rock and Roll Music*. *Rolling Stone*, February 7, 1970.

Album review: *The Allman Brothers Band*. *Rolling Stone*, February 21, 1970.

Album review: *Blond*. *Rolling Stone*, February 21, 1970.

Album review: Charlie Haden, *Liberation Music*. *Rolling Stone*, February 21, 1970.

Album review: Frank Zappa, *Hot Rats*. *Rolling Stone*, March 7, 1970.

Album review: Van Morrison, *Moondance*, by Greil Marcus and Lester Bangs. *Rolling Stone*, March 19, 1970.

Album review: *Rick Nelson in Concert*. *Rolling Stone*, April 2, 1970.

Album review: *Blue Cheer*. *Rolling Stone*, April 30, 1970.

Album review: The Doors, *Morrison Hotel*. *Rolling Stone*, April 30, 1970.

Album review: *B. J. Thomas Greatest Hits, Vol. 1*. *Rolling Stone*, April 30, 1970.

Album review: *Renaissance*/Blonde on Blonde, *Contrasts*. *Rolling Stone*, May 14, 1970.

Album review: Taste, *On the Boards*. *Rolling Stone*, May 28, 1970.

Book review: James Simon Kunen, *The Strawberry Statement: Notes of a College Revolutionary*. *Rolling Stone*, May 28, 1970.

Album review: Allen Ginsberg, *Songs of Innocence and Experience*. *Rolling Stone,* June 11, 1970.

Album review: Eric Burdon, *Eric Burdon Declares "War." Fusion,* June 12, 1970.

Album review: Mott the Hoople. *Fusion,* June 12, 1970.

Album review: Blues Image, *Open/Frijid Pink/Killing Floor*/Shakey Vick, *Little Woman You're So Sweet*. *Rolling Stone,* June 25, 1970.

Album review: Mystic Moods Orchestra, *Stormy Weekend*. *Rolling Stone,* June 25, 1970.

Book review: Jerry Rubin, *Do It: Scenarios of the Revolution*. *Rolling Stone,* June 25, 1970.

Album review: *Ritchie Valens in Concert at Pacoima Jr. High*. *Rolling Stone,* July 9, 1970.

Album review: The Yardbirds, *Five Live Yardbirds/Eric Clapton and the Yardbirds Live with Sonny Boy Williamson*. *Rolling Stone,* July 9, 1970.

Album review: John Cale, *Vintage Violence*. *Fusion,* August 21, 1970.

Album review: Love Sculpture, *Blues Helping*. *Fusion,* August 21, 1970.

Album review: Buddy Miles, *Them Changes*. *Rolling Stone,* September 3, 1970.

Album review: *Black Sabbath*/Gun, *Gun Sight*. *Rolling Stone,* September 17, 1970.

Book review: Charles Sopkin, *Seven Glorious Days, Seven Fun-Filled Nights*. *Rolling Stone,* September 17, 1970.

Album review: The Fugs, *Golden Filth*. *Creem,* August 1970.

Single review: The Who, "Anyway Anyhow Anywhere." *Creem,* August 1970.

Album review: John Coltrane, *The Best of John Coltrane: His Impulse Years/Transitions*. *San Diego Door,* September 17, 1970.

"Jimi Hendrix: Two Points of View" (Hendrix obit), by Roger Anderson and Lester Bangs. *San Diego Door,* September 24, 1970.

"I Remember Ray" (Ray Charles retrospective). *Creem,* October 1970.

Album review: The Pipkins, *Gimme Dat Ding! Rolling Stone,* October 1, 1970.

Album review: Blues Section, *Blues Section* and *Some of Love/Tasavallan Presidentti/International Harvester, Sov Gott Rose-Marie/Wigwam*. *Rolling Stone,* October 1, 1970.

Album review: *Crabby Appleton*. *Rolling Stone,* October 20, 1970.

Album review: *Cactus*. *Creem,* November 1970.

Album review: Junior Mance, *With a Lotta Help from My Friends*. *Creem,* November 1970.

"Of Pop and Pies and Fun: A Program for Mass Liberation in the Form of a Stooges Review, or, Who's This Fool? (Part One.)" *Creem,* November 1970. **CD, LB1**

Album review: The Rolling Stones, *Get Yer Ya-Ya's Out! Rolling Stone,* November 12, 1970.

Album review: The Doors, *Absolutely Live. Fusion*, November 13, 1970.

Album review: *Black Pearl Live. Rolling Stone*, November 26, 1970.

Album review: *Brownsville Station. Rolling Stone*, November 26, 1970.

Album review: The Byrds, *Untitled. Rolling Stone*, November 26, 1970.

Album review: *Led Zeppelin III. Rolling Stone*, November 26, 1970.

Album review: *Ry Cooder. Creem*, December 1970.

Album review: Früt, *Keep On Truckin'*, by "Calabash Bangs." *Creem*, December 1970.

Album review: Love, *Love Revisited, Four Sail, Out Here,* and *False Start. Creem*, December 1970.

Album review: *Mashmakhan,* by "Punko Bangs." *Creem*, December 1970.

"Of Pop and Pies and Fun: A Program for Mass Liberation in the Form of a Stooges Review, or, Who's This Fool? (Part Two.)" *Creem,* December 1970. **CD**

Album review: *Deep Purple in Rock/Gator Creek*/J. F. Murphy and Free Flowing Salt, *Almost Home. Rolling Stone*, December 2, 1970.

Album review: Frank Zappa, *Chunga's Revenge. Rolling Stone*, December 24, 1970.

Album review: John Mayall, *USA Union. Rolling Stone*, December 24, 1970.

"James Taylor Marked for Death." *Who Put the Bomp?*, winter/spring 1971. **CD, LB1**

Album review: The Doors, *Thirteen. Rolling Stone*, January 7, 1971.

Album review: *Ginger Baker's Airforce 2. Rolling Stone*, February 4, 1971.

Album review: *Dreams. Rolling Stone*, February 4, 1971.

Album review: Buddy Miles, *We Got to Live Together. Rolling Stone*, February 4, 1971.

Album review: *Steppenwolf 7. Fusion*, February 5, 1971.

Book review: Dotson Rader, editor, Defiance No. 1: *A Radical Review. Rolling Stone*, February 18, 1971.

Album review: *Amon Düül/Birth Control/Brainbox/Joy Unlimited/The Marbles/*The Cats, *45 Lives. Creem*, March 1971.

Album review: Captain Beefheart, *Lick My Decals Off. Creem*, March 1971.

Album review: Question Mark and the Mysterians, *96 Tears/*The Shadows of Knight, *Back Door Man. Fusion*, March 5, 1971.

"Fractured at the Stones Flick: Wondering Where to Lay the Blame" (*Gimme Shelter). The San Diego Door*, March 17, 1971.

Album review: Yoko Ono, *Plastic Ono Band. Rolling Stone*, March 4, 1971.

Book review: Jack Kerouac, *Doctor Sax/Mexico City Blues/Lonesome Traveler/Rolling Stone*, March 4, 1971.

"The Carpenters and the Creeps." *Rolling Stone*, March 4, 1971.

Album review: *Chicago III/*Cold Blood, *Sisyphus/If. Rolling Stone*, March 18, 1971.

Album review: Captain Beefheart, *Mirror Man. Rolling Stone*, April 1, 1971.

Album review: Peter Green, *The End of the Game*. *Rolling Stone*, April 1, 1971.

Album review: Zephyr, *Going Back to Colorado*. *Rolling Stone*, April 1, 1971.

Album review: Charles Mingus, *The Best of Charles Mingus*. *Fusion*, April 2, 1971.

Album review: Rahsaan Roland Kirk, *Rahsaan Rahsaan*. *Fusion*, April 2, 1971.

Album review: David Crosby, *If I Could Only Remember My Name*/Bruce Palmer, *The Cycle Is Complete*. *Rolling Stone*, April 15, 1971.

"Dead Lie the Velvets Underground, R.I.P.; Long Live Lou Reed." *Creem*, May 1971. **LBI**

Album review: *Brian Auger's Oblivion Express*. *Rolling Stone*, May 13, 1971.

Album review: Bread, *Manna*. *Rolling Stone*, May 13, 1971.

Album review: Jackson Heights, *King Progress*. *Rolling Stone*, May 27, 1971.

Album review: *Osmonds*. *Rolling Stone*, May 27, 1971.

Album review: Various artists, *Original Golden Oldies from the Fabulous '50s, Incense and Oldies,* and *American Rock Anthology*. *Who Put the Bomp?,* summer 1971.

Album review: Barbra Streisand, *Stoney End,* by "Lecher Bangs." *Creem*, June 1971.

Album review: *Black Pearl*. *Creem*, June 1971.

"Psychotic Reactions and Carburetor Dung: A Tale of These Times" (Count Five tribute). *Creem*, June 1971. **CD, LB1, LB2**

Album review: Grand Funk Railroad, *Survival*. *Rolling Stone*, June 10, 1971.

Album review: Atomic Rooster, *Death Walks Beside You*. *Rolling Stone*, June 24, 1971.

Album review: *Earth Wind and Fire/Mandrill*. *Rolling Stone*, June 24, 1971.

Album review: Crowbar, *Bad Manors*/King Biscuit Boy with Crowbar, *Official Music*/Ronnie Hawkins, *The Hawk*. *Fusion*, June 25, 1971.

Album review: Blue Cheer, *Oh! Pleasant Hope*. *Rolling Stone*, July 8, 1971.

Album review: *Black Oak Arkansas*. *Fusion*, July 9, 1971.

Album review: Ten Wheel Drive with Genya Ravan, *Peculiar Friends*. *Rolling Stone*, August 5, 1971.

Album review: *Weather Report/Zawinul*. *Rolling Stone*, August 5, 1971.

Album review: Booker Ervin, *That's It!*/The Cecil Taylor Quartet, *Air*. *Creem*, September 1971.

Album review: *Charles Mingus Presents the Charles Mingus Quartet/Town Hall Concert*. *Creem*, September 1971.

Album review: The Temptations, *Sky's the Limit*. *Creem*, September 1971.

Album review: *The Best Of Herbie Hancock/Mwandishi*. *Rolling Stone*, September 2, 1971.

Album review: The Mothers of Invention, *Fillmore East*. *Rolling Stone*, September 30, 1971.

Album review: *Mahavishnu*/John McLaughlin, *My Goal's Beyond*. *Phonograph Record Magazine*, November 1971.

"Free Form Music in San Francisco: San Francisco on Two Cents a Day." *Phonograph Record Magazine*. November 1971.

Album review: Hot Tuna, *First Pull Up, Then Pull Down*/Jefferson Airplane, *Bark. Rolling Stone*, November 11, 1971.

"Nico . . . A Kind of Frozen Purity." *Fusion*, November 12, 1971.

Album review: Black Sabbath, *Master of Reality. Rolling Stone*, November 25, 1971.

Album review: *The Grateful Dead. Creem*, December 1971.

Album review: *Sir Lord Baltimore/Dust. Creem*, December 1971.

"Do the Godz Speak Esperanto?" *Creem*, December 1971. **CD, LB1**

Movie review: *Medicine Ball Caravan. Creem*, December 1971.

Album review: Savage Rose, *Refugee. Rolling Stone*, December 9, 1971.

Album review: Crabby Appleton, *Rotten to the Core. Rolling Stone*, December 23, 1971.

Album review: Wayne Shorter, *Odyssey of Iska. Rolling Stone*, December 23, 1971.

"Alice Cooper, All American: A Horatio Alger Story for the Seventies." *Creem*, January 1972. **LB1**

Album review: Alice Coltrane, *Universal Consciousness. Phonograph Record Magazine*, January 1972.

Album review: *Rory Gallagher. Phonograph Record Magazine*, January 1972.

"California '99: Townshend or San Andreas at Fault?" *Phonograph Record Magazine*, January 1972.

Performance review: John Prine, the Troubadour, Los Angeles. *Phonograph Record Magazine*, January 1972.

Album review: Alice Cooper, *Killer. Rolling Stone*, January 6, 1972.

Album review: Don McLean, *American Pie. Rolling Stone*, January 20, 1972.

Album review: Led Zeppelin, *IV. Creem*, February 1972.

Album review: Little Richard, *King of Rock and Roll. Creem*, February 1972.

Album review: *Chicago at Carnegie Hall, Volumes I, II, III & IV. Creem*, February 1972. **CD**

Book review: Jonathan Eisen, *Forever Changes* and *Twenty-Minute Fandangos. Creem*, February 1972.

"Crabby Appleton Zaps the Zombies" by Lester Bangs and Andrea di Guglielmo. *Creem*, February 1972.

Album review: *The Dave Clark Five. Rolling Stone*, February 17, 1972.

Album review: The Rolling Stones, *Hot Rocks, 1964–1971. Rolling Stone*, February 17, 1972.

Album review: Yoko Ono, *Fly. Creem*, March 1972.

Movie review: *A Clockwork Orange. Creem*, March 1972.

Album review: *Papa John Creach*/Paul Kantner and Grace Slick, *Sunfighter. Rolling Stone*, March 2, 1972.

Album review: Emerson, Lake & Palmer, *Pictures at an Exhibition. Rolling Stone*, March 2, 1972.

Album review: King Crimson, *Islands. Rolling Stone*, March 2, 1972.

Album review: Captain Beefheart, *The Spotlight Kid. Rolling Stone*, March 30, 1972.

Album review: *Eddie Cochran. Rolling Stone*, March 30, 1972.

Album review: *Blue Öyster Cult. Rolling Stone*, March 30, 1972.

Album review: Carole King, *Music. Creem*, April 1972.

Album review: Mott the Hoople, *Brain Capers. Creem*, April 1972.

Album review: The Nitty Gritty Dirt Band, *All the Good Times. Phonograph Record Magazine*, April 1972.

Album review: The Guess Who, *Rockin'. Rolling Stone*, April 13, 1972.

Album review: Black Oak Arkansas, *Keep the Faith. Creem*, May 1972. **CD, LB2**

Album review: *Bullangus/REO Speedwagon. Creem*, May 1972.

Album review: Jon Lord and the London Symphony Orchestra, *Gemini Suite. Creem*, May 1972.

Album review: David Amram, *No More Walls. Phonograph Record Magazine*, May, 1972.

Album review: Wayne Cochran & the C. C. Riders, *Cochran*/Edgar Winter's White Trash, *Roadwork. Rolling Stone*, May 11, 1972.

Album review: Sonny and Cher, *All I Ever Need Is You. Rolling Stone*, May 11, 1972.

Album review: Deep Purple, *Machine Head. Rolling Stone*, May 25, 1972.

Album review: The Rascals, *Island of Real. Rolling Stone*, May 25, 1972.

Album review: The Allman Brothers Band, *Eat a Peach. Creem*, June 1972.

Album review: *America. Creem*, June 1972.

Album review: Dave Edmunds, *Rockpile. Creem*, June 1972.

Album review: Kris Kristofferson, *Border Lord. Creem*, June 1972.

Album review: Savoy Brown, *Hellbound Train*/Ten Years After, *Alvin Lee & Co. Creem*, June 1972.

"Anyone Tampering with This Machine: The Senior Prom of the '70s." *Creem*, June 1972.

Book review: Allen Katzman, editor, *Our Time: Interviews from the East Village Other. Creem*, June 1972.

"Bring Your Mother to the Gas Chamber, Part One: Black Sabbath and the Straight Dope on Blood-Lust Orgies." *Creem*, June 1972.

Album review: Janis Joplin, *Janis in Concert. Rolling Stone*, June 8, 1972. **LB2**

Album review: Jerry Lee Lewis, *The Killer Rocks On. Rolling Stone*, June 8, 1972.

Album review: Hawkwind, *In Search of Space. Rolling Stone*, June 22, 1972.

Album review: Loretta Lynn, *One's on the Way*/Conway Twitty, *I Can't See Me Without You*/Loretta Lynn and Conway Twitty, *Lead Me On. Rolling Stone*, June 22, 1972.

Liner notes: *Them . . . Featuring Van Morrison*. Released July 1972.

Album review: David Peel & the Lower East Side, *The Pope Smokes Dope.* *Creem*, July 1972.

Album review: *Lou Reed/The Velvet Underground Live at Max's Kansas City.* *Creem*, July 1972.

"Bring Your Mother to the Gas Chamber, Part Two." *Creem*, July 1972.

Album review: Miles Davis, *The Complete Birth of Cool. Phonograph Record Magazine*, July 1972.

Album review: Brownsville Station, *A Night on the Town. Rolling Stone*, July 6, 1972.

Album review: *Who Will Save the World? The Mighty Groundhogs! Rolling Stone*, July 20, 1972.

Album review: The Rolling Stones, *Exile on Main Street. Creem*, August 1972. **LB1, LB2**

Album review: *The Sidewinders. Creem*, August 1972.

Book review: Diane di Prima, *Memoirs of a Beatnik*/David Meltzer, *Orf. Creem*, August 1972.

"Loose as a Goose and Twice as Truthful: A Recounting of Some Times in the Season of Dust." *Creem*, August 1972.

"Women in Rock: They Won't Get Fooled Again." *Ms.*, August 1972.

Album review: *Carlos Santana and Buddy Miles Live. Rolling Stone*, August 31, 1972.

"Evel Knievel Bites the Dust." *Creem*, September 1972.

Album review: *Foghat. Phonograph Record Magazine*, September 1972.

Album review: Three Dog Night, *Seven Separate Fools. Phonograph Record Magazine*, September 1972.

Album review: *Them . . . Featuring Van Morrison*, by Richard Cromelin and Lester Bangs. *Phonograph Record Magazine*, September 1972.

Book review: Len Brown and Gary Friedrich, *So You Think You Know About Rock and Roll. Phonograph Record Magazine*, September 1972.

Album review: Jefferson Airplane, *Long John Silver. Rolling Stone*, September 14, 1972.

Album review: *Ramatam. Rolling Stone*, September 28, 1972.

Album review: Randy Newman, *Sail Away*/Nilsson, *Son of Schmilsson. Creem*, October 1972.

Album review: Alice Cooper, *School's Out*, by Lester Bangs and Ben Edmonds. *Creem*, October 1972.

Album review: *White Witch. Creem*, October 1972. **CD, LB2**

"Visual and Vocal: Linda Ronstadt." *Penthouse*, October 1972.

Album review: The Kinks, *Everybody's in Showbiz. Phonograph Record Magazine*, October 1972.

Album review: Slade, *Slade Alive. Phonograph Record Magazine*, October 1972.

Book review: Richard Meltzer, *Gulcher. Coast*, November 1972.

Album review: *National Lampoon Radio Dinner. Creem*, November 1972.

Album review: The Band, *Rock of Ages. Creem*, November 1972.

Album review: The Guess Who, *Live at the Paramount. Creem*, November 1972. **CD**

"John Coltrane Lives." *Creem*, November 1972. **CD, LB1, LB2**

Movie review: *Kansas City Bomber. Creem*, November 1972.

"Pharoah Sanders." *Creem* blues and jazz supplement, November 1972.

"The Shape of Jazz Today." *Creem* blues and jazz supplement, November 1972.

Album review: The Golddiggers, *Today! Phonograph Record Magazine*, November 1972. Reprinted in *Fusion* (by Lester Bangs and Judy Linn), January 1973, and *Oui*, March 1973.

Album review: Grand Funk Railroad, *Phoenix. Rolling Stone,* November 11, 1972.

Album review: Yes, *Close to the Edge. Creem*, December 1972.

"Deep Purple Ain't Schizoid! Maybe Just a Little Loony . . ." *Creem*, December 1972.

"Detroit's Rock Culture." *Phonograph Record Magazine*, December 1972.

Album review: *Buddy Guy and Junior Wells Play the Blues*/Cactus, *'Ot 'n' Sweaty. Creem*, January 1973.

Album review: Captain Beefheart, *Clear Spot. Creem*, January 1973.

"I Only Get My Rocks Off When I'm Dreaming: So You Say You Missed the Stones Too? Cheer Up, We're a Majority!" *Creem*, January 1973. **LB1**

"Sex Lives of the Rolling Stones Competition." *Creem*, January 1973.

Album review: Elvis Presley, *Burning Love and Hits From His Movies. Rolling Stone*, January 4, 1973.

Album review: The Raspberries, *Fresh Raspberries. Rolling Stone*, January 4, 1973.

Album review: Joni Mitchell, *For the Roses. Creem*, February 1973.

Album review: James Taylor, *One Man Dog. Creem*, February 1973. **CD, LB2**

"The Beatles' Moralizing Was Insipid and Self-Righteous" (from "Nine Ways of Looking at the Beatles 1963 –1973"). *Stereo Review*, February 1973.

Album review: *Duane Allman: An Anthology. Rolling Stone*, February 1, 1973.

Album review: The London Symphony Orchestra and Chamber Choir with Guest Soloists, *Tommy. Rolling Stone*, February 15, 1973.

Album review: David Bromberg, *Demon in Disguise. Creem*, March 1973.

Album review: David Clayton-Thomas, *Tequila Sunrise*/Little Jimmy Osmond, *Killer Joe. Creem,* March 1973. **LB2**

Album review: Creedence Clearwater Revival, *Creedence Gold. Creem*, March 1973.

Album review: *Full Moon/The Section. Creem*, March 1973.

Movie review: *Deep Throat. Creem*, March 1973.

"Scrooge McDuck—Dope Fiend!" *Creem*, March 1973.

"The Incredibly Strange Creatures Who Stopped Living and Became Mixed-Up

Zombies, Or, The Day the Airwaves Erupted." *Creem*, March 1973. **CD, LB1**

Album review: *One/Black Kangaroo*. *Phonograph Record Magazine*, March 1973.

Album review: Deep Purple, *Who Do We Think We Are!* *Phonograph Record Magazine*, March 1973.

Album review: The Guess Who, *Artificial Paradise*. *Phonograph Record Magazine*, March 1973.

"Bangs Keeps Score" (year-end awards, 1972). *Phonograph Record Magazine*, March 1973.

Album review: Neil Diamond, *Hot August Night*. *Rolling Stone*, March 15, 1973.

Album review: Ray Charles, *All-Time Great Country & Western Hits*/Curtis Mayfield, *His Early Years with The Impressions/Back in the Alley: The Classic Blues of B. B. King/The Best of B. B. King*. *Rolling Stone*, March 29, 1973.

"Rock Critics Rule! And Other Startling Musical Revelations" (short self-portrait). *Coast*, April 1973.

"A Rock Critic Will Be President! Sniffin' Out Meltzer's Future: Tomorrow's a Red Nose" (Bangs on Meltzer). *Coast*, April 1973.

Album review: *Derek & the Dominos in Concert*. *Creem*, April 1973.

Album review: The Rolling Stones, *More Hot Rocks (Big Hits and Fazed Cookies)*. *Creem*, April 1973.

"Alvin Lee: The Invulnerable Bullock—Just Ask the Rest of the Band. . . ." *Creem*, April 1973.

"Sex Lives of the Rolling Stones: Competition Results." *Creem*, April 1973.

"The Beach Boys Regroup." *Stereo Review*, April 1973.

Album review: The Move, *Split Ends*. *Rolling Stone*, April 26, 1973.

Album review: Blue Öyster Cult, *Tyranny and Mutation*. *Creem*, May 1973.

Album review: Dr. Hook and the Medicine Show, *Sloppy Seconds*/Shel Silverstein, *Freakin' at the Freakers Ball*. *Creem*, May 1973.

Book review: Maxene Fabe, *Death Rock*. *Creem*, May 1973.

"Jethro Tull in Vietnam: Their Rock 'n' Roll Circus Has a Really Big Top." *Creem*, May 1973. **CD, LB1**

"Cop a Taste of This Tome, Gate" (review of *Really the Blues* by Mezz Mezzrow). *Oui*, May 1973.

Album review: *The Best of Bread*. *Rolling Stone*, May 24, 1973.

Album review: Led Zeppelin, *Houses of the Holy*. *Creem*, June 1973.

Album review: Johnny Winter, *Still Alive and Well*. *Creem*, June 1973.

"Slade Don't Do No Rock Operas." *Creem*, June 1973. Reprinted in *Let It Rock*, October 1973.

Album review: Jefferson Airplane, *30 Seconds Over Winterland*. *Phonograph Record Magazine*, June 1973.

Album review: Sun Ra, *Atlantis*. *Phonograph Record Magazine*, June 1973.

"Brownsville Station: Rock and Roll Mania from Lester Bangs." *Phonograph Record Magazine*, June 1973.

Performance review: Kinky Friedman, Chicago, Illinois. *Phonograph Record Magazine*, June 1973.

Album review: Canned Heat, *The New Age*. *Rolling Stone*, June 7, 1973.

Album review: Kinky Friedman, *Sold American*. *Rolling Stone*, June 21, 1973.

Album review: *The Marshall Tucker Band*. *Rolling Stone*, June 21, 1973.

"Platform Shoe Rock" (glam rock). *Chicago Daily News*, June 23, 1973.

"Deaf Mute in a Telephone Booth: A Perfect Day with Lou Reed." *Creem*, July 1973. Reprinted in *Let It Rock*, November 1973. **LB1, LB2**

Movie review: *Lost Horizon*. *Creem*, July 1973.

"Paul and Pelvis: Down the Tube" (McCartney and Presley TV specials). *Creem*, July 1973.

Short Take: *Cesar and Rosalie*. *Creem*, July 1973.

Short Take: *The Thief Who Came to Dinner*. *Creem*, July 1973.

Album review: *Flo & Eddie*. *Creem*, July 1973.

Album review: Kim Fowley, *International Heroes*. *Creem*, July 1973.

Album review: Anne Murray, *Danny's Song*. *Phonograph Record Magazine*, July 1973.

Album review: Sparks, *A Woofer in Tweeter's Clothing*. *Let It Rock*, July 1973.

Album review: *The Pointer Sisters*, by Richard Meltzer and Lester Bangs. *Phonograph Record Magazine*, July 1973.

"Iggy (Pop) and the Stooges: The Apotheosis of Every Parental Nightmare." *Stereo Review*, July 1973.

Album review: Bruce Springsteen, *Greetings from Asbury Park, N.J. Rolling Stone*, July 5, 1973.

"The Alcohol Crisis and What You Can Do About It." *Punk*, July 30, 1973.

"Androgyny in Rock: A Short Introduction." *Creem*, August 1973.

Back in the U.S.A. column: "Nature of Rock." *Let It Rock*, August 1973.

Album review: Anne Murray, *Danny's Song*. *Creem*, September 1973.

Book review: Ron Peters, *The Big Stash*. *Creem*, September 1973.

"Mark Farner's State of the Nation Address." *Creem*, September 1973.

Album review: Mike Bloomfield, John Hammond, Dr. John, *Triumvirate*. *Gallery*, September 1973.

Album review: George Harrison, *Living in the Material World*. *Gallery*, September 1973.

Book review: Timothy Leary, *Confessions of a Hope Fiend*. *Gallery*, September 1973.

"Has Alice Cooper Sold Out? *Billion Dollar Babies*." *Stereo Review*, September 1973.

"Kesey's Catharsis: An Approach So Passé—It's Gauche." *Chicago Tribune* Book World, September 16, 1973.

"The New York Dolls" (part of "What's New: The Critics Choose Their Favorites"). *Real Paper*, September 26, 1973.

Album review: Jethro Tull, *A Passion Play*, in the form of a readers' survey. *Creem*, October 1973.

Album review: Mott the Hoople, *Mott. Creem*, October 1973.

Book review: William S. Burroughs, *Kentucky Ham*/Jack Kerouac, *Visions of Cody. Creem*, October 1973.

"You Rip Me, I'll Rip You" (New York Dolls). *Phonograph Record Magazine*, October 1973. **LB2**

Album review: Carole King, *Fantasy. Gallery*, October 1973.

Album review: *Chicago VI. Gallery*, October 1973.

"Hawkwind and Amon Düül II: Space Rock in Blind Alleys." *Stereo Review*, October 1973.

Book review: Richard Elman, *Uptight with the Stones: A Novelist's Report. Creem*, November 1973.

"Emmett Grogran Stops Lying," by Georgia Christgau and Lester Bangs. *Creem*, November 1973.

"Screwing the System with Dick Clark." *Creem*, November 1973. **CD, LB1**

Album review: *Eric Clapton's Rainbow Concert. Creem*, November 1973.

Album review: Van Morrison, *Hard Nose the Highway. Creem*, November 1973.

Album review: Cheech & Chong, *Los Cochinos. Phonograph Record Magazine*, November 1973.

Concert review: Mott the Hoople, the New York Dolls, and Dr. Hook and the Medicine Show. *Phonograph Record Magazine*, November 1973. **LB1**

"Music Round-Up." *Gallery*, November 1973.

Album review: The Carpenters, *Now and Then. Let It Rock*, November 1973.

"Review of *Music Is My Mistress* by Duke Ellington." *Chicago Tribune* Book World, November 11, 1973. Reprinted in *Creem*, January 1974.

"1973 Nervous Breakdown: The Ol' Fey Outlaws Ain't What They Used to Be" (the Rolling Stones). *Creem*, December 1973. **LB1**

Album review: James Brown, *Soul Classics Vol. 2*/The JB's, *Doin' It to Death*/The New Birth, *Birth Day. Creem*, December 1973.

Album review: Lou Reed, *Berlin. Creem*, December 1973.

Album review: Slade, *Sladest. Creem*, December 1973. **CD**

Album review: Uriah Heep, *Sweet Freedom. Creem*, December 1973.

Album review: David Bowie, *Pin Ups. Creem*, January 1974.

Album review: Hawkwind, *Space Ritual*/Amon Düül II, *Live in London. Creem*, January 1974.

Album review: Jethro Tull, *A Passion Play*, by *Creem*'s readers. *Creem*, January 1974.

Album review: Neil Young, *Time Fades Away. Creem*, January 1974.

"Eat Your Meat (Cereal Division): Consumer Guide to American Burger Stands." *Creem*, January 1974. **LB1**

Movie review: *Detroit 9000*. *Creem*, January 1974.

Off the Wall: Ned McCune, *The Gateway*. *Creem*, January 1974.

Off the Wall: Will Perry, *Death of an Informer*. *Creem*, January 1974.

"Savoy Brown Is Not Dead: Some Call It Blues, Some Call It Dues, But We Call It Carrying On (What Else D'ya Expect from a Pack of Limeys?)." *Creem*, January 1974.

"Critics Choice Poll." *Let It Rock*, January 1974.

Album review: Alice Cooper, *Muscle of Love*, by "Wally Cleaver." *Creem*, February 1974.

Album review: John Lennon, *Mind Games*. *Creem*, February 1974.

Book review: William S. Burroughs, *Exterminator!* *Creem*, February 1974.

Book review: James Morris, *The Preachers*. *Creem*, February 1974.

Book review: John Rechy, *The Fourth Angel*. *Creem*, February 1974.

Short Take: *Charlie Varrick*. *Creem*, February 1974.

"The Dr. Hook Story, or, Every Time You Try to Find the Bottom, It's Never There." *Creem*, February 1974.

"The Who's 'Manageably Pretentious' *Quadrophenia*." *Stereo Review*, February 1974.

"Blood Feast of Reddy Kilowatt! Emerson, Lake & Palmer Without Insulation! And You Wonder Why There's an Energy Crisis. . . ." *Creem*, March 1974. **LB1**

Back in the U.S.A. column: "My Top Ten." *Let It Rock*, March 1974.

Album review: Helen Reddy, *Long Hard Climb*. *Creem*, April 1974.

Book review: Jack B. Weiner, *The Morning After*. *Creem*, April 1974.

"Honey, Come & Be My Enemy, I Can Love You Too: Iggy and the Stooges Take America by the Spleen," by "Esther [Korinsky] and Lester." *Creem*, April 1974. **LB1, LB2**

Album review: Creedence Clearwater Revival, *Live in Europe*. *Let It Rock*, April 1974.

Album review: Lou Reed, *Rock 'n' Roll Animal*. *Creem*, May 1974.

"Dada at the End of a Fist: A Champagne Flight with Grace Slick." *Creem*, May 1974. **LB1**

"Lamont Blankenship: The Next Todd Rundgren?" *Creem*, May 1974.

Movie review: *Serpico*. *Creem*, May 1974.

Album review: Eddie Kendricks, *Boogie Down*/Herbie Mann, *London Underground*. *Creem*, June 1974.

"Transcendence of the Orgasm: Field Tripping with Deep Purple." *Creem*, June 1974.

Album review: Bryan Ferry, *These Foolish Things*/Roxy Music, *Stranded*. *Creem*, July 1974.

Album review: The New York Dolls, *Too Much, Too Soon*. *Creem*, July 1974.

"Pop Artist Lou Reed Reviewed." *Stereo Review*, July 1974.

Album review: David Bowie, *Diamond Dogs* (RCA). *Creem*, August 1974.

"Cybill Does It" (Cybill Shepherd press party), by "Garth." *Creem*, August 1974.

"'I Am the World's Greatest Guitarist,' Says Ted Nugent," by Lester Bangs and Jaan Uhelszki. *Creem*, August 1974.

"My Night of Ecstasy with the J. Geils Band: Well, There's a Little Bit of Groupie in All of Us. . . ." *Creem*, August 1974. **CD, LB1, LB2**

"Uriah Heep: Übershlock Declining." *Village Voice*, August 29, 1974.

"Barry Manilow: Fifth Reich Kitsch." *Creem*, September 1974.

Book review: Tony Scaduto, *Mick Jagger: Everybody's Lucifer. Creem*, September 1974.

Movie review: *Born Losers. Creem*, September 1974.

Rock-a-Rama: Steven Grossman, *Caravan Tonight. Creem*, September 1974.

"Stonewall Jackson Ain't No Nazi: Primeevil Career of Blue Öyster Cult." *Creem*, September 1974.

"Smack as Catch Can: The Shape of Dope Today." *Creem*, September 1974.

"Lou Reed Sings Gilbert O'Sullivan." *Shakin' Street Gazette*, September 1974. Reprinted in *Creem*, February 1975.

Album review: Brian Eno, *Here Come the Warm Jets. Creem*, October 1974.

Book review: Charles Bukowski, *Notes of a Dirty Old Man* and *Erections, Ejaculations, Exhibitions and Tales of Ordinary Madness. Creem*, October 1974.

"C'mon Sugar, Let's Go All-Nite Jukin' with Wet Willie." *Creem*, October 1974, **LB1**

Rock-a-Rama: *Queen II. Creem*, October 1974.

Short Take: *Quackser Fortune Has a Cousin in the Bronx. Creem*, October 1974.

Short Take: *Uptown Saturday Night. Creem*, October 1974.

Short Take: *Zandy's Bride. Creem*, October 1974.

"How to Be a Rock Critic." *Shakin' Street Gazette*, October 1974.

"Rock Decadence Sweepstakes" (David Werner, Kiss, Dana Gillespie, Wayne County). *Penthouse*, October 1974.

"It's Only the Rolling Stones." *Village Voice*, October 31, 1974.

Short Take: *Golden Needles. Creem*, November 1974.

"When in Doubt, Kick Ass! *Creem* Carpetbags Its Way Through a Few Pith-Ant Observations on the South, Where They Always Say, 'Howdy! Boy.' " *Creem*, November 1974.

"Better Than the Beatles: The Wackers." *Shakin' Street Gazette*, November 1974.

"Tot Rock: Wild in the Playpen." *Real Paper*, November 20, 1974.

"Sounds: Southern Bands." *Penthouse*, December 1974.

"ELO: Pomp and Circumfluence." *Village Voice*, December 9, 1974.

Album review: Randy Newman, *Good Old Boys. Creem*, January 1975.

"Johnny Ray's Better Whirlpool: The New Living Bowie." *Creem*, January 1975. **CD, LB1**

Album review: Hydra, *Seceding from the South. Penthouse*, January 1975.

"Killer Frogs in Transatlantic Blitz: A Franco-American Chronologue Starring Les Variations." *Creem*, February 1975. **LB1, LB2**

Movie review: *Lenny*. *Creem*, February 1975.

Short Take: *Blood for Dracula*. *Creem*, February 1975.

"What the Stones Fantasize About." *Hype*, February 1975.

"Jon and Barbra's Torch Song" (Barbra Streisand and Jon Peters). *Village Voice*, February 3, 1975.

Album review: George Harrison, *Dark Horse*. *Creem*, March 1975.

"Let Us Now Praise Famous Death Dwarves, or, How I Slugged It Out with Lou Reed and Stayed Awake." *Creem*, March 1975. **CD, LB1, LB2**

"Limey Foretrekkers, or, The Aldebarrian Old Guard" (Emerson, Lake & Palmer, Hawkwind, Mike Oldfield, and Yes). *Creem*, March 1975.

Rock-a-Rama: Sparks, *Propaganda*. *Creem*, March 1975.

"The Ex-Beatles Keep Trying." *Stereo Review*, March 1975.

Album review: Kevin Ayers, *The Confessions of Dr. Dream and Other Stories*. *Creem*, April 1975.

"Not Insane and Not Funny Either: The Firesign Theatre's Catalog of Misconceptions." *Creem*, April 1975.

Rock-a-Rama: Jack Bruce, *Out of the Storm*. *Creem*, April 1975.

Rock-a-Rama: *Kinky Friedman*. *Creem*, April 1975.

Rock-a-Rama: Love, *Reel to Reel*. *Creem*, April 1975.

Rock-a-Rama: The Ohio Players, *Fire*. *Creem*, April 1975.

"Dandelions in Still Air: The Withering Away of the Beatles." *Real Paper*, April 23, 1975. Reprinted in *Creem*, June 1975.

Album review: Paul Davis, *Rustic of the Hour*. *Creem*, May 1975.

"What Has 160 Teeth and Plays Soccer? The Faces, Who Are Still Kicking." *Creem*, May 1975.

"The Elton John Interview," by Lester Bangs and Jaan Uhelszki. *Creem*, May 1975.

"Bryan Ferry's Pursuit of Elegance." *Penthouse*, May 1975.

"Paul Davis: Rustic of the Hour." *Creem*, May 1975.

Album review: Kraftwerk, *Autobahn*. *Creem*, June 1975.

Movie review: *Savages*. *Creem*, June 1975.

"Alice Cooper: Punch & Judy Play the Toilets." *Creem*, July 1975.

"Rick Wakeman Drowns in Suds." *Creem*, July 1975.

"Boy Howdy's Greatest Hits" (joke record labels). *Creem*, July 1975.

Rock-a-Rama: Bob Dylan, *Blood on the Tracks*. *Creem*, July 1975.

Rock-a-Rama: Lou Reed, *Sally Can't Dance*. *Creem*, July 1975.

"John Cale and Nico: Up from the Underground." *Penthouse*, July 1975.

Album review: The Rolling Stones, *Metamorphosis* and *Made in the Shade*. *Creem*, August 1975.

Album review: Barry White, *Just Another Way to Say I Love You*. *Creem*, August 1975. **CD, LB2**

Rock-a-Rama: Magma, *Kohntarkosz. Creem*, August 1975.

Rock-a-Rama: Jerry Jordan, *Phone Call from God. Creem*, August 1975.

"Rock: Tangerine Dream—Sandmen of Alphaville." *Real Paper*, August 20, 1975.

Album review: Lou Reed, *Metal Machine Music. Creem*, September 1975. **LB1**

Album review: Frank Zappa and the Mothers of Invention, *One Size Fits All. Creem*, September 1975.

"Kraftwerkfeature, or, How I Learned to Stop Worrying and Love the Balm." *Creem*, September 1975. Reprinted in *New Musical Express*, September 6, 1975. **CD, LB1, LB2**

Movie review: *Nashville. Creem*, September 1975.

Rock-a-Rama: *Hype* fanzine. *Creem*, September 1975.

"Frankie Valli: The Screech That Roars." *Village Voice*, September 8, 1975.

"Boy Howdy's Top Ten: The Creem of Current Hootch." *Creem*, October 1975.

Rock-a-Rama: Brian Eno, "The Lion Sleeps Tonight (Wimoweh)"/"I'll Come Running" and Bryan Ferry, "You Go to My Head"/"Remake/Remodel." *Creem*, October 1975.

Rock-a-Rama: Kraftwerk, *Ralf & Florian. Creem*, October 1975.

Rock-a-Rama: Tangerine Dream, *Alpha Centauri* and *Electronic Meditation. Creem*, October 1975.

"The New Prefab Nihilism" (Blue Öyster Cult and the Dictators). *Penthouse*, October 1975.

"Paul and Linda: Alright Tonight" (Wings). *Stereo Review*, October 1975.

"Jazz: The Elegance of John Lewis?" *Real Paper*, October 8, 1975.

"Art: 2, Bangs: 0" (Art Garfunkel press conference). *New Musical Express*, October 11, 1975.

"Singles Reviewed This Week by Lester Bangs." *New Musical Express*, October 11, 1975.

"Getting Your Rocks Off: A Lustful Look at the Raunchy Side of Rock 'n' Roll." *Screw*, October 13, 1975.

Album review: Bruce Springsteen, *Born to Run. Creem*, November 1975.

"Don't Print This Lou Reed Story." *Creem*, November 1975.

"Dictionary of MOR Soul: Schmaltz with a Beat." *Real Paper*, November 5, 1975.

"It's the Last Bash on the Gridiron: Faces Huddle for Defensive Play." *Creem*, November 1975. Reprinted in *New Musical Express*, November 22, 1975.

Album review: The Grateful Dead, *Blues for Allah. Creem*, December 1975.

Album review: The Marshall Tucker Band, *Searching for My Rainbow. Creem*, December 1975.

Album review: *The Who by Numbers. Creem*, December 1975.

"Ted Nugent," by "Natty Bumppo." *Creem*, December 1975.

Album review: Lou Reed, *Sally Can't Dance. Denim Delinquent*, December 1975.

"Dr. Demento's Novrec MOR." *Village Voice*, December 22, 1975.

"First Came Art . . . Then Came Kmart." *Chic*, exact date unknown, 1976.

"Isis Is as Isis Does." *Chic*, exact date unknown, 1976.

Album review: The Allman Brothers Band, *Win, Lose or Draw*. *Creem*, January 1976.

"Jethro Tull: Naked Came the Codpiece," by Lester Bangs and "Mongo" Genheimer, *Creem*, January 1976.

"John Denver Is God." *Creem*, January 1976. **LB1**

"Letter from Britain: If It's Tuesday (or Wednesday or Thursday or . . .) This Must Be the Bar." *Creem*, January 1976.

Album review: Patti Smith, *Horses*. *Creem*, February 1976.

"From the Jefferson Airplane to the Starship Enterprise." *Creem*, February 1976.

"How to Succeed in Torture Without Really Trying, or, Louie Come Home, All Is Forgiven." *Creem*, February 1976. **CD, LB1, LB2**

Rock-a-Rama: The Dictators, *Go Girl Crazy! Creem*, February 1976.

Rock-a-Rama: The Allman Brothers Band, *The Road Goes On Forever*. *Creem*, February 1976.

Rock-a-Rama: Art Garfunkel, *Breakaway*. *Creem*, February 1976.

"A Good Show-Biz Biography Nowadays Is Hard to Find." *Chicago Tribune* Book World, February 1, 1976.

Album review: Neil Young, *Zuma*. *Creem*, March 1976.

The Greatest Album Ever Made, Just in Case You Ever Wondered" (*Metal Machine Music*). *Creem*, March 1976. **CD, LB1, LB2**

"Joey Gallo Was No Hero." *Village Voice*, March 8, 1976. Published in slightly different form as "Bob Dylan's Dalliance with Mafia Chic: He Ain't No Delinquent, He's Misunderstood." *Creem*, April 1976. **LB1**

Album review: David Bowie, *Station to Station*. *Creem*, April 1976. **CD**

"Death May Be Your Santa Claus: An Exclusive Up-to-Date Interview with Jimi Hendrix," by "Mort A. Credit as told to Lester Bangs." *Creem*, April 1976. Reprinted in *New Musical Express*, May 1, 1976. **LB1, LB2**

Single review: Willie "Loco" Alexander, "Kerouac"/"Mass. Ave." *Creem*, April 1976.

Album review: Lynyrd Skynyrd, *Gimme Back My Bullets*/Bad Company, *Run with the Pack*. *Creem*, May 1976.

Rock-a-Rama: Kraftwerk, *Weather Reconnaissance Balloon Farm*. *Creem*, May 1976.

Rock-a-Rama: Lou Reed, *Coney Island Baby* (RCA), by "Delmore Schwartz." *Creem*, May 1976.

Rock-a-Rama: Telly Savalas, *Who Loves Ya Baby? Creem*, May 1976.

"Venus & Mars & Paul & Linda: Wings on the Run." *Real Paper*, May 19, 1976. Reprinted in *Creem*, August 1976.

"Innocents In Babylon, Part One" (reggae feature). *Creem*, June 1976. **LB1, LB2**

Rock-a-Rama: Roxy Music, *Siren*. *Creem*, June 1976.

Rock-a-Rama: Bruce Springsteen, *Sentimental Journey*, by "Jean Genet." *Creem*, June 1976.

Rock-a-Rama: The Velvet Underground, *White Light/White Heat*, by "Bill Bored." *Creem*, June 1976.

"Miles Davis: Depression as an Art Form." *Phonograph Record Magazine*, June 1976. Reprinted in *New Musical Express*, April 30, 1983. **LB1, LB2**

Album review: The Rolling Stones, *Black and Blue*. *Creem*, July 1976. **LB1**

Album review: Bob Seger, *Live Bullet*. *Creem*, July 1976.

"*Creem* Celebrates the Bicentennial." *Creem*, July 1976.

"Innocents in Babylon, Part Two." *Creem*, July 1976. **LB2**

Rock-a-Rama: Kevin Coyne, *Matching Head and Feet*, by "the Hindenburg." *Creem*, July 1976.

Rock-a-Rama: Edgar Froese, *Epsilon in Malaysian Pale*, by "Aid to Dependent Lazlo." *Creem*, July 1976.

Rock-a-Rama: Magma, *Mekanik Destruktiw Kommandoh*, by "Aid to Dependent Lazlo." *Creem*, July 1976.

Album review: Blackmore's Rainbow, *Rainbow Rising*. *Creem*, August 1976.

"Bob Seger: Bringing Detroit Back to Michigan." *Phonograph Record Magazine*, August 1976.

"This Beer Belly Thinks Canadian Brew's Best." *Windsor* (Ontario) *Star*, August 21, 1976.

Album review: Jeff Beck, *Wired*. *Creem*, September 1976.

Movie review: *Buffalo Bill and the Indians*. *Creem*, September 1976.

Rock-a-Rama: The Beatles, *Rock & Roll Music*. *Creem*, September 1976.

Rock-a-Rama: Bohannon, *Dance Your Ass Off*. *Creem*, September 1976.

Rock-a-Rama: David Bowie, *Changesonebowie*. *Creem*, September 1976.

Rock-a-Rama: Bob Marley and the Wailers, *Rastaman Vibration*. *Creem*, September 1976.

Rock-a-Rama: *Ramones*. *Creem*, September 1976.

Rock-a-Rama: Rolling Stones, *Black and Blue*. *Creem*, September 1976.

Born in the U.S.A. column: "There Are Only Three Rock Groups in America." *New Musical Express*, September 18, 1976.

Album review: Aerosmith, *Rocks*. *Creem*, October 1976.

Album review: David Crosby and Graham Nash, *Whistling Down the Wire*. *Creem*, October 1976.

Rock-a-Rama: Miles Davis, *Filles de Kilimanjaro*, by "Ralph J. Gleason." *Creem*, October 1976.

"How the Eagles Cleaned Up the Wild West (and James Dean, and Tequila, and Divers Other Deviant Outcroppings)." *The Music Gig*, October 1976. Reprinted in the *New Musical Express*, October 16, 1976.

"Peter Frampton Is Nice Nice Nice." *Village Voice*, October 25, 1976.

"Sex and the Art of Rock 'n' Roll. Q: Does Sex Sell Records?" *Creem*, November 1976.

Album review: Linda Ronstadt, *Hasten Down the Wind. Creem*, November 1976.

Rock-a-Rama: Brian Eno, *Taking Tiger Mountain (By Strategy). Creem*, November 1976.

Rock-a-Rama: *Jonathan Richman and the Modern Lovers. Creem*, November 1976.

Rock-a-Rama: Buck Trent, *Bionic Banjo. Creem*, November 1976.

Rock-a-Rama: *The Runaways. Creem*, November 1976.

Born in the U.S.A. column: "I Ain't Voting." *New Musical Express*, November 6, 1976.

"Richman? Poor, Man" (Jonathan Richman). *New Musical Express*, November 13, 1976. Reprinted as "Twerp King at the Summit" in *Creem*, January 1977.

"The Future of Techno-Rock: Where's Boston?" *Real Paper*, November 20, 1976. Reprinted in *New Musical Express*, January 1, 1977.

"Uptown Rulers Take to the Warpath" (Wild Tchoupitoulas). *Village Voice*, November 22, 1976.

"Bob Dylan Versus Don Kirshner: Can You Tell the Players Without a Scorecard?" (*Hard Rain* and *Rock Music Awards* TV specials). *Creem*, December 1976.

Rock-a-Rama: *Bill Cosby Is Not Himself These Days, Rat On. Creem*, December 1976.

Rock-a-Rama: Bob Marley and the Wailers, *Rastaman Vibration. Creem*, December 1976.

Rock-a-Rama: *Ramones. Creem*, December 1976.

Rock-a-Rama: Lou Reed, *Blondes Have More Fun*/Patti Smith, *Teenage Perversity and Ships in the Night* ("bootlegs"). *Creem*, December 1976.

"Three Visions of Öyster Apocalypse" (Blue Öyster Cult). *Creem*, December 1976.

Album review: *The Beatles at the Hollywood Bowl. Circus*, exact date unknown, 1977.

Album review: The Captain & Tennille, *Come In from the Rain. Circus*, exact date unknown, 1977.

"The Punk Rock Machine." *National Screw*, exact date unknown, 1977.

"Ramones!" *Vortex*, exact date unknown, 1977.

Album review: Stevie Wonder, *Songs in the Key of Life. Creem*, January 1977.

"Blondie Is More Fun." *Village Voice*, January 10, 1977.

Album review: Deep Purple, *Made in Europe. Circus*, February 28, 1977.

Album review: *NBC's Saturday Night Live. Circus*, February 28, 1977.

Album review: Ted Nugent, *Free-for-All. Circus*, February 28, 1977.

"Get the Hook? The Strange Truth About the Jefferson Starship." *Creem*, March 1977.

Album review: *The Babys. Stereo Review*, March 1977.

Album review: Barclay James Harvest, *Octoberon. Stereo Review*, March 1977.

"Iggy Pop: Blowtorch in Bondage." *Village Voice*, March 28, 1977. **CD, LB1, LB2**

Album review: Leon Redbone, *Double Time. High Fidelity*, April 1977.

"How to Learn to Love Reggae." *Stereo Review*, April 1977.

Album review: Television, *Marquee Moon. Circus*, April 14, 1977.

"I Saw God and/or Tangerine Dream." *Village Voice*, April 18, 1977. **CD, LB2**

"Muzak with a Beat (What Is Jazz-Rock?)." *Real Paper*, April 23, 1977.

Album review: Jethro Tull, *Songs from the Wood*, by Eric Genheimer "with Robert Duncan and Lester Bangs posthumously." *Creem*, May 1977.

Album review: Natalie Cole, *Unpredictable. High Fidelity*, May 1977.

Album review: The Kinks, *Sleepwalker. High Fidelity*, May 1977.

"Hi! We're Still Dead: A Long Night with the Grateful Dead." *Chicago Daily News* Sidetracks supplement, May 12, 1977.

"Hey Johnny—There's a Geezer Out Here Says He's Got the Answer to All Your Problems . . ." (Sex Pistols). *New Musical Express*, May 28, 1977. **LB2**

"Van Morrison Makes Another Good Album . . . So?" by "Leicester Baines." *High Fidelity*, June 1977.

"The Aesthetics of Queen: Perspectives on A *Day at the Races* in Comparative Contemporary Music." *Hit Parader*, June 1977.

"The Ramones: The Laser Thin Line." *Stereo Review*, June 1977.

Album review: Pablo Cruise, *A Place in the Sun. Stereo Review*, June 1977.

Album review: *Piper. Stereo Review*, June 1977.

Album review: Iggy Pop, *The Idiot. Stereo Review*, June 1977.

"Back Door Men and Women in Bondage" (Cherie Currie fantasy). *Back Door Man*, July/August 1977.

"Meditations on John Coltrane's Ascension." *Gig*, July 1977.

Album review: Flame, *Queen of the Neighborhood. Stereo Review*, July 1977.

Album review: Bill Quateman, *Night After Night. Stereo Review*, July 1977.

"Gregg Allman: The Fink Has Soul," by "Les Baines." *High Fidelity*, August 1977.

"Everybody's Search for Roots" (Roots of Punk Part I). *New Wave*, August 1977. **LB1**

Album review: *Peter Gabriel. Stereo Review*, August 1977.

Album review: Jethro Tull, *Songs from the Wood. Stereo Review*, August 1977.

Album review: Elliott Murphy, *Just a Story from America. Stereo Review*, August 1977.

"John Cale's Best Cuts: A Welcome Combination of Rock, Brains, and Guts." *Stereo Review*, August 1977.

Album review: Utopia, *Ra. Stereo Review*, August 1977.

"Peter Tork at CBGB?" *Village Voice*, August 8, 1977.

"Peter Frampton Cures Schizophrenia." *Chicago Daily News* Sidetracks supplement, August 4, 1977. Reprinted in *New Musical Express*, August 13, 1977.

"Richard Hell and the Voidoids." *Waxpaper*, August 26, 1977.

"How Long Will We Care?" (a.k.a. "Where Were You When Elvis Died?") *Village Voice*, August 29, 1977. **CD**

Album review: Jeff Beck/Jan Hammer Group, *Live*. *Stereo Review*, September 1977.

Album review: *Cheap Trick*. *Stereo Review*, September 1977.

Album review: *Foreigner*. *Stereo Review*, September 1977.

Album review: Bob Marley and the Wailers, *Exodus*/Peter Tosh, *Equal Rights*. *Stereo Review*, September 1977.

"Peter Laughner: He Was a Friend of Mine." *New York Rocker*, September/October 1977. **CD**

"An-th-r B-ncha N-w Y-rk We-rdo-s" (Sic F*cks). *New Musical Express*, September 24, 1977.

Album review: Alice Cooper, *Lace and Whiskey*. *Stereo Review*, October 1977.

Album review: The Dictators, *Manifest Destiny*. *Stereo Review*, October 1977.

Born in the U.S.A. column: "I Don't Want to Talk About Satan, Just Want to See His Face." *New Musical Express*, October 8, 1977.

"Heavy Metal: The Sinal Folution." New Musical Express, October 8, 1977. Reprinted in *Hit Parader*, March 1978.

Movie review: *Short Eyes*. *Chicago Daily News* Sidetracks supplement, October 13, 1977.

"Dead Boys Almost Count Five." *Village Voice*, October 24, 1977.

"Admit It: You Like to Kick Cripples, Too (Especially If You Are One)" (heavy metal). *Gig*, November 1977.

TV column: "The Videot." *Gig*, November 1977.

"Th . . . They're the Dead Boys! Night of the Living Dead Boys." *Punk*, November 1977.

Album review: Burning Spear, *Dry and Heavy*. *Stereo Review*, November 1977.

Album review: Kiss, *Love Gun*. *Stereo Review*, November 1977.

Album review: *Steve Winwood*. *Stereo Review*, November 1977.

Performance review: "Iggy Suffers Metallic K.O., Ramones Rule, O.K.?" *New Musical Express*, November 5, 1977.

Album review: Nick Drake, *Bryter Layter*. *Stereo Review*, December 1977.

Album review: Jonathan Richman and the Modern Lovers, *Rock 'n' Roll with the Modern Lovers*. *Stereo Review*, December 1977.

"The Clash: Lester Bangs Falls in Love (And Sees the Promised Land), Part One." *New Musical Express*, December 10, 1977. **CD**

"Freddie Mercury's Supermarket Sweep." *Village Voice*, December 12, 1977.

"The Clash: Lester Bangs Falls in Love (And Sees the Promised Land), Part Two." *New Musical Express*, December 17, 1977. The entire article was reprinted in the *Clash on Broadway* box set, Epic/Legacy, 1991. **CD**

"Death Means Never Having to Say You're Incomplete: Richard Hell." *Gig*, January 1978. **CD**

"Out to Pasture with Les McEwen & the Rollers in Bay City, Michigan." *Phonograph Record Magazine*, January 1978.

Album review: Elvis Costello, *My Aim Is True*. *Phonograph Record Magazine*, January 1978.

Album review: Lily Tomlin, *On Stage*. *Stereo Review*, January 1978.

Movie review: *Renaldo and Clara*. *Chicago Daily News* Sidetracks supplement, February 2, 1978.

"Techno-Rasta, As I Would Say" (Big Youth and dub reggae). *Village Voice*, February 20, 1978.

"The Ten Most Ridiculous Albums of the Decade." *Phonograph Record Magazine*, March 1978.

"Jukejoy Comes to Soho (Almost)" (Delbert McClinton and Joe Ely). *Village Voice*, March 27, 1977.

"Eno Sings with the Fishes." *Village Voice*, April 3, 1978.

"Patti Smith's Top 40 Insurrection." *Phonograph Record Magazine*, May/June 1978.

"Lester Bangs's Introduction to Rock Cinema." *Phonograph Record Magazine*, May/June 1978.

"The Last Waltz." *Phonograph Record Magazine*, May/June 1978.

Album review: Bob Marley, *Kaya*. *Rolling Stone*, June 1, 1978.

"Growing Up True Is Hard to Do" (Bob Seger). *Village Voice*, June 5, 1978.

"What Rhymes with Orange, Bob?" (Bob Dylan). *Village Voice*, July 17, 1978.

Album review: The Rolling Stones, *Some Girls*. *Stereo Review*, August 1978.

"Jesse Winchester: A Patriotic Chore." *Village Voice*, August 21, 1978.

"Ramones Go Depresso—So Would You if Your Best Girl Left You for Suicide." *New Musical Express*, September 23, 1978. Reprinted in *Trouser Press*, November 1978.

"Blue Öyster Cult: One Enchanted Evening." *Village Voice*, October 9, 1978.

"A Sid Vicious Story: A Tale of Two Patsies." *Village Voice*, October 23, 1978.

LB2

"All That Jazz: Miles Davis Lives." *Gig*, November 1978.

"Homage to Charles Mingus: All the Things You Could Be by Now If Duke Ellington's Wife Was Your Mother." *Gig*, November 1978.

"Roots of Punk Part II." *New Wave*, November 1978.

Album review: Van Morrison, *Wavelength*. *Rolling Stone*, November 16, 1978.

Album review: *Ace Frehley*. *Circus*, November 21, 1978.

"Bob Seger: Music for the Aged." *Hit Parader*, December 1978.

"Twenty-five by Twenty-five: Twenty-five Top Rock Critics Pick Their Twenty-five Favorite Records." *Billboard*, December 2, 1978.

"Clash in the Crossfire." *Village Voice*, December 11, 1978.

Album review: Eric Dolphy, *The Berlin Concerts*. *Rolling Stone*, December 14, 1978.

Album review: Styx, *Pieces of Eight*. *Rolling Stone*, December 28, 1978.

"How I (Finally) Joined the Velvet Underground." *Hit Parader*, exact date unknown, 1979. **LB2**

"I Would Buy a Used Car from Meat Loaf: A Political Manifesto of Sorts." *Hit Parader*, January 1979.

"Jim Morrison: Ofus Laureate." *Village Voice*, January 8, 1979.

"Willie Nelson: Red-Headed Stranger or Drugstore Cowboy?" *Hit Parader*, February 1979.

"Roots of Punk Part III." *New Wave*, February 1979.

Album review: Alice Cooper, *From the Inside. Circus*, February 6, 1979.

"Whatever Happened to Reggae?" (Peter Tosh). Stereo Review, April 1979.

Album review: Village People, *Cruisin'. Rolling Stone*, April 14, 1979. **LB2**

"A Bellyful of Wire." *Village Voice*, April 23, 1979. **LB2**

"The White Noise Supremacists." *Village Voice*, April 30, 1979. **CD**

"Keith's Shag Has a Perm" (The New Barbarians). *Village Voice*, May 21, 1979.

"Ian Hunter: The Coots Are All Right." *Village Voice*, June 4, 1979.

Album review: Lou Reed, *The Bells. Rolling Stone*, June 14, 1979. **LB1, LB2**

"Heavy Metal: Testing the Limit—Van Halen, the Godz, and Assorted Dregs." *Los Angeles Herald-Examiner*, June 17, 1979.

Album review: Robert Gordon, *Rock Billy Boogie. Rolling Stone*, June 28, 1979.

"Fripp Must Be Suffering from Over-Exposure," by Lester Bangs and Galen Brandt. *Los Angeles Herald-Examiner*, August 12, 1979.

"David Byrne Says 'Boo!' " *Village Voice*, August 20, 1979.

"Old Pooh, New Paint: How Ian Dury Keeps Doing It Himself." *Los Angeles Herald-Examiner*, August 26, 1979.

"The Grooming of David Johansen." *Village Voice*, September 3, 1979.

"Preacher Van Is Looking for a New Tongue" (Van Morrison). *Chicago Sun-Times*, October 14, 1979.

"Elton John After the Fact." *Village Voice*, October 29, 1979.

"The Ambient Mr. Eno." *Musician*, November 1979.

Album review: Blondie, *Eat to the Beat. Stereo Review*, December 1979.

"Open Letter to Starship Kantner." *Village Voice*, December 3, 1979.

"Sham 69 Is Innocent!" *Village Voice*, December 17, 1979. **CD, LB2**

Pazz & Jop Decade Product Report. *Village Voice*, December 17, 1979.

"What If They Gave a New Year and Nobody Came?" *Village Voice*, December 31, 1979. **CD**

"Celebrities: So Human." *Reliable Source*, 1980.

"Ramones Get Technical." *International Musician and Recording World*, January 1980.

"Captain Beefheart's Iridescent Logic." *Musician*, January 1980.

"Rock in the Seventies." *Musician*, January 1980.

"Pop Music in the Eighties." *Stereo Review*, January 1980.

"The Undertones: Wholesome Becomes Hep." *Village Voice*, January 21, 1980.

Album review: The Heartbreakers, *Live at Max's Kansas City. Rolling Stone*, February 7, 1980.

Album review: Peter Tosh, *Mystic Man*/Toots and the Maytals, *Pass the Pipe. Rolling Stone*, February 7, 1980.

"Burning Spear: Poetry Is History." *Village Voice*, February 11, 1980.

"The Fire Next Time" (The Clash). *Soho Weekly News*, March 5, 1980.

Album review: ZZ Top, *Deguello. Rolling Stone*, March 6, 1980.

"A Kiss and a Boby Enchilada" (Joe "King" Carrasco). *Soho Weekly News*, March 19, 1980.

"John Lydon Across the Border." *Village Voice*, March 24, 1980. **LB2**

"Free Jazz: Punk Rock." *Musician*, April 1980.

Book review: Peter Guralnick, *Lost Highway. Los Angeles Herald-Examiner*, April 13, 1980. **CD**

" 'Rosco' Fripp's Funky Tape Loop." *Village Voice,* April 28, 1980.

Album review: Lydia Lunch, *Queen of Siam. Rolling Stone,* May 1, 1980.

"The Joy of Suicide." *Soho Weekly News*, May 28, 1980.

"I Have Seen the Past of Rock 'n' Roll and It Is ZZ Top." *Musician*, June 1980.

"Art Ensemble of Chicago: Rated G." *Village Voice*, June 2, 1980.

Album review: The Slits, *Cut. Rolling Stone*, June 12, 1980.

"Devo: Goodbye Bozos." *Village Voice*, June 16, 1980.

"Grace Jones Beats Off." *Village Voice*, June 25, 1980.

"Capetown Calling" (Max Roach's *We Insist! Freedom Now Suite*). *Soho Weekly News*, June 25, 1980.

"The Stones Cruise on Eighth Street." *Village Voice*, July 23, 1980.

"Whose New Wave?" *Musician*, August 1980.

"Pop Group: Cambodian Kitchen Sink." *Village Voice*, August 13, 1980.

"Captain Beefheart's Far Cry." *Village Voice*, October 1, 1980. **LB2**

"Going Beyond Music: A Consumer Guide." *Musician*, October 1980.

Album review: Jackson Browne, *Hold Out*/Bob Dylan, *Saved*/The Kinks, *One for the Road*/The Rolling Stones, *Emotional Rescue. Musician*, October 1980.

Music column: "Bob Dylan Meets God. Or, God Meets Bob Dylan." *Music and Sound Output*, November/December 1980.

Poem: "Trapped by the Mormons." *Contempo Culture*, December 1980.

"Otis Rush Mugged by an Iceberg." *Village Voice*, December 3, 1980. **CD, LB2**

"Thinking the Unthinkable About John Lennon." *Los Angeles Times*, December 14, 1980. **CD**

Liner notes: *Fugs Greatest Hits, Vol. I: Proto Punk* (PVC/Adelphi), 1981.

"Better Than the Beatles (And DNA, Too)" (the Shaggs). *Village Voice*, January 28. 1981. **LB2**

"Rock's Top Ten Guitarists—Another View." *International Musician and Recording World*, February 1981.

Music column: "Touring: Down the Road to Nowhere." *Music and Sound Output*, February/March 1981.

"Live from Austin, Texas." *Musician*, March 1981.

"Everything Above 14th Street Is Gila Bend, Arizona." *Village Voice*, March 24, 1981.

Music column: "You Can Get Anything You Want & Here's How." *Music and Sound Output*, April/May 1981.

"Big Youth Go Home." *Village Voice*, April 15, 1981.

"Jello Biafra Is No Cretin." *Village Voice*, April 29, 1981. **LB2**

Music column: "Recording: Less Is More." *Music and Sound Output*, June/July 1981.

"David Byrne: No Longer Paranoid." *International Musician and Recording World*, June 1981.

Movie review: *A Face in the Crowd. Psychotronic*, July 1981.

Movie review: *Forty Guns. Psychotronic*, July 1981.

"John Lennon Is Alive and a Voidoid: A Rock & Roll Fantasy." *Village Voice*, July 1, 1981.

"Au Pairs Say Sex Is Good!" *Village Voice*, July 1, 1981.

Music column: "Regionalism: Best Buy for the Polite Majority." *Music and Sound Output*, August/September 1981.

"Jim Morrison: Bozo Dionysus a Decade Later." *Musician*, August 1981.

"Dylan: Love or Confusion?" *Village Voice*, August 26, 1981.

"A Reasonable Guide to Horrible Noise." *Village Voice*, September 30, 1981. **CD, LB2**

Music column: "Every Song a Hooker." *Music and Sound Output*, October 1981.

"Stevie Nicks: Lilith or Bimbo?" *Village Voice*, November 25, 1981.

Music column: "Miles Davis: Music for the Living Dead." *Music and Sound Output*, November/December 1981.

Liner notes: *It Falleth Like Gentle Rain from Heaven—The Mekons Story* (British CNT), 1982.

Music column: "The Fix Is In." *Music and Sound Output*, January/February 1982.

"Yecch! An Interview with a Slob," by Stephanie Hill and Lester Bangs. *Village Voice*, January 13, 1982.

Pazz & Jop Critics Poll Protest Ballot. *Village Voice*, January 27, 1982.

"1994: A Projection, or, George Orwell Meets Kraftwerk (And Boogies, Even!)." *Music and Sound Output*, March/April 1982.

Music column: "We Are All Deadheads." *Music and Sound Output*, March/April 1982.

"Rod Stewart: Wake Up Rodney, I Think It's Time for You to Record," by Lester Bangs and Paul Nelson (book excerpt). *Music and Sound Output*, March/April 1982.

Book review: Jerzy Kosinski, *Pinball. Village Voice*, March 16, 1982.

"Jehovah Is Just All Right with Van." *Village Voice*, March 23, 1982.

"If Oi Were a Carpenter." *Village Voice*, April 27, 1982.

Music column: "Bad Taste Is Timeless." *Music and Sound Output*, May/June 1982.

"Nico: *The Marble Index.*" *What Goes On*, 1983 (written in October 1978).

"From *All My Friends Are Hermits.*" *Chemical Imbalance*, 1989 (written in fall 1980).

"Bye-Bye Sidney, Be Good." *Throat Culture #2*, 1990 (written in 1979).

"An Instant Fan's Inspired Notes: You Gotta Listen." Previously unpublished liner notes on the Comedian Harmonists (written in 1981). *The New York Times*, September 5, 1999.

Lester Bangs, Books

Blondie. New York: Fireside, 1980.

Rod Stewart. By Lester Bangs and Paul Nelson. New York: Delilah Books, 1981.

Psychotic Reaction and Carburetor Dung: The Work of a Legendary Critic: Rock 'n' Roll as Literature and Literature as Rock 'n' Roll. Edited by Greil Marcus. New York: Alfred A. Knopf, 1987.

Lester Bangs, Contributions to Anthologies and Encyclopedias

Bruce Springsteen, The Rolling Stone Files: The Ultimate Compendium of Interviews, Articles, Facts and Opinions from the Files of Rolling Stone. Edited by Parke Puterbaugh and the editors of *Rolling Stone.* New York: Hyperion, 1996. Includes Bangs's review of *Greetings from Asbury Park, N.J.*

The Doors Companion: Four Decades of Commentary. Edited by John Rocco. New York: Schirmer Books, 1997. Includes "Jim Morrison: Bozo Dionysus a Decade Later."

The Doors: The Illustrated History. Edited by Danny Sugerman. New York: William Morrow & Company, 1983. Includes Bangs's review in *Fusion* of *Absolutely Live*.

Elvis Presley: The Rebel Years. New York: W. W. Norton & Company, 1997. Photo book includes "From Notes for Review of Peter Guralnick's *Lost Highway*, 1980" from *Psychotic Reactions and Carburetor Dung.*

Musician, Player & Listener: The Year in Rock 1981–82. New York: Delilah, 1981. Bangs's contributions are "I Have Seen the Past of Rock 'n' Roll and It Is ZZ Top," "Jim Morrison: Bozo Dionysus a Decade Later," and "Austin, Texas."

The Penguin Book of Rock & Roll Writing. Edited by Clinton Heylin. New York: Viking, 1992. Bangs's contributions are "In Which Yet Another Pompous Blowhard Purports to Possess the True Meaning of Punk Rock" from *Blondie* and "Death May Be Your Santa Claus: An Exclusive Up-to-Date Interview with Jimi Hendrix."

Reggae, Rastafarians, Revolution: Jamaican Music from Ska to Dub. New York: Schirmer Books, 1997. Includes "How to Learn to Love Reggae."

Rock Revolution: From Elvis to Alice—The Whole Story of Rock and Roll. New York: Curtis Books, 1973. Edited by Richard Robinson and the editors of *Creem*. Bangs's chapters are "The Rolling Stones: Ecstasy and Evil," "The Progressives: Rock Stylizations from Brahms to the Auto-Destruct Guitar," "The Heavy Metal Kids," and "Glitter Rock."

Rock Revolution: From Elvis to Elton—The Story of Rock and Roll. New York: Popular Library, 1976. By the editors of *Creem* magazine. This edition reprints Bangs's chapters from the first book and adds "Rages to Come: *Creem*'s Predictions of Rock's Future" and "The Elton John Interview" by Lester Bangs and Jaan Uhelszki.

The Rolling Stone Book of the Beats: The Beat Generation and American Culture. Edited by Holly George-Warren. New York: Hyperion, 1999. Includes Bangs's obituary of Jack Kerouac and review of Allen Ginsberg's *Songs of Innocence and Experience.*

The Rolling Stone Illustrated History of Rock & Roll. New York: Random House/Rolling Stone Press, 1980. Edited by Jim Miller. Bangs's contributions are "The British Invasion," "Protopunk: The Garage Bands," "The Doors," "Bubblegum," and "Heavy Metal."

The Rolling Stone Record Review. New York: Pocket Books, 1971. Reprints nine reviews from *Rolling Stone,* 1967–70.

The Rolling Stone Record Review Volume II. New York: Pocket Books, 1974. Reprints sixteen reviews from *Rolling Stone,* 1970–72.

Stranded: Rock and Roll for a Desert Island. New York: Alfred A Knopf, 1979. Edited by Greil Marcus. Bangs writes about Van Morrison's *Astral Weeks.* Also reprinted in *Psychotic Reactions and Carburetor Dung.*

The Velvet Underground Companion: Four Decades of Commentary. Edited by Albin Zak, III. New York. Schirmer Books, 1997. Includes "Nico: *The Marble Index.*"

Lester Bangs, Letters

To Nancy Alexander. Mid-1974, winter 1975, spring 1977, spring 1979, summer 1980.

To Roger Anderson. Winter 1972; April 8, 1972; summer 1972; November 1972; and April 1973.

To Pam Brown. May 4, 1976.

To the editor, *Fusion.* October 30, 1970.

To the editor, *Phonograph Record Magazine.* December 1971, May 1972, and November 1972.

To the editor, *Teenage Wasteland Gazette.* Spring 1972.

To the editor, *Village Voice.* May 14, 1979.

To James Grauerholz. September 14, 1977, and April 1, 1980.

To Jean Holabird. Circa 1978.

To Barry Kramer. January/February 1976 and July 29, 1977.

To Greil Marcus. June, July, early August, late August, October 14, November 2, November 4, November 9, late November, early December, and late December, 1969; November 1970; December 1971; early 1972; April 9, 1972; 1974; spring 1982; and March 6, 1982.

To Richard Meltzer. Early winter 1973, late winter 1973, April 1973, and spring 1979.

To Fran Pelzman. January 6, 1981.

To Richard Riegel. Spring, summer, and fall, 1973; January, February, March, June, and October 1974; January, November, and December, 1975; June 1976; and February 1982.

To Lisa Robinson. February 1971.

To Lillian Roxon, "Body Shop" column, *Fusion*. March 5, 1971.

To Mike Saunders. Fall 1971, early spring 1972, late spring 1972, summer 1972, and February 9, 1977.

To John Sinclair. November 2, 1971.

To Nick Tosches. November 15, 1975.

To JoAnn Uhelszki. February 1982.

To Richard C. Walls. April 18, 1977.

Lester Bangs, Unpublished Manuscripts

The following is a list of unpublished works cited in the text. By no means is it a complete account of unpublished Bangs.

"A Letter from Fourteenth Street." Poem, circa 1977.

"Andy." Poem, circa 1968.

A Reasonable Guide to Horrible Noise. Book proposal, 1981.

All My Friends Are Hermits. Several fragments exist of Lester's novel in progress. I'm using this title for all of them, 1979 –82.

All the Things You Could Be by Now If Iggy Pop's Wife Was Your Mother: A Book of Jive 'n' Verities. Book proposal, 1977.

Andy. Poem, circa 1969.

Beyond the Law: Four Rock 'n' Roll Extremists. Book proposal plus sample chapter on Brian Eno, 1980.

Catholic School Girls in Trouble. Book proposal, 1981.

Catholic School Girls in Trouble. Fragments, book in progress, 1981.

"Concert review: Mars and the Contortions." Circa 1978. (The rant about *Metal Machine Music* was quoted in *Lou Reed and the Velvet Underground* by Diana Clapton.)

"Detroit Fragments." Various topics, circa 1972.

"Drunk." Poem, circa 1976.

Drug Punk. Unpublished autobiographical novel, circa 1969.

"End of the Year Ballot." Compiled for the *Rock Yearbook*, 1980.

Excerpt from *Rod Stewart*. Thirty-five pages excised from the finished book with Paul Nelson, 1981.

"Getting Bids on the Albatross: Or, How Does It Feel to Be Frank Zappa?" Column written for *Slash* magazine, circa 1981.

"Hey! You!" Fragment, circa 1975.

"I Ain't Pouting." Lyrics, circa 1977.

"I Saw God in a Bottle of Romilar." Rejected by *High Times*, circa 1979.

"It's Never Snowed in Austin." Lyrics, 1980.

"Jerry Rubin Plays Cupid." Rejected by the *Village Voice*, 1982.

Journal of a Blob. Unpublished autobiographical novel, circa 1970.

Lost Generation: American Kids Now in Their Own Words. Book proposal, 1980.

"Lester Calls Idi Amin." Transcript of unsuccessful phone interview, circa 1975.

"M.O.R.: Why Everything Stinks." Circa 1979.

"Nancy Two." Lyrics, circa 1979.

"New York Club Scene." Survey feature assigned and rejected by the *Village Voice*, circa 1980.

"Notes on Arizona." Circa 1979.

"Notes on Austin." Fall 1980.

"Notes on California." Circa 1980.

"Notes on Mingus." Circa 1970.

"Old Broads Like Me (For Genya Ravan)." Poem, circa 1978.

"Part One: What (Clenched)." Poem, circa 1981.

"Part Two: Permanent Dislocation (Letting Go)." Poem, circa 1981.

"Piss It Away." Poem, circa 1976.

Psychotic Reactions and Carburetor Dung: Lester Bangs's Greatest Hits. Book proposal, 1982.

"Ray Conniff: Please Come See Me. In the Citadel." Circa 1978.

Rock Gomorrah: The Scandalous Lies About the Woodstock Nation. Book proposal, 1980.

Rock Gomorrah/Tales from Beyond the Grooves. Unpublished book, 1982.

Rock Through the Looking Glass: A Book of Fantasies. Book proposal, 1980.

"Sexual History." Fragment, circa 1980.

"She Has Big Legs (I'd Like to Squomp)." Poem, circa 1976.

"Slow Times in Detroit." Circa 1978.

"Street Hassling." Rejected by the *Village Voice*, circa 1978.

"Stuck in Round of Nowhere." Fragment on women, circa 1975.

"The Count Five." Fragment, circa 1967.

"The Last Strat Manifesto." Rejected by *Musician*, circa 1980.

"The Widow That Won't Date." Poem, circa 1976.

They Invented It (You Took It Under): The Beatles. Book proposal, 1979.

"Truisms." Poem, circa 1978.

"We Have Been Defiled But." Poem, circa 1978.

Women on Top: Ten Post-Lib Role Models for the Eighties. Book proposal, 1980.

Lester Bangs, Recordings

"Let It Blurt" / "Live." Spy Records 45, 1979.

Lester Bangs and the Delinquents, *Jook Savages on the Brazos.* Live Wire LP, 1981. Reissued on CD by Moll Tonträger, Germany, 1995. Includes "I'm in Love with My Walls," "Life Is Not Worth Living (But Suicide's a Waste of Time)," "Accidents of God," "Legless Bird," "I Just Want to Be a Movie Star," "Nuclear War," "Grandma's House," "Kill Him Again," "Fade Away," "Day of the Dead," "Give Up the Ghost."

Birdland, *Birdland with Lester Bangs.* Add On Records LP, 1986. Reissued on CD by Bacchus Archives/Dionysus, 1998. Includes "Textbook Case," "Kill Him Again," "I'm in Love with My Walls," "Fade Away," "Accidents of God," "I Fought the Law," "Let All Come Down," "The Killer," and "There's a Man in There."

"Sister Ray," Birdland rehearsal tape. Flexi-disc included with *Throat Culture* #2, 1990.

Other Recordings and Videos

A Tribute to Lester Bangs. St. Mark's Poetry Project, May 15, 1992. Videotape.

Lester Bangs. Assorted interviews, *Living Together* feature, undated. Audiotape.

———. Interviews for *Catholic School Girls in Trouble.* Belair Escort Agency, New York, 1981. Audiotape.

———. Interview with Richard "DNV" Sohl. 1977. Audiotape.

———. Interview with Rob Tyner. September 1, 1977. Audiotape.

———. "Romilar rap." Undated. Audiotape.

———. Solo demos I–VI. New York, undated. Audiotapes.

Lester Bangs and Birdland. Live recording. Location and date unknown. Audiotape.

———. Rehearsal recordings I–III. Undated. Audiotapes.

Lester Bangs and the Delinquents at Duke's. Austin, Texas, November 7, 1980. Audiotape.

———. Rehearsal tape. October 16, 1980. Audiotape.

———. Rehearsal tapes I & II. Undated. Audiotapes.

Lester Bangs interviewed by Australian radio. New York, March 12, 1980. Audiotape.

Lester Bangs interviewed by Tish and Snooky Bellomo. New York, 1977. Audiotape.

Lester Bangs, Joan Goodwin, and Mike Goodwin. Radio discussion on the film *Jackson County Jail.* Undated. Audiotape.

Lester Bangs and Peter Laughner. Jam tape, Birmingham, 1976. Audiotape.

Lester Bangs, Peter Laughner, and Peter Stampfel. Jam tape. New York, May 1977. Audiotape.

Lester Bangs and Nancy Stillman. Jam tape. March 17, 1980. Audiotape.

Lester Bangs and "Tender Vittles" at CBGB. June 12, 1977. Audiotape.

————. Rehearsal tape. Undated. Audiotape.

Lester Bangs and Rex Weiner. Jam tape. March 27, 1981. Audiotape.

Lester Bangs watching *Hec Ramsey* and talking on the phone. Undated. Audiotape.

The Lester Bangs Experience. Rehearsal tape, New York. April 2, 1977. Audiotape.

————. Rehearsal tape. April 3, 1977. Audiotape.

Panel Discussion on the Legacy of Lester Bangs. South by Southwest Music & Media Conference, Austin, Texas. March 12, 1992.

Rock Critics' Symposium. Buffalo State University, May 11, 1974. Audiotape.

Mike Saunders. Demos of songs by Lester Bangs. Circa 1972. Audiotape.

Nancy Stillman. Demos of songs by Lester Bangs. Audiotape.

"Theatrical Rock" special, *All You Need Is Love* documentary series. EMI-TV, London, circa 1974. Videotape. Features several interview segments with Bangs.

Tour of *Creem* magazine's Cass Avenue office. WTVS-TV, Detroit, fall 1971. Videotape. Features roundtable discussion with Bangs, Dave Marsh, and Barry Kramer.

Other Authors, Articles and Reviews

Altman, Billy. Lester Bangs obituary. *Village Voice*, May 11, 1982.

————. Lester Bangs obituary. *Creem*, July 1982.

Anderson, Roger. "Growing Up with Lester." *Throat Culture #2*, 1990.

————. "The Gospel According to Lester Bangs." *East Bay Express*, November 27, 1987.

————. "The Last Anniversary: An Altamont Memoir." *East Bay Express*, December 8, 1989.

Arnold, Thomas K. "The Passing of Lester Bangs." *San Diego Reader*, May 27, 1982.

Associated Press news wire. "Rock Critic Lester Bangs Is Dead at 33." May 1, 1982.

Author unknown. "Man Dies in Flaming House Here." *Escondido Daily Times-Advocate,* August 5, 1957.

————. "Publisher's Death Accidental." *Detroit News,* February 1, 1981.

Barbaro, Kathleen. "Mo-dettes at Duke's." *Contempo Culture #4*, October 1980.

Beale, Lewis, "California Livin' Is Becoming a Reality for Ex-*Creem* Staffers." *Detroit Free Press*, April 29, 1990.

Bellomo, Tish and Snooky. "Sex and the Single Forkhead." *New York Rocker*, exact date unknown, 1977.

Berman, Laura. "Life After *Creem*." *Detroit Free Press*. February 16, 1986.

———. "The Queen of *Creem*: Connie Kramer Keeps Her Rock Publishing Dynasty Rolling." *Detroit Free Press*, March 17, 1985.

———. "Whipping Up a Lighter *Creem*." *Detroit Free Press,* December 5, 1985.

Birth announcement, Leslie Conway Bangs. *Escondido Daily Times-Advocate*, December 14, 1948.

Board, Mykel. "Lester Bangs Memorial at St. Mark's Church." *New York Press*, May 20, 1992.

Carson, Tom. "I'll Be Your Mirror: Lester Bangs's Naked Grunge." *Village Voice Literary Supplement*, December 1987.

Christgau, Georgia. Lester Bangs obituary. *Village Voice*, May 11, 1982.

Christgau, Robert. "Age of Rock Critics Too." *Fusion*, May 14, 1971.

———. Lester Bangs obituary. *Village Voice*, May 11, 1982.

City of Escondido. "Historical Information." Web site.

Cohn, Nik. "Disco's Homeboy Turns Hitman." *Weekly Mail & Guardian*, February 24, 1995.

Coley, Byron. "Lester Bangs and Birdland: The Silo That Sang." *Village Voice*, March 3, 1987.

Collins, Alice. "Rock Publisher Dies Here, Cause of Death Studied." *Birmingham Eccentric & Observer*, February 2, 1981.

Crowe, Cameron. Letter to the editor. *Creem,* July 1982.

Cruger, Roberta. "Twenty-Five Years of *Creem*, Part One: Flashbacks to Boy Howdy's Pre-Pubescence." *Creem*, January/February 1994.

Curley, Brian S. "Egg on Shirt." *Throat Culture #2*, 1990.

Curtis Circulation Company. "The Wild & Wacky Story of a Music Magazine." *Bestseller Business*, November 1972.

Denby, David. "The Moviegoers: Why Don't People Love the Right Movies Anymore?" *The New Yorker*, April 6, 1998.

The editors of *Fusion*. "An Armchair Guide to Rock's Critical Sixties." *Fusion*, June 12, 1970.

———. "*Fusion* Interview: Jon Landau, Writer-Producer," Parts I and II. *Fusion*, October 16 and 30, 1970.

Edmonds, Ben, and Richard Meltzer. "Jack Bonus Stole the Show: Grunt, What a Lovely Sound." *Phonograph Record Magazine*, November 1971.

Ehrmann, Eric. "Detroit's MC5 Kick Out the Jams." *Rolling Stone*, January 6, 1969.

El Cajon Chamber of Commerce. *El Cajon California*. Civic brochure, 1967.

———. *El Cajon California*. Civic brochure, 1969.

———. "List of Churches, 1971."

El Cajon Public Library. "El Cajon." Web site.

Escondido Chamber of Commerce. "Welcome to the History of Escondido, California!" Web site.

Goldberg, Michael. "Greil Marcus, World's Greatest Rock Critic." *Addicted to Noise* Web site.

Graff, Gary. "*Creem* Magazine Closes, Lays Off Staff Members." *Detroit Free Press*, August 20, 1985.

Gross, Jason. "Robert Quine Interview." *Perfect Sound Forever* Web site, November 1997.

Heimel, Cynthia. "Death on the F Train." *Village Voice*, December 21, 1982.

Holdship, Bill. "Lester Bangs—The Man Had a Heart." *East Lansing* (Michigan) *State News*. May 13, 1982.

———. "Lou Reed Interview." *Creem*, November 1987.

Hoskyns, Barney. "Rock 'n' Roll as Literature, Literature as Rock 'n' Roll." *Mojo*, March 1994.

Ilka, Douglas. "Barry Kramer, *Creem* Publisher, Dies At 37." *Detroit News*, January 30, 1981.

Ingersoll, Brenda. "The Rise and Fall of Deday LaRene." *Detroit News*, May 8, 1994.

Jones, Steve. "Re-Viewing Rock Writing: Recurring Themes in Popular Music Criticism." *American Journalism*, Spring/Summer 1992.

Julian, Ivan. "Cleaning House with Lester Bangs." *Throat Culture #2*, 1990.

Kakutani, Michiko. "Books of The Times: Psychotic Reactions and Carburetor Dung." *New York Times*, November 25, 1987.

Kent, Nick. "Ballad of a Loudhearted Man." *New Musical Express*, May 4, 1982.

———. "Doomed Guys Don't Go Pop!" *Arena*, summer 1988.

Kriner, Paula. "Ex-Inlander and Rock Music Critic Dies in N.Y." *Daily Californian*, May 27, 1982.

Laughner, Peter. Letter to the editor. *Creem*, April 1973.

———. Album review: Lou Reed, *Coney Island Baby. Creem*, March 1976.

Lengel, Allan. "Giacalone Lawyer Gets Year in Prison." *Detroit News*, May 5, 1994.

Lockwood, Herbert. "Flume Brought Prosperity to Cajon Farmers." *Daily Californian*, March 1, 1965.

Loder, Kurt. "Book Review: The Collected Lester Bangs." *Rolling Stone*, November 19, 1987.

Macrae, Scott. "Rock's New *Creem* of the Crop." *Vancouver Sun*, July 30, 1976.

Marcus, Greil. Lester Bangs obituary. *Village Voice*, May 11, 1982.

———. "Ripped to Shreds." *Rolling Stone*, July 24, 1980.

———. "Rock-a-Hula Clarified." *Creem*, June 1971.

Marsh, Dave, and Deday LaRene and Barry Kramer. Editorial (*Creem* mission statement). *Creem*, January 1970.

McFadden, Robert D. "New York's Power Restored Slowly; Looting Widespread,

3,300 Arrested; Blackout Results in Heavy Losses." *New York Times*, July 15, 1977.

Meltzer, Richard. "Antihero: Dead Men Don't Deconstruct." *Spin*, January, 1988.

———. Book review: Paul Williams, *Das Energi*. *Fusion*, December 1973.

———. "Caned Out: The Autobiography of Richard Meltzer." *Fusion*, January 1973.

———. "Get Behind the Blue Öyster Cult (Before It Gets Behind You)." *Creem*, February 1972.

———. "Lester Recollected In Tranquility." *San Diego Reader*, December 6, 1984.

———. "Rock Memories." *Spin*, April 1986.

———. "Sniffin' Out Music's Future: Tomorrow Never Nose!" *Coast*, April 1973.

———. "Vinyl Reckoning." *San Diego Weekly Reader*, January 28, 1999.

———, and Nick Tosches. "Richard Meltzer and Nick Tosches Shoot the Shit." *Throat Culture #2*, 1990.

Nelson, Paul. "Lester Bangs: 1948–1982." *Rolling Stone*, June 10, 1982.

Niester, Alan. Album review: Christopher Milk, *Some People Will Drink Anything* (Warner Bros.). *Creem*, January 1973.

Pareles, Jon. "Notes from Underground: Lester Bangs Gave Rock Criticism a Swift Kick in the Pretensions." *New York Times*, December 13, 1987.

Patoski, Joe. "Joe Nick Remembers." *Throat Culture #2*, 1990.

Pearlman, Sandy. "*Fusion* Interview: Richard Meltzer." *Fusion*, June 12, 1970.

Pelzman, Fran. "Everyday Shit." *Throat Culture #2*, 1990.

Powers, Ann. "What Do Indie Rockers Want?" *Village Voice*, May 16, 1995.

Presley, Sharon. "Birdland: The Flight . . . and the Fall." *New York Rocker*, exact date unknown, 1979.

Reay, Tony. "Letter from *Creem* Magazine to *Rolling Stone* Magazine." *Creem*, April 1969.

Ridgely, Roberta. "El Cajon—Whoosh!" *San Diego and Point Magazine*, July 1958.

Riegel, Richard. "Lester Bangs, Liberation Critic." *Throat Culture #2*, 1990.

Shaw, Greg, and Jon Tiven and David Newberger. "Fanzines: Surveying Them, Editing Them, Reading Them." *Fusion*, June 1972.

Shellenbarger, Pat. "Irreverence Fuels National Music Magazine." *Detroit News*, January 1975.

Simmons, Doug. "Cellars by Starlight: Lester Bangs, 1948–1982." *Boston Phoenix*, May 11, 1982.

Sinclair, Tom. "Lester Bangs: The Lost Interview." *Puncture*, summer 1989.

Singleton, Donald. "The Lights Go Back On: Subways Roll; Fires & Looting Ease; 3,400 Are Arrested." *New York Daily News*, July 15, 1977.

———. "The Price Tag: Billion-Dollar Blackout." *New York Daily News*, July 16, 1977.

Smith, Patti. "The monkey man swings home for a snort of Cognac with his pals, Bianca and Boy. He may top it off with a Cold Italian Pizza. Ook, ook." *Creem*, January 1973.

Stax, Mike, and Gary Rachac. "Growing Up in the Dark Ages: The Early Years of Lester Bangs." Unpublished manuscript.

Tosches, Nick. "The Heartbeats Never Did Benefits." *Fusion*, October 15, 1971.

———. "The Punk Muse: The True Story of Protopathic Spiff Including the Lowdown on the Trouble-Making Five-Percent of America's Youth." *Fusion*, July 10, 1970.

———. "Whiskey Is the Spirit of Christmas: Your De-Luxe Guide to Your Yuletide Econo-Hootch." *Creem*, January 1972.

Trakin, Roy. "Bangs and Whimpers." *Soho Weekly News*, exact date unknown, June 1977.

Trbovich, Marco. "Where *Creem* Is At: Who Woulda Believed America's Only Rock 'n' Roll Magazine Is Out There in Walled Lake?" *Detroit Free Press*, February 18, 1973.

Tyner, Rob. "Lester & Me." *Throat Culture #2*, 1990.

Uhelszki, Jaan. "Jaan Uhelszki Remembers to Forget to Remember." *Throat Culture #2*, 1990.

———. "Twenty-Five Years of *Creem*, Part Three: Look Back in Anger." *Creem*, May/June 1994.

Walls, Richard C. "Yeah, I Dunno." *Throat Culture #2*, 1990.

———. "Twenty-Five Years of *Creem*, Part Two: We Didn't Know What We Were Doing." *Creem*, March/April 1994.

Ward, Ed. "Lester Bangs Will Be Missed." *Austin American-Statesman*, May 7, 1982.

Watchtower Bible and Tract Society. "Family Responsibilities in Keeping Jehovah's Witnesses Pure," *The Watchtower*, September 15, 1981.

Wenner, Jann. "Records." *Rolling Stone*, November 9, 1967.

Wharton, David. "The Resurrection of *Creem* Magazine." *Los Angeles Times*, September 30, 1990.

Whitall, Susan. "Lester Lives on the Internet." *Bam*, April 5, 1996.

———. "Linda McCartney Knew How to Put Everyone at Ease." *Detroit News*, April 24, 1998.

White, William E. "The Dextromethorphan FAQ: Answers to Frequently Asked Questions About Dextromethorphan (DXM)." Web site.

Willis, Ellen. "My Grand Funk Problem—and Ours." *The New Yorker*, February 26, 1972.

Wise, Stewart. "Remembering Raul's and *Contempo Culture*." *Austin Chronicle*, April 7, 1987.

Wolcott, James. "The Noise Boys: Two New Collections of Old Rock Criticism Are Music to Deafened Ears." *Vanity Fair*, October 1987.

Other Authors, Books

Amburn, Ellis. *Subterranean Kerouac: The Hidden Life of Jack Kerouac*. New York: St. Martin's, 1998.

Andersen, Christopher. *Jagger Unauthorized*. New York: Delacorte, 1993.

Anson, Robert Sam. *Gone Crazy and Back Again: The Rise and Fall of the* Rolling Stone *Generation*. New York: Doubleday, 1981.

Bockris, Victor. *Transformer: The Lou Reed Story*. New York: Simon & Schuster, 1994.

Booth, Stanley. *The True Adventures of the Rolling Stones*. New York: Vintage, 1985.

Burroughs, William S. *Junky*. New York: Penguin, 1977.

Cherkovski, Neeli. *Bukowski: A Life*. South Royalton, Vt.: Steerforth, 1997.

Chernikowski, Stephanie. *Dream Baby Dream: Images from the Blank Generation*. Los Angeles: 2.13.61, 1996.

Christgau, Robert. *Grown Up All Wrong: 75 Great Rock and Pop Artists from Vaudeville to Techno*. Cambridge, Mass.: Harvard University Press, 1998.

———. *Christgau's Record Guide: Rock Albums of the '70s*. New York: Ticknor & Fields, 1981.

———. *Christgau's Record Guide: The '80s*. New York: Pantheon, 1990.

Clapton, Diana. *Lou Reed and the Velvet Underground*. London: Proteus, 1982.

Denisoff, R. Serge. *Solid Gold: The Popular Record Industry*. New Brunswick, N.J.: Transaction, 1990.

Dickstein, Morris. *Double Agent: The Critic & Society*. New York: Oxford University Press, 1992.

Drabble, Margaret. *The Ice Age*. New York: Alfred A. Knopf, 1977.

Draper, Robert. *Rolling Stone Magazine: The Uncensored History*. New York: 1990.

Duncan, Robert. *The Noise*: Notes From a Rock 'n' Roll Era. New York: Ticknor & Fields, 1984.

El Cajon Valley High School. *Legend* (school annual). 1965.

Gifford, Barry, and Lawrence Lee. *Jack's Book: An Oral Biography of Jack Kerouac*. New York: Penguin, 1979.

Gimarc, George. *Punk Diary: 1970–1979*. New York: St. Martin's, 1994.

Glessing, Robert J. *The Underground Press in America*. Bloomington, Ind.: Indiana University Press, 1971.

Goldman, Albert. *The Lives of John Lennon*. New York: William Morrow, 1988.

Goldstein, Richard. *Goldstein's Greatest Hits: A Book Mostly About Rock 'n' Roll*. Englewood Cliffs, N.J.: Prentice-Hall, 1970.

Goodman, Fred. *The Mansion on the Hill: Dylan, Young, Geffen, Springsteen, and the Head-On Collision of Rock and Commerce*. New York: Times Books, 1997.

Gray, Marcus. *Last Gang in Town: The Story and Myth of the Clash.* New York: Henry Holt, 1995.

Haden-Guest, Anthony. *The Last Party: Studio 54, Disco, and the Culture of the Night.* New York: William Morrow, 1997.

Harry, Debbie; Chris Stein; and Victor Bockris. *Making Tracks: The Rise of Blondie.* New York: Da Capo, 1998.

Heimel, Cynthia. *Sex Tips for Girls.* New York: Simon & Schuster, 1983.

Heylin, Clinton. *From the Velvets to the Voidoids: A Pre-Punk History of a Post-Punk World.* New York: Penguin, 1993.

Hinton, Brian. *Celtic Crossroads: The Art of Van Morrison.* London: Sanctuary Publishing, 1997.

Holmstrom, John, editor. *Punk: The Original.* New York: Trans-High, 1996.

Holzman, Jac, and Gavan Daws. *Follow the Music: The Life and High Times of Elektra Records in the Great Years of American Pop Culture.* Santa Monica, Calif.: First Media Books, 1998.

Howard, Gerald, editor. *The Sixties: The Art, Attitudes, Politics, and Media of Our Most Explosive Decade.* New York: Marlowe & Co., 1995.

Hunter, Ian. *Diary of a Rock 'n' Roll Star.* London, 1997: Independent Music Press.

Johnstone, Nick. *Patti Smith: A Biography.* London: Omnibus Press, 1997.

Kent, Nick. *The Dark Stuff: Selected Writings on Rock Music 1972–1995.* New York: Da Capo Press, 1995.

Kerouac, Jack. *The Subterraneans.* New York: Grove Press, 1971.

Kozak, Roman. *This Ain't No Disco: The Story of CBGB.* Winchester, Mass.: Faber and Faber, 1988.

Marsh, Dave. *Fortunate Son: The Best of Dave Marsh.* New York: Random House, 1985.

———. *Louie Louie: The History and Mythology of the World's Most Famous Rock 'n' Roll Song.* New York: Hyperion, 1993.

McDonnell, Evelyn, and Ann Powers. *Rock She Wrote: Women Write About Rock, Pop, and Rap.* New York: Delta, 1995.

McNeil, Legs, and Gillian McCain. *Please Kill Me.* New York: Grove Press, 1996.

Meltzer, Richard. *The Aesthetics of Rock.* New York: Da Capo Press, 1987.

———. *Gulcher: Post-Rock Cultural Pluralism In America (1649–1993).* New York: Citadel Underground, 1990.

———. *The Night (Alone).* New York: Little, Brown, 1995.

———. *Prickly Heat and Cold: Volume Two of Caned Out: The Authorized Autobiography of Richard Meltzer.* Los Angeles: Illuminati, 1984.

———. *17 Insects Can Die in Your Heart: Good Verse and Bad from Richard Meltzer's Golden Decade (1968–83).* Los Angeles: Ouija Madness Press, 1982.

Mendelssohn, John. *I, Caramba: Confessions of an Antkiller.* Los Angeles: Rhino Records, 1995.

Miller, Timothy, editor. *America's Alternative Religions.* Albany: State University of New York Press, 1995.

Mingus, Charles. *Beneath the Underdog: His World as Composed by Mingus.* New York: Vintage, 1991.

Morgan, Ted. *Literary Outlaw: The Life And Times of William S. Burroughs.* New York: Avon Books, 1990.

Orwell, George. *The Collected Essays, Journalism and Letters of George Orwell.* London: Secker & Warburg, 1968.

Penton, M. James. *Apocalypse Delayed: The Story of Jehovah's Witnesses.* Toronto: University of Toronto Press, 1988.

Reed, Jeremy. *Waiting for the Man: A Biography of Lou Reed.* London: Picador, 1994.

Reisfield, Randi, and Danny Fields. *Who's Your Fave Rave? 16 Magazine: Teen Idols as You Knew Them . . . AND as They Really Were!* New York: Boulevard, 1997.

Rosten, Leo, editor. *Religions of America: Ferment and Faith in an Age of Crisis.* New York: Simon & Schuster, 1975.

Sinclair, John. *Guitar Army: Street Writings/Prison Writings.* New York: Douglas Book Corporation, 1972.

Smith, Franc. *Harry Vernon at Prep.* New York: Signet, 1960.

Smith, Patti. *Complete.* New York: Doubleday, 1998.

Thompson, Hunter. *Hell's Angels: The Strange and Terrible Saga of the Outlaw Motorcycle Gangs.* New York: Ballantine, 1983.

Tosches, Nick. *Lester.* New York: Dreamland, 1992 (limited-edition monograph).

Walley, David. *Who Stole the Bomp?* New York: Anchor, 1998.

Watchtower Bible and Tract Society. *Knowledge That Leads to Everlasting Life.* New York: Watchtower Bible and Tract Society, 1995.

———. *Mankind's Search for God.* New York: Watchtower Bible and Tract Society, 1990.

Weinstein, Deena. *Heavy Metal: A Cultural Sociology.* New York: Lexington, 1991.

Williams, Paul. *The Map, or Rediscovering Rock and Roll: A Journey.* South Bend, Ind.: And Books, 1988.

———. *Rock and Roll: The 100 Best Singles.* New York: Carroll & Graf, 1993.

Willis, Ellen. *Beginning to See the Light: Sex, Hope and Rock-and-Roll.* Hanover, N.H.: Wesleyan University Press, 1992.

Wolfe, Tom, editor. *The New Journalism.* New York: Harper & Row, 1973.

Public Documents

Autopsy report, "Lester C. Bangs." City of New York, Office of the Chief Medical Examiner. May 1, 1982.

Birth certificate, Leslie Conway Bangs. San Diego County, California. December 13, 1948.

College transcript, Leslie Conway Bangs. San Diego State College. September 1968.

Conduct register transcription form (prison record), Conway Bangs. September 11, 1945.

Convict record ledger data, Conway Bangs. February 5, 1935.

Death certificate, Conway Leslie Bangs. San Diego County, California. August 4, 1957.

Death certificate, "Lester C. Bangs." City of New York, New York. April 30, 1982.

Death certificate, Norma Belle Bangs. San Bernardino County, California. March 13, 1982.

Extract of Registrant Classification Record, Leslie Conway Bangs. U.S. Selective Service System. File closed January 31, 1972.

FBI file, Barry Kramer. Closed December 29, 1972; unclassified April 28, 1999.

Laboratory findings, "Leslie C. Bangs." Director of toxicology, city of New York, Office of the Chief Medical Examiner. May 27, 1982.

Personal identification of body, "Lester Bangs." City of New York, Office of the Chief Medical Examiner. May 2, 1982.

Report of death, "Lesley Bangs" (*sic*). City of New York, Office of the Chief Medical Examiner. April 30, 1982.

State of Texas v. *Conway Bangs*, District Court, Delta County. January 16, 1935.

Telephone notice of death, "Leslie Bangs." City of New York, Office of the Chief Medical Examiner. April 30, 1982.

Acknowledgments

I am indebted first and foremost to the people who granted me interviews, all of whom are named in the sources. Many of them also shared photographs, clip files, tapes, and videos, as well as submitting to follow-up interviews and fact-checking. I appreciate the kindness extended by each of them, but several deserve special recognition.

Topping this list is Lester's nephew Ben Catching III, who not only shared his memories but invited me into his home and family. As Lester's literary executor, John Morthland gave me unhindered access to the Bangs archives; as Lester's best friend, he provided countless leads and innumerable insights. Billy Altman did the same with unfailing cheer. This book would not have been possible without the three of them. Thanks also to their loved ones: Joyce and Emma Altman, Midge Catching, and Thomas, Karen, and Matthew Hildebrandt.

Because of the feelings that my sometimes intrusive questions must have stirred, I am also especially indebted to Andrea DeLucia, née di Guglielmo; Kate Alexander, formerly Nancy; Kathy Miller; and Judith Wilmot. Their candor could not have been easily offered, but it was graciously provided nonetheless.

Cameron Crowe has been an enthusiastic supporter of this project since 1994. ("Dude, you gotta write the book; you caught the keys!") I was likewise buoyed by the support, advice, and consistent goodwill of Nick Tosches, who inspired me not only as a writer, but as someone who got the hell out of Jersey. Richard Meltzer was extremely accommodating, and, man, is he a goddamn great writer! Robert Quine and his wife,

Alice Sherman, and Robert Duncan and his wife, Roni Hoffman, were also very helpful, while Roger Anderson and Jaan Uhelszki provided more support and encouragement than I could ever measure. One of the best by-products of this book is that I now consider many of these people my friends.

In Ohio, Richard Riegel shared his memories and letters and spent hours searching for obscure clips. In Detroit, Susan Whitall gave me the grand tour of the *Creem* sights, Richard C. Walls introduced me to the joys of the Dream Cruise, and Charlie Auringer dusted off his recollections, files, and photos. In Los Angeles, Bill Holdship shared the Lester-in-*Creem* index that he compiled for *Psychotic Reactions and Carburetor Dung*, then exceeded the bonds of friendship by accompanying me on a road trip to El Cajon. (We spent two weeks there one night.) In San Diego, Gary Rachac provided a map to Lester's teen years via an oral history that he compiled with Mike Stax of *Ugly Things* fanzine, and Rob Houghton offered his recollections in interviews as well as in his own extraordinary written account of the high-school and *Drug Punk* years.

In addition to those who were interviewed, the photographers who shared their work included Roberta Bayley, John Collier, Bob Gruen, Ida S. Langham, Richard Lee, Michael Mayhan, Christina Patoski, Chuck Pulin, and Pennie Smith.

The never-ending search for information was aided by Dave Frazee in the Pioneer Room of the Escondido Public Library, Larry Todd at the Texas Department of Justice, Laura Saegert at the Texas State Library and Archives Commission, Melissa Beeler at the office of the Delta County District Clerk, the staff of the El Cajon Public Library, Nancy Gerry and William Melton at El Cajon Valley High School, Dana Quinter at Grossmont Junior College, Suzanne Montgomery at San Diego State University, Paula Sweeney with the U.S. Selective Service System, the staffs at the main branch of the Detroit Public Library and the University of Chicago Library Research Center, Linda Kloss at the Federal Bureau of Investigation's Freedom of Information Office, Dean Siegal at the Block Drug Company, and John Easton at the University of Chicago Medical School.

Many others helped by contributing missing facts, phone numbers, forgotten books, valuable perspectives, or just some encouragement along the way. They include Rick Addy, Lorraine Ali, Punch Andrews, Lance Bangs, Brian Beck, Bill Bentley, Leslie Berman, Hanne Blank, Mykel Board, Mike Bruno, Torry Bruno, Jon Carroll, Irwin Chusid, Gail

Colson, Jeff Condon, Lou DePinto, Dave DiMartino, Robert Draper, Dave Dunlap, Howard Fields, Stewart Francke, Mikal Gilmore, Matt Hendrickson, Dave Hoekstra, Tim Holmes, Lisa Holton, Barney Hoskyns, Tonya Hurley, Wendell Jamieson, Jeff Jarema, Aime and Lee Joseph, Cynthia Joyce, Sabrina Kaleta, Ira Kaplan, Steve Karas, Matthew Kaufman, Mark Kemp, Cristi Kempf, Monica Kendrick, Judi Kerr, Frank Kogan, Robert Kozloff, Lex Kuhne, Tuli Kupferberg, Bob Kurson, Ken Kurson, Steve Leiber, and Nick Logan.

Also: Ian MacDonald, Jed Mayer, Keven McAlester, Kevin McDonough, Mike McGonigal, Don McLeese, Jim Merlis, Kate Messer, Krista Mettler, Fred Mills, Robert Mizrachi, Casey Monahan, Rob Moore, Madeline Morel, Jeffrey Morgan, Charles Shaar Murray, Chris Nadler, Paul Natkin, Hank Neuberger, J. Niimi, Cathy O'Brien, Jim O'Donnell, Abe Opincar, Camille Paglia, Rob Patterson, Zach Paradis, Michael Pietsch, Steve Popovich, Mark Pucci, Jack Rabid, Sylvia Reed, John Reilly, Barbara Rice, Tim Riley, Ebet Roberts, Jim Rondinelli, Cynthia Rose, Ed Sanders, Vin Scelsa, Bud Scoppa, Debbie Sellnow, Paul Shefrin, Elaine Shock, Doug Simmons, Tom Sinclair, Bob Small, Mat Snow, Kelly Spector, Helene Stapinski, Jeff Stark, Shawn Stewart, Carrie Anne Svingen, Cathryn Swan, Jim Testa, Brad Tolinsky, Andy Wang, Bill Wyman, Kiki Yablon, Raymond Zoltowski, and of course Nigel Wade, John Barron, Jocelyn Winnecke, and all of my colleagues at the *Chicago Sun-Times*.

Bangs scholar Steve Czapla literally saved me hundreds of hours of work, and I was unbelievably lucky to draw on his knowledge and insights. Jeff Pizek and Michaelangelo Matos transcribed some of my interviews; Jason Gross and Gail Worley searched for pieces in the New York Public Library system, and Joshua B. Green scoured the Northwestern University library. My most dedicated assistant, Anders Smith-Lindall, transcribed, researched, and checked facts as well as helping me process a lot of this information. Theoretically these people were my interns, but they are all so talented I'm convinced I'll wind up working for them some day.

I knew that my agent, Chris Calhoun, was the man to sell this book when he told me he carried one of Lester's pieces about Blue Öyster Cult in his wallet through college. I appreciate his faith and persistence. I am also extremely grateful to my editor, Gerry Howard, for his belief in this idea, his hard work in crafting the finished book, and his decision to take me with him to Broadway/Doubleday. Thanks also to Amy Gray,

Linda Steinman, Maureen Sugden, Mark Hurst, Terry Karydes, and Carlos Brown at Broadway/Doubleday, and to Matthew Hamilton, William Webb, Mike Jones, Elizabeth O'Malley, Jocasta Brownlee, and everyone at Bloomsbury Publishing in the U.K.

My old friend Patti Kleinke and my sassy sister-in-law, Pam Kotars, also helped with the transcribing. My aunt, Kay Stapleton, housed and fed my family while I sped around Detroit like a maniac. My in-laws, George and Ellie Kotars, provided a home away from home for Kim and Melody when I was in book-hermit mode. Thanks also to my brother Michael and the rest of my family, especially my mom and dad, Helene and Harry Reynolds, who have not only put up with but actively encouraged my obsession since the spring of 1982.

Several of my closest friends served as volunteer readers, editors, fact-checkers, and always-reliable sounding boards. Rob O'Connor paved the way with the Bangs-tribute issue of *Throat Culture*, and his feedback was extremely valuable. My college buddy and walking rock encyclopedia David Sprague was always available to answer the most niggling questions, while Tony DiMurro offered long-standing friendship and insight into very difficult matters. Robin Daughtridge applied her peerless photo expertise to help choose the most striking images; J. R. Jones patiently read the early chapters and improved the writing immeasurably; Greg Kot, Jay Orff, Michael Stark, Phil Velasquez, Marc Weingarten, and Robert Wilonsky are quite simply Kings of Rock, and Keith Moerer and Susan Hamre remain trusted editors and true pals.

After Lester Bangs, no one has influenced my thinking about rock 'n' roll more than Professor Deena Weinstein, and I hope that I never graduate from her unending class.

Finally my wife, Kim, accompanied me on interviews, transcribed tapes, read every draft of every chapter, brainstormed on structure, hashed out difficult passages, speculated on various mysteries, and provided countless back rubs, pep talks, and slaps in the face when those were needed. She also put up with Lester as a permanent houseguest. Granted, he didn't smell quite as bad as he would have in the flesh, but he could still be loud and unruly. He took up an enormous amount of psychic space for several years of our lives, but the truth is that we miss him already.

Index

About the
Author

Born in Jersey City, New Jersey, the year the Beatles arrived in America, Jim DeRogatis began voicing his opinions about rock 'n' roll shortly thereafter. He is currently the pop music critic at the Chicago *Sun-Times* and a contributor to *Penthouse, Guitar World, World of Wrestling,* and the *Launch* and *Iron Minds* Web sites, among other publications. Together with Greg Kot—Siskel to his Ebert—he co-hosts *Sound Opinions,* the world's only rock 'n' roll talk show, on WXRT-FM. His first book, *Kaleidoscope Eyes: Psychedelic Rock from the '60s to the '90s,* was published in 1996 by Citadel Underground in the U.S. and Fourth Estate, Ltd., in the U.K. He has been known to annoy his wife Kim and daughter Melody by flailing away on the drums and playing Wire or the Flaming Lips entirely too loud. They retaliate with Barbra Streisand and Loonette the Clown from *The Big Comfy Couch.*